Anonymous

Muniments of the Royal Burgh of Irvine

Vol. II

Anonymous

Muniments of the Royal Burgh of Irvine
Vol. II

ISBN/EAN: 9783337081942

Printed in Europe, USA, Canada, Australia, Japan

Cover: Foto ©Andreas Hilbeck / pixelio.de

More available books at **www.hansebooks.com**

ARCHÆOLOGICAL
AND HISTORICAL COLLECTIONS

RELATING TO

AYRSHIRE AND GALLOWAY

400 Copies printed.

Of which this is No. 219

The Tolbooth of Irvine - 1860.

MUNIMENTS

OF THE

Royal Burgh of Irvine

VOL. II

Edinburgh
PRINTED FOR THE AYRSHIRE AND GALLOWAY ARCHÆOLOGICAL ASSOCIATION
MDCCCXCI

Printed by R. & R. Clark
FOR
DAVID DOUGLAS, EDINBURGH

AYRSHIRE AND GALLOWAY ARCHÆOLOGICAL ASSOCIATION

President.

The EARL of STAIR, K.T., LL.D., V.P.S.A. Scot., Lord-Lieutenant of Ayrshire and Wigtonshire.

Vice-Presidents.

The DUKE of PORTLAND.
The MARQUESS of BUTE, K.T., LL.D., F.S.A. Scot.
The MARQUESS of AILSA.
The EARL of EGLINTON and WINTON.
The EARL of GALLOWAY, K.T.
The EARL of GLASGOW.
The LORD HERRIES, Lord-Lieutenant of the Stewartry.
The Rt. Hon. Sir JAS. FERGUSSON, Bart., M.P., G.C.S.I., K.C.M.G., C.I.E., LL.D.
The Right Hon. Sir J. DALRYMPLE-HAY, Bart., C.B., D.C.L., F.R.S.
Sir M. SHAW-STEWART, Bart., Lord-Lieutenant of Renfrewshire.
Sir ANDREW AGNEW, Bart., of Lochnaw.
Sir WILLIAM WALLACE, Bart., of Lochryan.
Sir WILLIAM J. MONTGOMERY-CUNINGHAME, Bart., V.C., of Corsehill.
Sir HERBERT EUSTACE MAXWELL, Bart., of Monreith, M.P., F.S.A. Scot.
R. A. OSWALD, Esq., of Auchincruive.

Hon. Secretaries for Ayrshire.

R. W. COCHRAN-PATRICK, Esq., of Woodside, LL.D., F.S.A., Hon. Sec. S.A. Scot., Under Secretary for Scotland.
The Hon. HEW DALRYMPLE, F.S.A. Scot. (for Carrick).
J. SHEDDEN-DOBIE, Esq., of Morishill, F.S.A. Scot. (for Cuninghame).
R. MUNRO, Esq., M.D., M.A., F.S.A. Scot.

Hon. Secretaries for Wigtonshire.

The Rev. G. WILSON, Glenluce, C.M.S.A. Scot.
Sir HERBERT EUSTACE MAXWELL, Bart., of Monreith, M.P., F.S.A. Scot.

Hon. Secretaries for the Stewartry.

Capt. CLARK KENNEDY of Knockgray.   JAMES G. KINNA, Esq., Herron Cottage, Minnigaff.

Joint-Treasurers.

C. G. SHAW, Esq., and D. W. SHAW, Esq., County Buildings, Ayr.

Council.

The Right Hon. The EARL of GLASGOW.
The Hon. HEW DALRYMPLE, F.S.A. Scot.
Sir HERBERT EUSTACE MAXWELL, Bart., of Monreith, M.P., F.S.A. Scot.
Colonel HUNTER-WESTON of Hunterston, F.S.A.
F. T. R. KENNEDY, Esq., of Dunure.
J. MACDONALD, Esq., LL.D., F.S.A. Scot., Glasgow.
R. MUNRO, Esq., M.D., M.A., F.S.A. Scot., Kilmarnock.
J. SHEDDEN-DOBIE, Esq., of Morishill, F.S.A. Scot., Beith.
R. D. MURDOCH, Esq., Ayr.
J. F. DALRYMPLE HAY, Esq., of Dunlop.
R. M. POLLOK, Esq., of Middleton.
ROBERT GOUDIE, Esq., Ayr.

List of Members, 1891.

ABERDEEN UNIVERSITY LIBRARY.
AGNEW, Alexander, Procurator-Fiscal's Office, Court-House Buildings, Dundee.
AGNEW, Sir Andrew, Lochnaw, Stranraer.
AGNEW, R. Vans, of Barnbarroch, Stranraer Park, Stranraer.
5 AILSA, Marquess of, Culzean Castle, Maybole.
AITKEN, A., Solicitor, Stranraer.
ALEXANDER, Dr., Dundonald.
ALEXANDER, General Sir Claud, of Ballochmyle, Bart., Mauchline.
ALLAN, Rev. William, Manse of Mochrum, Port-William.
10 ALLISON, R. A., Scaleby Hall, Carlisle.
ANDERSON, W., 149 West George Street, Glasgow.
ANDREWS, David, Solicitor, Girvan.
ANTIQUARIES, Society of, Burlington House, Piccadilly, London, W.
ARMOUR, John, jun., Architect, Irvine.
15 ARMSTRONG, R. B., 6 Coates Crescent, Edinburgh.
ARTHUR, M., Fullarton House, Troon, Ayrshire.
ARTHUR, William, Arthur Seat, New Cumnock.
AYR, Burgh of.

BAILEY, J. Lambert, Banker, Ardrossan.
20 BAIRD, J. G. A., of Adamton, M.P., Monkton.
BLAIR, Captain, of Blair, Dalry, Ayrshire.
BLAIR, Rev. D. Oswald Hunter-, O.S.B., St. Benedict's Monastery, Fort Augustus.
BLAIR, E. Heron Maxwell, Penninghame House, Newton-Stewart.
BLAIR, F. C. Hunter-, F.S.A. Scot., Wine Merchant, Leamington.
25 BLANC, Hippolyte J., 73 George Street, Edinburgh.
BORLAND, J., Chemist, Kilmarnock.
BORTHWICK, Lord, Ravenstone, Whithorn.
BOSTON Public Library, U.S.A.
BOWIE, J. H., 16 Markland Terrace, Wilson Street, Hillhead, Glasgow.
30 BOYD, Colonel Hay, of Townend, Symington.

LIST OF MEMBERS.

BOYD, D. A., Seamill, West Kilbride, Ayrshire.
BOYLE, Col., R.E., 6 Sumner Terrace, Onslow Square, London, S.W.
BROWN, A. J. Dennistoun, of Balloch Castle, Dumbartonshire.
BROWN, D., Townend Cottage, Dalry, Ayrshire.
35 BROWN, J. Oswald, Orangefield, Monkton.
BROWN, J. T., Gibraltar House, Edinburgh.
BROWN, Miss, of Lanfine, Newmilns.
BROWN, Robert, Abercorn Bridge, Paisley.
BROWN, D., & Co., Stationers, 2 King Street, Kilmarnock.
40 BUTE, Marquess of, Mountstuart, Rothesay.

CAIRD, Sir James, K.C.B., 3 St. James's Square, London, S.W.
CAIRNEY, William, 4 Park Grove Terrace, West, Glasgow.
CALDWELL, James, Craigielea, Paisley.
CAMPBELL, Colonel Sir A., Bart., of Blythswood, M.P., Renfrew.
45 CAMPBELL, Captain R. M., of Auchmannoch, Glaisnock House, Cumnock.
CAMPBELL, Colonel W. H., Treesbanks, Kilmarnock.
CARFRAE, Robert, 77 George Street, Edinburgh.
CARMENT, J., LL.D., 32 Albany Street, Edinburgh.
CARRUTHERS, David, Market Lane, Kilmarnock.
50 CHRISTIE, William, Royal Bank, Irvine.
COMRIE, Alexander, Accountant, Dalry.
COOPER, Mrs. A. F., of Failford, Tarbolton.
CORRIE, A. J.
COWAN, Hugh, St. Leonards, Ayr.
55 COWAN, John, 12 Hill Street, Edinburgh.
CRAWFURD, T. Macknight, of Cartsburn, Lauriston Castle, Edinburgh.
CRUM, A., of Thornliebank, Glasgow.
CUNINGHAME, John, Ironmaster, St. Vincent Street, Glasgow.
CUNINGHAME, W. C. S., of Caprington, Kilmarnock.
60 CUNINGHAME, Sir W. J. M., Bart., V.C., of Corsehill, Kirkbride House, Maybole.
CUNLIFFE, Brooke Stewart, Chief Constable of Wigtonshire, Newton-Stewart.
CURRIE, Dr., Hydropathic Establishment, Skelmorlie.
CUTHBERT, Alex. A., 14 Newton Terrace, Glasgow.

LIST OF MEMBERS.

DALRYMPLE, Sir Charles, Bart., M.P., New Hailes, Musselburgh.
65 DALRYMPLE, Hon. Hew H., Lochinch, Castle Kennedy, Stranraer.
DALRYMPLE, Capt. The Hon. North, Lochinch, Castle Kennedy, Stranraer.
DALRYMPLE, Hon. Robert M., Lochinch, Castle Kennedy, Stranraer.
DAVIDSON, Patrick, Drumley, Tarbolton.
DAY, Robert, yr., 3 Sidney Place, Cork.
70 DICK, G. G., 3 Barns Street, Ayr.
DICKIE, Hugh, Rector, Academy, Kilmarnock.
DICKIE, James, Town Clerk, Irvine.
DICKIE, James, 13 Fenchurch Avenue, London, E.C.
DICKSON, George, Sheriff-Substitute of Galloway, Auchendoon, Newton-Stewart.
75 DICKSON, T., General Register House, Edinburgh.
DOBBIE, Robert, M.D., 3 Wellington Square, Ayr.
DOBIE, J. Shedden, F.S.A. Scot., of Morishill, Beith.
DODD, Mrs. Ashley, Stockton House, Codford St. Mary, Bath.
DONALDSON, J., Sunnyside, Formby, near Liverpool.
80 DOUGALL, D., Solicitor, Ayr.
DOUGLAS, David, 10 Castle Street, Edinburgh.
DOUGLAS, J. C., M.D., Whithorn, Wigtonshire.
DOUGLAS, W. D. Robinson, of Orchardton, Castle-Douglas.
DREW, James, Doonhill, Newton-Stewart.
85 DUNCAN, James Dalrymple, 211 Hope Street, Glasgow.
DUNLOP, David, Solicitor, Ayr.
DUNLOP, W. H., of Doonside, Ayr.

EASTON, John, C.A., 41 St. Vincent Place, Glasgow.
EGLINTON and WINTON, Earl of, Eglinton Castle, Irvine.
90 ELDER, George, Knock Castle, Largs.
EVANS, John, D.C.L., Nash Mills, Hemel Hempstead.

FAED, James, 7 Barnton Terrace, Edinburgh.
FAULDS, A. Wilson, Knockbuckle, Beith.
FERGUSSON, David, Solicitor, Ayr.
95 FERGUSSON, Right Hon. Sir James, Bart., K.C.M.G., of Kilkerran, M.P., Maybole.
FLEMING, John, 1 Scotland Street, Woodlands, Glasgow.

LIST OF MEMBERS.

FREW, William, M.D., Walmer, Dundonald Road, Kilmarnock.
FLEMING, James, jr., Kilmory, Skelmorlie.
FLINT, John, 2 Montgomerie Terrace, Ayr.
100 FORSYTH, John, Teacher, Castle-Douglas.
FOSTER, W. K., 45 Leinster Gardens, Hyde Park, London, W.
FRANKS, Augustus W., British Museum, London.
FRASER, Sir W., K.C.B., 32 Castle Street, Edinburgh.

GALLOWAY, Earl of, Galloway House, Wigtonshire.
105 GARDNER, Alexander, Publisher, Paisley.
GARDNER, William, Shawl Manufacturer, Paisley.
GEDDES, G. H., 142 Princes Street, Edinburgh.
GEMMELL, Thomas, Banker, Ayr.
GEMMELL, William, 150 Hope Street, Glasgow.
110 GILLESPIE, William, Solicitor, Castle-Douglas.
GILMOUR, A., Solicitor, Irvine.
GILMOUR, Allan, Woodend, Kilmarnock.
GIRVAN, J. Graham, 186 West George Street, Glasgow.
GLASGOW, Earl of, Kelburne Castle, Fairlie, Ayrshire.
115 GLASGOW, R. B. Robertson, of Montgreenan, Kilwinning.
GORDON, A. J., Factor, Kirkcudbright.
GORDON, George W. G. M., Corsemalzie, Whauphill.
GOUDIE, Robert, Sheriff-Clerk, Ayr.
GRAHAM, J., 212 West George Street, Glasgow.
120 GRAHAM, R. C., of Skipness, Argyleshire.
GRAY, G., Clerk of the Peace, Glasgow.
GREENWELL, Rev. Canon, Durham.
GREIG, T. C., Rephad, Stranraer.
GUTHRIE, Arthur, J.P., Ardrossan.
125 GRAY, John, 181 Renfrew Street, Glasgow.

HAMILTON, Captain, of Pinmore, Girvan.
HAMILTON, Frank S, Cairnhill, Kilmarnock.
HAMILTON, George, Ardendee, Kirkcudbright.
HAMILTON, H. M., 2 Harcourt Buildings, Temple, London.
130 HAMILTON, J., Town Clerk, Kilmarnock.
HAMILTON, J. Wallace, of Cairnhill, Kilmarnock.

LIST OF MEMBERS.

HAMILTON, John, of Sundrum, Ayr.
HAMILTON, Mrs. M. C., 13 Suffolk Square, Cheltenham.
HANNAH, A., Cairnsmore, Bellahouston, Govan.
135 HAY, J. F. Dalrymple, of Dunlop, Dunlop.
HAY, Right Hon. Sir John C. Dalrymple, Bart., of Park, Wigtonshire.
HENRY, David, Architect, Church Square, St. Andrews.
HERRIES, Lord, Kinharvey, New Abbey, Dumfries.
HILL, Daniel, Isalee Villa, Ayr.
140 HORNE, Robert R., 150 Hope Street, Glasgow.
HOULDSWORTH, William, Rozelle, Ayr.
HOWATSON, Charles, of Glenbuck, by Lanark.
HUME, Lieut.-Col., 8 Abbotsford Crescent, St. Andrews.
HUNTER, Andrew, Ayr.
145 HUNTER, David, Sea Tower, Ayr.
HUTCHISON, Graham, of Balmaghie, Castle-Douglas.

IRVINE, Burgh of.

JAMESON, Andrew, Advocate, St. Colme Street, Edinburgh.
JOHNSTON, D., 160 West George Street, Glasgow.
150 JOHNSTON, T. B., Geographer to the Queen, 9 Claremont Crescent, Edinburgh.
JONAS, A. C., 4 St. James's Crescent, Swansea.

KEITH, Rev. W. A., Burham Vicarage, Rochester.
KENNEDY, Captain Clark, of Knockgray, F.R.G.S., F.L.S., F.Z.S., Travellers' Club, Pall Mall, London.
KENNEDY, F. T. R., of Dunure, Ayr.
155 KENNEDY, J., of Underwood, 71 Great King Street, Edinburgh.
KENNEDY, J., yr., of Underwood, 71 Great King Street, Edinburgh.
KENNEDY, James, 25 Greendyke Street, Glasgow.
KENNEDY, Thomas, Glenfield, Kilmarnock.
KILPATRICK, William, Solicitor, Ayr.
160 KING, H. B., Commercial Bank, Kilwinning.
KINNA, James G., Riverstead, Creebridge, Newton-Stewart.

LIST OF MEMBERS.

KIRKCUDBRIGHT MUSEUM, per George Hamilton, Ardendee, Kirkcudbright.
KIRKHOPE, Thomas, Writer, Ardrossan.
KNOX, James, of Langlands, Dalry, Ayrshire.
165 KNOX, R. W., Moorpark, Kilbirnie.

LAING, Alexander, LL.D., Newburgh-on-Tay.
LAMB, J. B., Architect, Paisley.
LANDSBOROUGH, Rev. D., Kilmarnock.
LEADBETTER, Thomas, 122 George Street, Edinburgh.
170 LIVINGSTON, Rev. N., D.D., 7 Carrick Park, Ayr.
LOCKHART, John, 39 Sandgate Street, Ayr.
LONDON LIBRARY, 12 St. James's Square, London, S.W.
LORRAINE, Dr., Castle-Douglas.
LYON, D. Murray, Secretary to Grand Lodge of Scotland, Freemasons' Hall, Edinburgh.

175 M'ALISTER, J., Surgeon, Kilmarnock.
M'CALL, James, 6 St. John's Terrace, Hillhead, Glasgow.
M'CALL, James, Monreith Arms, Port-William.
M'CALLUM, Robert, Town Chamberlain, Ayr.
M'CHLERY, William, Balminnoch, Kirkcowan.
180 M'CLELLAND, A. S., 115 St. Vincent St., Glasgow.
M'CONNACHIE, J. A., C.E., 12 Victoria Road, Kensington, London, W.
M'CONNEL, William, of Knockdolian, Girvan.
M'COSH, James M., Solicitor, Dalry, Ayrshire.
M'CULLOCH, David, Beech Grove, Kilmarnock.
185 M'CULLOCH, Thomas, Founder, Kilmarnock.
M'EWEN, Robert P., of Bardrochwood, 16 Randolph Crescent, Edinburgh.
M'FIE, Alexander, Banker, Whithorn.
M'GIBBON, D., 65 Frederick Street, Edinburgh.
M'GIBBON, William, Draper, Stranraer.
190 M'HAFFIE, Wm. J., Torhousemuir, Wigton.
M'KERLIE, P. H., 26 Pembridge Villas, Bayswater, London, W.
M'KERRELL, R. M., of Hillhouse, Dundonald.
M'KERROW, George, M.D., 7 Barns Street, Ayr.

LIST OF MEMBERS.

MACARTHUR, Lady, 27 Princes Gardens, London, S.W.
195 MACDONALD, Alexander, 9 Montgomerie Drive, Kelvinside, Glasgow.
MACDONALD, A. G., The Crescent, Ardrossan.
MACDONALD, J., LL.D., 14 Kingsborough Gardens, Kelvinside, Glasgow.
MACDONALD, J. C. R., W.S., Dumfries.
MACDOUALL, James, of Logan, Stranraer.
200 MACDOWALL, Henry, younger, of Garthland, Lochwinnoch.
MACFARLANE, Dr., 6 Manchester Square, London, W.
MACKEAN, J. A., Maryfield, Paisley.
MACKENZIE, Alexander, 7 Gilmour Street, Paisley.
MACKENZIE, James, Solicitor, Stranraer.
205 MACKINNON, William, 115 St. Vincent Street, Glasgow.
MACLEOD, Rev. W., 112 Thirlestane Road, Whitehouse Loan, Edinburgh.
MACPHERSON, Professor Norman, 2 Randolph Cliff, Edinburgh.
MACRORIE, William, Solicitor, Ayr.
MARWICK, Sir J. D., LL.D., F.R.S.E., City Chambers, Glasgow.
210 MATTHEWS, Rev. G. D., D.D., 25 Christchurch Road, Brondesbury, London, N.W.
MAXWELL, Mrs., of Carruchan, Dumfries.
MAXWELL, Francis, of Gribton, Dumfries.
MAXWELL, Sir Herbert Eustace, Bart., M.P., of Monreith, Whauphill.
MAXWELL, Captain John Heron, yr., of Penninghame, Newton-Stewart.
215 MAXWELL, Sir W. F., Bart., Cardoness, Gatehouse.
MAXWELL, W. H., of Munches, Dalbeattie, Kirkcudbrightshire.
MAXWELL, Wellwood, of Kirkennan, by Dalbeattie.
MERCER, John, C.E., Ayr.
MIDDLEMAS, W., Town-Clerk's Office, Kilmarnock.
220 MITCHELL, Sir Arthur, 34 Drummond Place, Edinburgh.
MITCHELL, J. O., 69 East Howard Street, Glasgow.
MITCHELL, J. W., Lyon-Clerk Depute, Edinburgh.
MITCHELL LIBRARY, Ingram Street, Glasgow.
MONTGOMERIE, J. C., Dalmore, Stair.
225 MORRIS, A. Pollok, of Craig, c/o Messrs. M'Grigor, Donald, & Co., 172 St. Vincent Street, Glasgow.

LIST OF MEMBERS.

MORRIS, James A., F.R.I.B.A., 28 Canfield Gardens, South Hampstead, London, N.W.
MUNRO, Rev. Alexander, D.D., 52 Great Clyde Street, Glasgow.
MUNRO, R., M.D., Kilmarnock.
MURCHLAND, Charles, Publisher, Irvine.
230 MURDOCH, J. B., Barclay, Langside, Glasgow.
MURDOCH, John, Architect, Ayr.
MURDOCH, R. D., Fairfield Lodge, Ayr.
MURRAY, David, 169 West George Street, Glasgow.
MURRAY, William, Barns Park, Ayr.
235 MUTTER, James, of Meiklelaught, Ardrossan.

NIMMO, Mrs. E. H., Alcombe, Chippenham, Wiltshire.

OLIVER, Rev. J., Manse of Maryhill, Glasgow.
OSWALD, R. A., of Auchincruive, Ayr.

PARLANE, James, Appleby Lodge, Rusholme, Manchester.
240 PATERSON, A. T., Montreal, Canada, per John Paterson, Union Bank of Scotland, Irvine.
PATERSON, John, of Knowehead, Irvine.
PATERSON, Sheriff Orr, Ayr.
PATON, Hugh, Seedsman, Kilmarnock.
PATON, James B., Merchant, Ayr.
245 PATON, Robert, Gartferry, Ayr.
PATRICK, Miss Cochran, Ladyland, Beith.
PATRICK, R. W. Cochran, LL.D., of Woodside, Beith.
PATRICK, W. Ralston, of Trearne, Beith.
PICKEN, James, Hillhouse Lodge, Fenwick.
250 POLLOCK, William, Solicitor, Ayr.
POLLOK, R. M., of Middleton, Ayr.
PORTLAND, Duke of, Welbeck Abbey, Worksop, Notts.
POWLETT, Hon. A. L. Orde, Bolton Hall, Wensley, Yorkshire.
POWLETT, Hon. W. T. Orde, Wensley Hall, Wensley, Yorkshire.
255 PROCURATORS, Faculty of, Glasgow.

LIST OF MEMBERS.

RAFF, James, 14 Kingsborough Gardens, Kelvinside, Glasgow.
RAILTON, William, St. Marnock Place, Kilmarnock.
RAMSAY, Dr., Lochwinnoch.
RAMSAY, R., 33 Greendyke Street, Glasgow.
260 RANKEN, G. J., Solicitor, Ayr.
REID, Charles, Lily Mount, Kilmarnock.
REID, H. G., 11 Cromwell Crescent, South Kensington, London, S.W.
RENNIE, Thomas, Banker, Maybole.
ROBB, George, 11 Germiston Street, Glasgow.
265 ROSE, James, 11 Langlands Street, Kilmarnock.
ROWAT, William, St. Margaret's, Paisley.

SCOTT, John, C.B., Hawkhill, Greenock.
SELBY, R. R., M.D., Port-William.
SHAW, Charles G., Ayr.
270 SIGNET LIBRARY, Edinburgh.
SMITH, Rev. George Mure, 6 Clarendon Place, Stirling.
SMITH, J. Guthrie, Mugdock Castle, Milngavie.
SOMERVELL, James, of Sorn, M.P., Mauchline.
STAIR, Earl of, Lochinch, Castle Kennedy, Stranraer.
275 STEPHEN & POLLOCK, 31 Sandgate Street, Ayr.
STEVENSON, Allan, Architect, Ayr.
STEVENSON, T. G., 22 Frederick Street, Edinburgh.
STEWART, Gen. The Hon. A., Corsbie, Newton-Stewart.
STEWART, H. G. Murray, of Cally, Gatehouse.
280 STEWART, J., Heathfield, Irvine.
STEWART, Mark J., M.P., Ardwell, Wigtonshire.
STEWART, Sir Michael Shaw, Bart., of Ardgowan, Greenock.
STEWART, Robert Hathorn Johnston, Glasserton, Whithorn.
STRUTHERS, A. W., 3 Barns Terrace, Ayr.
285 STURROCK, Arthur, British Linen Company Bank, Kilmarnock.
STURROCK, J., junior, Solicitor, Kilmarnock.
STURROCK, Peter, Kilmarnock.
SYMINGTON, G., Banker, Glenluce.

THOMSON, Rev. J. H., Free Church Manse, Hightae, Lockerbie.

LIST OF MEMBERS.

290 THUREUEN, Lieut.-Col. F. A. V., Kirkfell, Highland Road, Upper Norwood, London, S.E.
TROTTER, Robert de Bruce, M.D., Tayview House, Perth.
TURNBULL, Andrew, Town-Chamberlain, Kilmarnock.
TURNER, F. J., Mansfield Woodhouse, Mansfield, Notts.
TURNER, J. H., Portland Estate Office, Kilmarnock.

295 VERNON, Hon. G. R., M.P., Auchans, Dundonald.
VIVIAN, A. P., St. James St., Buckingham Gate, London, S.W.

WALES, James, of Buckstone, Rawdon, Yorkshire.
WALKER, J., 74 Bath Street, Glasgow.
WALLACE, Charles, Dally, Kirkcolm, Stranraer.
300 WALLACE, Lieut.-Col. Sir William, Bart., of Lochryan, Stranraer.
WALLET, Duncan, 15 Billiter Street, London, E.C.
WATSON, J. C., 19 Kelvinside Terrace, Kelvinside, Glasgow.
WATSON, Peter, Cashier, Annbank.
WATT, J. R., M.D., Ayr.
305 WEIR, William, of Kildonan, Portland Ironworks, Kilmarnock.
WESTON, Col. Gould Hunter-, of Hunterston, West Kilbride.
WILLIAMSON, Walter, Solicitor, Beith.
WILSON, Rev. G., Free Church Manse, Glenluce, Wigtonshire.
WILSON, R. Dobie, 38 Upper Brook Street, London, W.
310 WOOD, Adam, Portland Villa, Troon.
WRIGHT, Hugh, of Altiery, Port-William.
WYLIE, R., Kilwinning.

YOUNG, David, Town Clerk, Paisley.

TABLE OF CONTENTS.

I.—MISCELLANEOUS MUNIMENTS.

		PAGE
1.	*Letters of Procuratory by the Burgh of Irvine to Mr. William Arthurle and others*—6th April 1472	1
2.	*Letters of Bailiery by the Burgesses of Irvine, to Archibald Mure, and four others*—11th October 1551	3
3.	*Letters of Procuratory by the Provost and Bailies of Irvine to William Kyle and others*—10th May 1552	4
4.	*Letters of Bailiery by the Burgesses and Community of Irvine in favour of Stephen Tran and others*—6th October 1552	5
5.	*Infeftment of John Wilson and Janet Sod his wife, in the half of the Loch Mill or Burgh Mill of Irvine*—9th February 1554-55	7
6.	*Discharge by Gavin, Commendator of Kilwinning, to the Burgh of Irvine for the Tax levied for reducing the Rate of Exchange of French money*—9th January 1556-57	9
7.	*Protest on behalf of the Burgh of Irvine for right to repledge a Burgess from the jurisdiction of the Bailies of Ayr*—23d August 1557	10
8.	*Letters of Bailiery by the Community of the Burgh of Irvine to Stephen Tran and four others*—4th October 1557	10
9.	*Inquest on the service of Hew Kyll as heir to Thomas Kyll his father, in the land of Gallowmuir*—20th April 1561	12
10.	*Discharge by Alexander Earl of Glencairn to the Burgh of Irvine for £52 : 6 : 8, towards furnishing Soldiers to take the Castle of Dunbarton*—27th December 1569	13
11.	*Commission for repledging Andrew Ross in Newmuir from the Sheriff-Court to the jurisdiction of Irvine*—6th October 1572	14
12.	*Contract between Hew Earl of Eglinton and the Burgh of Irvine as to their respective jurisdiction*—10th February 1572-73	15
13.	*Minutes of the Convention of Burghs at Glasgow*—1579	21
14.	*Agreement between the Commissioners of Ayr and Irvine respectively, in regard to their procedure before the Convention of Burghs about to meet*—15th February 1582-83	28

VOL. II

		PAGE
15.	*Letter from the Earl of Gowrie and other Lords to the Provost, Bailies, and Council of Irvine—21st September* 1584	29
16.	*Letter from Laurence Scott to the Provost and Bailies of Irvine anent the business of the Town—8th April* 1591	30
17.	*Letter from Laurence Scott to the Magistrates of Irvine referring to the legal interests of the Burgh—24th June* 1593	31
18.	*Convention of Burghs*—1595	32
19.	*Act of Deprivation of non-resident Burgesses of Irvine—9th June* 1595	36
20.	*Letter from William Scott to the Provost and Bailies of Irvine about the Convention of the Burghs—5th July* 1599	40
21.	*Petition of John Wyllie—post* 1601	42
22.	*Complaint by Helen Gray, to the Kirk Session of Irvine, against Janet Smyth—date wanting. Circa* 1601	43
23.	*Missive from the Magistrates of Selkirk to the Magistrates of Irvine, respecting the articles to be discussed at the Convention of Burghs at Selkirk—15th February* 1608	43
24.	*Articles for instruction of the Burghs, produced by Sir John Drummond, Commissioner to the Convention at Selkirk*—1616	48
25.	*Articles of the Convention of Burghs*—1641 [?]	50
26.	*Renunciation by James Blair and his spouse, in favour of the Magistrates of Irvine, of an annualrent of* 160 *merks furth of the Burgh Mills—27th May* 1642	53
27.	*Act of the Convention of Burghs for registration of Charter by David the Second, King of Scots, conferring privileges upon the Burghs—7th July* 1642	56
28.	*Petition of John Dunlop, late Bailie of Irvine, for satisfaction for his Losses in defence of the town against Montrose's Highlanders in* 1645	58
29.	*Tack by the Earl of Eglinton to the Burgh of Irvine, of the Hair Mill, for* 19 *years—23d July* 1645	60
30.	*Agreement between the Crafts of Irvine and the Magistrates in regard to the acceptance by the former from the latter of the Seal of Cause—3d July* 1646	64
31.	*Receipt by the Commissioners of Perth to the Treasurer of Irvine for Contribution of £*90 *for the help of the Poor of Perth in time of pestilence—1st December* 1646	69
32.	*Receipts for various sums connected with the levy and equipment of Troops—19th January* 1647	69
33.	*Letter from W. Bell, Dalry, to [William Wishart, Bailie of Irvine,] desiring payment of the allowance for the Families of Soldiers wounded or slain—6th February* 1648	70

TABLE OF CONTENTS.

PAGE

34. Receipts on behalf of several parishes in Ayrshire, to William Wishart, Bailie of Irvine, for the allowance due to the Families of Soldiers wounded or slain—February and March 1648 71

35. Warrant to Ninian Ross, late Treasurer of Irvine, to pay for the Confections used when the Laird of Ardkinglas was admitted Burgess—1st March 1648 73

36. Receipt for Maintenance paid by the Magistrates of Irvine for Colonel Montgomery's Regiment, from December 1645 to 1st March 1648—13th March 1648 73

37. Order by Alan Dunlop, Bailie of Irvine, to the Treasurer, for payment of 100 merks borrowed from James Blair—1648 74

38. Discharge by Henry Christie, Quartermaster of Argyll's Regiment, to the Magistrates of Irvine, for Maintenance Money—23d April 1650 . 74

39. Discharge by James Christie, Quartermaster of the Marquis of Argyll's Regiment, to the Magistrates of Irvine for Maintenance Money—19th June 1650 74

40. Backbond by Robert Galt, to the Magistrates of Irvine, in regard to the Multures of the Loch Mill and Water Mill—10th March 1652 . . 75

41. Minute of the Gentlemen and Heritors of Ayrshire anent payment of a Bed sent by the Town of Irvine to Broddic—30th May 1656 . . 76

42. Petition of Hew Ross, schoolmaster, to the Magistrates of Irvine—12th December 1656 77

43. Petition of Adam Fullertoun, for payment of money advanced to Duke Hamilton's Regiment, and the decision of the Magistrates of Irvine thereon—1st April 1659 78

44. Tack in favour of Robert Galt, of the two Burgh Mills of Irvine—27th May 1659 79

45. Petition of James Galt, smith, with account—1659 . . . 86

46. Discharge by the Earl of Eglinton to Robert Galt, for the silver duty of the Holme Mill—9th January 1660 88

47. Discharge by Hew Whyte, merchant, to the Magistrates of Irvine—8th August 1662 88

48. Bond by Henry Dyet in reference to shooting at the Papingo—29th August 1665 91

49. Discharge by Ninian Cuninghame to the Magistrates of Irvine for £6 sterling for behoof of the Manufactory of Montgomeryston—2d November 1665 . 92

50. Missive from the Provost and Council of Edinburgh to the Provost and Council of Irvine, with instructions regarding the next Convention of the Burghs—25th March 1667 93

	PAGE
51. Missive from the Provost and Council of Edinburgh to the Provost and Council of Irvine in regard to the next Convention of Burghs—16th December 1667 .	97
52. Discharge by John Smyth, mason, to the Magistrates of Irvine, for £1000, in payment of his work upon the Bridge of Irvine—23d December 1667 .	98
53. Letter, Sir Alexander Cuninghame of Robertland to the Magistrates of Irvine—23d September 1670	99
54. Discharge by the Earl of Eglinton to the Magistrates of Irvine for the outfit of their Militia horses—21st May and 8th June 1671	100
55. Discharge by the Earl of Eglinton to the Magistrates of Irvine for three years' maintenance of their Militia horses—1st July 1671 .	100
56. Discharge by the Earl of Eglinton to the Magistrates of Irvine for 200 merks, due for the town's Militia horses—13th December 1671	101
57. Order to the Treasurer of Irvine to pay to Mr. Robert Hunter, preacher, the interest on Bond for £1000, lent by him to the Burgh—2d September 1680	101
58. Discharge by Robert Hunter to the Magistrates of Irvine for the interest of £1000 lent by the late Robert Hunter of Hunterstone—2d September 1680 .	102
59. Order upon the Treasurer of Irvine to pay the Provost's expenses at the Funeral of the Laird and Lady of Kilbirnie—21st January 1681 .	102
60. Act of the Town Council of Irvine, appointing William Clerk schoolmaster of the Burgh for one year—16th April 1686 .	103
61. Act of the Town Council of Irvine appointing Auditors of the Tavern accounts—23d December 1686	104
62. Report by the Commissioners appointed by the Convention of Royal Burghs on the state and condition of the Burgh of Irvine—2d May 1692. [Miscellany of Scot. Burgh Record Society, p. 102.].	104
63. Act of the Town Council of Irvine in favour of the Incorporations of Trades thereof, granting liberty to improve their Seat in the Church of Irvine—4th November 1693	107
64. Agreement between Alexander Lord Montgomerie and the Magistrates of Irvine anent the Holm Mill—25th May 1694 .	108
65. Agreement between the Magistrates of Irvine and James Nisbet, Bailie, for the sale by the latter of a Tenement near the Cross—20th August 1694 .	109
66. Letter from Lord Findlater to the Provost and Magistrates of Irvine, requesting Contributions for the Harbour of Cullen—17th February 1697 .	111
67. Act of the Town Council of Irvine, allowing Mr. Andrew Tait, minister, to repair his Tenement in Irvine—1st May 1702 .	112
68. Gift by several Noblemen, Gentlemen, and others, of various sums, for maintaining a yearly Horse Race at Irvine—20th August 1702 .	113
69. Scroll Instrument upon the Election of a Commissioner to Parliament for the Burgh of Irvine—17th September 1702 .	115

TABLE OF CONTENTS.

xxi

		PAGE
70.	*Account by William M'Taggart, Dean of Guild of Irvine, of the Election of a Commissioner to Parliament for the Burgh*—17th September 1702	119
71.	*Instrument upon the Election of new Councillors for the Burgh of Irvine*—25th September 1702	122
72.	*Inventory of Goods seized by the Collector of Irvine, and publicly burned, with minutes thereof*—6th and 7th April 1704	124
73.	*Roup of the Market and Bridge Customs of Irvine*—1st November 1705	126
74.	*Act of Privy Council for a general Contribution for repairing the Harbour of Irvine*—12th February 1706	128
75.	*Roup of the Petty Customs of the Market, Bridge, and Anchorage of Irvine*—1st November 1706	129
76.	*Report by [Allan] Francis, Clerk of the Burgh of Irvine, to on the Council of the Burgh, and form of election of its Office-bearers*—29th June 1710. [*Miscellany* of Scot. Burgh Record Society, p. 195.]	131
77.	*Act of the Town Council of Irvine authorising the production of their Charter of Replegiation before the Justices at Ayr*—29th October 1711	132
78.	*Bond by Residenters in Ayrshire for payment of stakes for the Prize to be shot for yearly at Irvine*—1721	132
79.	*Act of the Town Council of Irvine erecting the Barbers of the Burgh into an Incorporation*—30th September 1723	134
80.	*Roup of the Customs of Irvine*—1st November 1732	135
81.	*Contract between the Magistrates of Irvine and Thomas Brown, mason, for building the Bridge anew*—15th January 1748	137
82.	*Commission to James Gemmell, Writer, to be Fiscal of the Admiralty of Irvine*—13th November 1752	140
83.	*Attestation of the date of the Seal of Cause*—24th February 1757	141
84.	*Proposed Address by the Freeholders of Ayr to the King in regard to arming the Inhabitants for defence of the Coast*—3d October 1759	141
85.	*Letter to the Magistrates of Irvine in reference to an Address by them and the Magistrates of Ayr to the King, regarding the arming of the Inhabitants*—15th October 1759	143
86.	*Papers in Process between the Magistrates of Irvine and Mr. Kemp, Teacher of English, etc.*—1755-1759	145
87.	*Commission by Archibald, Earl of Eglinton, Deputy Vice-Admiral of Irvine, to Anthony M'Harg, Town-Clerk, as his substitute*—15th November 1777	161
88.	*Memorial and Queries for the Magistrates of Irvine in reference to the use of the Bridge*—12th August 1783	163

MUNIMENTS OF THE BURGH OF IRVINE.

II.—COUNCIL BOOK OF IRVINE.

	PAGE
Beginning 6th December 1664 and ending 8th May 1668 .	165-238

III.—EXCERPTS FROM BURGH ACCOUNTS.

1. *Burgh Accounts*—1600-1601		239
2. *Burgh Accounts*—1601-1602		241
3. *Compt of borrowit Silver and depursings when the Town went to Dunbartane—Circa 1602*		243
4. *Burgh Accounts*—1607-1608		245
5. *Burgh Accounts*—1608-1609*		248
6. *The Toune's Compt auchtand to Margaret Hamilton, 1610*		250
7. *Towne's Compt*—1611		251
8. *Account for Refreshments to the Magistrates, etc.*—12th January 1648		252
9. *Account of Disbursements by John Dunlop for the Burgh—Circa* 1653		253
10. *Account by Bailie John Dunlop against the Burgh*—1653-57		254
11. *Account of proportion due by the Burgh to the Agent of the Royal Burghs*—1653-1654		257
12. *Account of Expenses incurred by the Magistrates for Refreshments*—29th August 1655		257
13. *The Compt of John Guthrie his chairges and depursings for the Town of Irvine in Edinburgh*—1656		258
14. *Order for payment to William Morison, "the Burgh's post," for carrying a Letter*—4th November 1656		259
15. *Account of Disbursements and Losses sustained by John Dunlop, bailie—Circa* 1656		259
16. *Account by Laurence Blair against the Magistrates for Refreshments*—28th April 1658		261
17. *Order for payment for carriage of a Letter to Edinburgh*—14th April 1659		261
18. *The Provost's Account—Circa* 1659		262
19. *Account between Provost Craig and David Calderwood for use of the latter's horse*—11th March 1662		263
20. *Account against the Magistrates for Refreshments*—1661-1662		263
21. *Account for Refreshments to the Magistrates and their Guests*—1663		265
22. *Account for Refreshments to the Magistrates*—1663-1664		266
23. *The Town's Account due to Janet Barclay*—1669-1670		267

TABLE OF CONTENTS.

xxiii

	PAGE
24. Account for Refreshments to the Magistrates, etc.—1670	270
25. Account for Refreshments—1670	271
26. Account for Refreshments—4th October 1676	274
27. Account between the Burgh of Irvine and their Agent—11th June 1677	275
28. Account for Refreshments—1679-1680	276
29. Account for Refreshments—1678-1680	280
30. Account for Candles for the use of the Guard—1678-1680	283
31. Account for Refreshments—1680	284
32. Account for Ironwork, etc.—18th November 1680	287
33. Account of John Dean, cooper, for making "new pecks" for the Town—March 1681	288
34. Account for Refreshments—1680-1681	289
35. Account for Refreshments—1681	291
36. Order for payment of quartering two Soldiers—April 1681	292
37. Order on the Treasurer to pay £19 to the smith for dressing the Town Clock, etc.—18th April 1681	292
38. Order for payment of various Town Charges—29th April 1681	293
39. Order on the Treasurer for the price of 6000 "skluitts"—5th May 1681	293
40. Order for payment of Account for Calseying the Bridge—7th May 1681	294
41. Order for payment of Salary to William Meldrum, the Town Marshal—16th May 1681	294
42. Order for payment of drawing 86 draught of Stones for the Bridge Calsey—25th May 1681	294
43. Order for payment of the price of ten Trees—28th May 1681	294
44. Order for payment of price of 10 loads of Coals for a Bonfire—30th May 1681	295
45. Order for payment of Skins for the Town's Drum—31st May 1681	295
46. Order for payment of Sand for the Kirk—14th July 1681	295
47. Order for payment of Lime for the Kirk—15th July 1681	295
48. Various Burgh Accounts—August and September 1681	296
49. Account of the Treasurer's Disbursements—1681	298
50. Order for payment to Hugh Montgomery of his Salary as Bailie, and other sums—19th August 1682	298
51. Order for payment on account of the Militia Horse for the Town—12th February 1684	299
52. Account between James Boyle, late Provost, and the Burgh—1679-1686	299
53. Account due by the Town to Janet Garven—1686	302
54. Account for Refreshments—1686-1687	313

		PAGE
55.	Account by John Murray, wright, for work done in the Church and School—1697	315
56.	Account between the Soldiers in the companies of Captains Mossman and Erskine and certain Inhabitants of Irvine—1700	316
57.	Account of Mathew Gray for repairing Newmurehouse—1702	318
58.	Order by Bailie Stevenson to pay for 14 bolls of Lime for new Bridge—25th August	319
59.	Account for work by David Mure—September 1742	319
60.	Account for Mason Work—1743	320
61.	Various Accounts—1744	321
62.	Account for Timber, etc.—1744	322
63.	Account for Slates and Timber—1744	323
64.	Account for repairs at the Meal Market—February 1745	323
65.	Accounts for carting materials for building the Prison—1744-1745	324
66.	Account of Refreshments to the "Carriers"—1744-1745	327
67.	Various Trades Accounts—1744-1745	330
68.	Account of Expense of rebuilding the Town House—anno 1745	333

INDEX   337

LIST OF ILLUSTRATIONS

THE TOWNHOUSE OR TOLBOOTH OF IRVINE, from the N.W. Drawn by Mr. W. H. Ross of Glasgow, from a Photograph taken *circa* 1860 . *Frontispiece*

SIGNATURES OF STEPHEN TRAN, PROVOST OF IRVINE, AND JAMES BROWN, TOWN CLERK, —1552 . . . . *Page* 4

SEAL OF THE BURGH OF IRVINE,—1552 . . . 6, 164

SIGNATURES OF GAVIN, COMMENDATOR OF KILWINNING, AND JAMES MAXWELL, BURGESS OF ROUEN,—1557 9

SIGNATURE OF ALEXANDER, EARL OF GLENCAIRN,—1569 . . 14

SIGNATURES OF HEW, EARL OF EGLINTOUN, AND HEW, MASTER OF EGLINTOUN,—1573 . 20

SIGNATURES OF THE EARLS OF GOWRIE, MAR, AND GLENCAIRN, AND THE ABBOTS OF CAMBUSKENNETH AND DRYBURGH,—1584 29

SIGNATURE OF ALEXANDER, EARL OF EGLINTOUN,—1645 . . . 63

SIGNATURES OF CRAFTSMEN OF IRVINE, viz. HEW BROUN, THOMAS GAIRNER, DANIELL DUNLOP, WILLIAM HENDRISOUN, ANDRO BORDLAND, LOURENC SPIR, ROBERT MEINZEIS, HEW THOMSONE, WILAM HENDRISONE, AND HEW THOMSONE,—1646 68

STAMP OF THE INCORPORATED TRADES OF IRVINE,—1646 . . 68

SIGNATURES OF GENTLEMEN AND HERITORS OF THE SHIRE OF AYR, viz. (LORD) COCHRANE; (SIR J. CAMPBELL OF CESNOK) Sr J. CESNOK; (BARRE of that Ilk) BARRE of y^t Ilke; J. CONYNGHAME; W. ROWALLANE, Yonger; DUNLOP; JO. HALDANE,—1656 76

SIGNATURES OF NOBLEMEN AND OTHERS, with their CONTRIBUTIONS for a YEARLY HORSE RACE AT IRVINE, viz. KILMARNOCK for ten ℔ sterling; MONTGOMERIE ane hundred and tuentie pounds Scots; F. MONTGOMERIE, sixtie pounds Scots; ALEX^r HOME, sixtie pounds Scots; CRAFURD OF KILBIRNY, sixty pounds Scots; WILL. COCHRANE, sixtie pounds Scots; J. MONTGOMERIE, sixty p^{ds} Scots,—1702 . 114

VOL. II *d*

LIST OF ILLUSTRATIONS.

	PAGE
SIGNATURE OF ARCHIBALD, EARL OF EGLINTOUNE,—1777	163
SCULPTURED STONE, containing the ARMS OF THE BURGH, which formed the centre of the pediment of the street entrance door to the OLD COUNCIL CHAMBER,—date supposed to be *circa* 1640	238
SEAL OF THE BURGH OF IRVINE as appended, in 1646, to the SEAL OF CAUSE ("Miscellaneous Muniments," No. 30), and the Matrix of which is now in possession of the TOWN COUNCIL. The Matrix, however, is of brass or copper, not silver, as stated in the "Introduction" to Vol. I. p. xxxiii	335

MUNIMENTS
OF
THE BURGH OF IRVINE

MUNIMENTS
OF
THE BURGH OF IRVINE

———▶◀———

I.—MISCELLANEOUS MUNIMENTS.

1. *Letters of Procuratory by the Burgh of Irvine to Mr. William Arthurle and Others.—6th April 1472.*

NOVERINT universi presentes litteras visuri nos burgenses et totam communitatem burgi de Irwyn fecisse constituisse et ordinasse necnon per presentes facere constituere et ordinare venerabiles et circumspectos viros videlicet magistrum Willelmum Arthurle decretorum doctorem dominos Johannem Umffalde vicarium de Kilmauris Johannem Robertoun Johannem Kerd capellanos et Finlaium Roys conburgensem nostros veros legitimos et indubitatos procuratores actores factores et negociorum nostrorum nuncios speciales dando et concedendo eisdem et eorum alteri conjunctim vel divisim nostram plenariam potestatem et specialem mandatum ad comparendum pro nobis et nomine nostro coram officiali Glasguensi suisve commissariis pluribus aut uno in omnibus causis nostris contra quoscunque motis seu movendis et specialiter in causa pro nobis mota seu movenda contra dominum Gilbertum Heward capellanum ad agendum defendendum commendum recommendum libellum prestandum libellos et quascunque pecunias recipiendum dandum recipiendum litem seu lites contestandum et contestari videndum de calumpnia et de veritate dicendum juramentum in animas nostras prestandum et a parte adversa prestitum requirendum ponendum et articulandum positionibus et articulis respondendum testes litteras instrumenta et quecunque probacionum genera producendum et procedendum . . contra testes a parte adversa productos videndum . . . . et eorum dicta dicendum et comparendum contra producta a parte adversa excipiendum replicandum duplicandum triplicandum quadruplicandum . . . . . et concludaudum sentenciam seu sentencias tam interlocutorias quam diffinitivas fieri petendum et audiendum aliasque necesse fuerit et quolibet alio gravamine auferendo semell vell plures . . . et appellandum appellacionem seu appellaciones intimandum . . . petendum et optinendum exspensas suas faciendas postulaciones . . . . seu causas absencie racione et quascunque alias excusaciones legittimas nomine nostro proponendum allegandum et probandum absolucionem supplicem et ad carceriam si opus fuerit petendum et optinendum judicium fieri implorandum . . . . seu procuratores locorum eorum substituendum juramentum deferendum concordandum et comprobandum et litteras quittancie dandum ac quecunque alia et singula faciendum gerendum et exercendum que veri et legittimi procuratores facere debent aut possent et que nosmet facerimus aut facere potuissemus si . . . . . personaliter interessemus Ratum gratum firmum atque stabile perpetuis temporibus habituros totum et quicquid dicti nostri procuratores aut eorum aliquis . . . conjunctim vel divisim nomine nostro in premissis vel premissorum aliquo duxerint vel duxerit faciendum.

In cujus rei testimonium sigillum nostrum commune presentibus est appensum apud burgum nostrum de Irwin sexto die mensis Aprilis anno domini millesimo quadringentesimo septuagesimo secundo.

[Seal wanting: parchment much wasted by damp.]

Abstract.

Letters of Procuratory by the burgesses and community of Irvine to Mr. William Arthurle, doctor of decrees, Sir John Umffald, Vicar of Kilmaurs, Sir John Roberton, Sir John Kerd, chaplains, and Finlay Ros, burgess, giving to them and each of them full power and special mandate to compear for and in name of the burgh of Irvine before the Official of Glasgow, or his commissaries, in all their causes against whomsoever, and especially in the plea between the town and Sir Gilbert Heward, chaplain. Dated at Irvine and sealed with the common seal of the Burgh, 6th April 1472.

2. *Letters of Bailiery by the Burgesses of Irvine, to Archibald Mure, and four Others.*—11th *October* 1551.

UNIVERSIS pateat per presentes nos burgenses et communitatem burgi de Irwin fecisse constituisse et ordinasse et per presentes facere constituere et ordinare delectos nostros comburgenses Archibaldum Mur Willelmum Kyll Johannem Wylsoun Johannem Auld Jacobum Broun nostros veros legittimos et indubitatos ballivos commissarios et nuncios speciales dando et concedendo prefatis nostris ballivis commissariis et nunciis et eorum cuilibet conjunctim et divisim latoribus seu latori presencium nostram plenariam liberam et legittimam potestatem ac speciale et expressum mandatum terras nostras assedandi firmas earundem et annuos redditus nostros levandi curias nostras tenendi exitus et amerciamenta earundem recipiendi transgressores puniendi comburgenses nostros stallangiatores et omnes inhabitantes infra burgum nostrum antedictum ac libertates eiusdem coram quibuscumque judicibus per quoscunque quibuscunque de causis attachiati arestati seu calumniati fuerint ad crucem et forum ac libertatem predicti burgi nostri replegeandi et reducendi Et generaliter omnia alia et singula faciendi dicendi gerendi et exercendi que ad officium ballivorum et commissariorum ad talia constitutorum de jure et consuetudine regni Scotie noscuntur pertinere Ratum gratum habentes et habituri totum quicquid prefati nostri ballivi commissarii et nuncii conjunctim et divisim in premissis et ea tangentibus duxerint vel duxerit faciendum In cujus rei testimonium sigillum commune predicti burgi nostri de Irwin est appensum apud dictum burgum de Irwin undecimo die mensis Octobris anno domini millesimo quingentesimo quinquagesimo primo.

[Seal broken.]

ABSTRACT.

Letters of Bailiery by the burgesses and community of Irvine, appointing their conburgesses Archibald Mure, William Kyll, John Wilson, John Auld, and James Broun, their bailies, commissioners, and special nuncios, with full power to set the burgh lands, hold courts, punish transgressors, and to do all other things which to the office of bailies and commissioners by the law and custom of the Kingdom of Scotland are known to belong. In testimony whereof the common seal of the Burgh is appended: Given at Irvine, and sealed with the common seal of the Burgh 11th October 1551.

3. *Letters of Procuratory by the Provost and Bailies of Irvine to William Kyll and Others.*—10th *May* 1552.

UNIVERSIS pateat per presentes nos Stephanum Trane prepositum de Irwin Willelmum Kyll Joannem Wylsoun ballivos ac Jacobum Brown scribam dicti burgi fecisse constituisse et ordinasse necnon facere constituere et ordinare tenore presentium honorabiles et probos viros Willelmum Kyll Robertum Scott magistros Jacobum M'Gill Joannem Spens Thomam M'Calzeane Jacobum Scott et eorum cuilibet conjunctim et divisim nostros veros legittimos et indubitatos procuratores actores factores et negociorum nostrorum gestores ac nuncios speciales dando et concedendo dictis nostris procuratoribus et eorum cuilibet conjunctim et divisim nostram veram legittimam et omnimodam potestatem ad comparendum pro nobis et nomine nostro coram dominis consilii supreme domine nostre regine ad producendum libros prothogollorum quondam Thome Cameroun clerici burgalis de Irwin ac omnia alia et singula facienda gerenda et exercenda que ad officium procuratorum ad talia constitutorum de jure et consuetudine regni Scotie noscuntur pertinere Et quod nos ipsi fecerimus si personaliter interessemus Ratum gratum habentes et habituros totum et quicquid prefati nostri procuratores conjunctim vel divisim in premissis et ea tangentibus duxerint faciendum sub ypotheca et obligatione omnium bonorum nostrorum presentium et futurorum In cujus rei testimonium sigillum nostrum commune presentibus est appensum unacum nostris subscriptionibus manualibus apud Irwin decimo die mensis Maij anno domini millesimo quingentesimo quinquagesimo secundo.

I, JHONE WELSOUNE, wht my hand one the penn.

[Small part of Seal remaining.]

[*On the back.*]

Decimo nono Maij anno, etc., v^o quinquagesimo secundo vise et admisse.   J. SCOTT.

ABSTRACT.

Letters of Procuratory by Stephen Tran, provost of Irvine, William Kyll, John Wilson, bailies, and James Broun, clerk of the burgh, appointing honourable and worthy men, William Kyll, Robert Scott, Masters James M'Gill, John Spens, Thomas M'Calzean, James Scott, and each of them, conjunctly and severally, their lawful procurators, actors, factors, and special messengers, and giving them power to compear on their behalf before the Lords of Council of their Sovereign Lady the Queen, to produce the Protocol Books of the deceased Thomas Cameron, clerk of the Burgh of Irvine, and to do all and sundry other things pertaining to the office of procuratory, according to the law and custom of the Kingdom of Scotland. Sealed with the common seal of the burgh, and subscribed at Irvine 10th May 1552.

[The signatures given in facsimile are :—I, STYNE TRAN, proveist, vyth my hand.   JACOBUS BROUNE, manu propria.]

4. *Letters of Bailiery by the Burgesses and Community of Irvine in favour of Stephen Tran and Others.*—6th October 1552.

UNIVERSIS pateat per presentes nos burgenses et communitatem burgi de Irwin fecisse constituisse et ordinasse et per presentes facere constituere et ordinare dilectos nostros conburgenses Stephanum Tran nostrum prepositum Joannem Gemmyle Joannem Pebilles Joannem Wylsoun Willelmum Kyll juniorem Magister Johannem Auld nostros veros legitimos et indubitatos ballivos commissarios et nuncios speciales Dando et concedendo prefatis nostris ballivis commissariis et nunciis et eorum cuilibet conjunctim et divisim latoribus ceu latori presencium nostram plenariam liberam et legittimam potestatem ac speciale et expressum mandatum terras nostras assedandum firmas earundem et annuos redditus nostros levandum curias nostras tenendum exitus et amerciamenta earundem recipiendum transgressores puniendum conburgenses nostros stallangiatores et omnes inhabitantes infra burgum nostrum antedictum ac libertates ejusdem coram quibuscumque judicibus per quoscumque quibuscumque de causis attachiati arrestati ceu calumniati fuerint ad crucem et forum ac libertatem predicti burgi nostri replegiandum et reducendum et generaliter omnia alia et singula facienda ducenda gerenda et exercenda que ad officium prepositi et ballivorum commissariorum ad talia constitutorum de jure et consuetudine regni Scotie noscuntur pertinere Ratum gratum habentes et habituri totum et quicquid prefatus noster prepositus et ballivi commissarii et nuncii conjunctim vel divisim in premissis et ea tangentibus duxerint vel duxerit faciendum. In cujus rei testimonium sigillum commune predicti burgi nostri de Irwin presentibus est appensum apud dictum nostrum burgum de Irwin sexto die mensis Octobris anno domini millesimo quingentesimo quinquagesimo secundo.

[On back.]

Die quinto mensis Decembris anno domini millesimo v^c lij° in curia burgi de Aire vise et admisse, etc.   S. D. PRESTOUN.

In curia viccecomitatus de Air pro nundinis xxvij Junij anno, etc. liij° vise et admisse.   H. PRESTOUN.

ABSTRACT.

Letters of Bailiery by the burgesses and community of Irvine, appointing their conburgesses Stephen Tran their provost, John Gemmyll, John Peebles, John Wilson, William Kyll, younger, and Mr. John Auld, their bailies, commissioners and special nuncios, giving full power and special mandate to them to set their lands, to uplift the fermes thereof, and the annualrents of the burgh, to hold their courts, and to take the issues and fines of the same, to punish transgressors, to repledge and bring back their conburgesses, stallingers, and all inhabitants within their burgh and liberties thereof, before whatsoever judges, by whomsoever, and for whatever causes they may be attached, arrested, or accused, to the cross and market and freedom of their foresaid burgh; and, generally, to do all other things belonging to the office of provost and bailies commissioners appointed for such purposes, as by the law and custom of Scotland are known to pertain. Sealed with the common seal of the burgh at Irvine 6th October 1552.

5. *Infeftment of John Wilson and Janet Scot his Wife, in the half of the Loch Mill or Burgh Mill of Irvine.*—*9th February* 1554-5.

Nono mensis Februarii anno, etc. liiii. The quhilk day in jugment Archebald Mure provest of the burgh of Irvin with consent and assent of the consale and communite of the said burgh hes admittit enterit and rasavit Alexander Scot sone and aire to umquhile William Scot eldar burges of Irvin his airis executouris and assignais in and to all and haill the tane half of the Lochmyln callit the borrowmyln with the pertinentis quhilkis the said umquhill William Scot and his subtennentes usit and brukit aboifoire The said Alexander and his forsaidis payand thairfor yeirly to us and our successouris proveist baillies and communite of the said burgh males and deueteis usit and wount providing that the said Alexander and his forsaidis observe and keip the use and consuetud of the said burgh usit abefoir conforme to the auld lovable use maid thairanent in tymes bigane And thairefter in jugment incontinent the said Alexander Scot with consent and assent of Kathrin Montgomery his mother resignit and ourgef simpliciter fra him his airis executouris and assignais all his rycht titill of rycht clame interes propirte possessioun and kyndnes quhilkes he hes had or may have in and to the tane half of the said Loch mylu callit the borrow mylne with the pertinentis quhilkis the said umquhile Williame Scot and his subtennentis usit abefoire with all and sindre fredoumes commoditeis and proffettis pertenyng thairto in the handis of the said Archebald Mure provest forsaid for the tyme of the said burgh as in the handis of thair superiour thairof in favouris of the saidis Johnn Wilsoun and Jonet Scot his spous and the langar levar of tham twa and thair forsaidis And thairefter the said proveist with consent and assent of the baillies consale and communite of the said burgh hes enterit admittit and rasavit thairto the saidis Johnn and Jonet and the langar levar of tham twa thair airis and assignais tennentis to tham to be brukit usit and josit be the saidis Johne or Jonet or the langar levar of thame and thair subtennentis and servandis ane or ma The saidis Johne and Jonet the langar levar of tham twa and thair forsaidis payand yeirly herfor to us and our successouris males and deuoteis usit and wount with this provisioun that the saidis personis keip and observe the custoume of the said burgh conform to the auld lovable consuetude and use thairof maid thairanent abefoir Apud acta Extractum de Libris actorum curie burgalis de Irvin per me Jacobum Browne scribam dicte curie propria manu.

Ita est Jacobus Browne scriba dicte curie notarius publicus manu propria.

Penultimo Januarii 1584, productum per HAY

GIBSOUN.

6. *Discharge by Gavin, Commendator of Kilwinning, to the Burgh of Irvine for the Tax levied for reducing the Rate of Exchange of French Money.*—9th *January* 1556-7.

WE Gawin commendatour of Kilwyning and James Maxwell burges of Rowane be the tennour heirof grantis us to haif ressavit fra Petir Craik messinger in name and behalf of the baillies counsale and communite of the burgh of Irewin the soume of thretty nyne pundis five schillingis money of this realme in compleit payment of thair pairt of the taxt maid uponne the haill borrowis of this realme for the doun getting of the impositioun of sexteine deneiris aboun four deneiris rasit in Rowane and Deip upoun the custum of ilk Frank waring bocht thair be the merchandis of the borrowis of this realme to be brocht within the samin conforme to the letteres of the lordis of counsale gevin thairupoun Of the quhilk soume of thretty pundis five schillingis money foirsaid in compleit payment of the foirsaid taxt for the pairt of the said toun of Irewin as said is we hald us weill content and thankfullie payit and for us our airis executouris and assignayis quitclames and discharges the saidis baillies counsale and communite of the said burgh of Irewin and thair successouris thairof for evir be thir presentis Subscrivit with our handis at Edinburgh the ix day of Januar the yeir of God I^m v^c lvj yeiris Befoir thir witnes Alexander Kaa Thomas Rychtpayth burges of Edinburgh maister George Freir notar publict and Gilbert Thorntoun with utheris divers.

7. *Protest on behalf of the Burgh of Irvine for right to Repledge a Burgess from the jurisdiction of the Bailies of Ayr.*—23d August 1557.

Jhesus.

Anno Domini millesimo quingentesimo quinquagesimo septimo die mensis Augusti xxiii Forsamekle as William Kyle ane of the balyeis commissariis in that part lauchfully constitute be the burgh of Irwin to replaig Jhone Montgumery burgess therof fra befoir the balyeis of Aire quha wes attechit at thair instance and past to the presens of the saidis balyeis of Aire for the tyme thai ar to say Master Mechaell Wallace and Jhon Lokart, and requirit the said Jhone Montgomery to be replagit first be vertew of his commissioun schawin and producit in jugement quhilk the sadis balyeis repellit quhill thai had sene ane greter evedent rycht And therefter the said William producit the Kinges confirmatioun that deit in Flowdoun of guid mynd quham God assolze and said it was ane our precious jowall to ony man within burcht to turs betuex bourghes bot that ilk burcht suld rathere set forwart utheris fredomes Quhilk chartour of confirmacioun of replaging under our said soverane lordes gret seill on be contemptioun the saidis balyeis of Aire repellit and gaif thair ansuer therupone And sua the said William protestit for rameid of law with tyme and place to call thaim therfor to underly the law for ther dissobedeance And therefter the said William departit but ony uther ansuer gevin to him Super quibus ipse Willelmus petiit instrumenta publica in pretorio dicti burgi de Aire in facie judicii coram his testibus Stephano Prestoun Johanne Mur notariis meis collegis Stephano Tran Johanne Chalmer Johanne Montgomery burgensibus de Irwin et Olivero Houstoun ballivo dicti burgi de Irwin cum multis aliis.

Jacobus Broun, *notarius publicus.*

8. *Letters of Bailiery by the Community of the Burgh of Irvine to Stephen Tran and four Others.*—4th October 1557.

Universis et singulis per presentes literas pateat nos communitatem burgi de Irwin fecisse constituisse et ordinasse et per presentes facere constituere et ordinasse dilectos nostros comburgenses Stephanum Tran urbis prefectum nostrum Oliverum Houstoun Jacobum Scot Jacobum Brown et Joannem Cuningham nostros veros legittimos et indubitatos ballivos commissarios et nuncios speciales Dando et concedendo prefatis nostris ballivis commissariis et nunciis ac eorum cuilibet conjunctim et divisim latoribus ceu latori presentium nostram plenariam et omnimodam potestatem speciale et expressum mandatum Terras nostras assedandi firmas earundem et annuos redditus levandi curias nostras tenendi exitus et amerciamenta earundem recipiendi trangressores puniendi conburgenses stallangiatores et omnes inhabitantes infra dictum nostrum burgum ac libertates ejusdem coram quibuscunque judicibus per quoscunque quibuscunque de causis attechiati arrestati ceu calumniati fuerint ad crucem forum et libertatem predicti burgi nostri replegiandi et reducendi cautionem de jure parti querenti inveniendi et generaliter omnia alia et singula faciendi ducendi gerendi et exercendi que ad officium ballivorum commissariorum ad talia constitutorum de jure et consuetudine regni Scotie noscuntur pertinere Ratum gratum firmum et stabile habentes et habituri totum et quicquid nostri memorati ballivi commissarii et nuncii conjunctim et divisim in premissis et ea tangentibus duxerint ceu duxerit In cujus rei testimonium sigillum nostrum commune presentibus est appensum apud dictum burgum nostrum de Irwin quarto die mensis Octobris anno domini millesimo quingentesimo quinquagesimo septimo.

[Half of seal remaining.]

Dorso.

Septimo mensis Maij anno, etc. lviiij° productum per Jacobum Broune.
W. HEGAIT *subscripsit.*

Octavo die mensis Julij anno domini lviij° productum per Jacobum Broun in judicis presencia in curia vicecomitatus de Air.
JAMES BLAIR.

ABSTRACT.

Letters of Bailiery by the community of the Burgh of Irvine, appointing as their bailies, commissioners, and special nuncios, their conburgesses Stephen Tran, provost of the burgh, Oliver Houstoun, James Scot, James Broun, and John Cuningham, giving to them full power and special mandate to set the burgh lands, uplift the fermes and yearly rents thereof, hold courts, receive the fines thereof, punish transgressors, repledge and bring the burgesses, stallingers, and all inhabiting within the burgh and liberties thereof, before whatever judges, by whomsoever attached, arrested, or accused, to the market-cross and liberty of the said burgh, to find caution according to law to the party complaining; and generally, all other things to do which to the office of bailiery appointed for such purposes are known to belong by law and custom of the realm of Scotland. Given and sealed with the common seal of the burgh, at Irvine, 4th October 1557.

9. *Inquest on the service of Hew Kyll as Heir to Thomas Kyll his Father, in the land of Gallowmure.—20th April 1561.*

CURIA burgalis de Irwin tenta in pretorio ejusdem vicesimo die mensis Aprilis anno Domini millesimo quingentesimo sexagesimo primo per Jacobum Scot urbis prefectum Thomam Broun et Joannem Gemmyll ballivos dicti burgi sectis vocatis curia confirmata in debita forma, etc.

Inquisitionis Nomina.

Williame Kyill.	Jhone Sympsoun.
Stene Tran.	Olever Houstoun.
Robert Conyngham crucis.	George Broune.
Jhone Chalmeris.	Jhone Wilsoun younger.
Jhone Gemmyll elder.	Jhon Cumyng eldar.

Willeame Pawtoun.
Thomas Smyth.
Peter Goltray.
Jhone Deyne.

The quhilk day the provest balyeis counsell and comonitie of the Burght of Irwin all in ane voce hais interit rentallit admittit and rasavit Hew Kyll sone and aire to umquhile Thamas Kyll burges of the foirsaid burght lauchfull kyndlie and just tennand of lyne and bluid in and to the twenty schilling land of Gallowmur of auld extent with the pertenenttis befoir the dait herof occupyet be umquhile Jhone Kyll and Thomas Kyll guidschir and fathir to the said Hew all lyand within the terretorie and fredome of the foirsaid burght parochin of the samyn balyeary of Conynghame and schirefdome of Aire payand tharfore yerly the said Hew his ares and assignayes to the comunitie and thesaurer of the foirsaid burgh males

gersumes and deweteis of the auld usit and wount Provyding all wayes
that the said Hew his ares nor assignayes induce nor mak na gretar
possessioner assignaye nor tennand in degre to the forsades landes nor na
part tharof nor himself and gif swa be thes present writ to exspyre and be
of nane availl Alswa in and to the quhilkis landes the sades provest balyeis
and comunietie hes ryplie and delegently consederit be dyvers actis of court
contenit within the court bukes of Irwin that the sades umquhile Jhone
and Thomas Kyilles guidschir and father to the said Hew wer lauchfull
rentalleris and possessionares of the foirnamit landes unto the tyme of
thare deceis and never sauld nor disponit the rycht tharof to na persoun
nor persones nor yit lykwyis the said Hew disponit nocht na rycht that
he culd clame tharto of the samyn in all tymes bypast unto the dait herof
Tharfore the forsades provest balyeis and comunitie hais interit rentallit
and resavit the forsaid Hew his ares and assignayes nerast and lauchfull
tennand to the foirnamit landes with the pertenenttes in maner abone
writtin quhome to the sades landes pertenes be just kyndnes and rycht
apud acta extractum de libro actorum curie burgalis de Irwin per me
Jacobum Broun notarium publicum ac scribam dicte curie manu mea
propria, etc. JACOBUS BROUN, *notarius publicus,*
manu propria.

10. *Discharge by Alexander Earl of Glencairn to the Burgh of Irvine for £52 : 6 : 8, towards furnishing Soldiers to take the Castle of Dunbarton.*—27*th December* 1569.

WE Alexander Erle of Glencairne grantis us to heif rasavit fra the handis
of Hew Campbell burges of Irwine the soum of fyfte tua pundis vjs viijd
monye in nayme and behaif of the provist ballies and communite thairof at
the request of the Lord Regentis Gracis wrytting direct to thame for
furnissing of certen men [of] weir for obtenyng of the castell of Dunbartoun
and that in compleit payment of the moneth of November togidder with
uthir thre monethis preceeding the said moneth of November as our
discharge beris gev[in] to the saidis provist and ballies Of the quhilk soum
of fyfte tua poundis vjs viijd of the moneth of November quhilk makis
fowr monethis in the haill we grantis us weill content and compleitlie
payit of the haill fowr monethis foirsaid and exoneris and dischargis the
saidis provist balleis and communite for now and ever. Subscribit with

our hand at the Finlastoun the xxvij day of Decembar the yeir of God jᵐ vᶜ thre scoir nyne yeris.

11. *Commission for repledging Andrew Ros in Newmuir from the Sheriff-Court to the jurisdiction of Irvine.*—6th October 1572.

JHESUS

To all and syndry quham it afferis We Hew Campble provost of Irwin Hew Scott and Jhon Gemmill balyeis greting in God omnipotent: Forsamekle as Andro Ros in Newmuir dwelling within our terretorie and fredome is techet be ane precept at the instance of Jhone Twedy oye and air to umquhile Robert Twedy burges off our burgh to compeir in the shiref court of Air the sevint day of Octobre instant thare to answer for the violent occupation of our saides landes of Newmuir extending to ane merk land being ane pairt and pertinentes of our burrowlandes And becaus we ar onlie juges competent to the said Andro and alsua the caus and landes pertenyng to us as said is Tharfor be the tenor herof we haif constitut and ordanit honorable men James Broun Thomas Broun Allan Ros our comburgesses or ony ane of thaim our balyeis commissioneres and deputes in the premisses with power to thaim or ony ane of thaim to replaig the said Andro to the liberte and jurisdiction of our burgh, caution of law for administration of justice to fynd, courtes to sett and assign, actes, instrumentes and documentes to ask lift and rais, etc., and generallie all uther thinges to do as we war present, firm and stabill, etc., be this present commission gevin under the testimonie of our seill of office as use is, and subscription of our commoun scribe at Irwin the sext day of Octobre 1572.

    Jacobus Broun scriba communis burgi de Irwin ac notarius publicus hic me subscribente in testimonium premissorum.

                                          JACOBUS BROUN, *Scriba.*

    Vij Octobris 1572.— Producta in judicio in curia viccomitatus de Air visa et admissa.   GEORGIUS ANGUS.

12. *Contract between Hew Earl of Eglinton and the Burgh of Irvine as to their respective jurisdiction.*—*10th February* 1572-3.

AT the burgh of Irwin the tent day of Februar the yeir of God j^m v^c lxxij yeiris It is appointit aggreit and finallie endit betuix ane nobill and mychtie lord Hew erll of Eglintoun lord Montgomerie baillie of Coninghame and Hew maister of Eglintoun his sone and appering air fear thairof and the said Erll his fathir as lauchfull tutour administratour to him of the law and als takand the burdin on him for his said sone on that ane pairt, Hew Campbell provest of Irwin Hew Scott Robert Kile baillies of the said burgh for thameselflis and taking the burding apoun thame for the remanent haill comburgessis of the said burgh of Irwin inhabitantis thairof quhatsumevir present and thair successouris on the uthir pairt in maner following That fforsamekill as the said Hew erll of Eglintoun having respect to the gret luife, kindnes, amitie, cumpany, societie and favour that wes betuix his predecessouris baillies of Coninghame and the said provest baillies counsale and communitie of the said burgh of Irwin, and willing the same luife kindnes amitie cumpany societie and favour that wes betuix his fathir and predecessouris and the saidis provest baillies and communitie suld continew and induir presentlie betuix the said erll his sone and in all tyme cuming betuix his airis and successouris and the saidis provest baillies and communitie present and thair successouris in all tymes cuming and that na occasioun sall fall owt in ony tyme heireftir betuix the said erll his sone and successouris and thame and thair successouris quhilk in onywyis mycht dissolve the samin And the said erll belevand that the punischement of slauchteris mutilationis bludes thyftis spoilzeis and uthiris violences and crymes committit within the said burgh of Irwin burro ruidis or burro landis and commontie pertening and belonging thairto haid pertenit to his office of the balliarie of Coninghame quhairthrow debaitt and controversie wes usit and movit betuix his lordschip on that ane part and the provest baillies counsale and communitie of the said burgh of Irwin befoir the lordis of counsale and yit dependis anent the using of the samin But now eftir perfit advisement and consultatioun haid thairintill and for removing of all occasioun pley and controversie in tyme cuming the said Hew erle of Eglintoun hes foundin and perfytlie understandis that the provest baillies of the said burgh of Irwin and commontie thairof ar als frelie infeft in burgage with jurisdictioun criminale and all liberteis and priveleges belanging thairto as ony uthir burgh within this realme and hes usit and execut the ordinar jurisdictioun thairof in punischement of slauchtiris mutilationis bludes thyftis tuilzeis violences and uthiris crymes quhatsumevir committit within thair freidome and boundis foirsaidis in all tymes bygane past memour of man Thairffoire the said Hew erll of Eglintoun for himself and takand the burding on him for the said Hew maister of Eglintoun his aires and successouris baillies of the said baillierie of Coninghame to the end and fyne that mutuale luife, amitie, freindschip, cumpanye, societie and favour may still continew betuix thame on the ane part and the saidis provest baillies counsale and communitie on the uthir part (nocht importing servitud upoun the said burgh in ony sort) as thai did of befoir with the said erllis fathir and predecessouris be thir presentis renuncis all actioun and caus presentlie depending befoir the saidis lordis of counsale betuix the saidis Hew erll of Eglintoun on that ane part and the saidis provest baillies and communitie on the uthir, anent the jurisdictioun abonespecifeit and all rycht and titill that he hes or may ask or clame thairto fra thin furth for evir and is bundin and oblist be the teunour heirof his airis and successouris nevir to molest trubill vex or inquiet the saidis provest and baillies and communitie nor thair successouris in na tyme cuming in peciabill joising using of the said ordinair jurisdictioun sitting apoun slauchtiris mutilationis bludes thiftis violences committit be the inhabitantis of the said burgh nor sall pretend na rycht nor titill thairto in tyme cuming nor in using of ony uthiris thair priveleges and putting of thame to executioun within the boundis of thair saidis liberteis and fredomes thairof nowthir in the law nor by the law nor sall nocht be himselff his airis nor successouris nor be na uthir mid persoun in his nor thair names procuir solist nor obtene be commissioun infeftement or be ony uthir maner of way at our soverane lordis handis his grace successouris thair justice chalmerlanis or uthir minister of the law quhatsumevir havand his grace auctoritie and powar present and to cum ony jurisdictioun intromissioun or melling in ony sort be way of justice nowthir civilie nor criminalie with the saidis provest baillies and communitie thair boundis and jurisdictioun thair personis and guddis nor sall mak thame stop lett hindir or impediment in purchessing ony new priveleges liberteis fredomes powar auctoritie or jurisdictioun that thai may obtene at our soverane lordis handis or his grace successouris thair justice chalmerlanis or ony uthiris thair graces officiaris havand powar as said is within thair boundis and liberteis of thair toun and haill indwellaris thairof foirsaidis

bot sall help furthir supple and assist thame thairintill at his and the said
Hew his sone fear foirsaid his airis and successouris gudlie powar   And als
it sall nocht be lesum to the saidis provest baillies and commonitie to purches
ony new faculteis privilegeis or fredomes quhilk may give thame jurisdictioun
in onywyis without the boundis of the said burgh burrow ruddis fredome
and commontie thairof in prejudice of the said erlis bailliery of Coninghame
and regalitie of Kilwining as ane seperat jurisdictioun by the toun   Attour
it sal be lesum to the said erll the said Hew his sone thair airis and
successouris baillies principale of Coninghame and thair deputtis having the
use and rycht of the keiping of the heid fair of the said burgh halding
yeirlie at our first terme day quhilk is the xv day of August past memour
of man to keip the samin siclyke in tyme cuming and to hald courtis for
administratioun of justice That is to say ane court eftir the fair for punische-
mant of sic faltis and complaintis as salhappin to be committit in the said
fair   Lykas the said erll and his predecessouris hes bene in use of bygane
sall uplift sic stressis and customes as he and his predecessouris hes bene
in use of be thameselflis or thair deputtis to tak up and uplift at the said
fair but hurt or dirogatioun of the saidis provest baillies and commonteis
privileges bot that thai thair haill communitie inhabitantis strangeris
merchandis seymen and marineris resortand to thair port and waltiris with
servandis guddis and geir in the menetyme preservit in sic integritie as
thay war of befoir and fra sic courtis to be alluterlie exemit Providing that
it salbe lesum to the said erll Hew his sone and thair successouris be thameselflis thair servandis and deputtis to uplift the custome ale the tyme of
the fair as he and his predecessouris did of befoir   Providing also that
give it hapynnis (as God forbid) that the said erll his airis successouris
or servandis freindis or uthiris landwart men dwelling within the said
bailliery of Coninghame beand na indwellaris within the said burgh nor
libertie thairof nor pertinentis of the samin to committ slauchtir or
mutilatioun amangis thameselflis within the libertie of the said burgh and
boundis thairof in tyme cuming, in that caice it salbe lesum to the saidis
provest and baillies to use and exerce thair auctoritie and jurisdictioun
thairanent conform to thair ald use and possessioun   That is to say the
saidis provest and baillies counsall and communitie and thair successouris
sall intromett with sic landwart personis as sal happin to committ the saidis
crymes in maner following videlicet to tak thame to tolbuith cognosce and
decerne thair apoun the wrang and distrubulance of the burgh and to tak

up sic unlawis as concernis thame thairthrow and to tak cautioun for furthir distribulance of the said burgh in tyme cuming as efferis And give the cryme beis ane blud but danger of slauchtir or mutilatioun they sall suffir the committeris thairof beand landwart men as said is to depart butt farthir payment of ony bludwett bot paying allanerlie ane unlaw for the wrang and finding cautioun for the distribulance of the toun in tyme cuming as said is, and give the cryme beis slauchtir or mutilatioun the saidis provest baillies and thair successouris eftir thai have apprehendit the said landwart men committeris thairof sall cognosce apoun the wrang and distribulance of the burgh and tak thair unlawis and cautioun thairupoun as efferis within   houris eftir thair apprehending and taiking and the said erll his airis and successouris and thair deputtis havand thair powar and jurisdictioun thairto the said space of   houris being bipast sall presentlie ressave furth of the handis of the saidis provest and baillies for the tyme all sic landwart personis as sal happin to committ the saidis crymes of slauchtir mutilatioun thyft or uthir crymes abonespecifiet eftir the ische of the saidis houris that the saidis provest baillies hes cognoscit apoun the said distribulance and put ordour thairto within the tyme foirsaid and thaireftir the said erll his airis and successouris baillies of Coninghame sall warrand the saidis provest and baillies present and to cum at the handis of our Soverane lord foirsaid and his grace successouris thair justice chalmerlanis and all uthiris ministiris of the law quhome it efferis anent the deliverance to him his airis and successouris of the committeris of the saidis slauchteris for quhome fra thinfurth thai salbe haldin to answer And give the said Hew erll of Eglintoun Hew maistir of Eglintoun his airis and successouris baillies of the said bailliery of Coninghame and thair deputtis refuissis to ressave sic landwart personis committeris of the said crymes or neglectis thair dewtie thairintill furth of the handis of the said provest and baillies the saidis faltouris beand apprehendit and tane be thame and tane cautioun of the distribulance of the toun in maner foirsaid the saidis erll Hew maistir of Eglintoun his sone his airis or thair deputtis ane or ma beand requirit to tak deliverance of the saidis faltouris the said space of   houris being bypast the saidis provest and baillies to punische the saidis crymes of slauchtir and mutilatioun according to thair jurisdictioun and powar as they sall answer to the authoritie or to present the committeris thairof to my lord Justice or his deputtis as be thame salbe thocht maist expedient for the tyme and this ordour to stand betuix the saidis parteis tuicheing the crymes of slauchtir and mutilatioun that salhappin to be committit within the said burgh boundis and fredome thairof be landwart men And the saidis erll Hew maistir of Eglintoun his airis and successouris or thair deputtis beand present within the said burgh and boundis thairof is contentit to concur and assist to the saidis provest and baillies in taiking of the saidis landwart personis as salhappin to committ the saidis crymes within the said burgh and fredome thairof and the said faltouris beand tane be the saidis provest and baillies the said erll his airis and successouris nor deputtis salhave na intrometting with the saidis personis until the tyme the saidis provest and baillies have decernit apoun the wrang and distribulance of the said burgh and tane cautioun thairupoun in maner and within the tyme and space abonewrittin And it sall nocht be lesum to the saidis erll Hew maistir his sone his airis successouris nor thair deputtis nawyis to serche seik or ryip ony houssis within the said burgh libertie and fredome . . . . . any persoun or persounis committeris of the saidis crymes landwart persoun or uthiris Bot give the saidis provest or ony of the [baillies] counsale or communitie thair tenentis indwellaris within the boundis of the said burgh and fredome thairof or uthiris merchandis strangeris be sey or land seymen marineris fischeris or uthiris resortand be sey towart the said burgh and thair servandis or ony ane of thame salhappin to be partie to the said landwart personis in committing of the saidis crymes or slauchtir mutilatioun bludes toilzeis and utheris foirsaidis, in the quhilk caice the saidis provest and baillies salhave the full jurisdictioun of sic landwart personis alswele as of ony uthir persoun or personis dwelling within the fredome of thair said burgh, and the saidis provest baillies nor thair successouris sall nocht be haldin to deliver to the said erll the said Hew his sone his airis and successouris his nor thair deputtis sic landwart men as salhappin to be partie to ony persoun dwelling within the said burgh and boundis thairof or thair adherentis abone exprimit Providing alwayis that it sall nocht be lesum to the saidis provest and baillies nor thair successouris present and to cum to intromet or uplift be thair jurisdictioun ony landwart menis escheittis that happinis to committ slauchtir mutilatioun or uthiris crymes abone specifeit And the saidis provest and baillies present nor thair successouris tocum presentlie nor yit hereftir sall cum andir league or band with na maner of persoun bot stand immediate to our Soverane lord and his successouris exceptand the league maid with my lord erll of Ergile be the saidis provest and baillies for sawftie of thair personis and gudis quhen thay travell within the said erlis boundis to stand in effect allanerlie And furthir the said erll for himselff and his said sone bindis and oblissis him his airis and successouris to caus his said sone ratifie and appreve this contract at his perfite age of xxj yeris in all pointis eftir the forme and tennour thairof and this contract nawayis to be prejudiciall or hurtfull to the inhabitantis of the Regalitie of Kilwining liberteis and previleges thairof in ony sort and ather of the saidis parteis faythfullie bindis and oblissis thame thair airis and successouris ather to uthris to observe keip and fullfill all and sindry the premissis ilkane of thame for thameselffis undir the paine of perjury defamatioun inhabilitie and never to have fame nor honour in tyme cuming in caice thay contravene this present or part heirof and ar contentit and consentis that this present contract be insert and registrat in the buikis of counsale and to have the strenth force and effect of ane act and decret of the saidis lordis in tyme cuming and executoriallis to pas heirupoun in forme as efferis and to that effect makis constitutis and ordanis honourabill men thay ar to say

thair lauchfull and undoutit procuratouris committand to thame thair full frie plane powar to compeir befoir the saidis lordis quhatsumevir day or dayis place or places and in thair names consent to the registering and inserting of this present contract in thair said buikis to have the strenth force and effect of thair act and decret and executoriallis of horning to pas thairupoun aganis the partie failzeand at the instance of the partie complenand and observand.—In witnes heiroff the said parteis hes subscrivit this present contract in maner following day yeir and place abonewrittin Charles Mowat of Busbie William Montgomery brothir german to the said erll Johnne Peiblis Thomas Broun burgessis of Irwin William Heigait burges in Glasgow Gawin Baillie and Johnne Baillie servandis to the said erll witnessis to the premissis.

hes maister of Eglintonn

13. *Minutes of the Convention of Burghs at Glasgow.*—1579.

At Glasgow in the Conventione and Assimble of Borrowis halding thair the xxiiij xxv xxvj and xxvij dayis of Fabruar the yeir of God j^m v^c (1579) yeiris comperit the Commissioneris undirwrittin of the Borrowis of the realme be thair Commissiones undir the Commone Seillis and pairt thairof undir the subscriptiones of the commone Clerkis thairof of quhome ther names eftir followis—

  Edinburcht   *Dundey*
Henry Neisbit baillie   Alexander Scrymgeour baillie
Henry Chartouris   Richart Blytht
  Air   *Hadyntone*
George Lokhart   Robert Neisbit proveist
George Cochren   Alexander Symsoun
  Cowper   *Dunbartane*
David Philp, thesaurer Maister Williame Houstone
  Irvin   *Glasgu*
Hew Campbell proveist Georg Elphinstone
Gavin Nasmyth   Williame Cunynghame bailleis
  Craill   *Peblis*
David Ramsaye   Gilbert Tweyde thesaurer
  Lynlythgu   *Dunbar*
Andro Ker   Maurice Lawder
  Striviling   Williame Kellie
Robert Alexander   *Abirdene*
  Pertht   Williame Menzies
Dionis Conquerour   *Sanctuadras*
Maister Patrik Quhitlaw of Maistir David Russall
  Newgrange
  Lanerk   *Pettynweme*
David Brentene   Stene Mairtene
Williame Wilkene   *Renfrew*
  Ruyland   Adame Hall
David Spens baillie   Patrik Jaksone

Comperit Johne Wyse burges of Glasgu and producit ane Commissione to compeir for the Proveist bailleis and communitie of Wigtone and desirit to be admittit as commissioner for thame Quhilk desyir the foirsaid haill commissionaris repellit becaus thai comperit na burges of Wigtone with the samyn instructit be thame and thairfoir the said tone was unlawit as absent.

Comperit Nicoll Palmer as ane messinger direct be the bailleis and communitie of Dumfreis and presentit ane Lettre of ratificatione of all thingis to be done in this present conventione to be concludit upone subscrivit be the commone Clerk quhilk the said commissionaris rasavit nocht as ane commissione.

The quhilk day Stevin Mairtene [comperit] and produceit ane commissione for the bailleis counsale and communitie of Pettynwene and desyrit to be admittit as commissionar for thame Quhome the haill commissioneris of Burrois present with his commissione admittit and rasavit as commissionar for thame without prejudice of the libertie of the burcht of Craill and the Actione intentit and depending bitwix thame presentlie befoir the Lordis of Session, etc.

Protestit David Ramsay commissioner for Craill that the admissione and receate of the said commissioner of Pettinveing and his commissione prejuge nocht the rycht and privilege nor yit the Actione depending betwix thame thairupone befoir the Lordis and disassentit fra his admissione becaus as he allegit Pettynvene wes and is within the boundis of the fredome and libertie of Craill and thairupone askit actis and instrumentis, etc.

Comperit Allexander Scrymgeour and Richar Blyth commissionares of Dundiey and ratifeit and apprevit the Act maid at Striviling in ane Conventione of Borrowis haldin the xxv of October 1574 bering that quhair quhatsumevir contentione beis betwix Borrowis concerning thair liberteis salbe proponit in generall Conventionis of Borrowis and referrit to certane to be chosen be thame thairfoir as in the said Action is at mair lenth content And leikwise Dionise Conquerour and Maister Patrik Quhitlaw commissionares for Pertht ratifeit the samyn and thairupone the saidis commissioneris for Pertht tuk nocht with provisione that the said retificatione maid be thame of Pertht prejug thame not tuiching the prioritie of thair place albeit thai be secund in ratificatione as said is, etc.

Protestit Robert Allexander commissionar for Striviling that quhatsumevir thing beis done or decernit betwix the burchtis of Dundie and Perthe tuiching the secund place of Borrowis clemit be ather of thame prejug not Striveling and the privilege it hes to the secund place of Borrowis thairupone tuik instrumentis, etc. Item forsamekill as be Act of Parliament maid at Edinburche last the questione and debate betwix Pertht and Dundey anent thair place in Parliament was referrit to the decisione of the commissioneris of Borrowis to be decydit be thame at this Convention of Borrowis now in Glasgu And eftir lang ressoning thairof be the saidis commissionaris it wes ernistlie requeistit be thame in respect of hie and wechtie materis now to be trettit tuiching the weilfair and libertie of the haill Borrowis that the saidis commissioneris of Pertht and Dundie suld tak up in hoip of concord the said mater debetabile and questionable betwix the said twa Borowis swa that perpetuall amitie may heireftir ramane amangis thame At the quhilk ernist requeist and for the caus foirsaidis the saidis commissioneris of Perth and Dundey hes obeyit the saidis haill commissioneris hes continuit thair conclusione thairintill quhill nixt Conventione with consent of pairteis as the mater standis now but prejudice of Act of Parliament thairanent and athir of thair rychtis and thairfoir the saidis Commissionaris of Perthe and Dundey hes faythfullie promesit to caus thrie honest indwellaris gild brethir of the said towne to cum to the Kirk of Beyte on the Wednisday immediatlie preceding Palm Sonday nixt tocum and leikweis the said commissionaris of Dundey hes promeist in leik maner to caus thrie honest men indwellaris gild brethering of thair toune to cum on the said day to the Kirk of Beate and the saidis thrie or twa of thame in ilk syde as the Counsales of the said burchtis sall think expedient to accept the decisione of the saidis materis upone thame togidder with ane ourisman to be chosin on this maner that ather Dundiey sall cheis burgessis indwellaris within severall burghis of the quhilk Pertht sall have ther cheis of ony of the said five men to be ourisman as thai sall happin to aggrey upon twa tikatis to be put in ane hatt the ane to contene five names and the uther nane and quhilk of the townes that gettis the tickat continand the namis that towne sall nominat the men and the uther towne sall haif ther choise quhilk of the five men thai wall cheis to be oursman for thame boith And the jugis and oursmen to decreit thairanent as thai sall aggrey within sic space as thai sall appoynt ther metyng providing that the writing of the names of Perth or Dundey on this present Act prejuge naine of thame of the prioritie of thair places clamit, etc.

The haill commissiones of borrowis presentlie convenit hes with ane consent pronuncit to pas all togidder to Striviling halilie in proper persones that convenit at the leist evirie towne ane commissionar and Edinburght twa to gif thair answeris to the Kingis Majestie to his Grace's petitiones and pas furth of this towne of Glasgu on Sonday nixt the xxviij of Februar instant to be thair that nycht in Striviling God willing ilk towne convenit present undir the pane of xx^{lib} of thame that failleyis.

The haill Commissiones presentlie convenit hes maid creat and constitut Henry Neisbit Henry Chartouris commissionaris of Edinburght Richart Blyth in Dundey George Lokart in Air George Elphinstone in Glasgu Moreis Lawder in Dunbar Robert Neisbit proveist in Hadyntone and Alexander Symsone thair commissionaris and procuratouris to pass to Edinburght and thair to persew suite and craive Mungo Russall the compte the kuyngis [kuthergis?] and payment to be maid be him to the Burrowis of the superplus and rest of the extent and bulzerum gadderit and collectit be him and immediatlie to pas to that effect furth of Striviling to performe the samyne with power to substitute procuratores be and alls to thame to compone and aggrey thairupone and to gif discharges of thair rasat in ample forme and thair expenssis to be tane simplie as of the said compt And the rest that happins to be resavit to be furth cumand to the haill Borrowis and brocht in to thame at thair nixt Conventione providing that thair expenssis exceid nocht xx pund.

Item the haill commissionaris of Borrowis present hes fund the towne of Haldintone to have transgrasit and brokin the Act maid at Striviling the xxv of October 1574 in persewing the towne of Dunbar befoir the Lordis of Cessione not being first menit nor compleuit on in the Convention of Borrowis becaus thai bayth be thair commissionaris was present at the making of the said Act and thairfoir the haill commissionaris of Borrowis present with the commissionaris of boithe the saidis burchis contendaris hes deput and chosin thir persones following, viz. Henry Neisbeit baillie of Edinburght James Oliphant Johne Wilsone and Henry Chartouris burgessis of Edinburght or ony twa of thame as jugis for Hadyngtone and Maistir Robert Glen Maistir Johne Prestone Francis Lyntoun and John Arnet burgessis of Edinburght or ony twa of thame jugis chosin for Dunbar And in cais of thair varians with power to the four jugis exceptaris to cheis and ordene ane oursman and that to decyde upon the questiones movet betwix ather of the saidis townes and speceallie concerning the contentis of the twa libellit summondis rasat be athir of thame againis utheris befoir the Lordis of Cessione hinc inde as salbe contenit in clames And the said jugis to convene in Edinburght the nynt day of Mairche nixt and to decerne thairanent betwix and the twenty day thairof with power to the saidis jugis and ourisman to proroge for aucht dayis nixt thaireftir Providing in cais the Proveist of Hadyngtone conducendis to this present compromit and apprevis the samyn the haill commissionares present absolvis thame fra the penaltie breiking of the said Act maid at Strivilang utherweyis boith the saidis pairteis contendaris to be frie for persuit and defensse of ther summondis hinc inde as thai intentit as they micht befoir this present Act making and in that cais the said towne of Hadyngtone to incur the penaltie of the Act maid at Striviling and the haill Borrowis to tak pairt with uther conforme thairto.

Item the haill commissionaris of Borrowis presentlie convenit hes ratifeit and apprevit as be thir presentis ratifeis and apprevis in the Act maid in Conventione of Borrowis haldin in Striviling the xxv of October 1574 bering that all commone controverseis and questiones debetable and actiones amangis the Borrowis concerning thair liberteis salbe befoir all processis or pleyis to be proponit in the generall Conventione of Borrowis and the samyn referrit to thrie or four that sall be chosin be commone consent to desyid thairintill as in the said Act at mair lenthe is contenit Quhilk thai ordanit to be observit inviolable in tymes cuming with this additione following that thrie or four that salbe chosin and nominat be consent of the maist pairt of the commissionaris present at the Conventiones quhen thai sall happin albeit the peirteis contendland consent nocht thairto and als that the peirtie contraviner of the said Act by the panis contenit in the Act ellis maid at Striviling sall paye of penaltie to the peirtie willing to abyid at the samyn the sowme of ane hundreth pundis money for cost skayth and dammage susteinit and to be susteinit thairthrow.

Item the commissionaris of Hadyngtone disassentit fra the appoyntment of the said sowmes of penaltie and protestit that it prejuge thame nocht and thairupone askyit instrumentis.

Item anent the complaynt gevin in be Hew Campbell and Gavin Nasmyth commissionaris of Irvine first gevin in to the Kyngis Grace and Lordis of Sacreit Consall and thairfra remittit to be desydit in this present Conventione tueching the abuse of the taxatione and Stent Roll making within the towne of Irvine allegine the samyne to be sett in quartis of the tone not haveand respect to thame that hes the guddis thairto in the said compleynt wes at mair lenthe contenit The haill commissionaris of Borrowis presentlie havand considderatione thairof and avysing thairwith ordanis quhen ony taxationes sall happin to occur that the said towne of Irvine suld be stentit and taxt and ane taxt roll maid thairof conforme to the use of uther Borrowis To wit the provest bailleis and consale thairof sall caus and deput certane sworne men of the toue to taxt everie allery ane within the samyn according to thair abilitie.

Item Maistir Williame Houstone commissioner of Dunbartane protestit that the said ordinance be nocht prejudiciale to the burght of Dunbartane anent the use of stenting and thairupone tuik note.

Item anent the complent gevin in be David Brentone and Williame Wilkene commissioneris of Lanerk against the proveist bailleis and consale of Rugland comperand be David Spens thair commissioner for the wrange committit be thame in makieng of ane grit number cuntre lauvert men not dwelland nor willing to dwell within the burght burgessis and frie men with thame as was at langer contenit in the said complayint Ordanis the provest bailleis and consall of Ruglan to caus wairne and charge all and sundry persones quhome thai have maid frie men not duelling within the towne to cum duell and ramane within the samyn within xl dayis eftir thai be chargit thairto with certificatione gif thai failzie that thai salbe put furth of the rollis their fredomes cryit dune to have na libertie nor privilege and decreit againis thame to the nixt Conventione of Borrowis undir the pane of x^{lb} and in tyme cuming ordanis thame to retreit nor admittit na burgessis bot according to Actis of Parliament and lawis of burgthe, etc.

Item anent the Supplicatione gevin be Georg Lokart for himself and John Lokart Robert Chalmer Edwart Walles and George Kennedy burgessis of Aire desyring support and contribatione for the grit expenssis maid be thame in mentinence and persut of thair privilege tuiching of thair provest and bailleis anent the Schireffis of Air as in the said super locutione at mair lenthe is contenit The haill commissioneris present ordanis ilk commissione now present to declare and oppin the samyn every ane to thair nychtbouris respective and to reporte thair answeris and fullilie instructit quhat thai wil do thairanent the nixt Conventione of Borrowis.

Item it is statut and ordanit be the haill commissiones of Borrowis present that the proveist and bailleis within evirie burght fra Glasgu eist quhair ony heryng salmont killing or uther fisches ar packit sall diligentlie visie and seycht that the barrallis and treis quhairin thai ar packit be of just mesour conforme to auld use and wont and the samyn to be brynt and markit with the mark of the towne and that all fisches that ar to be saltit be weill and sufficientlie saltit and the samyn veste be the beste men of everie toune quhome into it apertenis or salbe apointit thairto be the provist bailleis and counsell theirof under sic panes to the transgressouris as the said provist baillies and counsell sall appoint.

Item it is statute and ordinit be the haill commissioneris and borrowis present for executioun of the Actis of Parliament grantit to the libertie and privilege of Borrowis and tyme cuming the privalege given to provist and baillies of borrowis within thair awin jurisdictionne that the saidis provestis baillies sall caus execut the saidis Actis conforme to the tenour of the samyn and to be answerable thairfoir in every Conventionne of Borrowis as thai salbe accusit thairupon under the pane of xx^{lib}.

Item the haill commissioneris of Borrowis presentlie convenit hes at the request and desyir of the Kingis Majestie continuet and superceidit as thai continew and suppereeides ane procideing agans Maister George Halkat conservitour in Flanderis quhill thair nixt Conventionne of Borrowis.

Item the haill commissioneris present hes promisit to asist for lyf and concur with the towne of Peblis in defence of the caus persewit contreir thame be my Lord Newbothle as becumis thame to do conforme to the Actis of Borrowis maid of befoir.

Item the Commissioneris of Borrowis present ordanis the townes that ar appoynit to visie the havin of Elay sall at thair convening in Sanct Andros visie the schoir and havin of Sanctandros and tak cognitioune give the haell mony appointit for the reparage thairof be wairnit and to requeist the proveist ballyes and consell of Sanctandros to caus the collector of the Stent mak compt and reekning how he hes bestowit the samyn upon the repairing of the saidis schoir certifeing the saidis proveist baillies and consell gif thai failze the haill commissioneris and Borrowes will [make] complent to the Kingis Grace and his Counsell thairupon for ordour to be tane thairanent.

Item the haill commissioneris of Borrowis present hes fund everie ane of thir townes following to have incurrit x^{lib} for the pane of unlaw for thair not complenand to this present Conventioun as thai quho war lauchtfulle wairnit thairto according to the Act maid in the last conventioune of townes viz' Innerness Elgine Forrast Muntrois Jedbruche Dumfreis Kirkcudbryght Wigtoun Quhithoirne Kirkadie Dysert Forfar   and for uptaking of the saidis unlawis ordanes Edinburgh to caus Lettres to be rasit for poynding thairfoir and sum officeir in armes to inbring the samyn and

Edinburgh to be furth cumand and comperable thairfoir to the nixt Conventiones of Borrowis.

14. *Agreement between the Commissioners of Ayr and Irvine respectively, in regard to their procedure before the Convention of Burghs about to meet.*—15th February 1582-3.

At Edinburgh the fiftene day of Februare the yeir of God J^m v^c fourescoir twa yeiris. It is appointit aggreit and finalie compromittit betuix George Cochrane burges and commissioner of the burgh of Air ffor himself and takand the burding upone him for the provest baillies counsale and communitie of the said burgh of Air on that ane part and Hew Campbell provest and Thomas Broune court clerk of the burgh of Irwing for thameselfis as commissioneris for the said burgh and takand the burding upone thame for the baillies counsale and communitie of the said burgh of Irwing on that uthir part In the haill commissioneris of burrois at the nixt conventioun to be convenit at Edinburgh the twenty foure day of Februar instant as juges arbitratouris and amicabill compositouris commonly chosin be bayth the saidis partyis Anent the lettres of horning and executioun thairof purchest be the said burgh of Air aganis the said burgh of Irwyng upone ane unlaw and penalte for thair allegit absence fra the last conventioun of burrois haldin at Perth And siclike anent the lettres of horning and executioun thairof purchest be the said burgh of Irwyng aganis the said burgh of Air for allegit nompayment of thair brig stent And ffor all actionis that hes followit or may follow thairupone for ather of the saidis actionis and caussis as at lenth salbe contenit in thair clames to be gevin in be thame hinc inde in the saidis materis. And the saidis commissioneris of burrois as juges forsaidis sall meit upone the said xxiiij day of Februar instant in the said burgh of Edinburgh at the said conventioun and thair accept the saidis materis in and upone thame and sall deliver thairin with all gudely expeditioun as thai sall think maist expedient And bayth the saidis partyis for thameselflis and takand the burding upone thame respective as is abone specifeit be thir presentis bindis and oblissis thame faythfully to abyde underly and fulfill the decrete laude sentence and deliverance of the saidis juges in the saidis materis respective but ony appellatioun reclamatioun or agane calling quhatsumevir Providing always that the lettres purchest be ather of the saidis burrois respective and all

executions thairof and all actionis that hes followit or may follow thairupone sall ceis and haif na effect in the menetyme quhill the saidis juges haif pronuncit thair decrete thairin.—In witnes of the quhilk thing bayth the saidis partyis for thameselflis and takand the burding upone thame as is abonespecifeit haif subscrivit this present compromit with thair handis day yeir and place forsaidis befoir thir witnessis David Lawte writer Adame Lawte his sone Thomas Stene Alexander Hagy and Daniell Hay servandis to the said David with utheris dyvers.   GEORGE COCHRANE.
HEW CAMPBEL.
THOMAS BROUN.

15. *Letter from the Earl of Gowry and other Lords to the Provost, Bailies, and Council of Irvine.*—21st September 1584.

RYCHT traist freindis. Eftir our hartlie commendaciones we have declairit our mynd to my Lord Boyde to be schawin to yow in sum materis of consequence tending to the suirtie of Godis trew religioun and professouris thairof the weilfair of the Kingis Majestie and commoun welthe of the haill realme quhairanent we desyr yow effectuuslie to gif him firme credite as gif we wer all present with yow. Sa we commit you to God. At Striveling the 21st of September 1584.—Your loving Freindis

[Dorso.]

To our traist freindis
    The provest baillies and counsall of the burcht of Irwing.

16. *Letter from Lawrence Scott to the Provost and Bailies of Irvine anent the business of the Town.*—*8th April* 1591.

RYCHT Honorable Siris. Eftir all hartlie commendatiounes with service Pleas ressave fra the beirar hereof ane Act and Lettre to summond your unfriemen trublaris of your mercattis of new agane seing of the Lordis ordinance As for the blank contenit in the lettir to summond witnesses yea need nocht to summond ony becaus yea charge thame only to heir and sie thame decernit to decist and ceis and nocht for dammage and skayth yea haif sustenit be thame quhairin I am informit be Masteris Alexander King and Oliver Colt your procuratouris that the samyn neidis na probatioun bot onlie your gift concernyng your libertie quhilk contenis the boundis annexit to your libertie with the last Decreit gottin aganis certane utheres unfriemen quhairof thai desyrit me to adverteis yow thairof quhilk gift and decreit remanis in my hand quhilk God willing salbe saiflie keipit to the finell end and decisioun of the caus. This Lettre being usit send me the samyn back agane with the Act and God willing at the day I sall do diligence thairin and na forder delay fund. The occasioun that the samyn tuik nocht ane end the last Sessioun consistit in yourselftis seing of the lang tary of the gift and the samyn could nocht be put to ane poynt quhill the samyn first come for instructing of your summondis. It was allegit be Master William Oliphant (efter the lang delay hie usit and efter the preponing of mony uthir frivoll ressoumes in ane supersing of delay quhilkis war all repellit) that the Lettres requyrit continewatioun and the defendaris aucht to be of new summond seing the samyn importit ane dead quhilk was fund relevant be the Lordis. As for my debursingis I will superseid the payment thairof and geving up of my compt till the samyn tak ane end and find me wirdy ane rewaird with my debursingis. Swa committis yow quho mot preserve yow all. Frome Edinburgh the aucht day of Apryle 1591. Youris awin to power with service to be commandit.

L. SCOTT.

[*On the back.*]

This ar direct to the . be Lawrence Scott anent . . sure keping of the said . . Chartor of Boundance etc.
To the Rycht Honorable and speciall freindis
Patrick Tran W. . provestis and in thair absence Broun to be deliverit at his . . .

17. *Letter from Laurence Scott to the Magistrates of Irvine, referring to the legal interests of the Burgh.*—24th June 1593.

RICHT honorable Siris. Eftir hartlie commendatiounes ye sall witt that sen my last lettre I have gottin the gift of your haill unfriemen past the King and compositioun and that upoun my great moyane very ressonablie To witt every persoun contenit in this ticket quhais name is contenit in the gift ffor fyve merkis the peice and ane restrictioun bak to me giff thair be ony persoun that I think gude to deleit furth of the signatour the rest omittit in the signatour sall pay na mair nor fyve merkis. I have gevin by handis to Johnne Oliphant and Maister William Broun to the furtherance of me in this turne xx merkis seing they are the men quha ar readeris of the signatouris and ressavearis of the offir fra the partie to be reportit to the chaker lordis componaris of the signatour ffor ye maun understand that nathing is past furth of chakker and without thair help nathing could tak effect. And I have insert donatour in the signatour of escheat Stevin Gemmill calling him burges of Irving at quhais handis ye sall gett all securitie neidfull to the use of the haill towne. Thairfoir siris be advysit heirannentis and luik the haill names insert in the signatour quhilkis ar heir contenit in this ticket and giff thair beis ony ye wald deleit do as ye think gude and the samyn sallbe obeyit. Siris we knaw quhat ye have to do in this turne and quhat this doing may work and forder the towne to ane commown weill of burch. And send me with all expeditioun possible ane boy directit bak with your answer heirintill giff ye think this compositioun ressonable or nocht and giff ye will agrie thairto ffor in my opinioun I think to caus ane of the personies pay the haill compositioun and put the rest in ane great thralldome agreing to the townes weill. And in caice of your agriement heirto luik that thair be na particular factionis amangis yow nor respecter of persones in this turne bot denunce the haill persones immediatlie eftir the ressait of this my lettre. And send me the denunciatioun with the executionis bak with the first beirir ffor I upoun my honestie hes promeist to report bak answer betuix this and the last day of this moneth of Junij with the compositioun of the escheat quhilk lykwayes ye sall send me with your beirar. And the haill commoditie of this turne sall redound to the use of yourselflis and nathing to me exceptand I refer my travellis in this turn to your awin discretioun. I pray yow Siris be als diligent to keip to me as I have bene earnest to keip to yow ffor in caice I violat promeis I am tuichit in my honestie and be my promeis-making I will nocht be estemit in tymes cuming nathir yit will my credeit at thair handis be in ony tyme heireftir sa far be extendit. Swa to remember ye have onlie to satisfie this my lettre that the bak return of your answer be reportit bak agane betuix this and the foirsaid last day of Junij. And sa mony as ye think ye ar to deleit furth of the signatour wryt thame in ticket and the samyn salbe obeyit. And send the horneing with the compositioun as said is bak your answer giff it be possible uthirwayes send me the compositioun with the persounes ye desyr deleit and I sall nocht dait the signatour to your denunciatioun returne bak and the signatour salbe agrieable to the horneing. Bot giff possible all can be obeyit do diligence uthirwayes do as said is. I mister nocht to insist in forder wryting bot ye knaw yourselff quhat this turne may furthir yow mair better nor I can wryt quhilk I refer to your wisdomes lipining ye will be the mair earnest heirin seing the samyn tuichis me as said is upoun promeis. Swa in haist to your answer committis yow to God. Off Edinburgh the xxiiij day of Junij 1593. Youris obedient servitour to liftis end salbe

LAURENCE SCOTT.

As for your generell lettres aganis all uthires youris unfriemen salbe send to you eftir your answer and luik aboue all thingis the composition of escheat be reportit with your answer.

[*Addressed.*]

To the Rycht honourable the provest and baillies of Irwing and ffailzeing of thame to Hew Broun thair court clark giff this.

18. *Convention of Burghs.*—1595.

Att Glasgu the xxiiij day of Aprile the yeir of God j^m v^c lxxx fyfteine yeris :—

THE quhilk daye comperit the Commissioneris of the Burrowis in the west efterspecifeitt be missives send be ather to utheris to advyse treitt and conclude upoun certane effairs for the weill of the Burrowis sic as to putt ordour to the gadge of hogheidis and barrellis and restrauyng of unfremenis trafficquyng and als to putt remeid and ordour to burgessis fremen nocht dwelland nor bering commonne chargeis within thair burghtis and every commissioner producit and presentit ane commissioune directt fra the towne he wes commissioner to as followis, videlicet—

George Cochren baille of Air.

James Stewart, baillie of Glasgu, with Thomas Muir and James Tempill for Glasgu.

William Scott commissionar for Irvyn.

William Conynghame commissionar for Dunbartane.

Johnne Jacksoune and Adam Knok bailleis and commissionaris for Renfrew.

Johnne Stenarde burges and commissioner for Rothsaye.

Johnne Riddell baille and commissioner for Rutherglen.

The samyn daye it wes aggreitt and concluditt be the commissionaris foirsaid for observing of the privilege of the Burchtis conforme to the Act maid in the general conventioune of Burrowis haldin last in Stirveling that the Magistrattis of everie ane of the townes sall caus all persones maid burgessis be ony of the townes that duellis nocht nor makis actuall residence thairinto and ar trafficqueares as fremen or hes ony commonne landis within ony of the Burghis foirsaid to be chargeit be thair names in speciall ather personaly or at thair mercat croces respective upoun ane mercat daye in tyme of mercatt be thair officers to cum and resorte to the towne qubair they wer maid fre wyth thair familie and thair to mak actuall residence and duelling within the samyn and to do sic thingis as becumis thame and onderly the chargeis of the towne as uther fremen dois betuix and the xv daye of Junj nixt makand publict intimatioune and certificatioune to thame giff they failze thair fredomes salbe cryitt downe and thai fra that daye furth to be repute haldin and useit as unfremen and have na privilege of fredome thairinto.

And siclyik the saidis commissionaris hes statute and ordanit that in tyme cumyng thair salbe na persounne maid freman and burges in ony of the saidis townes bot sic as ar actuall induellares resident within the samyn and mak securite for remanyng and induelling thairinto and doing of his dewtie in the samen as becumis ane freman and in caice he makis nocht residence to tyne his fredome ipso facto and to be repute unfre in all respectis fra thin furth.

Item that everie ane of the townis sall be thair commissionaris geve upe and reporte the haill names of all unfremen that useis trafficque of fremen within thair townes and bowindis to the nixt generall assemblie of Burrowis that thai may be persewit be the aigent of Burrowis thairfore.

Att Glasgu the xxv daye of Apryle 1595 :—

The quhilk daye the haill commissioneris of Burrowis befoir wryttin haveand consideratioune that upoun ernist suite the gadge of Hering quhitefische and salmond the Hogheid was reduceit fra xviij gallounes to xv gallounes and now having reasonit and weill advysit that for skarsnes of tymmer in this west cuntrey and for scrowis for making of treis in sic greit quantite to be very rair and scant to be goitten and thairfore harde it is to keip the said greit gadge albeit in very deid thai ar maist willing to caus the samen of xv gallounes sa neir as gudle thai may for satisfactioune and obedience of the auld Statutes and constitutiounes sett downe thairanent Thairfor all in ane voce hes concludit and be thir presentis bindis and obleissis thame and thair Burghis foirsaid ilk ane to utheris to caus every couper craftismen makeris of Hogheidis and barrellis in thair said townes respective to mak the saidis Hogheidis to be of xv gallounes or at the least xiiij gallounes and ane half and the barrellis to be of the half thairof And sua mony as sall nocht exceid that quantite of xiiij gallounes and ane half and the barrell the half of the samen salbe confiscatt be the Magistrattis and Visitoris of ilk Burgh as salbe appointit thairfore in the samen respective and ilk Burgh thairof quhais Magistrattis and Visitoris faillis thairintill and dois nocht thair extreme and exact diligence for executing thairof sall paye of penaltie to the said remanent Burrowis keiparies of the samyn the sowme of ane hundreth lbs. money.

And for the better observatioune of the premisses it is concludit and consentit thairto be the sadis commissioneris that everie couper maker of the saidis treis sall stamp ilk Hogheid and barrell wrocht be him and mark the samyn with his awin ordiner mark that it may be knawin both to be sufficient work and als of the quantite foirsaid viz. ilk Hogheid xiiij gallounes and ane half at the leist and the barrell the half of the samen And that of all sic treis as thai salhappin to mak for paking of salmound hering and quhyte fische allanerly And that thai mak nane of les quantite to that effect onder the pane of ten pundis mony ilk falt to be upliftit and convict be the Magistrattis of the Burgh quhair thai duell And that ilk Burgh caus mak ane stamp to be commonne for all and delyver it to the

Visitor within the samen quha sall mark all the treis foirsaid thairwith and
that nane tre that wantis the said commone mark salbe useit be ony freman
to the effect foirsaid And gif ony Visitor salhappin to mark ony trie with
the said townes mark being of les quantiteis nor is foirsaid he sall incur the
paine and unlaw of ane hundreth lib. and the towne quhairin he duellis
togidder And farder for restranyng of unfremen fra useing of fremenis tree
in paking and peilling it is statute and ordanit that na Visitor within ony
of the saides Burrois sall affix the said townes commone mark upoun ony
treis to be maid or sett upe to ony unfremen quhatsumever bot only to
fremen burgessis duelland within Burghis and being fre Kingis Burghis
allanerly keipand the quantite abone rehersit And that na freman
quhatsumever by ony pakit Hering fra ane unfreman nor yit na uther
pakit hering fra ony utheris except the samyn be markitt with sum of the
saidis townes markis onder the pane of j^c lib. And that na freman couper
or utheris sall sell ony treis stampitt with the townes mark to ony onfremen
except thai first stryik of and putt awaye the townes mark thairfra onder
the said pane of j^c lib. And alsua that thai have ordanit that na awner
nor skippar nor maisteris of ony schip bark or boyt ressave in the samen
ony unfremenis gudis quhatsumever nor yit ony hering salmount or
quhyte fische of ony fremenis bot sic as salbe stampitt with ony of the
saidis townes markis onder the pane of j^c lib. And the haill penalteis abone
wryttin sa oft as thai fall and be convict to be upliftitt be the Magistrattis
and Visitor of ilk Burgh quhar the contravener duellis and to be bestowit
upoun the commoune weillis thairof All except the penalteis appointit for
ilk Burgh quhairof the Magistratis and Visitor be thair negligence or
utherwyis ar contravenaris and nocht puttares this act to executioune
concernyng the said gadge the samen to be upliftit be the general Agent of
the Burrois to the utilite of the remanent Burrois keiparies and observers
of the ordinanceis and statutes abone specifeitt And for tryall and
probatione of the contraventiounes the haill commissioneris foirsaidis
consentis and ar content that ony honest inhabitantis of the saidis Burghis
or ony of thame salbe admittit in sufficient witnes for preving of the said
contraventiounes quhen the samen salhappin to be persewit befor quhatsumever Juge nochtwithstanding ony exceptiounes of the law that may be
allegeit or proponit in the contrair renunceand the samen for thame and
thair Burghis respective forsaid for ever.

And that the actis befor wryttin in this Conventioune may be observit and corroratioune thairof the foirnemit Commissioners sall caus the commissioneris of every ane of the townes that salbe direct to the nixt general assemblie of Burrovis to craiff and maist ernistlie and gentillie suite the assistance confirmatioune approbatioune of the samen be the haill commissioneris of Burrois that salbe present at the said general conventioune that thair authoritie may be interponit thairto and executioune follow thairupoun as efferis.

In taikin of the premissis all beforwryttin the saidis haill commissioners hes subseryvitt the samyn as followis at Glasgu the xxvj daye of Aprile 1595. Followis the subscriptiounes George Cochren baille commissioner for Ayr William Scott as commissioner for Irvyn James Steuarte baille and commissioner for Glasgu Thomas Muir ane of the commissioneris of Glasgu James Tempill ane of the commissioners of Glasgu Williame Conynghame for Dunbartan John Jaksoune baille and commissioner for Renfrew and Adame Knok baille of Renfrew Johnne Steuarde commissioner for Rothsaye and Johnne Riddell baille of Rutherglen with our handis at the pen led be the nottaris onderwrittin : Ita est Henricus Gibsoune notarius de mandato dictorum commissionariorum scribere nescientium manibus suis ad hoc calamum tangentium manu propria subscripsi Ita est Jacobus Wynrame notarius publicus ac connotarius ad premissa requisitus manu sua Extractum de libris actorum burgi de Glasgu per me magistrum Henricum Gibsone notarium ac communem scribam ejusdem testantibus meis signo et subscriptione manualibus. H. GIBSOUN.

19. *Act of Deprivation of non-resident Burgesses of Irvine.*—
9th June 1595.

In pretorio burgi de Irwene nono die mensis Junii 1595 coram honorabilibus viris Hugone Nevene urbis prefecto et Alexandro Dunlope ballivo.

THE quhilk day the provest and baillie foirsaid with advyse and consent of the counsale and communitie of the said burgh haveing takin considderatioun that upoun the xxviij day of Apryle last bypast in ane burrow court haldin be thame in the tolbuith of the said burgh it wes statute and ordanit conforme to the first act and article set doun and conteinit in the statutes maid be the commissioneris of the west burrowis in Glesgow the xxiiij day of the said moneth and conforme to the Act of burrowis the tyme of the last generale conventioun that the haill personis maid burgessis of this burgh that duellis nocht nor makis nocht actuale residence thairinto and ar traffiqueris as friemen or hes onie commoun land within the samin sould be charged be thair names in speciale at the mercat croce of this burgh upoun ane mercat day in tyme of mercat be the townes officeris to cum and resort to this burgh with thair famelie and to mak actuale residence and duelling within the samin and to do sic thinges as it becumes thame and to underly the cherge of the toun as uther friemen betuix and the first day of Junii nixt thaireftir and now bygane With certificatioun and intimatioun to be made to thame that failzeis thair fredome sould be cryit doun this day being Witsonmonunday and they fra this day furth sould be haldin reput and used as unfriemen and have na previledge nor fredome thairinto as at mair lenth is conteinit and set doun in the Act foirsaid maid thairanent And that thairupoun the saidis provest and bailleis of the said burgh directit thair precept at the instance of William Scot thair procuratour fischal Be vertew of the quhilk Alexander Barcley ane of the officeris of this burgh upoun the fyft day of Maii last bypast in tyme of mercat being ane mercat day past to the mercat croce of the said burgh and thair be oppin proclamatioun lauchfullie warnit the haill persones underwrittin burgessis and friemen of the said burgh that duellis nocht nor makis nocht actuale residence thairinto and ar traffiqueris as friemen Thay ar to say, Alexander Blakburne in Fairlie, David and Patrik Aitkynis thair. William Thomsone thair, Stevin Wilsone in Larges. James Broun in Salteoittis, Johnne Dunlope beyond the goit thair, Johnne Boyd in Meinfurd, Johnne Couper thair, Johnne Blak in Kilmernok. Robert Harper thair, Robert Fultoun younger in Kirkwode, James Walker James Montfoid in Salteoitis, Gilbert Hunter in Blook, Johnne Hunter thair, Archibald Bair thair, Johnne Craufurde in Kilmernok, James Cuninghame in Peirstoun. Robert Biggart in Cuninghameheid, David Stewart thair, Robert Cuning in Balgrey. Johnne Findlay in Robertoun Walkmylne, Alexander Stevinstoun flescheowr, Johnne Robesone in Salteoitis Montgomery, James Robesone thair, Robert Andro in Larges. Johnne Boyd sone to the Laird of Portineroce, Robert Ewing in Southemmane, Johnne Or in Fairlie, Duncane M'Gibbonn in Larges, Walter Stewart in Cuninghameheid. Johnne Boyd in Kirkdyk, Kilmernok. To have cum and resortit to the said burgh with thair famelie and to mak actuale residence and duelling within the samin and to do sic thingis as it bicome thame and underly the cherge of the toun as uther friemen dois betuix and the said first day of Junii nixt thairefter and now bygane and maid certificatioun and intimatioun to thame that failzeit thair fredome and libertie sould be cryit doun upoun this day being Witsonmonunday And fra this day furth sould be reput haldin and used as unfriemen and have na priveledge nor fredome within the boundis and libertie of the samin Efter the forme and tennour of the said Act as at mair leuth is conteinit in the precept and executiones of the samin And becaus the said persones and ilk ane of thame hes disobeyit the command of the said precept and hes nocht cum to this burgh with thair famelie and maid actuale residence within the samin efter the forme and tennour of the said Act Thairfoir the saidis provest and bailleis with consent of the counsale and communitie of the said burgh hes depryveit and simpliciter dischargeit and be the tennour of this present act depryves and simpliciter discharges all and sindrie the foirsaid persones and ilk ane of thame of all libertie fredome and previledge within the boundis and libertie of this burgh And retreittis cassis and annullis thair and ilk ane of thair creationis and actes of burgesschippis respective And decernis and ordanis thame and ilk ane of thame to be reput haldin and used as unfriemen and to have na previledge nor fredome within the boundis and libertie of the samin Efter the forme and tennour of the said Act : and that thir presentis be publisched and intimat presentlie at the mercat-croce of this burgh that nane pretend ignorance of the samin apud acta Extractum de Libro actorum curie burgi de Irwene per me Hugonem Garven notarium publicum dictique burgi scribam sub meis signo et subscriptione manualibus.

HUGO GARVEN.

[*Dorso.*]

The names of unfrie traffiqueris within the boun[dis] of the libertie of this burgh by thais within wrettin quha ar depryved.

  George, Robert, and William Forgussillis in Kilbryid.
  Robert Lochrig thair.
  David and William Stewartis in Fairlie Crevoch.
  Williame Galt thair.
  Alexander Galt in Chapeltoun.
  Robert Fultoun elder in Kirkwode.
  David Biggart in Cuninghamcheid.
  Johnne Biggart in Walkmilne thair.
  Johnne Kirkwode in Kilbirnie.

David Archibald thair.
Rid Johnne Huntar in Blook Walkmilne.
Johnne Finla in Walkmilne Robertoun.
James Walker in Crevoch.
William Galt thair.
Thomas Stewart in Dykheid.
Johnne Hunter elder.
Archibald Bar in Blook.
Connell Kar in Blook.
Archibald Fultoun thair.
    Peblis thair.
Andro Speir in Colishill.   Speir his sone.
    Barkeris cikit sensyne.
Johnne Connell in Kilbirny.
Walter Robesone in Kilbirny.
Michaell Dysert in Blair.
    Walkeris in Cunynghame that trafliques to Wigtoun and use mercheandyce with clayth.
James Moreis in Kirkwod.
Robert Lochrig in Kilbryid.
William Forgussoun thair.
James Peblis in Blook.
Archibald Fultoun in Blook.
Johnne Huntar walkmilne.
Johnne Finla younger in Robertoun.
William Cuming in Robertoun.
Johnne Biggart in Lairdbra, Cunynghamheid.
David Biggart thair.
    Newmilnes.
David Broun elder walker.
James Broun his sone.
David Broun his sone also.
James Patoun in Kilmernok.
William Quhyt in Newmilnes.

    [*Indorsed.*]

Act of Deprivatioun of the outtintoun burgessis,
    with sum names on the bak thairof of unfrie trafliqueris.

20. *Letter from William Scott to the Provost and Bailies of Irvine, about the Convention of the Burghs.—5th July* 1599.

RYCHT honorabile and wilbelovit nybouris and mesteris eftir my very hertle commendationis of servic by and incertand the fourt articill conser[n]yng the reseving of the forlat and pek of Lichgu, and becauys na diligence was done be vis therintile in respect the hell borrowis we except hakl resavit the mesuris as Andro Kar verytiit our burche was onlawit and be my gret travellis was forgevin upon this Convention I sould presently resef the saidis forlat and pek and willis yow meist crnistle that viij lib. be send with all deligence with the berar heirof This Convention is nocht abile to dissole befoir Saterday nixtocom for by the discussion of the myssyf ther mekil ado with the conservatour and with William Huntar quha is recommandit be his M[ajestie] to be appontit conservatour within Ingland, besyd syndry utheris ocationis as to all my uther particularis committit to me shall God willing discharge to your contentamentis. I am very expensyf heir quhilk I am nocht to eschew Sua with my hertle commendationis to the provest balyies Archibald Georg, Jhone Pebillis provest, and Stevin Robeson and remanent nybouris Sua lukis for the hestie retornyng of the berar with the 8 lib. committis yow ther in the protection of Almychtie—fra Lichtgu this Thursday the 5 of Julij at 3 houris efternone Be youris servitour to power 1599.   WILLIAM SCOTT.

To my Welbelovit fryndis and mesteris the provest balyes
    Jhone Pebillis Archibald Georg Stevin Robeson burgessis
    and Hew Garvane court clerk of Irvin—gif this.

[*Written on back.*]

Largis

David Fair in Largis	Martene Andro merchand
Alexander Speir in Largis	James Connell merchand
Stevin Wilsoun	Johnne Aitkin merchand
Robert Andro thair	George Cochrane merchand
Johnne Jamie thair	Archibald Connell thair

MISCELLANEOUS MUNIMENTS.

Robert Jamie thair
Johnne Clark
George Fraser
Johnne Or, William Hude
Thomas Symsoun in Haly

Mathew Wilsoun thair
Henric Kelso
Mathew Gogosyid
Cudbert Fraser
    Muling thair

Kelburne

William Aitkin in Wattersyid
Johnne Bell in Cumroy
Andro thair   Andro his sone

Duncan Airdis
Johnne M'Gibboune in Kelburn
William Davie thair

Fairlie

David and Patrik Aitkynis
John Foster
Robert Foster in Fairlie
Johnne Boyd thair
Rober Or thair   Johnne Or thair

George Boyd thair

Johnne Boyd wy^t thair
Alexander Blakburne thair
William Thomsone thair

William Kirkwode in Southennane

Thomas and Johnne Dikeis thair
Robert Ewing thair

William Boyd thair
William Symsoun in Glenheid

Kilbryid

Hew Boyd thair
Robert Traing thair
William Boill sone to Archibald
    Boill in Chappelton

Johnne Boyd son to the L. of
    Portincors
Thomas Foid thair
James Hog thair
James Wodsyid thair
Archibald Wodsyid thair

Saltcottis

James Broun thair
Johnne Robesone thair
James Robesone thair
Thomas Lope beyond the goit
Johnne Boyd thair
James Howie thair
James Montfoid thair
Mathew Makkie
Robert Blak

Thomas Wilsoun thair
Allester Gastoun thair
Joseph Cunynghame thair
James Gilleis thair
Thomas Harbert thair
James Ros thair
Robert Montgomery thair
Hew Quhyt   Johnne Quhyt
Johnne and Hew Bowtone

Hew M'Kie   Johnne Dunlope   Blak Joky Stene
                             Johnne Braidschaw thair
                             Adame Mongomery thair
Alexander Lope thair   Adame Lope sone
Peitter Lope his sone   to umquhile Michael Lope
Johnne Miller

Irvene

Mr. Robert Barcley   Archibald Howie

Newmilnes

Thomas Adame merchand thair   Thomas Craig merchand thair

Kilmernok

Alexander Finlay mercheand
George Jamesone thair   William Cruikis mercheand
William Slos skynner
Robert Richie skynner   Johnne Hilhous mercheand
Adame Norvell   Johnne Patoun mercheand
Robert Broun mercheand   Robert Hume mercheand
James Andro mercheand   James Boyd mercheand
Hew Mur mercheand   Johnn Quhyt in Nethertoun
Robert Tailziour mercheand   Andro Tailzeour mercheand
Archibald Tannochill mercheand Robert Tailziour barker
Johnne Craufurde thair   Robert Gillespie barker
William Mur mercheand   Robert Harper in Hedge

21. *Petition of John Wyllie.*—[*Post* 1601.]

UNTO your Lordschipis wisdomes humblie and maist lamentablie schawes I John Wyllie quhair I am havilie distressit be your Lordschipes messengeris about the xxj day of Julij or thairby last bypast in the violent dispossessing me out of my houssis and yarddis quhilk I suld have payit maill for besyd the spilling of my brewing of aill quhilk I had in the fattis; promissing to releve me of the foirsaid maill and dewtie and to furneis and restoir me to ane uther hous quhairof I am altogiddir trublit thairfoir Quhairfoir I maist humblie beseik your Lordschipes to wey and considdir my pair estait in the premissis and to releve me of the foirsaid maill and dewtie according to promeis quhilk the provist William Scot being provist ffor the tym and Allexander Dunlop (his saull prais the Lord) being baillie for the tym promittit faythfully to observe: As also beseikes yow to considdir my estait in the outhrawing and spilling of my brewing of aill all being set out in the closs being in the fattis quhilk I culd nawayes gett sauld nor a penney for: And your godlie consellis answer and supplie maist humble and lamentablie I beseik.

22. *Complaint by Helen Gray, to the Kirk Session of Irvine, against Janet Smyth.*—[*Date wanting. Circa* 1601.]

UNTO your godlie Wisdomes minister elderes and deacones of the kirk of Irwin humlie meanes and schawes I Helene Gray servant upon Jonet Smyth spous to Hew Parker That quhair upon Mononday the nynt day of Februar instant the said Jonet Smyth movet in her mynd be ane evil spreit and set upon me at the Well brae of Gilbert Gibsounes and thocht to have castin me in the said well and haveand me be the hair of the heid scho ordaned to have bereft me of my lyfe wer not help come and tuik hir handis out of my hair and releisit me thair And forder the said Jonet callit me in presence of the proveist and William Muir baillie and sindrie utheris ane commoun theif huir and upon the hie streit scho said scho wald prove me baith theif and huir and that I had skaillit twa housses to wit John Wilsounes the skipperes and John Neveines hous and give it be sa as scho hes said of me it wer guid that I wer away And for remeid and justice and your wisdomes answer I humlie requyre.

23. *Missive from the Magistrates of Selkirk to the Magistrates of Irvine, respecting the articles to be discussed at the Convention of Burghs at Selkirk.*—15*th February* 1608.

RYCHT honourabill and our weill belovit brethrene efter all hartly commendatiounis forsamekill as the Commissiouneris of Burrowis in thair last generall Conventioune haldin at the burcht of Dumbertane hes afixit and sett the nixt generall conventioune to begin and hald at this our brucht of Selkirk the fyft day of July nixtorum with continewatioune of dayis for intreiting upoun thair commoun effairis and hes continewit the heidis and articklis following to be decydit thairintill ordaineing ilk brucht to be adverteisit heirof be this generall missive and send thair commissiouneris to the said conventioune sufficiently instructit to that effect To wit first that your commissiouner be ane of the trew and reformit Religioun presently professit and allowit be the lawis of the Realme and that your commissioun givin him testifie the same in expres and plane termes under the pane of xx^{libs} to be payit be you to the saidis burrowis in caice ye failzie Item that ye shaw and produce to the said nixt conventioune your exact diligence in writt in restraining and punisching unfrie trafficqueris sailleris without ticketis regraitteris foirstalleris and unfremen within your liberties usurpand the libertie of the frie burcht and of depryving outland burgessis and to give compt to the burrowis theranent of the offenderis and places quhair thai duell under the pane foirsaid Item that the burcht of Renfrew prosequite thair actiounis and suspentiounis raisit betuixt thame and certane unfriemen regraitteris and foirstalleris within thair liberties and report thair diligence thairupoun to the nixt conventioune under the pane of xl^{libs} and that ye caus Robert Fynnie thair new maid burges mak his residence in the burcht or discharge his libertie and shaw thair diligence thairupoun conforme to the act of Burrowis maid thairanent Item that the burcht of Wigtoun send thair commissiouner sufficiently instructed to the said conventioune nochtwithstanding thair exemptioune with thair forder diligence in writt agaynis thair unfrie tredderis conforme to the act maid thairupoun under the pane of ane hundretht pundis Item that the burchtis of Drumfreis and Kirkcudbrycht yit as of befoir rais lettres of captioun upoun thair horningis execute agaynis certane regraitteris and forstalleris and pute the samene to forder executioune and report thair diligence to the said conventioune under the pane of xl^{libs} conforme to the act maid theranent. Siclyke that the burcht of Lanark insist upoun the lettres of Suspensioune raisit be thair unfrie trafficqueris and report thair diligence thairof to the nixt conventioune under the said pane Item that ilk burcht that hes ony burgessis quha pass outwith the burcht as to landwart kirkis and clauchane tounis and thair baldis buythtis and sellis stepill wairis and leaves the same thair to be sald be unfremen restrane thair nychtbouris fra that kynd of tred and unlaw the transgressouris in ane unlaw of xl^{libs} and that thai report thair diligence thairupoun to the nixt conventioune Item that ye send your advyse with your commissiouner for taking ordour with sic as cumis to fairis and publict mercatis and byis thair wairis befoir the mercat be proclamit Item your advyse for making the mesure of the barel of salmond throw al the realme conforme to the mesure of Abirdene and the barel of hering conforme to the mesure of Leith Item that the burchtis of Glasgow Dumbertane and Renfrew schaw thair diligence in punisching sic personis within thair boundis as polutis and defylis the watter of Clyde with deid cariounis bukies and siclyke filth hurtfull to the fisching Item that the burcht of Glasgow schaw thair diligence in reforming thair trone wecht and conforming to the wecht of Lanark and thair trois wecht acording to the Frenche wecht Item that ilk burcht be thair commissiouner bring and produce to the said conventioune thair pairtis according to the taxt roll of burrowis of the sowme of twa thousand and sevin hundretht pundis awand be the burrowis to Thomas Fischer and William Speir merchantis and burgessis of Edinburgh conforme to the actis maid theranent ilk burcht under the pane of xl^{lib}. Item that the burcht of Dumbertane exchibit and produce in autentick forme to the said conventioune the maner and forme of thair electioune of the Magistratis and Counsell presently usit be tham to be considderit be the saidis burrowis gif the same be ordourlie proceidit and done conforme to the actis and parliamentis and burowis under the pane of ane unlaw of ane hundretht pundis Item that ye send your commissiouner sufficiently instructit and informit with power to decyde the plaintis and greifis following 1. To wit the complaint of Lychtquo agaynis [the burcht] of Edinburgh for taking custom of thair burgessis at thair portis and at Leith and agaynis Dumbertane for exacting greitter dewties of thair burgessis nor thai tak of utheris burrowis the tyme of the tak of the hering. 2. The complaint of Abirdene agaynis John Finlasone in Dundie and dyveris utheris that tredis with the bying of salmond in the north for merking thair barrelis of salmond with ane conterfite birning irn of the birne and mete of Abirdene and that the said burcht of Dundie warne and caus the said John to compeir to answer to the said complaint. 3. The complaint of George Brysone and George Hall burgessis of Renfrew agaynis the burcht of Glasgow for trubling and molesting the saidis personis in bying of merchandyce without thair awin burcht and harberie thairof and for unlawing tham and thair cautioneris. 4. The complaint of Drumfreis agaynis Wigtoun for taking of custome of thair nychtbouris quhairof thai have no rycht. 5. The complaint of the agent agaynis Dumbertane for suffering unfremen to pack and peill within thair liberties and taking of dewties for the samyn contraire the actis of burrowis maid theranent of

befoir And that all the said pairties compeir and bring and produce thair
clames that press and alledgances to the said burrowis ilk partie under the
pane and unlaw of xx^{lbs} and with certificatioune to bayth the saidis pairties
that the saidis burrowis will proceid and minister justice in the premissis
Item that your commissiouner bring and produce with him your pairt
acording to the taxt roll thereof of the sowme of fyve hundretht thrie scoir
merkis to be delyverit to the burcht of Irvyn and grantit unto thame be
the burrowis conforme to sundrie actis maid thairupoun under the pane of
twentie pundis Item that ye send your answer with your commissiouner to
the suplicatioune of the burrowis following To wit 1. The suplicatioune of
Bruntyland craving help to thair harberie and augmentatioune of thair
anchorage and that the said burcht produce thair rychtis of infeftmentis
quhairby thai aledge thame to have als grit liberties and previleidgis grantit
to thame as ony uthir hes in frie burrowis. 2. The suplicatioune of
Drumfreis craving support to the help of thair burcht and inhabitants quho
wer brynt with fyre. 3. The suplicatioune of Craill desyring support for
helping the ruffe of thair kirk thair harberie and bulwark with the biging
of thair Tolbuytht. 4. The suplicatioune of Anstruther Easter and
Innerkeithing desyreing help and support for reparatioune of thair harberies.
5. The suplicatioune of the burcht of Dysart and Kirkcaldie craving ane
new impost for reparatioune of thair harberie and schoir and thai to produce
thair last giftis of ony impositioune grantit of befoir to be sene and
considderit be the burrowis gif the same be expyrit Item that ye send
your commissiouner sufficiently instructit with your advyse and consent
for provyding ane minister to remane within the toun of Campheir with ane
sufficient stipend conforme to ane act maid thairanent Item your advyse
and consent for impositioune of ane unlaw upoun the burrowis that cumis
nocht to the Parliamentis and upoun thame that cumis and depairtis befoir
the dissolutoune thairof Item that ye send with your commissiouner your
pairt of the Clark and Agent fies to be payit to tham quhilk is the dowbill
of your pairt of the taxatioune of ane hundretht pundis under the pane and
unlaw of twentie pundis togither with all uthir taxatiounis and sowmes
quhilk ye sall find awand to the burrowis under the said pane Thairfoir
we ernestly desyre you to send your commissiouner sufficiently instructit
with power to convene at this our burcht with the rest of the commissioneris
of burrowis the said day with continewatioune of dayis to intreit reason
vote and decerne the heidis and articklis befoir mentionat and all uthir

matteris to be proponit in the said conventioune that may tend to the glorie of God the obedience and honour of our Soverane lord the Kingis Majestie and for the weill of this Realme and our estait of burrowis under the pane of ane unlaw of twintie pundis and sua to forder occasioune we commit you to God from Selkirk this fyfteine day of Februair the yeir of God 1608 yeiris.

Your loveing brethrene the Proveist Baillies and Counsell of the burcht of Selkirk our common clark subseryvand at our command.

GEORGE WOOD.

[In another handwriting.]

It is statut and ordanit that evere commissioner speik thair burcht to prepare Inns and have singis at thame at the Kingis requeist.

It is statut and ordanit that na swine be keipt within townis nor midinnis be on the streitis under the pane of xl^{lib} and to report diligens the nixt conventione.

It is desyrit be his Majestie that the habit of wimens buskis be conforme to Ingland and all the rest of thair apperell conforme thairto and that na clokis nor plaidis be worne. Item It is statut and ordanit that na wemen tapsteris be in ony burcht.

Item It is statut and ordanit that na samont be packit in hogitis bot in barellis baith quhat cum in the cuntre as they that be slane and that the barrellis be of ane gage: Item That thair be na hering be saltit in barrelis bot efter the gage of Leith and that the westland hogit be xv gallownis under the pane of ane hundreth pund. That ilk burcht shaw thair diligence at the nixt conventione.

Item It is statut that evere burcht cum tua or thrie dayes afor the parliament under the pane of fourte pundis.

It is statut that everie burch ostrar all unfrie trafiquikeris within thair libertes and to schaw thare dilligence: Item It is statut ordanit that nane within burch keip liquere in ony clachan under the pane of xl^{lib} Allis tuiching the samont and hering ordanis diligence to be producit under the pane of j$^{c lib}$. Item It is ordanit that Edinburgh Glasgoe Sterling Air Irving to meet in Dumbartane the xvi day of Agust nixt.

[*Addressed.*]

To the Rycht honorabill and our weilbelovit brethrene the provest baillies and counsaill of Irving.

[*Indorsed.*]

Thomas Boyd provest his report fra the conventioun at Selkirk.

24. *The Artikles for Instructioun of the Borrowis produceit be Sir John Drummond commissioner dereetit be the Kingis Majestie to the Commissioners and Conventioune haldin at Selkirk.*—1616.

And for als muche as we understand that you have buldit ane verrie fair Inne for the commodious resait of all passingeris within our burgh of Linlythgow and being desyrous that the lyk suld be bulditt in all utheris burghs and cietties of our kingdome and knawing no mair meit than yourself to be a presedent in Lynlythgow we ar thairfoir to will you to attend the meitting of commissioneris quhiche will be in Julij and thair to delyver unto them this our utheris letters and to insist for ane resolvit answer from them everrie poynt thairof as speciallie.

That in everrie burgh or cietties of this our kingdome thair may be according to the quantetie thairof and frequencie of travellouris a mor sewer Innes buldit according to the apoyntment and discretioun and thais to be buldit so neir the forme heir as may be with all possibill easment and provesioun for man and horse and als that mair thair may be singes hung at everrie hous efter the forme of this kingdome.

And in regaird that the lying of muck and fewell in greit heippis and middlingis upone the hie streittis, or within ony uther places of our saidis burghs and cietties is not onlie noysume to all straingeris and passingeris bayth in smell and sycht but is daingerous also in tyme of plaig being ane speciall nurischer thairof that thairfoir thai suld apoynt the streitis of thair townes to be keipit clein as also that within thair greit cities and townes skaflingeris may be apoyntit efter the forme heir used for cariage furth of thais townes of all sort of filth that so thair contre attending us in our intendit jurnay thidder the nixt yeir may not reproche the uncleinnes of the townes and cietties of that our kingdome.

And als that all suche filthie beastis as swyne be not sufferit to hant in the oppin streittis.

And because the habeit and heid attyre of the wemen and speciallie within the burghs and cieteis of that our kingdome is no way comlie decent in the weiring of clokis and plaiddis is all togidder scoffat at by straingeris being utheris wyse mast costlie than the habeittis and garmentis used heir that thairfoir the burrowis at this our meitting wald consult upon sume decent and handsume comlie sort of habeit apperell and heid attyre for the wemen within distinctione according to thair severall qualeteis and that the same be apoyntit to be observed heirefter thair being no doubt at all it will be some eneuch followit in the contrie.

And speciallie that no wemen nor maiddis do draw any wynes or aill bot to be done be men and boyis for avoyding of all suspicioun of the uther uncleinnes behaviour and carcage.

Answeris

And as to the first conteining the bigging of Inns becaus it is ane mater that will requyre ane lairg tyme and no les expenss to that effect and is to be done be particular personis in everie cittie quhais hurtis may be movit thairto be tyne the saidis commissioneris declairis that at thair return thai suld mak report to thair magistratis and his Majesties counsall and desyre to do thair indevour to move thame thairto according to thair habillities and the lyk answer thai mak to the singis to be hung in everie hous.

And as to the nixt heid conserning to the muk fewall and swyne declairis that in ilk burgh thair is everie yeir thair particular actis and statutis sett doune for removing of all sik fylthe and swyn and thairfoir thai ordan that ilk burgh sall caus put the samin to executioune nair cairfullie and delegentlie nor hes ben done hertofoir within xx dayis nixt efter the returne of thair present commissioneris and the said swyne and filth to be removit thairefter within fortie aucht houris and to renew thair yeirlie statutis thairupone for the better expeditioun of his Majesties will and intentionis and that ilk burgh hintenewit his ordenance to thair burgh and report thair deligence thairupone to the nixt convention under the pain of ane unlaw of xl$^{lib.}$

Annent the third heid concerning the atyre of wemen thairfoir thai ordan that ilk commissioner sall mak thair report of his Majesties provesion to thair Magistratis and counsall and desyre thame to consult and deliberat thairupone and to send thair commissioner suficent instructit to the nixt conventioun of borrowis thair advyse and judgment upone the alteratioun of the said attyres and habet of wemen and deferent formis thairof according to his Majesties will and mynd under the pain of xx^{lib}.

And anent the last part of the artickle concerning the wemen taveroneneris the saidis commissioneris thinkis the samyn maist resonable and thairfoir ordanis that ilk burgh sett furth thair particular actis and ordenanceis for dischairging the said wemen taverneris and tapsteris of wyne beir and dry aill tapsteris and put the samin to sufficient executioun and report thair deligence thairupone the nixt conventioun under the pain of ane unlaw of xx^{lib}.

And that this thair answer may be the mair better knawin to ilk burgh the saidis commissioneris ordanis that ilk commissioner present sall tak ane copie of this present act and instructions that nain pretend ignorance.

25. *Articles of the Convention of Burghs.*—[1641?]

1. THAT all comissioune heireftir be subscryvit be the magistratis and clark and seill of the burghe or ellis be ane act judiciallie be the clark and that all comissioneris be actwall treder exerceising the tred of merchandeis or hes beine.

2. That the burchis of Innernes Irwenn Wigtoun Muros unlawit in 20^{lib} ffor not reporting in wryt the 467 act in intimating of thame to thair . . .

3. Item that theis that dryveis cattell out of the kingdome soulld be burgessis.

4. Item that ilk burghe gif ane leist of thair names outlane burgessis and exact deligence at the nixt generall conventioune.

5. Item thair was ane informatioune geflin to the erill of Lauthiene quhane he went to France to treit anent the 6 act of the last conventioune concerning the aulld alayance betuix us.

6. Item anent the 9 act thair is ane chartour grantit in favouris of the haill bourrowis be King David that no man sould exerceis the traid of marchandieis bot onlie marchantis of frie burous and that no mairchant exerceis the tred of merchandice in the libertie of uther burowis except he

be ane burges of that burgh that ilk burgh extract the chartour to ley by thame.

7. Anent maistiris and auneris of schypis that thay giff no les nor 2000 weght for ilk tune of moirtchairge as madir and allum or ony uther deid weght and to report their deligence in wryt unto thair nychtbouris under the pane of 20^{lib}.

8. Thair is ane signatour to be drawin up to be subseryveit be the King and Admirall for gitlin pwer to the burrowis to set doun lawis and statoutis for the abuis of maistiris and marineris done to marchantis and that no auner nor maistir giff ony portage to marineris and that the toune of Edinburtgh caus pas the signatour.

9. Anent the 14 act for the remeid of unfrie men ratillies the act maid thairanent and ordanis the same to be put to executione and that nane by ony forrane wair fra any unfrie mane quha ar not burges without the libertie of the burche and the report be maid heirof in wryt at the nixt generall convention under the pane of 20^{lib} unlaw.

10. That all strong wattiris broght in from forane pairtis be confiskit quhair evir it can be aprehendit and to be intimat to the bureth and report maid in wryte at the nixt conventioun under the pain of 40^{lib} the ane half to the burowis and the uther hallf to the aprehender and gif in caice the maisterat put not this act to executioun to be fynit.

Mueros unlawit in 20 lib. but ane uther unlaw forgitlin him.

11. Item that no frie man within burghe sell ony mair wair to unfrie bot alls muche as he may carie on his bak for his awin use undir the paine of 40 lib.

12. Anent the 17 act that all inhabitantis be subject to thair magistratis in all thingis siweill and politik for the weill of the burche and the affairis thairof undir the pane of deprevationne quhairupone Abirdein protestit in the contrair that it soulld not be prejudece to the toun of Abirdein.

13. Glasgowe unlawed in 10 lib for not producing thair inhabitantis quha vent by the Stepill port and to produce thame at the nixt Conventioune.

14. Ranfrowe and Lanerick quha hes delapidat and set takis of thair landis and anent the forme of thair magistratis and counsell to be seine at the nixt generall conventioune.

15. Kirkenbrycht to give accoumpt of the bulding thair bulwarkis to be a heid of the nixt missive.

16. Rosa unlawit in 40 lib. for admitting David Boll thair burgess and not residing within thair brugh.

17. Restis of the money deu to Edinburgh tred to Picardie and Normandie in France 1912^{lib} all being coumptit to 1642.

18. The deuis is to be upliftit be the sessioune at Campheir for thrie yeiris to cum the superplus to pius usis.

19. Continewes the stablisching of conservator and collector at Campheir to the particullar conventioune at Edinburgh and to advyse the maner withe laweris—the meitting the 8 of Agust nixt.

20. Ilke brucht to cum sufficiently instructed anent the inrollin of Wick.

21. Ilke fair withine the kingdome to be directlie on the day insert in thair infeftment and not to be proclamed before the fair day brucht cum sufficiently instructed The Agent to suplicat the Lordis of Privie Counsell that the barrounis and gentrie may caus keip the direct day of the merkat. The agent to report his deligence the nixt conventioune.

22. Item that everie frie burghe intromet and seis upone ony unfriemanis guidis quhair thay can aprehend thame.

23. Item that everie burghe produce thair decreitis that thay haife obteinit againis the unfrie men againis the nixt conventioune.

24. Item that no frie mane within burghe sall sell ony moir merchand wairis to ony unfrie mane bot as much as he is aibill to carie on his bak for his awin proveisioune except it be meit or drink.

25. Item that no unfrie man by onie mair wair noir to suplie himsellf and that he by nain to sell in uther burrowis.

26. Item that no man sall beir offeice within burgh bot sik as is actuall mairchantis trafikeris or hes bein.

27. Iteme thame that gaiff in thair suplicatioune for thair lossis soulkd cum to Edinburght the 7 day of Agust to the comitie apoyntit for that effect.

28. Item ane act maid in favouris of James Airnet in Edinburgh for keiping of the conservarie hous in Campheir.

29. Item 1000 mark grantit to the burghe Air to be payit in twa yeiris

tym. Item ane uther grantit to Arbroith of 1000 mark in twa yeiris tyme to pay it. Item 1000 mark grantit to Inverkiething to be payit in twa yeiris tyme.

The count of the Chairgis in going to the Conventioune :—

Imprimis ane pynt of wyne with the comissioneris of Air and Wigtoun . . .	0^{lib}	12^s	0
Mair for my fraught and my manes . .	0^{lib}	10^s	0
Mair for alevin maillis of meit in Dunbartane with our wyne	14^{lib}	13	4
Mair for James Greiris dyet thair 3 dayis .	02^{lib}	06	0
Mair for his wagis . . .	02^{lib}	13	0
Mair for my dyet on Sonday and Manounday .	02^{lib}	10	0
Mair for my hors hyr .	03^{lib}	0	0
Mair to the keiper of the doir . .	00^{lib}	12	0
Mair to the tounis drumour . .	00^{lib}	12	0
Mair to the agent at the resait of the monyis .	05^{lib}	6	8
	32^{lib}	8^s	0
Item the denis of the messir includand clerk and agent fies . .	xx^{lib}	7^s	0
Item for ane unlaw	xx^{lib}	0	0
Summa totalis	lxxij^{lib}	vij^s	0

26. *Renunciation by James Blair and his Spouse, in favour of the Magistrates of Irvine, of an Annualrent of 160 merks furth of the Burgh Mills.—17th May 1642.*

WE James Blair younger merchand burges of Irving and Marioun Whyt spowssis grant us be thir presentis both with ane consent to haif actuallie ressaved at the making heirof from Allan Dunlop provest of the said burgh Maister Williame Cauldwall and Johne Reid baillies of the samyn and Robert Dunlop present thesaurer of the said burgh and in name and behalf of the counsell and communitie of the samyn All and haill the soume of twa thousand merks guid and usuall money of Scotland with the annual-rent thairof of all yeiris and termis bygain restand awand unpayit sen the

dait of the alienatioun and infeftment eftirspecifeit and that for the lawfull
redemptioun lousing and outquytting be thame from us of ane annualrent
of aucht scoir merks be yeir annalied be thame to us to be yearlie upliftit at
tua termis in the yeir Witsounday and Mertymes proportionallie furth of
the equall half of thair tua burrow mylnes of Irving commounlie callit
Lochmyln and Wattirmyln half Lochmyln lands astrict multuris sequilis
and pertinents thairof and aiker of land beyond Annock watter lyand
within the territorie of the said burgh bailliarie of Cunynghame and
Shirefdome of Air Quhairof the saids provest baillies counsall and
communitie acquyrit of late fra umquhill James Pebles of Knodgerhill the
richt of proppertie conform to ane heretabill securitie and richt of woodsett
gevin to us of the said annualrent be the provest baillies counsall and
communitie of the said burgh for the tyme of the dait the penult day of
December j^m vj^c threttie seven yeires and infeftment following thairupone
of the dait the twentie tua day of Januar 1638 Reddemable alwayis and
under reversioun be thame from us and our airis upoun payment of the
principall soume of tua thousand merks money and all byrune annualrents
of the samyn awand for the tyme upone any Witsounday or Mertimes evin
in quhatsumevir yeir of God thaireftir following upoun ffourtie dayis
premonitioun of befoir in maner more fullie contanit in the said heretabill
wodset and infeftment foirsaid Off the quhilk principall soume abone
writtin and all byrun annualrents thairof restand awand unpayit sen the
dait of the said richt of wodset we hold ourselfflis weill content satisfied and
payit and for us our airis and executouris exoner and simpliciter discharge
the saids provest baillies and thair said thesaurer and als the counsall and
communitie of the said burgh and thair successoris of the samyn and of the
exceptioun of not numerat money and all utheris of the law prejudiciall
heiranent for now and evir And thairfoir we be thir presentis both with
ane advyce and consent as said is grant and confes the said annualrent to
be dewlie and lawfullie redemit lowsit and outquyt from us and our foirsaids be the saids provest baillies counsall and communitie of the said
burgh and thair said thesaurer be real and thankfull payment making and
delyverance be thame to us of all and haill the said principall soume of tua
thousand merks money quhairupone the samyn was impignorat and
redemable as said is and of the saids bygain annualrents thairof of all yeires
and termis bygain restand awand unpayit sen the dait of the said richt of
wodset And the said richt of wodset and reversioun foirsaid thairin

contanit to be dewlie satisfied obtemperit and fulfillit be thame to us
conforme to the tennor of the samyn in all poynts And we in consideratioune thairof both with ane consent be thir presentis renunce and
simpliciter dischargeis fra us our airis and assigneyis to and in speciall
favours of the saids provest baillies counsall and communitie of the said
burgh and thair foirsaids the said annualrent with all richt and titill of
richt quhatsomevir we or our foirsaids had hes or can pretend thairto in
tyme cuming with the said richt of wodset charter and seasing following
thairupone quhilkis we have presentlie delyverit aback to thame to be
cutted cancellat and destroyit and quhilk we for us and our foirsaids
consent to be null and of nae availl strenth force nor effect and nevir to
mak faith in judgment nor outwith in tyme cuming Lykas we be thir
presentis for the said provest baillies counsall and communitie and thair
foirsaids bettir securitie tuitching this our renunceatioun aboue writtin and
to the effect that we may be habili modo denudit of our heretabill richt of
wodset aboue specifeit we have maid and constitute and be thir presentis
mak and constitute   and ilk ane of them conjunctlie and
severallie our lawfull procuratoris to the effect underwrittin and committis
to thame conjunctlie and severallie as said is our full power warrand and
commissioun for us and in our names and upone our behalf to compeir
quhatsumevir day or place lawfull and convenient befoir the saids provest
baillies counsall and communitie of the said burgh our immediat superioris
of the said annualrent and thair with all dew reverence purelie and simplie
be staff and bastioun as use is to resigne surrander and simpliciter upgeiv
and ovirgeiv Lykas we be thir presentis resigne surrander and simpliciter
upgeiv and ovirgeiv fra us our airis and assigneyis in the hands of the saids
provest baillies counsall and communitie of the said burgh our immediat
superiors of the said annualrent our right of proppertie thairof to and in
favours of the saids provest baillies counsall and communitie of the said
burgh my immediat superiors of the said annualrent and thair foirsaids for
evir that so our richt of proppertie foirsaid of the said annualrent may be
consolidat and establisht in thair persones and favours with ther richt of
superioritie of the samyn ad perpetuam remanentiam that so they and thair
foirsaids may from hencefurth for evir bruik joyse and posses thair said half
Burrow Mylns and lands foirsaids with the pertinents without ony burdings
of the said annualrent as thair awin proper heritage in that same forme and
maner as if the samin had nevir bein effected with the said annualrent actis

instruments and documents thairupone to ask lift and raise and generallie etc. ffirme and stable promittentes de rato Quhilk acquittance renunciatioun discharge and grant of redemptioun abone writtin we obleiss us our airis and successouris to warrand to the saids provest baillies counsall and communitie and thair foirsaids to be guid and sufficient at all hands and aganis all deidlie as law will And for the mair securitie we ar content thir presentis be insert and registrat in the buiks of Counsall and Sessioun to haiff the strenth of ane act and decreit of the Lords thairof and thair auctoritie to be interponit heirto that lettres and executoriallis of horning may pas heirupone if neid be upone ane simple charge of ten dayis onlie And for this effect constituts   our procuratouris promittentes de rato.—In witnes quhairof writtin be George Garvane servitor to Robert Broun clerk of the said burght we have subscryveit thir presentis with our hands at Irving the twentie sevint day of May j^m vj^c fourtie tua yeires befoir thir witnessis James Blair ane of the lait baillies of the said burgh my father the saids Robert Broun and George Garvane.

JAMES BLAIR, younger.
MAREON WHYT.

James Blair, elder, *witnes.*
R^t Broun, *witnes.*
Geo. Garvane, *witnes.*

27. *Act of the Convention of Burghs for registration of Charter by David the Second, King of Scots, conferring privileges upon the Burghs.* 7th July 1642.

In the generall Conventioun of Borrowis haldin at the burgh of Dundie this sevint day of July the yeir of God ane thousand sex hundreth fourtietua yeiris be the Commissioneris of borrowis thair conveynit The quhilk day the saids Commissioneris being conveynit anent the sext Act of the last particular Conventioun of Borrowis haldin at the burgh of Edinburgh the sext of August last ordayning ilk burgh to send thair Commissioneris sufficientlie instructit to this present Conventioun to decyid and defyne what liberties and priveledges the friemen of eache burgh hes or may have with the friemen of uther burghis or within the liberties of anie uther burgh in buying or selling of fforraine or hammell waire according to the lawis and liberties of this Kingdome and priveledge of the borrowis Compeired the Commissioneris of the burgh of Edinburgh and producit ane Transumpt of ane Chairtour grantit be King David to the burgessis of this Kingdome Which being sein and considderit be the Borrowis and that it may cum to the knowledge of the whole borrowis for thair better informatioun gif this or the lyik questioun sall happin to be mooved heirefter They ordaine the said Chartour to be registrat in ther buikis quhairof the tennor follows: David Dei gratia Rex Scotorum Omnibus probis hominibus totius terre suæ clericis et laicis Salutem Sciatis nos cum consilio concessisse dilectis nostris burgensibus Scoticis facultatem emendi ac vendendi liberamque ubique infra libertatem suorum burgorum Prohibemus etiam ne episcopus prior vel persona ecclesiastica Comes Baro vel persona secularis emat lanam pelles coria aut alia mercimonia sub quocunque colore cujuscunque fuerit status neque vendat nisi a solummodo a mercatoribus burgorum infra quorum libertatem resident quibus præcipimus quod hujusmodi mercimonia presentent apud forum et crucem burgorum ut mercatores emant et ipsis effectualiter proferant sine fraude et ibidem persolvant custumam Regis Prohibemus etiam ne aliqui extranei mercatores cum navibus et mercandisis venientes vendent aliquod genus mercimoniorum nisi mercatoribus nostrorum burgorum nec aliquos emant nisi a manibus mercatorum burgorum sub pœna Regis defensionis nostre Quæquidem concessiones libertates constitutiones perpetuo duraturas tenore præsentis Chartæ nostre confirmationis. In cujus rei testimonium presenti Chartæ nostre confirmationis sigillum nostrum apponi præcipimus testibus honorabilibus in Christo patribus Gulielmo episcopo Sancti Andree Patricio episcopo Brechinensi cancellario Senescallo Scotie nepote nostro Willielmo comite de Douglas Roberto de Erskene camerario nostro apud Perth vigesimo octavo die mensis Martii anno regni nostri trigesimo quarto As also ordanis the extract hereof to be givin to all who sall acquyre for the same thairefter and that ilk Burgh be requyrit to send thair Commissioners sufficientlie instructed to answer to the foresaid question contenit in the said Act of the particular Conventioun of Borrowis haldin at Edinburgh in November last and ilk burgh to report thair diligence heiranent to the nixt general Conventioun of Borrowis And this to be ane heid of the nixt missive.

> Extract furth of the Register of the Actes of the Conventioun of Borrowis be me Maister Alexander Guthrie commoun Clerk of Edinburgh and clerk also to the saids Borrowis witnessing heirto this my signe and subscriptioun manuall.   A. GUTHRE.

28. *Petition of John Dunlop, late bailie of Irvine, for satisfaction for his Losses in defence of the town against Montrose's Highlanders in* 1645.

My Lord Proveist Baillies and Counsell of this Burghe, Unto your Lordships humelie meanes and schawes I John Dunlope sumetyme ane of the Baillies of the samyne that whair I being ane of the baillies of this burghe in the yeir 1645 yeiris the deceist Allan Dunlope being then proveist and John Guthrie being the uther baillie for the tyme the samyne being the yeir of Muntrois troubling of this land and when Allester M'Coill came with his associats upon thir pairts and heir to this burghe among the rest many yea I may say the most considerable persones and most powerfull within this burghe and ane great many mae who could win away and our Ministeris heir having fled and transportit thameselvis thair wyffis bairnes servands familie guids and geir yea even as we say bag and baggage so much as they were habile to get transportit to Yrland or uthir partes beyond sey whair they might get any scheltring for the tyme untill that greate storme and calamitie wes past thair being universallie upon all ranks but exceptioun a universall panik fear all looking for a totall overrynning and destructioun and robbing of thame of all that thay had yea also fearing thair lyves to be in hazard and our inhabitantes who ducht not win away by sey money having withdrawne thameselves to some desolat places to hyd thameselves as wes weill known to many heir in this place and now we thrie who war magistratis for the tyme having sent away our awin wyflis over sea with our guids transportabile and being making away ourselves the whole crafts and commonalitie who could not win away came to us and besocht

cause not to goe off toun ourselves becaus say thay iff we sould remove and so sould leave the toune altogidder it was the hie way to mak them sack rase and distroy the whole toun in   that thair sould not be a memorie hearefter of a toun and causit our minister Mr. Hew M[1]

with us for that effect and said thay sould beir all our lose and if we left the toun [we sould] gett many a curse Whairon we did stay and gat tollerabile quarters of Allister and his [associats bet]ter nor wes expectit sume of us being in acquantance with him And he himself having declairit to us [wha] went to him upon his ordours sent to us from Caprontoun for meiting of him at Killm   that if we had left the toun and done as he hard uthirs had done it would not have byn in his power to have gottin

[1] Hew MacKaile, Minister, 1642-1649.—*Fasti Eccles. Scot.*

the toun keeped from a unsolt and more scaith and hairscheip than he
could speak of And what fears turmoylls travells and chargis we war in
in getting of immunitie and protectioun to the toun thes who abod heir
perceyit in some measour and did then blisse God mony a tyme in our
behalfs for our stay and what we did for thame and such in the toun who
made transportatioun els whair wer glaid from thair harts that we baid
still and acknowledged that under God that the samyne wes a meane that
they had aither house or hold undestroyit to returne unto and would have
borne thriefold burdine what would haive bene befailing thame to pay to
have borne of that which wes impendit for the touns saiftie and immunitie
And I for my part being fyndit in the somme of four scoir merkis for what
I did in complyence as it was callit as ane of the baillies of the burghe
and for taking of protectioun to the toun being urgit to pay the samen to
Mr Shill (?) for all the means I could use in the contraire as sall be maide
manifest to your Lordships and being put to great trouble pains cost
chargis and expencis and haifing givin out much quhairof I haife not as
yet gottin repayment and which I haife sett doun in ane particular compt
drawn upe apart heir ommitit for brevities cause and it being according
to God's word and a good conscience that what I as ane of the toun
Magistrats for the tyme suffirit and laid out for the toun and what it is
cost me in that accompt I haifing done the same for the toune's guid and
at thair desyres whairas I might have turned my bak upon the toun and
gone [over] sea as weill as uthiris if I had bene frie of that charge which
lay upon me as   weight being so importunatlie dealt with be the
tounschip for my stay and   what is aforsaid that I sould be
repayid thairof Heirfore I must [earnestlie] beseike your Lordships to
reid and peruse my said accompt and to tak the same into your wise grave
and christian consideratioun joyning thairwith my present conditioun and
[greate] afflictioun and troubile I haife bene under this long tyme bygane
not being as yet weill convalesit and what loss uthirwayes I have sustind
which renders me unable to bear such lose and especiallie it being for the
toun whairof I had charge for the tyme as ane of the Magistrats and which
is not pertinent to me to branch out and mak mor known nor it is And
that your Lordships would doe in this mater to me according to equitie
and a guid conscience as God will direct you Taking allongs with you
what the Magistrats of neighbour Burrowes who actit for their Brueghs in
the lyk mater the tyme aforsaid gatt done for them And your Lordships
answer heirupon most humblie I crave.

29. *Tack by the Earl of Eglinton to the Burgh of Irvine of the Hair Mill, for 19 years.—23d July 1645.*

AT the burgh of Irving the twentie thrid day of July the yeir of God j^m vj^c fourtie fyve yeiris It is appoyntit aggriet and finallie endit betuix ane noble and potent erle Alexander erle of Eglintoun lord Montgomerie and Kilwyning heretour of the corne myln and utheris underwrittin on the ane pairt and the provest baillies counsall thesaurer and commoun clerk of the said burghe undersubscryveris heirof for thameselffis and takand the burding in and upoun thame for thair successoures in thair offices rowmes and places and for the commounitie of the said burghe on the uther pairt in maner following That is to say, That forsameikle as the said noble erle for the yeirlie dewtie underwrittin hes sett and in tak and assedatioun lattin and be thir presentis settis and in tak and assedatioun lattis to the said Provest bailleis counsall thesaurer and commoun clerk of the said burghe and thair successoures in thair said offices roumes and places and commounitie foirsaid of the said burghe and to thair subtennentis ane or mae All and haill that the said noble erle's corn myln underwrittin callit the Hair myln with hir haill graith as the samin presentlie goes in wheilleis stones stoullis and haill remanent pertinentis thairof alsweill not namit as namit, with the mylne laid dam and wattir geang thairof with the myln-lands houssis biggingis yeardis kill and pertinentis thairof whatsumevir presentlie possest be James Galt and his subtennentis lyand within the parochin of Irving bailliary of Cunynghame and scherefdome of Air Togidder also with the said noble erle's thirlit multoures of all aittis allanerlie growand or that sall grow on the proppirtie of the said noble erle's ellevin merkland of his Ten pund land of Stane astrictit and thirlit to the said corne myln according to the threttie tua fatt as hes bene payit for the samin of befoir with the priveledg of casting of turff faill and divott on the moore of Dreghorne, alsweill for mending bigging and reparatioun of the said corne myln, houssis biggingis and kill thairof as of the laid and dame of the said corne myln as occasioun sall requyr and that induring the haill space yeires and termes of Nynteine yeires nixt and immediatlie following thair entrie thairto, whilk sall be reput to haif bein and begun to the saidis myln landis at Hallomes last bypast in anno j^m vj^c fourtie four yeires and whilk sall be and begin to the said corne myln houssis biggingis yeardis and kill and pertinentis thairof at Lambmes now approching in

the samin yeir of God j^m vj^c fourtie fyve yeires (at whilk time the said
noble erle oblissis him to mak the samin voyd and red and to enter the
saidis provest bailleis counsall thesaurer clerk and commounitie thairto), to be
fra thyn furth peceablie bruikit joysit and possest be thame and thair
subtennentis at thair plesour dureing the said space ffrilie quyetlie but ony
restrictioun. Provyding that the saidis provest bailleis counsall thesaurer
clerk and commounitie foirsaid and thair subtennentis do not at any tym
heireftir call truble nor persew the said noble erle's tennentis of his lordships
awin proppirtie of Stane foirsaid present nor to cum for thair saidis
abstractit multouris befoir ony uther judg bot befoir the said noble erle
himselff and his aires and thair awin baillis in thair baroun court of
Eglintoun whair the said noble erl promitis and oblissis him and his
foirsaidis to do to thame justice abiding to the lawis of this kingdome and
to caus his officiaris put the decreittes to be obtenit thairfoir to dew
executioun As alse provyding that the said noble erle and his foirsaidis at
all occasiounes when his uther mylns about sall ather be bund up, thair
dames out or wantis wattir, or when that the wattires ar grit that the
samin can not be gottin guidlie crossit, or utherwyes whensoevir, that the
said noble erle's uther mylns about ar not for the tyme serviceable that the
millar or millares to be placit in the said myln sall grind both reddilie and
sufficientlie to the said noble erle and his foirsaidis all wheitt and malt
that the said noble erle or his servandis in his name send to the said myln
at thes occasiones multur frie and frie of all uther dewtie sic as sall be for
the said erle and his hous awin use allanerlie under the pane of four merk
for ilk boll that the said millar failzeis in grinding when the samin beis
brocht to him both reddilie and sufficientlie, and payment to the said noble
erle and his foirsaidis and to his tennentis foirsaidis of all skaith they sall
incur be the grinding of thair stuff unsufficientlie or spilling thairof; and
for the doing whairof the saidis provest bailleis counsall thesaurer and
clerk sall caus thair millares and subtaxmen of the said myln bind thame
to the said noble erle for that effect: Lyckas it is heirby declairit that the
said noble erle's tennentis foirsaidis of his awin proppirtie of the Stane sall
not pay any mair nor yit any les for the grinding of thair saidis aittes
evirie way bot in that samin quantitie as thay war in use to pay of befoir to
the said James Galt As alse it is heirby declairit that howbeit the said
burgh hes takin tak fra the said noble erle of the said corne myln for
helping of thair awin suckin that yit when this tak expyres that thair

cummyng to the saidis myln with thair staff and grinding the samin thairat now, sall not infer on thame a thirlag heireftir but that both the said noble erle and the said burgh sall be in thair awin places thairanent as they war of befoir Quhilk tak abonewrittin the said noble erle oblissis him and his aires to warrand to the said provest bailleis counsall thesaurer clerk and commounitie and thair foirsaidis to be guid and sufficient during the space foirsaid at all handis and aganes all deidlie as law will ffor the quhilkis caussis the saidis provest bailleis counsall thesaurer and clerk obliss thame and thair successouris in thair saidis offices to pay thankfullie to the said noble erle his airis or assignayis thair factoures and chalmerlanes in thair names yeirlie and ilk yeir during the space of this present tak All and haill tuelff bollis guid and sufficient ferme ait meill at Candilmes and Lambmes proportionaly within the said burgh of Irving with the said burghes awin mercatt scalit furlott used for the tyme in the commoun mercat thairof, and ane hundreth eight merkis money of Scotland of silver maill at the Lambmes yeirlie, begynnand the first termes payment of the said half ferme meill at Candilmes nixt in anno j^m vj^c fourtie sex and first yeires payment of the said silver maill at Lambmes thaireftir in the said yeir, whilk tuelff bollis maill payable at Candilmes and Lambmes j^m vj^c fourtie sex and silver maill foirsaid payable at Lambmes in the said yeir sall be for the said burghes possessioun for the first yeir and sa furth yeirlie thaireftir during the said tak Lyckas they obleis thame to flitt and remove fra the said myln and utheris foirsaidis at the outrynning of this present tak gif the said noble erle or his foirsaid pleiss but ony warneing: And becaus that the said James Galt hes sawin the mylnlandis this present cropt, thairfoir the said noble erle promittes to giv to the said burgh content in the first end of thair rent dew for the first yeir for the want thairof be the sight of tua honest skillit men newtrallie or equallie to be chosin for that effect And as touching the said corn myln laid dam houssis and biggingis and kill foirsaid the samin ar appoyntit to be sightit at the said burghes entrie thairto, and whilk the said taxmen obliss thame to leiv at thair removall in als guid estait be the sight of aucht honest sworn skillit men to be chosin equaly betuix the saidis pairtis for that effect or maist pairt of thame being on lyiff for the tyme And gif the samin sall be ather bettir or wors at the outrynning of this present tak ather of the saidis pairteis obliss thame hine inde to mak reparatioun to utheris as affeires be the sight of the saidis sworn men or maist pairt of thame being on lyiff for the tym at the said removall And baith parteis ar content thir presentis be insert and registrat in the buikis of counsall and sessioun to have the strenthe of ane act and decreitt of the lordis thairof and thair act to be interponit heirto that lettres and executoriallis of poynding warning and hornyng may pas heron on sex dayes onlie And for the effect they constitut thair lauchfull procuratouris promittentes de rato In witnes herof (writtin be Robert Broun commoun clerk of the said burgh; baith the saidis pairtis haif subscryvit thir presentis with thair handis day moneth yeir of God and place abonewrittin, befoir thir witness George Garven notar in Irving, Hairie Lyn servitor to the said Robert Broun, and Thomas Young burrow officer of Irving, and Quintyn Mure notar thair, and Ninian Barclay servitor to the said noble erle.

Eglintoun

Johne Dunlop baillie.
James Blair conceller.
John Reid counseller.
Adam Fullertoun counseller.
James Blair younges, thessourer.
William Wisheart counseller.
Hew Line counselour.

Robert Cunyghame consellour.
John Davisoune counseller.
Moncow Cornwall counselour.
Johne Wricht counseller.
Johne Dean counseller.
William Galt counseler.
Johne Muir conneller.

R. Broun, Clerk.

Hendrie Lyn, *witnes*.
Ninian Barclay, *wittnes*.
G. Garven, *witnes*.
Quintyne Mure, *witnes*.

30. *Agreement between the Crafts of Irvine and the Magistrates in regard to the acceptance by the former from the latter of the Seal of Cause.—3d July* 1646.

WE Hew Broun Thomas Gariner Daniell Dunlop and Hendrie Dyet younger smythis Williame Hendirsone Lowrence Speir Hew Thomsone and Johne Miller tailzeoris Robert Mainzies wricht Andro Bordlan and Hew Thomsone weivers and James Walker glover all burgessis of the burgh of Irving grant us be thir presentis to haif resseavit from the proveist and baillies and counsall of the said burgh ane Seall of Caus of the dait of thir presentis quhairby they for the reassonis and upoun the considerationnis thairin conteinit did direct our severall crafts following, To wit the smyth craft includane and comprehendan the haill hemmirmen thairintill, the wobster craft, the tailzeor craft, the cordiner craft, the skinner craft, the wricht craft includane and comprehendan thairintill the haill joyners carpenters squarmen and cowpers all quhilk does mak up in haill the intyre and full number of Sevin crafts by and attour these annext to the smyth craft and wricht craft and ilk ane of them in ane frie craft to be only wroght usit and exercit be friemen sick as sal be admittit thairto be the severall deacones of the saids crafts respective and swae many maisters as sal be choysin be the deacon of thair awin craft inhabitantis within the said burgh and actuall burgessis thairof in all tyme cumyng And for that effect they haif givin and granted full power libertie and licence to the friemen of our saidis sevin severall crafts respective foirsaid indwelleris within the said burgh and actuall burgessis thairof present To convein within the said burgh how soon we pleis eftir the subscryving of the said seall of caus ilk severall craft be ourselflis allon and to chuse to ourselflis ane deacon of our awin crafts respective foirsaid to serve thairintill quhill Michaelmes nixt to cum and to us and our successouris friemen of the saidis crafts indwelleris within the said burgh and actuall burgessis thairof To convein yeirly thaireftir at the said burgh and to elect nominat and chuse to ourselflis in our awin severall meitings ane deacon of ilk ane of our awin sevin severall crafts respective foirsaid to serve thairin for that yeir to cum Togidder with ane boxmaister to ilk severall craft to keip our boxis quhen we sall haif power to chuse for that effect ay as we chuse our awin deaconis and quhilks haill severall deacons respective foirsaidis with so many of the friemen maisters of the

saidis crafts respective sal be choysin yeirlie as assessouris to thame sall
haif power to try the haill unfriemen of thair awin haill severall crafts
respective foirsaid and to resseave and admit thame in friemen of the saidis
crafts and to depose and debar all unfriemen frae all useing or exerceing of
the saidis sevin crafts and treddis respective foirsaid within the said burgh
and territorie thairof yeirlie in all tyme cumyng and to resseave prenteissis
to ourselflis of our awin severall crafts respective foirsaid and to uplift and
resseave all compositions penulties and fyns from the contraveiners of the
saidis deacons respective and thair assessours ordinances to be put in and
keipit in thair awin severall boxis and to be bestowit and imployit be our
saidis deacons respective and thair bretherin for the help of the puir agit
and decayit bretherin thair wyffs and bairnes and sick uther reassonable
usses as they think expedient upoun this speciall proviso alwayis and no
utherwayis videlicet that it sall not be liesum to ony of our saidis deacons
of the saidis crafts respective foirsaidis and thair assessours to impose or
exact any compositioun or fyn frae any quhome they admit in friemen of
thair awin crafts respective foirsaid bot allanerlie alsmutch as the twa pairt
of thair burgess fie extendis to quhilk sal be the just rewll and proportioun
to be exactit for the saidis craftismens fyn for evir in all tyme cumyng and
quhair it sall happin the saidis Magistrats and counsall and thair successouris to admit ony craftismen of our saidis severall crafts respective foirsaid
burges of the said burgh fyne frie that it sall not be liesum to the saidis
deacons and thair assessours foirsaid to exact above Ten merkis of fyn from
these craftismen admittit burgessis fyn frie as said is and quhilkis haill
bretherin of the saidis craftis ar haldin to acknowledge and obey thair awin
severall deacons and thair assessouris and boxmaisteris in all liesum things
concerning thair saidis crafts and weill thairof   And quhilkis deacons respective foirsaid with thair awin severall assessouris hes power to cognosce
decyd and tak tryell upoun unsufficiencie of work and maters debetable
betuix the maisteris servandis and prenteissis concerning and depending
thair saidis crafts allanerlie and to unlaw for unsufficient work and con-
traveineris of thair acts and ordinances and to uplift thair unlawis to be put
in thair awin severall boxis respective and to book thair prenteissis names
in the buiks of thair crafts and to tak up thair dewties for the samyn in that
same quantitie and maner as the deacons of the crafts and thair bretherin
does within the burgh of Air in the lyk caice and that nae persone nor

persones sall heireftir be friemen of the saidis crafts within the said burgh bot be the saidis deacons and assessours of the saidis crafts respective nor yit to use any of the saidis craftis occupatiouns and treddis respective foirsaid within the said burgh and territorie thairof bot be the saidis deacons and thair assessouris liberties and permissiouns obleissand the saidis magistrats and counsall and thair successouris to fortifie concur and assist with the saidis deacons in putting of thair acts and ordinances to executioun and in poynding for thair unlawis at all tyms and as neid and occasioun sall requyr the saidis magistratis putteris of the samyn to executioun getting alwayis the fourt penny of sick fyns unlawis and penulties as they sall concurre in with the saidis deacons and gettis payment to thame of obleissand also thame yeirly to chuse twa of the deacons of the saidis crafts upoun the counsall of the said burgh wha sal be of severall crafts quha sal be ather of the deacons then standing in place the tyme of the electioun of the toun counsall or wha hes bein deacons at ony tyme whatsumevir of before and quhilks twa deacons counsellouris sal be chaingit yeirly and uther twa put in thair places and quhilk does also beir ane declaratioun that the saidis deacons and thair assessouris sall not haif power to resseave any to be friemen of thair craft bot sick as sal be lauchfully creat burgessis first within the said burgh And quhilk seall of caus foirsaid hes relatioun that the expeiding thairof hes bein delayit this whyll bygain upoun sum differences betuix the saids magistratis and counsall and us the saids crafts tuitching thair feir of our arysing in ane mutinous and hostile way against the saidis magistratis and thair successouris In the quhilk caice they did strictlie urge ane claus irritant for foirfaulting and loseing to the craft or crafts so arysing of our seall of caus and libertie thairin conteinit and quhairunto we wald not agrie and eftir agitatioun thairof be us against thame before the burrowis the commissioneris of burrowis be thair act of thair generall conventioun haldin at Lanerk in Julij 1645 did allow our agriement swa far as we did mutually aggrie upoun and did moderat the penultie in the cais foirsaid to be as followis: Videlicet, that if our saidis crafts sould ayther togither or any ane of the saidis crafts for the maist pairt sould aryse in ane mutinous and hostile maner against the saidis magistratis and thair successouris for the time or sould mak any convocatioun contrair to the lawis of this kingdome the craft or craftis for quhom the deacon or deacons and the remanent craft or crafts sould be answerable for the samyn and the pairtie making the convocatioun ilk ane of thame sould pay ane unlaw of ffourtie pundis without prejudice alwayis of farder censure to be inflictit upoun the transgressouris be the saidis magistratis and counsall and thair successouris for the tyme conforme to the lawis of this kingdome And that the saidis burrowis did ordain the saidis Magistrats and counsell to give unto us our said seall of caus conforme to the said agriement upoun the penultie foirsaid and that the saidis magistratis and counsell hes givin to us the said seall of caus accordinglie conform to the said agriement and burrowis act and ordinance foirsaid and upoun the quhilks expres provisions conditiouns limitatiouns and restrictiouns particularly foirsaid both tuitching the liberties abonewrittin grantit be thame to us in forme and maner abonementionat and in thair same selff extent and upoun the penulties and utheris censures moderat be the saidis commissioners of burrows in the caice foirsaid the saids magistrats and counsall hes be the said seall of caus declarit thameselffs to haif givin the samyn to us and no utherwayis And hes also conditionat that how soon the walkers of the said burgh quha ar not for the present of ane competent societie to mak up ane incorporat pollitick bodie attains unto ane competent societie and number to mak up ane incorporat pollitick bodie that they sall give thame thair seall of caus friclie but compositioun with the lyk privilegis as we haif ours and upoun the alyk caveatis restrictions and penulties foirsaid and in the meintyme to debar all unfriemen quha ar not burges of the said burgh to exerce the said walker craft as the said seall of caus of the dait of thir presentis proportis And quhilk seall of caus we for our parts ilk ane of us for our awin severall crafts respective foirsaid doe heirby declair as for us and our successouris of our saids crafts to haif acceptit and imbraicit from the saids magistrats and counsall upoun the saids haill severall conditiouns provisiouns restrictiouns caveats and extent and undir the penulties and censuris particularly foirsaidis mentionat in the said seall of caus and act of burrowis And we are content for us and our successouris friemen of the saidis crafts thir presentis be insert and registrat in the buikis of counsall and sessioun thairin to remain ad futuram rei memoriam, and for this effect we constitute   our procuratouris promittentes de rato In witnes quhairof (writtin be George Garven servitour to Robert Broun comoun clerk of the said burgh) we haif subscrivit thir presentis with our hands as followis: At Irving the Thrid day

of Julij j^m vj^c fourtie-sex yeiris before thir witnessis James Harper and
Adame Cunynghame eldir merchandis burgessis of Irving.

We HENDRIE DYETT youngar smythe JAMES WALKER glover and
JOHN MILLAR tailyeour abonnamit with our handis at the pen
led be the notaries following at our command becaus we cannot
wrytt ourselffs.

Ita est Robertus Broun notarius publicus ad premissa requisitus de
mandatis antedictorum Testantibus his meis signo et subscriptione
manualibus.

Ita est Georgius Garven conotarius ad premissa requisitus de mandatis
antedictorum teste manu propria.

James Harper, *wittnes.*
Adame Conyghame, *witnes.*

At Edinburgh the Tent day of Junij 1656.—I undersubseryvand compeir
as procurator for Hew Broune Thomas Gairdner Daniel Dunlope and Hendrie
Dyet younger smithes William Hendersone Laurence Speir Hew Thomsone
and John Miller tailzeours Robert Menzies wright Andrew Bordlan and
Hew Thomsone weivers and James Walker glover all burgessis of Irvine

and consents for them to the registratioun heiroff in the Court buikis of Justice.   A. ABERNETHIE.

> The principall band withinwrittin within one sheit of paper presentit be George Garven wreitter in Irvine and registrat be me William Downie ane of the clarks of the Court of Justice as witues my subscription manuell.   W. DOWNIE.

31. *Receipt by the Commissioners of Perth to the Treasurer of Irvine, for Contribution of £90 for the help of the Poor of Perth in time of pestilence.*—1st *December* 1646.

WE Mr. Alex^r [Rol]lok minister at Perth and David Sharpe counseller ther comissionars from the said towne for acquainting the burghs upon the west syd off the said towne with the lamentable conditione thereof by the plague of pestilence and for seeking support for the poor theroff from the borroughs forsaid grants us to have receaved from Jhone Davidsone thesaurer to the Sessioune of Irowing in name of contributioune for helping the poor foirsaid the sowme off foirscoir ten libs. Scotts—In witness wheroff thir presents ar subseriwed by [our] hands at Irowing the 1 of December 1646.

Mr. ALEX^R ROLLOK, minister at Perth.
DAVID SCHARPE.

32. *Receipts for various sums connected with the levy and equipment of Troops.*—19th *January* 1647.

AT Irvin the 19th day of Januarii 1647 receivit fra Johne Reid balye of Irvin thrie notis under the hand of umquhile Mr. Adam Cunyngham beirand in haill the sowme of sex hundrethe threttein poundis 18^s 8^d. As also ane warrand under Earle of Eglingtoun his hand conforme to ane act of the Estates to pay to the laird of Girvanmains the sowme of sex hundrethe poundis Scotis money quhilk with the sowme of four hundrethe sextein poundis 16^d for the levi and transport money and bagadge horse and men their levi and transport money effeirand to the number of thretty sex foot sojouris as being their number they instruct the outreik of the samyn and two hundrethe merkis aledgit be the said Johne Reid bayle forsaid for outreiking of the Lord Chanchleris levi He lykwyse instructing the samyn compleitis the sowm of ane thowsand sevin hundrethe thriescoir thrie poundis Scotis money quhilk is the full proportioun of loane and taxt laid upon the town of Irvin be me. S. J. STEWART.

At Irvin the 19 day of Januarii 1647 receivit fra Johne Reid balye of Irvin twentie fyve poundis Scotis money As also two notis under umquhile Mr. Adam Cunyngham his hand beirand the sowm of thrie hundrethe fyftie thrie poundis As also a note under captain James Brownis hand be the sowm of ane hundreth merkis money receivit be the said James fra John Reid balye forsaid in name of umquhile Mr. Adam Cunyngham also a note under Collonel Robert Montgomeries hand beirand four hundreth and fourtein poundis Also a discharge under Archibald Sedserfis hand beirand two hundrethe and sevin poundis Also thrie notis for quartering under the hand of Collonel Hume and his officeris beirand the sowm of sevin hundreth fourscoir sevinttein poundis fyve shilling money forsaid quhilk compleitis the sowm of ane thowsand eight hundreth thriescoir thrie poundis as being the first nyne moneths mantinance imposit upon the town of Irvin be me.

S. J. STEWART.

[On back.]

Discharges pertaineing to the toune of tinnance deu to my Lo. Humbie. 17 munths man-

33. *Letter from W. Bell, Dalry, to [William Wishart, Bailie of Irvine], desiring payment of the allowance for the Families of Soldiers wounded or slain.—6th February* 1648.

WORTHIE FREIND

These ar to desyre yow to delyver to the bearer William Dowell apointed be our Sessioune to that effect that proportione of money whilk fals to this parish for the widows and orphans therin and tak aue lyne under his hand of the recept of the sam whilk sal be sufficient for your exoneratioune therof committing yow to God, I rest youres in the Lord,

W. BELL.

Dalry February 6, 1648.

34. *Receipts on behalf of several Parishes in Ayrshire, to William Wishart, Bailie of Irvine, for the allowance due to the Families of Soldiers wounded or slain.—February and March* 1648.

I Mr. Ralph Rogers grantis me to have received from William Wshert baylie of Irvin the sowm of an hundreth lxxxvij merkis and an half for the widows and orphanes of the parish of Ardrossan at Irvin February 8 1648.

RALPH ROGERS.

I Mr. Williame Russell minister at Kilbirnie grants me to have receivide frome Williame Wishart ane hundreth sixtie tuo markis 6ˢ 8ᵈ of that moneye quhilk was awand to the widows fatherles and lamed and that for the paroche of Kilbirnie as witnes thir presentis subscryvide with my hande att Irwine the 9 of Februarie 1648.   Mr. WILLIAME RUSSELL.

Resaved be William Kelso in Hingdoge from the handes of William Wishart the soum of tuo hundreth and fyftie merkis of the moneys allowed upon widewes and orphants and lamed souldiores within the parish of Dalrye as witnes my hand this eight of Februarie 1648.

WILLIAM KELSO.

I Mr. William Guthrie Minister at the new kirk of Kilmarnock grants me to have receaved from William Wishart the sowme of two hundreth sixtie two merks six shilling eight pennies which is the part of the contribution allowed by the estats for the widows bairns orphans and maimed within the new parioch of Kilmarnock as witnesse my hand at Irvine 9 Februarie 1648.   Mr. WILLIAM GUTHRIE.

Receaveit by me Hew Smythe portioner of Ridstoun the sowme of thrie hundrethe merkes Scottes money of the contributioun grantit for the widowes bairneis and orphantes and lame of the parische of Kilwynning as witness may hand the 1 Februarie 1648 yeiris.   H. SMYTHE.

I Thomas Patoune grantes me to have receaved from William Wisheart four hundreth merkis of that mony quhilk was allowed to the widowes fatherles and lamed, and that for the parishe of Stewartowne as witnes thir presentis subserived with (my) hand at Irvin February 8 day 1648.

THOMAS PATOUNE.

We James Campbell and Robert Nisbet elders of the kirk of Lowdoun grantis us to have receavid fra William Wischart baillie of Irvine the sume of thrie hundreth sextie two merkis appointed be the Presbetrie of Irvine to be gevin to the widows barnes orphans and maymed within the said paroche be thir presentis writtin and gevin under thair handis at Irvine the 1 of February 1648. JAMES CAMPBELL.
ROBERT NISBITT.

Receivit by mee Alan Dunlope youngar of Craig for the contributionne grantid for the widous bairns and orfants etc. for the parishe off Kilmars the soume off 74^{lib} 13^s 4^d Scots as wittnes my hand the 1 off February 1648. A. DUNLOP.

I Robert Huntar youngar of Huntarstoune grants me to have resavit from Williame Wishart bailyie of Irvine ane hundrithe thrie score fifteine merkeis money being appoynted for the widowes and orphanes withine the parochine of Kilbryd as wittnes my hand at Irvine the 9 February 1648.
R. HUNTARSTOWNE.

I Mr. Robert Aird minister at Girvan grant me to have receaved fra William Wshart bailyie of Irvin aucht punds halfe ane merk as our proportioun of the moneys appoynted be the estaits for supplie of widows orphans and lame souldiers be their presents writtin and subscryved with my hand at Irvin the 9 of Februar 1648. Mr. ROBERT AIRD.

Receaved from William Wishart baylyie of Irwing the sowme of ane hundreth merkis Scots for the proportiowne of the parish of Stevenstowne of the moneys belonging to the widowes as witnes thir presentis writtine and subscryvet with my hand at Irwing 8 March 1648.
J. CONYNGHAME.

Receivit by me David Boyll feir of Kelburne from William Wishert baylyie of Irving the sowme of sevin hundreth and thretie sevin merks six shillings 8^d dew to the widowes and orphannes within the pairishe of Lairges conforme to the comissionne givin to me by the sessionne of the said paroshe subscryvit with my hand at Irving the 14 of March 1648.
DAVID BOYLL.

I Robert Patoun merchand in Kilmarnock grant me to have receaved from William Wyshart baillie of Irwing the sowme of four hundreth seventie

fyve pund acording to his not therin for the pareish of Kilmarnock this
9 of Februar 1648 yeiris. ROBERT PATOUN.

Receavit farder xix^{lib} xvj^s R. PATOUN.

I Master Patrick Colvill minister at Bieth grantis me to have receavit
from William Wisheart bailyie of Irvin all and whole the soum of four
hundreth and tuentie fyve pundis six shillingis and eight pennies and that
as our proportionne of the moneyes appoynted for the widowes and
orphanes be this my hand at Irwine the first of March 1648.

Mr. PA. COLVILL.

35. *Warrant to Niniana Ros, late Treasurer of Irvine, to pay for the Confections used when the Laird of Ardkinglas was admitted Burgess,—1st March 1648.*

NINIANE Ros lait thesaurer and who is not as yet absolvit of your compts yea
sall not faill to mak payment to Hew Cunynghame of the somme of thrie
pund for tua pund and ane half of confectiones whilk wes gotin fra him
the tyme when the Laird of Arkinles wes maid burges And the samen
sall be alowit be us to yow in your acompts keipand thir presentis to be
your warand Be thir presentis subscryvit with my hand the first day of
March 1648. A. DUNLOP, *Bailie.*
R. BROUN, *Clk*

36. *Receipt for Maintenance paid by the Magistrates of Irvine for Colonel Montgomery's Regiment, from December 1645 to 1st March 1648.*

Irving, Martij 13th 1648.

RECEAVED be me Williame Wallace of Faillford Collectour of the Shyre of
Air ffrom the Magistrattis of the burgh of Irving compleitt peymentt of
all mantinence granted by the Parliament As also of all mantinence
appoynted by the Shyre for Colloneel Montgomery his Regiment And that
ffrom December 1645 to the first day of March 1648 As witness my hand
All quarters within the said space to the first of Merch is allowed by me.

W. WALLACE.

37. *Order by Alan Dunlop, Bailie of Irvine, to the Treasurer, for payment of 100 merks borrowed from James Blair.*—1648.

JAMES BLAIR wheras ther is imposid upon the brugh off Irvein ane soume off mony exacted bee Lieutenant Colonell Livistoune Lieutenant Colonell to my Lord Calander off the quhilk soume yow wes appoynted to lend ane hundreth merks quhilk wes performid bee yow And in resspeiet off the dystractions and confusiounes that arr att present thes arr too appoynt the tresourer off the brugh too mack yow pyment orr then to detein in your oune hands the equivalent soume Subscryveit with my hands att Irvein 1648. A. DUNLOP, *Bailie.*

13 December 1659.

   Apruvin be Magistratis and Counsel.

                 R. BROUN.

38. *Discharge by Henry Christie, Quartermaster of Argyll's Regiment, to the Magistrates of Irvine, for Maintenance Money.*—23d April 1650.

I HENRIE CHRYSTIE quartermaster to the Marques of Argyllis Regiment doe heirby confes and declair that I haif receawit ffyve hundreth and fortie pundis money Scotis fra the Collectour of the burgh of Irwing in name of the Magistrats of the said burgh of Irwing conforme to my severall receipts given thairupoun of this dait Quhilk sowme is as compleit payment of the mantenance of the said burgh for the monethes of December 1649 Januarij and Februarij 1650 quhairof exoneres the saidis Magistrats and of all monethes preceiding allocat to the said Regiment be thir presentis written and subscryveit at Irwing the tuentie thrid day of Apryll 1650.

            HEN. CHRYSTIE, *Quartermaster.*

39. *Discharge by James Christie, Quartermaster of the Marquis of Argyll's Regiment, to the Magistrates of Irvine, for Maintenance Money.*—19th June 1650.

I JAMES CHRYSTIE quartermaister to my lord Marques off Argyll his regement grants me to have reseived ffrom the Magistrats off the brough off Irwing the somme off thre hundreth and thre scoir pond Scots monijs and that ffor complit payment off the mentinance off the brough dew to my lord Argyll his regement ffor the months off Apryll and Maii 1650 provyding the notts of rescepts that I have given to the subcolectors in the brough ffor the rescept of the monijs be maid null without chellings and descherges the fforsaid Magistrats at all hands whatsomever.

Given under my hand at Irwing the 19 off Junij 1650.

JA. CHRYSTIE.

10. *Back Bond by Robert Galt, to the Magistrates of Irvine in regard to the Multures of the Loch Mill and Water Mill.*—*10th March 1652.*

I ROBERT GALT youngest lawful sone of umquhile James Galt in Newmyln Dregorne notwithstanding of the Tak set to me this day be the proveist and baillies of the burgh of Irwing of thair tua burrow mylns callit Loch myln and Wattir myln with the astrict multouris thairof mentionat in the said tak and amongst the rest of all corns grindable remainand within the said burght and suckin thairof be the space of twintie four hours according to the twintie fyft fact as the tak beiris yit I obleis me to the saids proveist baillies and counsell that leist the thirlage foirsaid of stuff remainand within the suckin during the space foirsaid sould hinder the incumyng of stuff and boothing of the samyn within the said burgh, I sall not persew for the multor of stuff cumyng be sea and remaining within the suckin be the space foirsaid befoir ony uthir judges bot only befoir the saids proveist baillies and counsell thamesellis in thair awin Court And that I sall not exact ony mair of the said multor for the samyn bot what the saids proveist baillies and counsell pleiss modifie to me according to thair awin discretioun To whom in that behalf I doe heirby submitt myself simpliciter if in caice the inbringers thairof and I cannot aggrie amongst oursellis. And I am content and consentis thir presentis be insert and registrat in the bnikis of Counsell and Sessioun or burrow Court buikis of Irving thairin to remain ad futuram rei memoriam And for this effect I constitute   my procuratouris promittens de rato, etc. In witnes quhairof (written be George Garven notar in Irving) I haif subseryveit thir presentis with my hand at Irving the tent day of March j^m vj^c fliftie tua yeiris befoir thir witnessis Robert Broun toun

clerk of Irving Hew Galt in Newmyln Dregorn and the said George
Garven. ROBERT GALT.

 R. Broun, *witnes*.
 Hew Galt, *witnes*.
 G. Garven, *witnes*.

  41. *Minute of the Gentlemen and Heritors of Ayrshire anent payment of a Bed, sent by the Town of Irvine to Broddie.—*30th *May* 1656.

Kilmarnock 30th May 1656.

THE whilk day the Gentlemen and Heritors of the shyre of Ayr being conveined compeired Mr Robert Barclay proveist of Irving and craved that some course might be laid doune for payment to them of ane Bed sent be the toune of Irving to Broddie since the Collectour had taken course with the rest of the Beds sent be them And thairfoir the saids Gentlemen and Heritors appointed the said Bed to be laid on with the rest of the assesment And the generall Collectour to uplift the samen accordinglie and he to pay in the samen to the toune of Irving.

42. *Petition of Hew Ross, Schoolmaster, to the Magistrates of Irvine.—* 12*th December* 1656.

To the Right Honorabill the Magistrats and Councell of the Burgh of Irvin.

HUMBLIE showing unto your honours that whereas a bargane and condition was made with me by some of your number sent from you in Apryl 1652 for keeping the Schoole to be doctour to the children which were learning to reade and wryt in the which condition their was agreed and promised to give unto me fourtie merks in the yeare. Of the which I have gotten nothing but onlie twentie merks. And now it is foure yeares and ane half bygane since the condition was made with me I did supplicat your honours befor and you promised to take some course in it but hes done nothing to my knowledge. Therfor I beseech your honours that yow would consider my poore condition haveing a familie and not able to sustaine them by reason of the want of meanes and daylie keept in the schoole that I can use no other meane for their reliefe. And haveing also contracted upon myselfe some debt for their supplie expecting alwayes some helpe from your honours according to condition. Therfor I desyre your honours to take ane course heirin and to cause your thesaurer to pay me otherwayes I will be forced to goe out of the towne a beggar. And your honours answer humblie I crave, your honours servant,

HEW ROSS.

[*In Dorso.*]

12 December 1656.

THE Magistratis and Counsell nowayes acknowledging what is mentionat in this supplicatioun anent a yeirlie closur of xl merk, etc. On consideratioun of the suplicantis present conditioun ordanes yow Robert Talyiour thesaurer to pay to the supplicant twentie merkis Scottis for supleing of his present necessity and thir presentis sall be your warrand. Subscrivit at Irving the said day.

M. Ro^t BARCLEY, *Provest.*
H. CUNYNGHAME, *Baily.*

43. *Petition of Adam Fullertoun, for payment of money advanced to Duke Hamilton's Regiment, and the decision of the Magistrates of Irvine thereon.—1st April* 1659.

My lord Proveist baillies and counsell of this brughe and unto your Lordships Humblie meanes and shaues I Adame Fullertoune elder merchant burges of this brughe that whair I haveing in Junij 1647 yeires at the earnest desyre of the Magistrats of this bruighe for the tyme and such of thair counsell as wes then present did lend ane houndireth pound Scoats as ane part of the somme of ffive houndireth pound Scoats grantit to Duik Hamiltouns regment quartert within this bruighe for the tyme and whairof   Levistoune of Westquarter had the charge and that for the said regments removell aff this bruighe which the lait Proveist Craig who had the pryme charge at that tyme and who acted werie mutch for getting of the said regment removit receavit from me to be given to them upon the clerks table upon faithfull promise of ane band to have bene given to me thairof beiring annualrent be the Magistrats and counsell of this bruighe to have bene draun upe be the clerk aforsaid and to have bene subscryvit upon the first day of the meitting of the saidis Magistrats and counsell after the said regments removell as is weill known to the said lait Proveist Craig and maist part of the counsell and clerk aforsaid and whairof I have oft and diverse tymes made representatioun to your Lordship for payment to me of my said principall somme and annualrents thairof now ann to me for the same by the space of ten yeires and   . scoar tuell pound . .   as yet I am not cume to any poynt   .   . ching the payment to me neither of my principall somme aforsaid nor yet of my bygane annualrents thairof yow haveing onlie found that I sould be payit of my said principall somme yow haveing takin to your consideratioun the payment cravet be me of my said bygane annualrents. And since that I yet lye furth of all both principall [and] annualrents which are to me just debt and whilk of all both conscience and equitie I ought to have als weill as uthirs gatt who lent moneyes for the same use and so much the more because ther wes ffyve houndireth merkes of the same money receivit be the provist from Westquarter applyit to the use of this bruighe and that I both have borne and does beir great burdein with this bruighe both in assessments and quarterings as is weill known to your Lordships which I dow not beir heirefter.

Heirfor I must humblie beseik your Lordships to tak present course for payment to me of my somme aforsaid and bygane annualrents thairof that so I may be now at last put to ane poynt and may not still be giveing in supplications and to be delayit as heirtofore I have bene over lang and your Lordships answer heirupon I most humblie crave.

Primo Aprilis 1659:

Presentes

Mr. Robert Barclay, *Provest*	Hew Montgomery
Provest Craig	Alexander Dyett
William Wishart	Laurence Anderson
Gilbert Wyllie	Williame finlay
Allan Cunyngham	Andrew Henderson

The Magistrats and Counsel condiscend to give the principall sum of ane hundreth pundis Scotts to the supplicant but refuissis to give any annualrent thair not being a contrary voic gevin in the mater.

R. Broun, *Clerk*,
at command of the Magistrats and Counsell.

Hew Montgomerie lait thesaurar who is not as yit absolvit of your comptis ffaill not incontinent efter the sight heirof to pay to Adam Fullartoun elder within and abonenamit ane hundrethe pundis Scottes award be us to him in maner mentionat in his withinwrittin suplicatioun; conforme to the act and determinatioun abonewrittin of us Magistrats and counsale and the samin sall be allowit be us to yow in your accompts upoun productioun heirof: Givin under our hands at Irvin the last day of May 1659.

Mr. Ro^t Barclay, *Provest*.
William Wishart, *Bailie*.
H. Cunynghame, *Bailye*.

44. *Tack in favour of Robert Galt, of the two Burgh Mills of Irvine.— 27th May 1659.*

At the burghe of Irving the tuentie sevint day of Maij the yeare of God J^m vj^c and fiftie nyne yeires It is appoyntit aggriet and finallie contractit and endit betwix the parties following To wit Mr. Robert Barclay provest of the said brughe Hew Cunynghame and William Wischart baillies

of the same for thameselves and with expres advyce and consent of the
counsell of the said bruighe and the saids proveist baillies and counsell
taking the burdeing in and upon them and thair successors for the commounitie of the samyne one the ane part and Robert Galt indueller at the
Loch mylnes of the said bruighe on the uthir part in maner following
That is to say That for someikle as the saids proveist baillies and counsell
for thameselffis and as burdiners forsaid haif for the yeirlie ferme and
deutie underwrittin Sett and in tak and assidatioun lattin and be thir
presentes Setts and in tak and assidatioun latts to the said Robert Galt
and his aires assignayes and subtennents ane or mae being of no hier degrie
nor himself that is to say honest yeomen folks fermoureres and mylners
of the corn mylnes underwrittin and lawbourrers of the grund and actuall
residenters and duellers at the said burghe of Irvings awn proper corne
mylnes underwrittin callit Loch Mylne and Wattir Mylne efterspecifeit
allanerly and to na utheris All and haill thair saids tua burrow mylnes
underwrittin designit as aforsaid with the mylne lands astrict multers
thairof underwittin sequeills laids dames and priviledgis of the wattir
drauchts thairof with the mylne houssis of the samyne yairds kill and uthers
biggings belonging or that can be known to belong thairto with thes lands
commounly callit the Lochmylne lands and thair aiker of land lyand
beyond the wattir of Annok as the samyne is and hes beine possest be the
said Robert Galt himself last fermourer and taksman thairof all lyand
within the teritorie of the said bruighe and that for all the dayes space and
yeires of flive yeires compleit nixt and immediatlie following the said
Robert Galt and his forsaids entrie thairto which wes and began to the
saids lands at Alhallowday last by past and wes and began to the yairds at
the labouring tyme of yairds last by past and which was and began to the
saids tua burrow mylnes and houssis biggings at Beltan last by past and
sall from thencefurth continue and indure and be peacabilie bruikit joysit and
possest be him and his forsaids dureing the said space sic lyk and as friclie
in all respects as the said Robert Galt himself last fermoroure and taksman
thairof possest the samyne of before with full power to him and his forsaids
be themselves and thair under mylners and servants in thair name to exact
and uplift the multoures particularlie efter specifeit To wit the tuentie-
fyft veschell of all maner of corne beir wheit peis ry and uthir stuff
grindable growand and that sall happen to grow upon the ground of all
lands quhatsumever belonging to the said bruighe in propertie and

tenandrie lyand within the parachon of Irving (except of malt allenerlie) which sall pay the multer and knaiveschipe eftermentionat and sic lyk the said Tuentie fyft veschell of moulter of the alyk qualitie of all maner of stuff grindable remayning and abyding within the bounds of the said sucken be the space of Tuentie four houres and does also still astriet and thirle as of before to the saids cornes mylnes all malt that sall happen to be broun within the said bruighe for the which the said Robert and his forsaids sall have right and libertie to exact and uplift for the grinding of ilk boll thairof that same self just particular quantatie of multour with that same self measur as he upliftit the samyne thir last sevein yeirs bygane and that dureing the space forsaid and which quantaties of moulter respective aforsaid sall be in full contentation to the said Robert and his under mylners and servants both for thair moulter bannok and knaveschipe and all that they can crave for the grinding of the said malt and becaus that the saids proveist baillies and counsell of the said bruighe upone consideratione of the inhabilitie of thair aun burrow mylnes aforsaids to serve the said sucken oftymes throw the want of water and uthirwayes hes taken in tak and assidatioun from the Airle of Eglintoune his mylne callit the Holme Mylne alias Hair Mylne with the mylne lands houssis biggings yairds kill dame wattergang astriet moulters sequeils and pertinents thairof lyand within the said parachon of Irving quhairof ther are divers yeires as yet to rin for the yeirlie payment of the deutie efterspecifeit mentionat in the said take which they did sett in subtak to the said Robert Galt with the mylne howssis kill yairds and biggings thairof for the last sevein yeires which outrynnes at Lambmes nixt for his releaving of them at the hands of the said earle of Eglintoune of the particular tak deutie thairin mentionat Thairfore the saids proveist baillies and counsell for thameselffs and taking the burdein in and upon them and thair successors in thair officis for the communitie of the said burghe hes for the said Robert Galt and his forsaids inhabeilling to serve the said sucken sett and in subtak and assidatioun lattin and be thir presentes setts and in subtak and assidatioun latts to the said Robert Galt and his forsaids fermourers and taksman of the saids tua burrow mylnes of Irving aforsaid All and haill the said corne mylne callit Holme Mylne alias Hair Mylne with the saids mylne houssis mylne lands kill yairds dame watergang astriet multers sequeils and pertinents thairof for the saids space of five yeires nixt and immediatlie following his entrie thairto which sall be and begin be vertew of this present subtak to the said mylne houssis biggings yairds kill dame moulters and sequeils thairof at Lambmes nixt to cume and to the said mylne lands thairof and sall begin to the lands at Hallowday nixt and sall from then forth be possest be him and his forsaids during the haill space (as being the onlie space and yeires which is to rin of the tak aforsaid which the saids proveist baillies and counsell themselffs hes thairof of the said earle of Eglintoune) with the haill priviledgis and liberties mentionat in the said bruighe of Irvings aun tak thairof and as the samyne wes and is possest be the said Robert Galt himself With full power to him and his forsaids to exact therat the just alyk quauntatie of multer abovewrittin of all cornes grayne and stuff thirlit to the saids burrow mylnes that sall happen to be ground at the said Holme Mylne alias Hair Mylne in that same maner as if the samyne wer ground at the saids tua burrow mylnes togidder with the multer of all cornes astrictit thairunto and if neid be to call and persew the abstracters of the stuff forsaid thirlit to the saids burrow mylnes before the saids proveist and baillies of the said bruighe present and to cume as accords of the law decreits ane or mae against thame thairupon to obtaine . . . executioun caus be put transact commoune and aggrie thairanent acquitancis and dischargis thairupon to give and . . . samyne to use and dispone at thair pleisor and generallie etc. ffor the whilk effect the saids proveist baillies and counsell obleiss thame and thair successors to hold and keipe multer courts quarterlie or oftiner as the said Robert and his forsaids sall think expedient and administrat justice thairintill to him and his forsaids as accords of the law lyk as the saids proveist baillies and counsell does heirby for them and thair forsaids ratifie allow and approve the possessioun which the said Robert Galt hes of the said burrow mylnes and uthir corne mylne particularie aforsaid callit the Holme Mylne alias Hair Mylne and of the said mylne lands astrict multers sequeils houssis biggings yairds parts pendicles and pertinents thairof and uthirs aforsaid be vertew of the former take and subtak he hes of them of the samyne consenting heirby he and his forsaids peacabilie bruik joyse and possese the samyne sic lyk and the same forme and maner as he possest the samyne before and that induring the haill space and yeirs of this present tak and subtak abovewrittin without any revocatioun or againe calling quhatsumever And which tak and subtak abovewrittin the saids proveist baillies and counsell for themselves and as burdinars aforsaids for the said communitie of the said bruighe binds and obleissis them and thair successors in thair officis to warrand to the said Robert Galt and his forsaids to be good and sufficient in all and be all things as is abovewrittin dureing the haill space and yeires of the samyne particularlie aforsaid at all hands and against all deidlie For the which caussis the said Robert Galt as principall and John Davisone merchant burges of the said burgh as cautionar souertie and full debitor for and with him to the effect underwrittin be thir presentes binds and obleissis them conjunctlie and severallie thair aires and executores successors to them in thair lands and heritagis and intrometers with thair rents guids and geir whatsumever to mak guid and thankfull payment to the saids proveist baillies counsell and communitie of the said bruighe and thair successors and to thair successors thesaurers in thair names present and for the tyme being indureing the haill space and yeires of this present tak particularlie aforsaid of all and haill fourscoir fyve bolls good and sufficient victuall the ane just and equal half thairof oatmeill als guid and sufficient as ony meill that sall be sauld in the mercat of Irvine (ane sek being onlie acceptit) and the uthir halfe guid and sufficient malt with the old scallit furlot of the said bruighe useit in the mercat thairof before the last reformatioun of measoures and whairwith the samyne wes useit to be payit of before and that for the tak deutie of the saids tua burrow mylnes of Irvine lands houssis biggings astrict multers and uthirs aforsaid belonging thairto and that at Candilmes Beltan Lambmes and Allhallowday proportionalie beginand the first quarter's payment thairof at Lambmes nixt to cume and that for his possessioun thairof from Beltan nixt to cume until the said terme and so furth quarterlie therefter at the saids four termes yeirlie dureing the space forsaid As also to releive and disburdine the saids proveist baillies counsell clerk and communitie of the said bruighe and thair successors at the hands of the said earle of Eglintoune and his aires successors and assignayes and thair factores and chalmerlands in thair names tuitching the payment to thame of tuelfe bolls oat meill and thriescoar tuelfe punds Scoats of silver meall dew be thame of tak deutie to the said earle for the said corne mylne callit Holme Mylne alias Hair Mylne mylne lands multers and uthirs aforsaids belonging thairto and that yeirlie from Lambmes nixt to cume dureing the space of this present subtake according as they are obleist thairby and of all that can be demandit be the said earle of them for the samyne dureing the said space and to report to thame yeirlie the said earle and his forsaids acquittance and dischargis thairof As als that the said Robert Galt and his forsaids sall actualie dwell and resceid at the saids tua burrow mylnes and that he shall hold and keep faithfull honest and sufficient under-mylners and servants in the saids thrie mylnes for the saife keiping and preserving of all stuff that sall be brought to the saids mylnes to be grund therat and for the deutifull eufauld and reddie serving of the inhabitants and for afftaking and unlaying of thair loads for whom the said Robert Galt and his forsaids sall be answerable and sall uphold the said thrie mylnes sufficient geangand mylnes to the effect forsaid and that the said Robert and his forsaids sall let out the clouse of the saids burrow mylnes that leids to the high mylne yeirlie dureing the space of this present take for drying of the Loch lands and uthirs adjacent thairto yeirlie at the seveintein day of March unto Allhallowday conforme to the former use and custom observit thairanent of before   And as to the saids thrie corne mylnes and haill severall houssis biggings and kills thairof [is] be the first tak and subtak thairof set be the saids proveist baillies and counsell of the said bruighe to the said Robert Galt of the samyne which wes in the moneth of Mairch j^m vj^c fiftie tua yeires now expyrit appoynted to have bene sighted at his entrie to the same be John Guthrie then ane of the baillies of the said bruighe John Dunlope then dean of gild Hew Broun dagmaker George Mortoun in Barrassie and   Boile in Perstoune as persones chosen for that effect both at the said Robert Galt his entrie thairto (and which wes accordinglie sighted be them) and wer appoynted also to be sighted be them or most part of them being on lyf for the tyme at the experation of the said first act and the said Robert Galt his removall thairfra that so aither partie might then hine inde satisfie and repair uthirs be the sight aforsaid of whatever the saids mylnes houssis biggings and uthirs aforsaids sould be fund at the said Robert his removell to be aither better or worse then the samyne wes at the said Robert his entrie thairto   So be reasoune of this present tak and subtak as abovewrittin sett now to the said Robert Galt and his forsaids of the samyne dureing the space and yeires particularlie aforsaid and of the said Robert his keeping still the possessioun of the said mylnes and uthirs aforsaid the saids thrie mylnes houssis biggings and kills thairof aforsaid are lykewayes appoyntit at the experatioun of this present tak and his removeall thairfra to be sighted be the persones aforsaid or most part of them being on lyf for the tyme and whatever the same sall then be fund be thame to be aither in better or worse condition then the samyne wes at the said Robert his first entrie thairunto aither of the saids parties be thir presentes binds and

obleis them and thair forsaids hinc inde to make satisfactioun and
reperatioune to uthirs be the sight aforsaid Lyk as the said Robert Galt
and his said cautioner bind and obleiss them and thair forsaids conjunctlie
and severalie that the said Robert Galt and his forsaids sall remove from
the saids thrie severall corne mylnes lands howssis biggings kills and
uthirs aforsaid at the experatioun of this present tak and subtak abovewrittin under the pain of tua hundireth punds money of Scoatland of
liquidat penultie presentlie aggreit upon to be payit be thame to the saids
proveist baillies counsell and communitie and thair said thesaurer in thair
names and that by and attour the doeing thairof As also the said Robert
Galt obleissis him and his forsaids not to persew any of the inhabitants of
the said bruighe for abstractit multers before any uther judge or judges but
onlie before the saids proveist and baillies thameselffs and which persuits
sall be yeirlie within the spaces following To wit for the abstrictit multers
of malt within half ane yeir yeirlie and for the abstractit multers of uthir
cornes and grayne grindable astrictit and thirlit to the said burrow mylnes
within the space of a yeir uthirwayes hee not to be hard in persewing of
the samyne And als the said Robert obleissis him and his forsaids to
keipe ane horse for homebringing to the inhabitants of the said burghe of
thair malt to be grund at the saids mylnes and for the homebringing
whairof the said Robert and his forsaids sall onlie have for ilk boll ane
peck of draff according to the old accustomit order or uthirwayes Ten
pennyes thairfore at the optioune of the carier who shall be ane man hable
both to beir on and off the said malt Lyk as I the said Robert Galt be thir
presentes binds and obleis him and his forsaids to warrand frie relive
harmeles and scaithles keepe the said Jhonne Davisone his cautioner abovementionat and his forsaids of his said cautionarie and of all perrell danger
cost skaythe dammage expenssis and intrest hee or his forsaids can or may
or sall happen to sustein and incur throw his said cautionarie in ony sort
And finallie the said proveist baillies and counsell obleiss them and thair
successors in thair offices to releive and scaithles keepe the said Robert Galt
and his forsaids of all taxt and impositioune that can be imposit or
reqwyrit of him for the rent of thair ann tua burrow mylnes aforsaid and
lands thairunto belonging sett to him in tak as said is be them and that
indureing the wholl space and yeires abovewrittin of this present tak And
for the mair securitie both the saids parties are content and consents that
thir presents be insert and registrat in the court buiks of justice or burrow

court buiks of the said bruighe or in the buiks of any uthir judicatorie within this natione for the tyme to haife the strenth of ane act and decreit of ony of the judges thairof respective aforsaids and thair auctorities to be interponit heirto that leters and executorialls of puynding warding and hornying may pas heirupon if neid be upon ane simple charge of sax dayes onlie and for this effect they constitute thair lauchfull procuratouris etc.—In witnes whairof (wryttin be James Finlay servitor to Robert Broun common clerk of the said bruighe) baith the saids parties have subseryvit thir presents with thair hands day moneth place and yeir of God abovewrittin before thir witnessis the said James Finlay and Alexander Iseat one of the burrow officars of the said burghe (Signed) Mr. Ro^t Barclay proveist, H. Cunynghame bailye, William Wisheart bailie. John Guthrie dein of gild, J. Dunlop counselor, Allane Cuninghame counsel^r, John Porter cownseller, Gilbert Wylky counseller, Alex^r Dyett cownseller, Robert Stewart cownseller, Hew Montgomre consler. Robert Galt. John Davisoune cautioner. James Finlay witnes, Alex^r Eisat witnes. R. Broun clerk.

Irving the 8th August 1667.

James Hunter procurator for the within namet Magistratis of Irving, and George Garvan procurator for the within namet Galt and his cautioner consents to the registratioune heirof in the borrow court bookis of Irving.

45. *Petition of James Galt, Smith, with Account.*—1659.

UNTO the Richt Honourable the Proveist Baillies and Counsell of this Burgh humelie meinyes and supplicattis I James Galt smith ane of your comburgessis That quhar thair is dewlie awand to me be your Honouris eightein poundis Scottis restand of brewine Beir be my wyff to the garisoun of Eglintoun Mair thair is awand to me sex poundis money for Speddis and Schuiles gevin be me to the said garisoun at command of Hew Cunninghame baillie Mair thair is awand to me uther sex poundis money for schoeing of sex horss to the Associat Raid at command of the Proveist Mr. Robert Barclay Mair thair is awand to me ffyve poundis tuentie pennes for tuentie pound and ane half of new maid work in mending of the Counsell Hous chymney at command of the Proveist Mair thair is awand to me of locall quarteris of Leivtennant Collonell Cotlars sojouris eight poundis

money   Mair thair is awand to me for quheit Breid I coft to the sojouris
quhill they war put in the Tolbuith for the Associat Armie threttie eight
shillingis money at command of Proveist Craig   Quhilkis soumes extendid
altogidder to ffourtie sevin poundis wanting four pennies Scottis and
is now of long tyme awand to me Heirfoir I intreatt your Honouris to
caus mak me payment of the foirsaidis soumes extending as said is ffor I
haif mutche adoe thairwith being awand to severall others myselff. And
your Honouris ausuer humelie I crave.

xvij Martij 1659.

The Magistrateis and Counsale recommend to the tua Baillies and Dene
of Gild to meitt and to tak dew cognition and tryale what is justlie dew to
the Petitioner and to report the nixt Counsale day And the Petitioner to
convine them and if he be *in mora* and doe not convine thame he not to
be hard after.

8 April 1659.

Thes to whome that is committit in the fornemmit findis the Toun to
be justlie awand to the suplicant 32^{lb} 19^s 4^d and ordanes him before he be
payit to first convine with the Thesaurer and pay what he sall be awand.

R. BROUN.

For Beir brewine to the garisounne of Eglingtoune	17	13	0
Item for sex Spaid heads at	4	0	0
Item for Shoeing sex horse	4	16	0
Item for 20 pound of made work to the Chemney	4	12	4
For wheat Bread	1	18	0
	32	19	4

Hew Magumrie Theaussurer who hes not as yeit perfytted your accompt
ye sall paye to James Gallt smith for the within wryttine compte Threttie
two pound 19^s 4^d, and the saming sall be allowed at your compte making.
Irvin the penullt June 1660.   F. DUNLOP, *Proveist.*

JOHN GUTHRIE, *Baillie.*
JAMES BLAIR, *Baillie.*

46. *Discharge by the Earl of Eglinton to Robert Galt, for the silver duty of the Holme Mill.—9th January* 1660.

GRANTS us to have ressavit frome Robert Galt for the silver dewty and victuall for the Holme Mylne sett be us to the town of Irwin compleit payment for all preciding yeirs to the first of August j^m vj^c fyftie nyne yeirs allowand to him ane chalder of corne gottin frome Johne Galt in Irland and the publick burdins to July 1659 as witnes our hand at Eglintoun the 9 day of Januar 1660. EGLINTOUN.

47. *Discharge by Hew Whyte, Merchant, to the Magistrates of Irvine.— 8th August* 1662.

BE it kend till all men be thir present lettres Me Hew Whyt merchant burges of Irvine the onlie lawfull sone of umquhill Steven Whyt somtym Proveist of the said burgh That forsamikell as I having compearit before the Magistrats and Counsell of the said burgh for the tyme upon the sixt day of Junij j^m vj^c fiftie seven yeirs and having then remonstrat to them that I was to transport myself with my wyfe bairns and my familie of this burgh to Irleland and because that I had made heretabill venditione of my lands within this burgh and my lands of Lochwards to James Blair then present din of gild of the said burgh my brother in law and that I was auand for the said lands to the thesaurer of this burgh diverse and sundrie yeirs fewit dewties therof and the teynds of the said lands diverse and sundrie yeirs and that I was obleist to the said James Blair and uthers to whom I had sold my lands of Lochwards to satisfie the bygane fewit dewties and bygane teynds therof As also I had conditioned to the said James Blair to releeve him at the touns hands theranent and anent the half of qulatsomever composition the said magistrats and counsell soold tak from the said James Blair for receiving of him their imediat heretabill vassell in the said lands of Lochwards and that trewlie he had sufferit much damage the tym after the death of his umquhill mother both of his goods and rents dew to him as heretour of the said lands he as heretour haveand right therto before that whittsonday term (he sawing the cropt therof upon the ground the said yeir) the toune having sensyn much of the corus be staking the samyn in William Wallace barne yeard destroyit be the Inglishes, and be his wanting of his heirscape goods both of silver work and uthers be deficiencie of the magistrats who had the charge therof as he alledgit and to be weell known And therfor most humblie craving a favour and ease of his said bygane teynd and future and in relation of his half composition afoirsaid in maner conteinit in his said supplicatioun and remonstrance afoirsaid The saids magistrats and counsell having taken the said mater to their consideratione over and above that yeirs teynd wherof all gat a deduction so he among the rest Hes condescended and be thir presents condescends that the said Hew Whyt shall have doun thirtie four pound Scots of his bygane teynd and declars they will tak from the said James Blair three score pounds and does simpliciter quatt the said Hew Whyt of thirtie pound therof (of the said Hews half of the same) he causing pay the rest of his teynds fewit dewties and uthers dew to the toune and which the said Hew accepted as a favour and therfor he did quatt the toun of what he could claime of them simpliciter in anie of the relations afoirsaid and quhat else he could demand of the toun or of the magistrats be their intromission directlie nor indirectlie in anie sort in maner and at length conteinit in the act made theranent sett doune in the borow court books of the said burgh before his said magistrats counsell of the same of the dait foirsaid And I the said Hew Whyt now compearand this day befor the baillies and counsell of the said burgh they being dewlie conveined within the counsell hous of the said burgh and having supplicat the said magistrats and counsell of the said burgh that they wold yet doe him that favour as to exoner and discharge him and these to whome he had made vendition of his tenements of land respective lyand within the said burgh and these persons eftirnamit to whom he sold the same To witt James Wodsyd merchant burges of the said burgh to whom he had sold heretabillie and irredimablie that his tenement of land with the yeard rig and pertinents accquyrit be his umquhill father from Mr Robert Tran and the said Hew and Alexander Cochrans merchant burges of the said burgh to quhom he made vendition of his said umquhill fathers fore tenement of land and uthers disponit therwith be him to the said Alexander and the reliet and airs of umquhill Robert Cochran who bought from the said Hew his oun back tenement of land with the pertinents therof of the ground annualls dew and payable for the same and that of all yeirs and terms preceiding this respective disposition of the same whilk was preceiding the yeir fiftie one in maner conteinit in my supplication given to them theranent The

saids magistrats and counsell out of the respect and favour they have
toward me in the mater afoirsaid having grantit to me the desyre of my
said supplication in the matter afoirsaid by their giving of discharges both
to me and the persons afoirsaid to quhome I did make heretabill vendition
of my said tenements of land in maner respective abovementionat of the
whole ground anualls dew and payable for the same before the said yeir of
God j^m vj^c fiftie one the quhilk yeir I disponit to the said umquhill Robert
Cochran in quhat relats to him therof for the said yeir fiftie one and to the
saids Alexander Cochran and James Wodsyd in quhat relaits to their respective tenements disponit be me to them before the yeir j^m vj^c fiftie eight
as their accquittances respective givin to me and them therupon mair fullie
proports. Therefor and in consideration of the former favour done to me
be the said magistrats and counsell of the said burgh for the tym I be thir
presents exoner quyt claime and simpliciter discharge the proveist baillies
and counsell of the said burgh and their whole communitie and ilk ane
of them their aires executors and successours of all and quhatsomever that
I my aires or asignayes can or may in anie wayes ask or claime of them or
anie of them be and throw their or anie of ther intromission with my
moveable heirscape guids and geir falling to me be deceis of my said
umquhill father and of the corns and cropt belonging to me of that yeir of
my said umquhill mothers deceise or anie other maner or way directlie or
indirectlie in that accompt admittand be thir presents the generallitie afoirsaid to be als sufficient in all respects as if evrie particular that I can crave
of them or anie of them in the matter afoirsaid wer particularlie and per
expressum sett doune and denominat therintill and obleissis me my aires
and executors to warrand to them and ilk ane of them and their foirsaids
this my accquittance and discharge abovewrittin to be good and sufficient
for their exoneration of the same at all hands and against all deidlie And
for the mair securitie I am content and consent that thir presents be insert
and registrat in the buiks of counsell and sessioune or in the court buiks of
anie other judicatorie within this kingdome for the tym to have the strength
of ane act and decreit of anie of the judges therof respective and their
auctorities to be interponit heirto as weell for conservatione therof forever
as that the samyn to have the strength of ane act and decreit of anie of
the judges therof respective and that letters and executorialls of poynding
warding and horning may pas heirupon upon ane simple charge of six dayes
onlie if neid be And for this effect I constitute   my

lawfull procurators In wittnes quhairof (writtin be Robert Service servitour to Robert Broun toun clerk of Irvine) I have subscryvit thir presents with my hand at Irvine the eight day of August j^m vj^c threescore tuo yeirs before thir wittnessis the said Robert Broun and the said Robert Service wryter heirof. H. WHYT.

R. Broun, *wittnes*.
R. Service, *wittnes*.

48. *Bond by Henry Dyet in reference to Shooting at the Papingo*.— 29th August 1665.

BE it kend till all men be thir present lettres Me Hendrie Dyet smyth burges of Irwing that fforsameikle as the Magistrats of this burgh haveing conforme to the old antient practeis appoyntit the Paippingoe to be set up and that whasoever burgessis pleasit to adres thameselffs thairto with thair bowis and arrows for schooting thairat might have full friedome and libertie upoun deponing the ordinarie consignatione And that severall dayis being appoyntit for schooting thairat and at last this day as being the last day that whosoevir sould ding the samyn doun sould be capitan and have ane Benne or Scarff consisting of the value of twelff pundis Scotts or thairby the said capitan giveing in securitie for produceing the Papingoe with ane scarff of the value afoirsaid with twintie ellis of small silk ribbens of the value of fourtie pennyis the ell and that ilk persone that sall schoot the nixt ensewing yeir sall give in and consigne in the hands of the said Capitan befoir they be suffered to schoott threttein schilling four pennyis Scottis to be disposit upone be the said Capitan at his pleasure in regaird of his furneisching of the said Scarff or Benne and ribbens afoirsaid to be poynts quhilk is to be done yeirlie the first Tysday of Maij being the first day appoyntit for schooting And to continew tuo dayis thaireftir as salbe appoyntit being thrie dayis and the fourt day the Papingoe to be maid louse for schooting hir af And it falling out that I have attaint to the honor this day in being Capitan throw my schooting doun of the Papingoe and haveing receavit ane scarff of the value afoirsaid Thairfore and for observing of the said ordinance witt yee me as principall and with me Johne Thomsone flescher burges of the said burgh as cautioner and souertie for me to be bound and obleist lykas we be thir presentis faithfullie bind and obleis us conjunctlie and severallie our airis and executoris to the

Magistratis of this burgh present or for the tym being that I the said Hendrie Dyet sall upone the first Tysday of Maij nixt to cum j^m vj^c thriescoir six yeiris exhibit and produce ane Papingoe with ane silk scarff of the value of twelff pundis with twintie ellis of ribbens of the value afoirsaid that so the said antient practeis may be keipit up in all tym cumying both with us and our posteritie and burgessis of this burgh under the pain of ffourtie punds Scotts of liquidat penultie by and attour the performance And at the performance quhairof the consignationes ar to be maid in manner foirsaid And this to be observit yeirlie in all tym cuming by all who sall succeid in the roume and place of me the said Hendrie and I the said Hendrie obleis me and my foirsaids to releiv my said cautioner and his foirsaids of his said cautionrie And we ar content and consentis thir presentis be insert and registrat in the buikis of Counsell or Burrow Court buikis of Irwyng to have the strenth of ane decreit that lettres and executoriallis neidfull may pas heiron if neid be on six dayis onlie And for this effect we constitute   our procuratoris, etc. In witnes quhairof wrytten be George Garven nottar in Irwin we have subscryvit thir presentis as followis at Irwin the twintie nynt day of August j^m vj^c thriescoir fyve yeiris befoir thir witnessis Hew Whyt Lawrence Blair merchands James Franck chirurgian and Robert Francis all burgessis of Irwing.

 Ita est Georgius Garven notarius publicus in premissis specialiter requisitus de mandato dicti Hendrici Dyet scribere nescientis ut asseruit ac calamum tangentis testantibus his meis signo et subscriptione manualibus. G. GARVEN.

   JOHNE THOMSONE, *Colectour of Consignationes.*

H. Whyt, *witnes.*   Robt Francis, *witnes.*
Ja^s Franck, *wittness.*   Laurence Blair, *witness.*

49. *Discharge by Ninian Cuninghame to the Magistrates of Irvine for £6 sterling, for behoof of the Manufactory of Montgomeryston.—2d November 1665.*

I NINIANE CUNINGHAME baillie of Montgomerystoun Collector appoynted be the masters of the Manufactorie of Montgomerystoun for uplifting of the contributione appoynted be Act of Parliament ffor the use of the said Manufactorie in relatione to the poor that wer to be leivied out of ilk parochine be thir presentes grant me to have receaved ffra Arthur Hamiltone toun clerk of Irving in name and behalff of the Magistratis and Counsell of the brught of Irving the sowme of six pund Sterling money ffor the said brught of Irving ther first yeires proportione imposit upone tham for the use of the said Manufactorie ffor tua poore that sould have bein outriked furth of the said burght for the use of the said Manufactorie and dischargis the saids Magistratis and Counsell of the said brught off the said six pund Sterling money receaved be me for the use above writtin for now and evir In witnes quhairof I have subscryvit thir presentis with my hand written be James Huntar servitor to the said Arthur Hamiltoun att Irving the second day of November j^m vi^c thriescoire ffyve yeires beffoire thir witnessis Mr. James Cuninghame Shereff Deput of Air and the said James Huntar. NINIAN CUNINGHAME.

J. Cuninghame, *wittnes*.
Ja. Hunter, *witnes*.

50. *Missive from the Provost and Council of Edinburgh to the Provost and Council of Irvine, with instructions regarding the next Convention of the Burghs.—25th March* 1667.

RIGHT HONOURABILL and our loveing freinds and nighbouris Efter hearty comendationes. Wheras the Comissioners of borrowes mett at Edinbrugh in the last Generall Convention did affix and appoynt ther nixt Generall Convention to be and begine at ther brugh of Edinbrugh the first Tuesday of Julij nixt 1667 being the second day of the said moneth with contiuuation of dayes and have continowed the heads and articles following to be resolved agried and concludit upon therin :

1. Item ilk burgh to send ther Comissioners sufficientlie instructed for keeping of the said Convention with ther comissiones under the comon seall of ther burgh and subscription of ther Magistrates or comon Clerk testificing them to be men fearing God of the true protestant religion presentlie in publict professed and authorized be the lawes of this Kingdome without suspition in the contrair expert in the affairs of borrowes merchand-

traffequers and inhabitants within ther burghes bearing portable charges therin with ther nighbours And that they be such as may tyne and winne in all ther caussis under the paine of 20^{lib} to be payed to the borrowes.

2. Item ilk burgh to report ther diligence in intimateing to ther severall burghes that no measure of victuall shall be keiped within ther respective borrowes bot conforme to the standert of Linlithgow under the paine of 20^{lib} ilk burgh conforme to 5 Act of the last General Convention of borrowes holdin at Edinbrugh in the moneth of Julij last.

3. Item that ilk burgh report ther diligence to the nixt Generall Convention in intimateing to the severall brughes at the homecomeing ther ratification and approbation of all Acts made against unfrie traders and against frie burgesse residentars in unfrie places and that the same be putt to due execution under the paine of 20^{lib} conforme to the 6 Act of the said last Generall Convention.

4. Item the Agent to report his diligence the nixt Generall Convention in concurring with the brugh of Perth, Stirling and uther royall borrowes who shall requyre him to the prosecution of ther Acts against unfrie traders conforme to the 7 Act of the Generall Convention.

5. Item the brugh of Dundie and Arbroth to report ther diligence in meiting at the brugh of Monros at some convenient day befor the nixt Generall Convention anent the reviseing of the measure of Salt of the said brugh and makeing it conforme to the measure of Dundie and the said brugh to conveine the rest under the paine of 20^{lib} conforme to the 8 Act of the said last Generall Convention.

6. Item the brugh of Edinbrugh to report ther diligence to the nixt Generall Convention in dealing with His Majesties Comissioner, Lords of Privie Counsell and uthers in power in recoverie of the borrowes friedome of trade and navigation with Ingland conforme to the 9 Act of the said last generall Convention.

7. Item the Clerk to report his diligence in wryting to the conservator for his appearance at the nixt Generall Convention of borrowes for subscryveing such Acts and Ordinances as Sir Patrick Drumond and uthers his predicessors had done before conforme to the 10 Act of the said last Generall Convention.

8. Item the brugh of Edinbrugh with the Agent to report their diligence

the nixt Generall Convention and give in concurrance to the brugh of Linlithgow in obtaineing all veshells that shall louse or load on the south syde of the Water of Forth to louse or load at the port of Blacknes provydeing the samen being above the port of Leith the said port of Blacknes being the onlie frie port conforme to the 11 Act of the said last Generall Convention.

9. Item ilk brugh to report ther diligence in intimating to the severall brughes at ther homecomeing that ane uniformitie be keiped of the measure of the eln reil and foot of measure throw the haill brughes of the Kingdome And for that effect ilk brugh shall procure the said measure of ane elne reil and foot from the Dean of Gild of Edinburgh marked with the toun and Dean of Gild their mark and that noe brugh presume to challeng any of the saids measures bot by the measure so marked As also that ilk brugh have the standert of the weights from the brugh of Lanerk and the Jadge or Jug from the brugh of Stirling and the furlet from the brugh of Linlithgow and uthir standerts from the respective brughes that keips the samen conforme to the 12 Act of the said last Generall Convention.

10. Item the brughes that did convein at the particular Convention at Edinburgh the 2d Julij j666 and for attending the Convention of Estates to report their diligence to the nixt Generall Convention makeing application to His Majesties Comissioner the Lords of his Privie Counsell and uthers it may concerne in procureing ane exoneration to the merchands of twelfe pund Scots imposit upon the boll of bay salt and 50 solze upon the tun of goods exported and imported to and from France and the exorbitant custome upon the duell hundred of plaidin and procureing ane convoy for guarding his ships tradeing to and from forraigne places and secureing ther coasts for preservation of trade And in caice of noe redres to choice Comissioners of ther number to goe to His Majestie for that effect And this recomendit cheiflie to the brughs of Edinburgh, Perth, Dundie, Aberdein, Lithgow, St. Andrews and Glasgow and to report ther diligence heiranent conforme to the 13 Act of the said Generall Convention.

11. Item the brugh of Queensferrie to report ther diligence in selling a peice of ther comon land quhich wes usles for ther brugh and imploying the money therof to the behove of ther comon good under the paine of 20^{lib} conforme to the 15 Act of the said last Generall Convention.

12. Item the Agent to report his diligence in concurring with the brugh

of Linlithgow in the stopping of the signatour for erecting borrow stands in a frie royall brugh conforme to the 16 Act of the last Generall Convention of borrowes.

13. Item the brughes of Perth, Dundie, Aberdein, Monros, Couper in Fyfe, to report ther diligence in the nixt Generall Convention in meiting at the brugh of Brichen the first Wednesday of September nixt and therefter at any tyme they should appoynt for composeing the difference betwixt the discontented persones in that brugh anent the constitution of the Magistrats and Counsell of the said brugh with power to the said brughes or any thrie of them to call before them all parties interested and to hear quhat shall be proponed be each partie and to consider the originall rights and priviledges of the said brugh and efter hearing both parties in consideration of the saids priviledges to deall for ane freindlie agriement conforme therto And failyieing therof to determine and decyde in the said matter as they or anie thrie of them shall upon the consideratioues forsaid find just and reasonable under the paine of 20^{lib} ilk brugh butt prejudice to aither the saids parties who shall find themselves interessed be the said determination to make ther adresse to the nixt Generall Convention of burrowes.

14. Item ilk brugh to send with ther Comissioners the proportiones of the soume of 2147^{lib} 6^s debursed be the Agent by order of the borrowes at the last Convention and for payment of the Clerk and Agent's fees and the Agent's sallarie at Court conforme to ane particular accompt to be given in therof And that under the paine of 20^{lib} ilk brugh.

Therfore we desyre your Wisdomes to send your Comissioners sufficientlie instructed for keiping of the said Convention as ye tender the weill of the state of burrowes under the paine of 20^{lib} ilk brugh in caice of failyie And till farder occasion we bid you fareweill. Your affectionat freinds and nighbours the proveist baillies and Counsell of Edinbrugh subscryveing be Mr. Thomas Young our comon clerk and generall clerk to the borrowes. Tho. Young.

Edinbrugh 25 March 1667.

[*Dorso.*]

ffor The Right Honorabill The Provest Bailzies and Counsell of the burgh of Irwing These.

51. *Missive from the Provost and Council of Edinburgh, to the Provost and Council of Irvine, in regard to the next Convention of Burghs.* 16th December 1667.

RIGHT honoorabill and verie loveing freeinds and nighbours The particullar Conventione of the Borrowes which mett heir the begining of this moneth haveing had severall important bussiness under ther consideration particullarly the setling of the staple port, the fiftie solze upon the tun, the tuelf pound upon everie boll of forraigne salt, with the abuses comitted be David Weymes in uplifting the penalties contained in the Act of Parliament, anent the breedth off lining cloath, and finding the same to be a too generall concerne for a particullar Conventione to engadge in and the matters being such as requyre a speedy dispatch the Conventione thought fitt that ther should be a generall Conventione of the Royall Borrowes heir at Edinburgh the first Tuesday of March nixt being the third day of the said moneth These ar therfore to give yow notice of ther resolutione to the end yow may send heir your Comissioner againe the tyme appointit fullie instructed and impoured to consult treat and conclude with the rest of the Comissioners anent the particullars above writtin and wholle bodie of the last generall missive already direct to yow and what shall farder be then offerred which may concerne the good and weelfair of the Royall Borrowes and ther particullar state, with all remembering the Clerks and Agents fies with the former missives dewes quhairof ye have ane accompt, and so till forder occatione we bid yow fairweell and rests your affectionat freinds and servands The Provest, Baillies and Counsell of Edinburgh, Subscryved be Mr Thomas Young our common clerk at our comand.

THO. YOUNG.

Edinburgh the 16th day of December 1667.

[*On the back.*]

For the Right Honourable the Provest Baillies and Counsell of the Burgh of Irving These.

52. Discharge by John Smyth, Mason, to the Magistrates of Irvine, for £1000, in payment of his work upon the Bridge of Irvine.—23d December 1667.

I JOHNE SMYTH macsson in Kilmars be thir presents grant me to have receaved fra Robert Cunynghame proveist of the brugh of Irving Henry Lyne and Lawrence Blair bailzies of the said brugh compleit payment and satisfactione of the soume of ane thousand pounds Scotis monie ffor the building of the secound bow of the bridge of Irving nearest the east end thairof and repairing of the tuo pillaris quhairupone the said bow is foundit conforme to ane minut of agriement past betuixt the saids proveist and baillies one the ane pairt and me one the uther part of the dait the twentie ffyft day of Maij j^m vj^e thrie scoir sevine yeares Quhairof I hold me weill satisfied and thairfor I be thir presentis exoner quytclame and simpliciter discharge the said proveist and baillies thair aires and executoris and als the counsell of the said burgh with all uthers quhom it effeires of the foirsaid soume of ane thousand pounds money foirsaid quhilk the saids proveist and baillies wer obleist to pay to me be vertew of the said minut of agriement ffor building of the said bow and repairing of the saids tua pillars and off the samin minut of agriement haill heids articles conditiones and claussis thairof onywayes conceaved in my favor or ony wayes obleist be them to me thairby in all tyme comeing Quhilk discharge above writtin I be thir presentis binds and obleis me my aires and executoris to warrand acquyt and defend to the saids proveist and baillies to be guid valeid effectual and sufficient at all hands and against all deidlie as law will And ffor the mair securitie I am content and consentis thir presentis be insert and registrat in the bookis of Counsell and Sessione Borrow Court bookis of Irving or any uther Judges bookis competent within this kingdome that lettres and executoriallis neidfull may be direct heirupone in fforme as effeirs And for this effect constitutis   my procuratoris, etc. In witnes quhairof I have subscryvit thir presentis with my hand (written be Alexander Montgomerie wreitter in Irving) att Irving the tuentie thrid day of December j^m vj^e thrie scoir sevine yeares befoir thir witnessis Bryce Muir messenger Alexander Montgomerie and Robert Cuninghame servitoris to Arthur Hamiltoun toun clerk of Irving and Johne Dunlop tailzeour burges of Irving.

Ita est Arthurus Hamiltone Notarius publicus in premissis requisitus de mandato dicti Joannis Smyth scribere nescientis (ut asseruit) calamumque tangentis scripsit.

Ita est Jacobus Hunter connotarius in premissis de mandato dicti Joannis Smyth testantibus manu mea propria signoque.

Bryce Mure, *witnes.*	Ro. Cuningham, *witnes.*
John Dunlop, *witnes.*	Al. Montgomerie, *witnes.*

53. *Letter, Sir Alexander Cuninghame of Robertland to the Magistrates of Irvine.*—23d *September* 1670.

Robertland, 23 September 1670.

MUCH HONORED

I most intreat yow to have patience untill Mononday come eight dayes quhich is the thrid of October For this day I can not keipe in regaird the Ministers apointed be the Counsell are come west and some of them are with me And all the nixt weake I will be abroad about businesse so that I can not apoint ane day before the foresaid thrid of October And that my cautioners and I be not troubled according to your promise and then I shall releive them of my cautiourie and give yow all satisfactioun in reasoun as ye will oblidge, Sir, your most assured friend to serve yow, AL. CUNINGHAME.

[*Addressed.*]

For his much honoured the proveist,
  bailies, and counsell of Irvin these.

[*In another hand.*]

INTERROGATIONIS.

Whither we most scite Jo. Reid or no.

Whither our peipell will be admitted witneses or no.

Whither the depositiounes we have allredie takein of straingers will be sustined or no.

Whither Robertlan maye rease criminall Letters to compeir befor the Justis Generall or no.

Whither

54. *Discharge by the Earl of Eglinton to the Magistrates of Irvine for the outfit of their Militia horses.*—21st May and 8th June 1671.

I GRANT me to have receaved from the Magistratis and brugh of Irvin ffull and compleit payment and satisfaction for the outricking and mentenance of there Melitia horsses according to the bargain betwixt them and me for the yeare sewinty as wittnes my hand at Edinburgh the 21th of May 1671.
EGLINTOUN.

I grant me to have receaved from the Magistratis and brugh of Irvine the soum of two hundreth Merkis Scottis money for the mentinance of thair Militia hors for ane year according to the bargain betwixt my Lord and them If the abone wryten discharg be not valled that my [lord] shall subscrive to them an new on as wittnes my hand at Irwen the eight day of Junij 1671.
H. MONTGOMERIE.

55. *Discharge by the Earl of Eglinton to the Magistrates of Irvine for three years' maintenance of their Militia horses.*—1st July 1671.

WEE Alexander Earle of Eglintoune lord Montgomerie and Kilwynning be thir presentis grant us to have ressavit fra James Blaire proveist of Irving Allane Cuming and Henry Lyne baillies therof for themselves and in name and behalf of the haill inhabitantis of the said brucht compleit payment and satisfactione for thrie yeirs maintenance and outreik of tua Militia horses furnished outreikit and mainteined be us with their ryders And that fra Witsunday j^m vj^c thrie scoire eight yeirs untill Witsunday last j^m vj^c thriescoire ellevin yeirs being tua hundreth merkis Scotis yeirlie conforme to ane agriement maid betwixt us and the toune of Irving therauent And therfore we be thir presentis Exoner and simpliciter dischairge the saids thrie yeirs mainteinance of the said tua Militia horses and their ryders during the space above specifeit for now and evir Declairing alwayes all former ressaites given be us to the Magistratis of the samen of the saidis Militia horses and ryders ther mainteinance preceiding this dait to be includit within this present dischairge and sall infer no double payment therof In witnes quhairof we have subseryveit thir presentis with our handis at Eglintoune the first day of Julij j^m vi^c thriescoire ellevin yeirs befoire thir witnessis Joseph Cunynghame of Carling and Arthir Hamiltoune wreitter heirof. EGLINTOUN.

 Jo. C. Carlung, *witnes.*
 Art. Hamiltone, *witnes.*

56. *Discharge by the Earl of Eglinton to the Magistrates of Irvine for 200 merks, due for the town's Militia horses.*—13*th December* 1671.

WEE Alexander Earle of Eglintoun grant us to have receved from the Magistrats of Irwinge the soume of tuo hundreth merks accordinge to agrement ffor the ffourth yeirs answering ffor ther Militia horsses lyable for ther said towne to appear, and discharges them therof And oblidges me to renew this discharge in more fforn if need be when required. In witness wherof we have subscribed thir presents with our hand at Eglintoun this thretin day of December j^m vj^e sevinty one years befor thir witnes Patrick Hunter of Hunterston and Robert Home writter herof.
                  EGLINTOUN.

 Pa. Huntar, *witnes.*
 Robt Home, *witnes.*

57. *Order to the Treasurer of Irvine to pay to Mr. Robert Hunter, preacher, the interest on bond for £1000, lent by him to the Burgh.* 2*d September* 1680.

ROBERT BRYSSOUNE thesaurer of the burgh of Irving ffaill not upon sight heirof to pey to Mr Robert Hunter preacher of the Gospell the soume of threescoir punds Scotts money being ane yeirs annualrent of the principall soume of ane thowsand punds Scotts dew be this burgh be bond to the said Mr Robert, quhilk yeires annualrent is from Wittsunday j^m vj^c sevinty nyn yeires to the terme of Wittsunday j^m vj^c ffour scoir yeires And take his discharge thairoff quhilk sall be allowed in your thesaurer compts Given att Irving the second of September 1680. A. BOYLE.
                  HEW MONTGUMRE.

58. *Discharge by Robert Hunter to the Magistrates of Irvine, for the interest of £1000, lent by the late Robert Hunter of Hunterston.— 2d September 1680.*

I Mr ROBERT HUNTER brother-german to Patricke Hunter of Hunterstoune grants me to have receaved from Robert Brysone thesaurer of the brughe of Irwin, in nam and behalfe of the Proveist, Baliffs, Councill, and comunitie of the said brughe of Irwin, the sowme of threescor Scottis punds money, as being on years ordinarie annualrent of the principall sowme of a thousand punds Scotts money conteaned in a bond granted by the Proveist, Bailiffs and Councill of the samin brughe to umquhill Robert Hunter of Hunterstoune my father, and failling of him be deceise to me the said Mr Robert Hunter his son, of the dait the twelveth day of Maij jᵐ vjᶜ seventie fyve years. The quhilk years annualrent being from the feast and term of Whytsonday jᵐ vjᶜ seventie nyn years to Whytsonday jᵐ vjᶜ and eightie years, quhairof I hold myself weel satisfied. And therfor I be thir presentis exoner, quytclaim and simpliciter discharg the forsaid Proveist, Baliffs, and Councill and comunitie of the said brughe and ther successors in office of the forsaid years annualrent and of all annualrents endew by them to me uppon the said principall sowme preceiding the term of Whytsonday jᵐ vjᶜ and eightie years. In wittnes quhairof I have both writtin and subseryvit this discharg with my hand at Irwin the second day of September jᵐ vjᶜ and eightie years befor thir wittnesses Mr Alexander Crauffurd of Fergushill and William Francis clerk deput of Irwin. Mn R. HUNTER.

    Alexr Craufurd.
    W. Francis, *witnes*.

59. *Order upon the Treasurer of Irvine to pay the Provost's Expenses at the Funeral of the Laird and Lady of Kilbirnie.*—21st January 1681.

UPON the eighteine day off November last quhen the Provist off Irving went to Killburny and his Ladies burriall both one that daij by the Provist directioun gave to tuinty six men and horsse in Kilburny toun and some morre with drink to the men and stra to ther horsses the sume which the said Robert Lrysoun being this yeir tressurie eight yeir off God was four

pund two shilling Scots by the Provist orders and morre upon the tuinty
one daij off Januar ane thousand and six hundreth and eight one yeer by
the Provist order to William fforgiesell the sume is thrie pund Scots and
this shall bee alloued in your thesaurie comptts.   J. BOYLE.

60. Act of Town Council of Irvine, appointing William Clerk Schoolmaster of the Burgh for one year.—16th April 1686.

AT Irving the sixteinth day of Apryll j^m vj^c ffourscore six years The quhilk day the Sederunt following viz. John Montgomerie proveist Mr. John Boyd baillie Robert Weir theasaurer of the burgh of Irving forsaid and John Blair of Burrowland Hugh Montgomerie James Mitchell John Hutchesone Michael Glasgow William Rodger John Crawfurd George Erskine and Andrew Hendersone counsellors of the samen burgh have aggreed with William Clerk Schoolemaster att Beith for serving as Schoolemaster of this burgh for the space of ane year commencing from this day and date, for payment to him of the soume of two hundreth merks for the said years service, and the ordinar casualities of Baptismes and Marriages quhich were formerlie in use to be uplifted be the Schoolemasters of this burgh: And on the other part the said William Clerk obleidges him to serve as Schoolemaster of the said burgh for the space of ane year and to teach such schollars as shall come to the schoole dureing the same space, and to remove himselfe from the said office of Schoolemaster imediatlie eftir the expireing of the said year, without any proces of law, if the said Magistrats and Counsell or their successores shall requyre him soe to doe, or otherwayes to serve as Doctor to the said Schole for the ordinarie casualitie and fie used to be given to the Doctors of the said Schoole: And in the meantyme in caice the said William Clerk shall dureing the forsaid space of ane year intromett with the casualities of Baptizmes and Marriages dew to the Doctor of the said Schoole hee oblidges himselfe to be comptable thairfor conforme to the saids Magistrats and Counsell their determinatione Sic subscribitur Jo. Montgomerie provest Jo. Boyd baillie Robert Weir theasurer William Clerk John Blair John Hutchesone James Mitchell Hugh Montgomrie John Crafurd William Rodger Michaell Glasgow Andro Hendirsoun   Extractum de Libris actorum dicti burgi per me

                                                 Jo^n HAMILTONE, *Dpt.*

61. *Act of the Town Council of Irvine appointing Auditors of the Tavern Accounts due by the Burgh.—23d December 1686.*

ATT the Burgh of Irvine the twenty thrid of December j^m vj^c eighty six yeeris The whilk day the Provost Baillzies and Councill of the said burgh of Irvine appoints Mr John Boyd and Patrick Boyll baillzies John Blair of Burrowland and James Hay clerk to state and peruse the wholl Tavern Accomptis due be the said burgh and to make there report thereof to the said Magistrats and Councill at their nixt meeting. Extracted be me

JA. HAY.

62. *Report by the Commissioners appointed by the Convention of Royal Burghs on the state and condition of the Burgh of Irvine.—2d May 1692.*[1]

IRVINE, the second day of May j^m vj^c and nyntie two years. Compeired befor James Fletcher, provost of Dundie, and Alexander Walker, baillie of Aberdeen, commissioners appointed be the convention of the royal borrowes for visiting the wholl royall burghs be west and south the river of Forth, the present magistrates and towne clerk of the burgh of Irvine, who gave in ane accompt of their patrimonie and comon good, together with ane answer to the saids visitors instructions as followes :—

1. As to the first article, it is answered that there comon good, *omnibus annis*, will extend to the sowme of 1791^lib 18^s Scots, and that ther debts will amount to 11,636^lib 5^d whereof there is 4133^lib 13^s 4^d in dependance befor the parliament, being for the plack on the point in King James tyme.

2. As to the second article, it is answered that they have no mortifications belonging to them.

3. As to the third article, its answered that they are no ways concerned therein, haveing a harbour of ther own.

4. As to the fourth article, its answered that they are no ways concerned therein.

5. As to the fifth article, its answered that they have produced ther

---

[1] *Miscellany*, Scottish Burgh Record Society, p. 162.

thesaurer's books for fyve preceeding years which is considered and stated in the answer to the first article, and that ther equeis amounts to, with the clerks and other dewes, 17^{lib} 10^s.

6. As to the sixth article, its answered that these fyve preceeding years all the forraigne trade they have hade is the particulars following, viz., ane ship of 70 tunn burden from France loadned with salt and brandie; item, another small veshell from Norway, loadned with tarr and daills, of burden about 30 tunns: and that they have exported about thritie pack of wooll or thereby yeirly for these two years bygone, each of which packs weighs about twelve stone; also about seaven or eight small barks, about 20 tunn the piece, loadned with victuall, the beginning of the Irish troubles, anno 1689 and 1690, wherein there were some strangers concerned, and a fourth pairt of ane small veshell from Norway, there pairt of the loadning therof came to 600 daills; and ane other ship from France, of 70 tunns, loadened with salt, and a small litle brandie. And that ther inland trade is verie inconsiderable, and what they have is by retaill of some brought from Glasgow, and other royall burghs, and that they have vented about a tunn of wine, seck, and brandie, each year, these fyve years bygone; and that they will consume about fourty bolls of malt, Lithgow measour, weekly, and that they hade a small quantity about twelve dacres imported by strangers.

7. As to the seventh article, its answered that they hade eight small ships, barks, and boats belonging to them, whose burden value and how imployed is conform to ane particular accompt in answer to this article given in under ther hands to the saids visitors, of which eight ships they have latly lost one.

8. As to the eight article, it is answered that they are concerned in matters of shipping in soe far it is mentioned in the above mentioned article, and that they are no other wayes concerned with unfree traders in matter of trade.

9. As to the nynth article, it is answered that ther cesses is pairtly payed by tax on ther inhabitants and pairtly out of ther comon good, as is at more length contained in ther answer to the nynth article.

10. As to the tenth article, it is answered that ther pairt of ther minister's stipends, schollmaster, and other publict servants, are payed and mantainet out of ther comon good.

11. As to the eleventh article, it is answered that all ther publict works are mantaneit out of ther comon good.

12. As to the twelth article, its answered that these houses where the heretors themselves doe stay are not stented, and the remainder posest be tenents payes monthly thrie pennies on each mark piece of rent by a stranger and two pennies by a freeman, and the rent of ther haill sett houses extends to 1621^{lib} 13^s 4^d, but of these there are a great many waist and that ther borrow aikers payes two pennies on each mark rent without any rebatement.

13. As to the thretteen article, it is answered that they have one yearly fair which begins the 8th and endest the 13 of August, wherof the Earls of Eglintowne are keepers, by ther deputs, fiscalls, and tenents, and have the one half of the customes; and they have two weekly marcats or fair dayes, and that the customes of the same are a pairt of ther comon good and soe stated in answer to the first article, and that ther are no other fairs in use to be held at the said burgh albeit by ther charter they have right to another which is no wont of use to be keeped.

14. As to the fourteenth article, its answered that the burghs of barronies and regalities lyeing within ther precinct are as followes, viz., one burgh of regality, Killwining; and of barronies, Kilmarnock, Kilmaars, Newmilns, Stewartoun, Beeth and Largs, which are very prejudiciall to them in point of trade, and serve the most pairt of the countrey with goodes by retaill and that ther houses are better and more of them then many royall burghs, particularly Kilmarnock, which hath a comon good and keeps a marcat. A more particular [account] therof ther commissioner will represent to the nixt conventione of borrowes.

15. As to the fyfteenth article, it is answered that a litle casuall comon good accrewes to them by fines and burges admissione but not worth the mentioneing.

This is the trew accompt of the state and conditione of the said burgh of Irvine in answer to the forsaid instructiones, as it is given up upon oath by the saids magistrates and towne clerk, under-ubseryveing, to the best of ther knowledge and surest informatione they can have to the saids visitors day and dait forsaid. Sic subscribitur: John Gray, baillie; James Mullivine, baillie. Ja. Nisbet, dean of gild. Jn. Hamiltoune, clerk.

63. *Act of the Town Council of Irvine in favour of the Incorporations of Trades thereof—granting liberty to improve their Seat in the Church of Irvine.—*4th November 1693.

ATT the burgh of Irving the flourth day of November j^m vj^c nyntie three years. The quhilk day anent the Petition presented before the Provest Baillies and Counsell of the said burgh of Irving by the Boxmaster and severall Deacons and Incorporationes of Trades within the samen burgh of Irving, makeing mention That quhair that Loft or Seatt appointed for and possessed by the petitioners in the west end of the Church of Irving, lyes att ane considerable distance from the pulpit, and is not so profiteablie placed for hearing as the samen might be: And there is ane litle roume or seatt att the end of the Counsells seat in the Church which is before the petitioners Loft, and is constantlie taken up by such as are unfitt to occupy such ane place, and being of the rabble doe often creat disturbance in the Church Whereas if the Honorable Magistrats and Counsell would grant libertie to the petitioners to bring forward their said loft or seatt to the westmost end of the penn as the Magistrats and Counsell enters in to their seatt in the Church which will no wayes prejudge their Honors seatt nor the fabrick and decorum of the Church, bot rather better the samen, and would be ane great comfort and encouragement to the petitioners to hear the Word of God preached and to attend upon the ordinances Craveing therefore and humblie intreating that the saids Magistrats and Counsell out of their true zeal and tender care for the good of their inhabitants would take the premissis to their consideration and give all possible encouragement to such as designe to hear the Word of God preached And that they would grant libertie to the petitioners to bring forward their said Loft to the westmost end of the forsaid penn att least so farr as the saids Magistrats and Counsell should think fitt, not wronging their oun seatt, as the said petition in itself more fully bears Which petition being att length read heard seen and consiidered be the saids Magistrats and Counsell of the said burgh of Irving, they in answer to the said supplicatione have unanimouslie condescendit unto and granted libertie and allowance, and doe hereby give and grant licence libertie and allowance to the severall Incorporations of the Trades of the said burgh of Irving to advance and bring foreward their said Loft so far upon that end of the Counsells Seatt opposite thereto as may be sufficient to furnish the saids Trades with roume for tuo seatts more to be added to the fore pairt of their said Loft according to the measure agreed unto by the written determination made by the Magistrats my Lord Montgomery and other heretors and members of the Kirk Session recorded in the Session Books quhich is tuentie sevin inches for each seatt in wideness provydeing alwayes that there be sufficient roume left ffor accomodateing the Toun Counsell to sitt into in the forescatt of the said Counsell Loft And als that the saids Trades doe raise the Magistrats and Counsells Loft als much higher then it now is as shall be aggreed upon by the saids Magistrats and Counsell (The Toun giveing to the saids trades tuentie shillings Sterling on that account for their help thereto) And remitted and hereby remitts the petitioners to the members of the said Kirk Session ffor procureing their libertie ffor advanceing the said Trades Loft alss farr into the body of the Church as is hereby condescendit unto, the same should be brought upon the end of the said Counsell Loft. Sic subscribitur Alex^r Cuninghame provost. Thos. M^{c}goune baylie; Ja. Nisbet baylie. James Millikin D : G : Wiliam Cuninghame treasurer. W. Stevenson counceller. J. Thomsone Counseller. Andrew Gemill. Andrew Spark. W. M^{c}taggart counseller. Hugh Love. Hugh Garven. John Thomson.

   Extractum de Libris actorum dicti burgi per me

                Jo^s Hamilton, *Cls.*

64. *Agreement between Alexander Lord Montgomery and the Magistrates of Irvine anent the Holm Mill.—25th May* 1694.

Att Eglintoun and Irving the tuentie fyfth and   dayes of May j^m vj^c nyntie four years It is aggreed betwixt ane noble and potent Lord Alexander Lord Montgomery and Kilwinning on the ane pairt and the Magistrats and toun Counsell of Irving on the other pairt as followes That is to say the said noble Lord hath prorogat and herby prorogates and protracts the former Tack sett of the Holm myln by his Lordship to the said Toun in the haill claussis tenor contents conditiones and obleisments thereof untill the terme of Lambmes j^m vj^c nyntie fyve years notwithstanding that the said tack expyreth att Candlemes nixt and wes overgiven to his Lordship by the toun Lykeas the said noble Lord hereby

obleidgeth himself to be att and bear the just and equall half of the
expenssis and charges to be debursed in removing of the said Holme mylne
to such a place as the saids Magistrats shall think fitt and of the imputting
of the said mylne damm and in doing other things requisite for the
advantage and convenient situatione of the said mylne and that betwixt
and the said terme   And on the other pairt   The saids Magistrats and
Counsell have also prorogate and hereby prorogates the said former tack
of the said mylne in the haill claussis contents conditions and obleisments
thereof ay and quhill the said terme of Lambmes j^m vj^c nyntie fyve years
and hereby obleidge themselves and their successors in office to be att and
bear the other just and equall half of the saids charges in removing the
said mylne and doing other things for the convenience thereof and of the
imputting of the said mylne damm betwixt and the forsaid terme and to
pay to the said noble Lord his Lordships factors or chamberlands in his
name the usuall and ordinary rent that wes in use to be payed by the
said former tack   In witnes quhairof thir presents (written by John
Hamilton wryter in Irving) are subseryveit by the saides pairties day
places moneth and year forsaid before thir witnessis respective, viz. to
the said Lord Montgomery his subscriptione att Eglinton the said tuentie
fyfth day of Maij Sir James Agnew younger of Lochnaw the said John
Hamilton and Robert Dunlop smith in Irving and to the subscriptione
of the saids Magistrats and Counsell of Irving att Irving the said tuentie
fyfth and   dayes of Maij   The saids John Hamilton and Robert
Dunlop and   MONTGOMERIE.

    S. J. Agnew, *witness*.

    Jo^n Hamilton, *witnes*.

65. *Agreement between the Magistrates of Irvine and James Nisbet, bailie,
    for the Sale by the latter of a Tenement near the Cross.*—20th
    August 1694.

ATT Irving the tuentieth day of August j^m vj^c nyntie four years   It is
aggreed betwixt the Magistrats and Toun Counsell of Irving on the ane
pairt and James Nisbet one of the baillies thairof on the other pairt as
follows, viz., The said James hereby oblidges him betwixt and
to sell and dispone to the saids Magistrats and Counsell and their

successors in office all and haill that ruinous Tenement on the east syde of the Cross of Irving betwixt the tenement belonging to Robert Weir couper on the north and that belonging to [William] Burns on the south with the haill stones lying before the same and belonging thairto and these within the Close thairof att least that he shall freelie consent to the valueing and appryseing of the said ruinous tenement and stones thairof by men to be chosen and sworne by the saids Magistrats in the termes of 6th Act Parliament 1, Session 3d King Charles the 2d, in order to their building a meill mercatt house thairupon And shall consent to the charge given to him thairanent and executions thairof Reserving alwayes to the said James his backhouse possest by Andrew Jack with the yaird and three riggs and pertinents thairof with tuo elnes broad for ish and entrie betwixt Burns gavill and the designed meill mercatt. Together with tuo elns of ground free betwixt the said backhouse and the said meill mercatt The east wall quhairof is to run in a streight lyne to that dyke betwixt the said tenement and Robert Weirs: For which cause on the other pairt the saids Magistrats and Counsell hereby obleidged them and their successors in office to pay and delyver to the said James Nisbet his aires or assigneys the soume of tuo hundreth and ffourscore merks Scotts betwixt and   with ffyftie pounds of penaltie in caise of failzie and annualrent thereafter dureing the not payment And to putt up a hewen door for entrie to the said James his backhouse, to be att the expenses of takeing away the rubbish of the said ruinous tenement and in repairing of Burns gavill and of what wryts shall be necessar for the Touns securitie in the premisses To quhich agreement both parties bind and obleidge themselves to stand and abyde thereat and the pairtie failzier to pay to the pairtie observer or willing to observe their pairt thairof the soume of ane hundreth merks Scotts attour performance And executione is hereby declaired shall passe hereon (if neid be) for implement to the Toun of their pairt thairof att the instance of the Toun Theasaurer or Procurator-fiscall. And both pairties consent to the registratione hereof in the books of Counsell and Session or Toun Court books of Irving that lettres of horning on six dayes and others neidfull may pass hereon in forme as effeirs and hereto constitutes   their procurators etc. In witnes quhairof both pairties have subseryved thir presents (written be John Hamilton clerk of Irving) day place and year forsaid before thir witnessis Robert Muir Surveyor of their Majesties Customes att Irving

William Stevinson and John Marschell wryters there and the said John Hamilton.
JA. NISBET.

ALEX^r CUNINGHAME, provest
THOS. MONTGOMRE, bayle
JAMES MILLIKIN, D : G :
JOHN GRAY, counseller
JOHN THOMPSON
ALEX^r DYETT, counsseller

ANDREW GEMILL, counssuler
ANDREW SPARK, counseller
J. THOMSONE, counseller
W. M'TAGGART, counseller
W. STIVENSON, counseller
HUGH GARVEN, counseller

Rob. Mure, witnes.
Jo. Marshell, witnes.

66. *Letter from Lord Findlater to the Provost and Magistrates of Irvine requesting Contributions for the Harbour of Cullen.—17th February 1697.*

GENTLEMEN,
    YOUR Towns Contribution for repairing the harbour of Cullen being as yet uncollected, the particular interest which my son the Secretary and I have in the place, and the trust committed to us anent the improving of the said contributions, doe oblidge me to intreat your assistance to this work, in extending your contribution to it as farr as possibly ye can For it is weell knowen to you that if the contributions of such good towns as yours to any publick work of this kinde be not more considerable then these of the country parishes, the work will prove ineffectuall, and though this town be but one of the meanest burghs of the kingdom for the tyme, yet if this work prove effectuall (as I am confident it will doe so) it may come to conduce something for the publick interest of the kingdome, but more especially that of the Burrows And I assure you your concurrence and assistance herein will prove a singular favour to my son the Secretary and will also most singularly oblidge Gentlemen, your ashured friend to serve you

                   FINDLATERR.

Cullen House, ffeb. 17, 1697.

[*On the back.*]

For the Provest and Magistrats off Irvine These

67. *Act of the Town Council of Irvine, allowing Mr. Andrew Tait, Minister, to repair his Tenement in Irvine.*—1st May 1702.

Att the burgh of Irving the ffirst day of Maij j^m vij^c and tuo years: WHEREAS by contract and agreement past betwixt the Magistrats and Counsell of the said burgh of Irving for the tyme on the one pairt and James Nisbet late baillie thereof (therein designed one of the present baillies of the said burgh) on the other pairt of the date the tuentieth day of August j^m vj^c nyntie four years The said burgh have right to that tenement then ruinous whereupon the meill mercat house is now builded bounded betwixt Robert Weirs tenement on the north and that tenement latelie belonging to William Burns and now to Master Andrew Tait Minister of the Gospel att Carmunock on the south Reserveing to the said James Nisbet tuo elnes breadth for ish and entrie betwixt the said meill mercatt house and the said William Burns now Master Andrew Taits gavill And now the Magistrats and Counsell of the said burgh afternamed considdering that att the building of the south wall of the said meill mercat house the Magistrats and Counsell of the said burgh for the tyme did (for the conveniencie of the said neighbouring south tenement and for the outward policie decorement and ornament of the said burgh) cause build a stone brace in the south wall of their said meill mercatt house opposite to the forsaid other south tenement upon designe that the said proprietars thereof might have the benefite of adjoyneing their said tenement to the said meill mercatt house Reserveing the breadth forsaid for ish and entrie as above said And lykewayes considdering that the said Master Andrew Tait is weill satisfied and pleased to adjoyne his said fore tenement to the said meill mercatt house and to build up ane gavill thereupon And in order to his reformeing of his said fore tenement is resolved to take doun his present ruinous gavill which is apparentlie dangerous and very uncomelie Therefore ffor the said Master Andrew Tait his encouragement therein the saids Magistrats and Counsell doe unanimouslie and cheerfullie for themselves and their successors in office hereby allow him under and with the reservation of the said tuo elnes breadth for ish and entrie to the said James Nisbet his aires and successors to their backhouses and yaird To take doun his said old ruinous gavill and to advance his said foretenement from thence to the said meill mercatt house south wall and to build his new gavill thereupon and to carry up vents therein, which is hereby declaired to be incorporate with his said fore south tenement, and is to be repute and holden as pairt and pertinent thereof in all tyme hereafter The said Master Andrew Tait alwayes building and setting up a hewen gate or door for ane entrie to the said James Nisbet his said backhouse and yaird And for the said Master Andrew Tait and his forsaids their further securitie thereanent the saids Magistrats and Counsell doe hereby assigne and dispone to them the said Master Andrew and his forsaids the contract and aggreement above narrated past betwixt them and the said James Nisbet in so farr as relates to or concernes the concession and grant above specified Promiseing hereby for them and their saids successors in office provest baillies dean of gild theasaurer and counsellours of the said burgh never to quarrell impugne nor come in the contrair of this their present grant allowance and concession forsaid conceived in favours of the said Master Andrew Tait and his aires and successors in any tyme coming And allowes extracts to be given them hereof Sic subscribitur Alex^r Cuninghame Provest. W. Stevenson Baylie. W. M'Taggart Dean of Gild. J. Thomsone counsler. Geo. Monro Counseller. Ro^{tt} Hastie Cowl^r Michael Glasgow Con^{lr} John Caldwall Cownsler. Samuel Duncan Counsler.

Extractum de libris actorum dicti burgi de Irving per me

Jo^s Hamilton.

68. *Gift by several Noblemen and others, of various sums, for maintaining a yearly Horse Race at Irvine.*—20th August 1702.

Wee undersubscryvers Noblemen Gentlemen and others ffor the love and respect wee have and bear towards the good Toun of Irving and our kynd friends therin doe by thir presents Mortifie Dedicate and Gift to the said good Toun the soumes of money respective under writtin adjoyned to our severall subscriptions: And ffor that effect wee hereby bind and obleidge ourselves each of us for our severall proportions efter specified to make good and thankfull payment to the Theasaurer of the said Burgh and successors in office of the saids severall soumes of money adjoyned to our saids respective subscriptions, and that betwixt and the terme of Whitsunday next to come j^m vij^c and three years : And quhich soumes are so mortified by us to the effect that the interest thereof may be applyed yearlie by the Magistrats of the said Burgh that a yearlie pryze of a silver plate may be furnished by the saids Magistrats ffor a horse race to be runn yearlie att the said burgh To the quhich premissis wee hereby firmelie and faithfullie obleidge ourselves In witnes quhairof wee have subscryved with our hands thir presents and adjected the severall soumes dedicated by us to the effect forsaid (writtin by John Hamiltone clerk of Irving att our speciall direction) Att Irving this twentieth day of August and   day of   j^m vij^c and tuo years and j^m vij^c years And whatever the yearlie interest of the saids mortified soumes shall amount to, the Provest of the said burgh of Irving hereby obleidges him and his successors in office to add a third pairt more thereto ffor makeing the silver pryze for the said horse race more valueable.

Kilmarnock ffor ten £ sterling

Montgomerie ane hundered and twentie pounds scots

H Montgomerie sixtie pounds scots

Alexr Hume sixtie pounds scots

Craufurd of Kilburny sixty pounds scots

Will: Cochrane sextein pounds scots

J Montgomerie sixty pistols

69. *Scroll Instrument upon the Election of a Commissioner to Parliament for the Burgh of Irvine.*—17*th September* 1702.

Att the Burgh of Irvine the 17 day of September 1702 yeirs and of her Majesties reigne the first year:—

THE quhilk day the Magistrats and Counsell of the said Burgh of Irvine being conveened within the Counsell house thairof in order to the choosing of ane Commissioner to represent the said Burgh att this ensueing Parliament indyted by her Majestie to sitt at Edinburgh the 12 November next Master Alexander Cunynghame of Collellan present Provost of the said Burgh imediatly after constituting the said meeting of Counsell in the usuall maner ordered the Nottar publict undersubscryveing Toun Clerk of the said Burgh to read in presence of the said Counsell her Majesties proclamatione to the effect forsaid Whereupon William M'Taggart present Dean of Gild of the said Burgh before reading the said proclamatione told that James Boyle sone to James Boyle of Montgomriestoun late Provost of Irvine was desyring acces to the said Counsell that he might be admitted burges of the said burgh and give his oath de fideli and submitt himself to the determinatione of the Magistrats and Counsell for his fyne The said provost answered that the Queens busines which concerned the publict being now tabled no privat busines ought to be obtruded to interfier thairwith and that after that was over M' Boyle should have access Upon quhich the said William M'Taggart desired the libertie of a vote of the whole Counsell seing the provost had refused Which vote the said provost refuseing the said William M'Taggart for himself and in name of the said James Boyle protested that seing he the said William and his adherents who he said were the pluralitie of Counsell desyred the libertie of the forsaid vote it was a thing unpresidented for the preces of the Counsell to refuse what was desyred by a considerable part of their number to be voted. Quhairto it was answered by the said provost That the Queens busines being tabled as said is nothing ought to justle it out Quhairto the said William replyed that there was yet tyme enough for voting a Comissioner it being a considerable tyme to sitting doun of Parliament and upon the whole took instruments Whereupon the provest desyred the said William M'Taggart to cary himself suteably and as became him in presence of the

Magistrats and Counsell And the said William insisting, the provest repeited that the Queens busienes ought to be prefered ut supra and ordered the election to go on Whereupon the said William said that the Toun was come to so low a pass that they were not in a capacity to allow anything for the Commissioners expenssis bot will be obleidged to choose one who would serve the Toun gratis. To quhich no reply was given but that the Counsell would think on that. And the election going on William Stevinsone Baillie his vote being asked he voted the said Mr Alexander Cunynghame as Commissioner to the forsaid Parliament Thereafter the said William M'Taggart Dean of Gild his vote being asked he answered that Mr Boyle being willing to serve the Toun gratis and to receive instructions he voted the said James Boyle to be Commissioner Upon quhich the provest offered also to serve gratis To quhich the said William answered The provest wes too long in saying so much, and that he continued firme in his resolutione and adhered to his vote for Mr Boyle And the votes going round the said James Boyle had eight voters who voted for him viz. The said William M'Taggart John Calderwood thesaurer John Thomsone late bailly and William Broun Robert Hastie John Caldwall Michael Glasgow and William Thomsone Counsellers And the said Mr Alexander Cunynghame provest had four voters besyd his own viz. The said William Stevinsone Baillie Mr William Cunynghame late provest and George Monro and Alexander Dyet Counsellors After which election the provest alleadged that James Boyle was not qualified for representing the Burgh of Irvine in Parliament not being ane actuall burges thairof Whereto William M'Taggart for himself and in name of these who voted for the said James Boyle answered That James Boyle haveing formerly offered himself to be made burges, ut supra, and for that end was waiting access and it is not his default that he is not burges, being required and refused And being now chosen by plurality of votes to be Comissioner he adhered to the election and thairupon took instruments a second tyme, and added that it was very hard and without a president that one in Mr Boyles circumstances the sone of a provest and als considerable ane heritor as any at the table should be refused especially seing it was the desyre of the plurality to have him admitted burges Quhairto the provest repeating ut supra answered that it was in the Magistrats power to allow or refuse as they please Unto quhich it was replyed That quhatever priviledge the Magistrats out of Counsell had to creat honourary burgessis yet in a constitute Counsell

especially when it was the desyre of the plurality it was not in the
Magistrats power to refuse, ffor if that should be sustained then the
Counsell were to expect no burgess but if the preces please, quhich is
equal to a negative vote, a thing never pleaded by any inferior Magistrat.
The provest answered that the Exchequer refused to receive vassals sometymes. Whereunto William answered that was nothing to this Counsell
and thought that after constituting that honourable Meeting if the receiving
a vassall was desyred by the plurality the Chancellour could not weill refuse.
Thereafter the provest having retired from the Counsell table and after
having walked a little alone he called all those who had voted for Mr Boyle
three excepted and discoursed with them; Dureing quhich space the said
William M'Taggart for himself and in name and behalf forsaid alleadged
that the provest in ane most unusual maner did insinuate upon the said
voters one by one to pass from their votes and to vote the said provest of
new, and did severall tymes protest against the same as a singular method
quhich he alleadged could not be parallelled, that men after they had
publickly declared the sentiments of their mynd should be so harrassed and
that such violence should be offered to their naturall libertie alledging they
were attacked some tuice and some thryce for their votes. And the provest
haveing again returned to the Counsell table requyred the Counsell to vote
of new again in respect they had voted a person not qualified according to
law not being ane actuall burges. Whereto it was replyed by the said
William M'Taggart that he resumed his former protests and adhered to
the former votes and protested against voteing of new and thairupon took
instruments. And the votes haveing gone round again the haill forenamed
persones who voted formerly for James Boyle adhered to their former votes
except the said John Calderwood who being called to give his new vote
answered Since it is so I vote your brother viz. Mr William Cunynghame
late provest as Comissioner. Whereupon Mr William Cunynghame late
provest protested that such as voted for Mr Boyle were not faithfull to their
alleadgence, and had not acted according to their oath of fidelity in respect
they had not voted a persone who was ane actuall burges and that therein
they had acted contrair to the law and priviledge of Burrowes. Quhairto
the said William M'Taggart answered that he and adherents did nothing
but what was highly consistent with ther alledgence and their oaths as
burgesses and Counsellers, etc. And that the said John Calderwood was
insinuat upon and harrassed to that degree that he gave his last vote in a

confusion. The said Mr Alexander Cunynghame provest replyed that there was no harrassing in the case, and that seing the pluralitie had refused to vote a person qualified according to law viz. ane actuall burges and that he haveing severall votes and his oun and being qualified and the other not he himself viz. the said Mr Alexander Cunynghame was dewly elected. Quhairupon the said Mr William Cunynghame protested and the said present provest adhered thereto. Thereafter the said William M'Taggart for himself and in name of adherents desyred that the minuts of Counsell and instruments might be read that it might be knowne if all was right written And in regard the provest refused to cause read the same instantly but delayed the same to the next sederunt and promisceing the minutts sould be then read The said William thereupon did again take instruments. After all which compeared personally the said James Boyle who gave in the minut of protestatione written with his oun hand and thereupon took instruments the tenor of quhich minut followes and is thus : Att Irvine the 17 day of September 1702. The quhilk day compeared personally I James Boyle sone to James Boyle late provest of Irvine within the Tolbuith of Irvine and past to the personall presence of Mr Alexander Cunynghame provest and William Stevinsone bailly sitting in Counceill with the members of toun Counsell, and desyred and required that they might enter and receive me conforme to the custome of Burgh to be ane burges thereof I being the sone of a burges most willing and ready to give my oath de fideli and pay all dewes requisite instantly and fulfill and performe whatever is usuall and incumbent in law for intrant burgessis to doe, and that the saids Magistrats might instantly administrate the necessar and usuall oath to me and order me to get ane extract from the Clerk on reasonable expensses and in case of refusall or unjust delay protested for coast skaith dammage and remeid of law. And farder adds that I have attended within the Tolbuith since the doun sitting of the Counsell in order to be made burges, quhich was deneyed, and I being now elected Comissioner to the insueing Parliament by plurality of votes of the Toun Councill protested against any new election and declaired I was willing to be burges and take all oaths requisite qualifieing myself for the said office. And I haveing entred the Counsell house door in order to take instruments in the Toun Clerks hand I was forced out of the door by the said Mr Alexander Cunynghame by thrusting me by the shoulder out of the said door. To the quhich minut of instrument it was answered by the said Mr Alexander

Cunynghame provest that Mr Boyle haveing violently intruded himself into the Counsellhouse door when the provest had opened the door himself calling for ane officer, the said James Boyle did violently thrust himself upon the provest, who thereupon demanded what he meant by such violence, if he had anything to say to the Counsell he should be called in dew tyme Quhairupon he thrust himself violently in upon the provest as said is and threw in a piece of money takeing instruments. Upon all and sundry quhich premises the saids haill parties hinc inde asked and took instruments ane or mae ut supra in the hands of me notar publict Comon Clerk of the said Burgh undersubseryveing. All thir things were done within the Counsellhouse of the said Burgh betwixt three and fyve hours in the afternoon day month yeir of God and yeir of her Majesties reigne respective abovewrittin in presence of the saids members of Councill above named and als in presence of John Gray late bailly of Irvine and John Boyd merchant there who were witnesses to the said minut of instrument given in and instruments taken thereon by the said James Boyle.

70. *Account by William McTaggart, Dean of Gild of Irvine, of the Election of a Commissioner to Parliament for the Burgh. 17th September 1702.*

ANE account of the most materiall things that passed September 17, 1702, att the electing James Boyle sone to Provest Boyle of Montgomeriestoun Commissioner to represent this burgh of Irving att the Parliament endyted by Her Majestie, as given in by William McTaggart present Dean of Gild of Irving.

Immediatlie after constituteing our meeting the Provest told the designe of that Counsell wes to nominat a Commissioner to represent us in Parliament, and wes about to have ordered the clerk to read the proclamatione, upon quhich William McTaggart said that Mr Boyle wes desyreing access that hee might be admitted Burges, give his oath de fideli, and submitt himself to the determinatione of Magistrats and Counsell for his fyne, which the provest refuseing, William in his own, and name of adherents who were the pluralitie desyred the libertie of a vote, which also being denyed, William ut supra protested and took instruments That it wes a thing unpresidented ffor our preses to refuse what wes desyred by a considerable pairt of our number to be voted. Hee answered The Queens bussienes must be preferred. It wes replyed There wes yet tyme enough for voteing a Commissioner. (It being a considerable tyme to the dounsitting of the Parliament.)

Thereafter the Provost desyred that the election of the Commissioner might goe on. Upon which William said That our Toun wes come to so low a passe that wee were not in a capacitie to allow anything for the Commissioners expence but would be obleidged to choose one who would serve gratis. To quich no reply wes given but that the Counsell would think on that. Thereafter Baillie Stevinsones vote wes asked who voted provest Alexander; after that Williams vote being asked, said that Mr Boyle being willing to serve the Toun gratis and to receive instructions hee voted him. Upon quhich and not before the Provest offerred to serve the Toun gratis. To quhich William answered hee wes too long in saying so much, and that hee continowed firme in his resolutione and adhered to his vote. So it went round Mr Boyle having eight votes and provest Cunynghame only flour. Upon which William ut supra adhered to his former instrument and took a 2d. That Mr Boyle wes by pluralitie of votes elected Commissioner. To quhich the Provest answered, Mr Boyle wes not qualified not being burges, William ut supra replyed Mr Boyle wes and is still desyreous to be admitted and for that end waites access, and added, that it wes very hard, and without a precedent that one in Mr Boyles circumstances the son of a Provost of this Burgh, and als considerable and heretor as any att the Board, should be refused, Especiallie sieing it wes the desyre of the pluralitie to have him admitted. It wes answered it wes the Magistrats prerogative to allow or refuse as they pleased. William replyed that whatever priviledges Magistrats extra Concilium had to creat honorarie Burgesses, yet in a constitute Counsell, especiallie when it wes the desyre of the pluralitie it wes not in the Magistrats power to refuse, flor if that should be sustained then wee are to expect no burgess but if our preses please, quhich is equall to a negative voice, a thing never pleaded by any inferior Magistrat The Provest replyed that the Exchequer refused to receive vassalls sometymes. William answered that wes nothing to us, and presumed to think that after constituteing that honourabill meeting if the recciveing a vassall wes desyred by the pluralitie the Chancellour could hardly weill refuise: Much tyme wes spent in discourseing hinc inde upon this and the lyke subject too tedious to narrate: After voteing the Provest wes pleased to retire from the table, and having walked a little alone, hee called all those who had voted for M'r Boyle, 3 excepted, and in a most unusuall manner did insinuate upon them one by one to passe from their votes and vote him of new. His expressions would be too tedious and hardly convenient to narrate, dureing quhich att severall tymes William supra did protest against such a singular method, and said it could not be parallelled that men after they had publicklie declaired the sentiments of their mynds should be so harrassed, and that such violence should be offered to their naturall libertie. This did not prevail with the Provest, but round he went, and becaus they stood their ground some were attacked tuyce others thryce. After all hee came to the Board and said it wes necessary they should vote again, becaus one not qualified wes chosen. For answer William ut supra resumed the former protests, adhered to the former vote, and protested also against voteing of new, and took instruments. But this could not prevail, a new vote must goe on, when it came to William hee adhered to his former protest and vote. After this provest William after some privatt conference with his brother protested that such as voted for M'r Boyle, were not faithfull to their allegiance, and had much bold and darring discourse to force our partie from their ground.

William answered wee did nothing but what wes highlie consistent with our allegiance and to our oaths as Burgessis and Counsellours, etc.

Thereafter a vote of the rest wes demanded, and when they adhered, they were asked a 2d tyme, yea some more then thryce, butt all in vain, excepting one, who when apart and called to give his new note (as they called it) wes so insinuat upon and harrassed to that degree that in a confusion hee said, Weill then, since it must be so I vote your brother, viz. provest William.

After this wes ended and some tyme spent in discoursing on what passed, William ut supra desyred that the minutts and instruments might be read, that it might be known if all wes right written, quhich being refused hee took instruments, etc.

71. *Instrument upon the Election of New Councillors for the Burgh of Irvine.*—*25th September* 1702.

Irving 25 September 1702 att the Tolbuith Stair foot betwixt 10 and 12 before noon :—

Mr ALEXANDER CUNYNGHAME present provost requyred Baillie M'Taggart Dean of Guild and William Thomsone shoemaker both toun Counsellers to be present in the Counsell house this hour and place in order to their concurring in the choise of a new Counsell of the said Burgh for the year to come, and protested against the said William M'Taggart Dean of Guild that he not only declyned himself to be present, but that hee withdrew and took away the said William Thomsone Counseller from the meeting of the said toun Counsell to the effect forsaid contrair to his allegiance and oath of fidelitie as a burges and a Counsellour, and thairupon took instruments in presence of James Nisbet late baillie W. Cr. James Muir and Hugh Buckle officers and Hugh Henderson gardiner.

Eodem die et hora :—

The haill Counsellours called thryce by ane officer audible att the Tolbuith stair head None compeared to elect a new Counsell, except these named in this dayes sederunt, whereupon the provest protested that such of their number as are this day present might proceid to their choise of a new Counsell, and protested against all these who withdrew that they had acted contrair to their burges oath and their allegiance, and oath de fideli, and thairupon took instruments in presence of the witnesses forsaid.

Ditto in Moses Crawfurd's house circiter quartam post meridiem :

The provest having withdrawen from the Counsell went with me nottar publick to the dwelling house of Moses Crawfurd, and to that roume quher the said William Thomson wes present in company with John Thomson late baillie Thomas Gray merchant and Moses Crawfurd wryter, and efter knocking severall tymes att the said chamber door, requyred in her Majesties name and in his oun as provest of the said Burgh the saids John Thomson Thomas Gray and Moses Crawfurd to open the said chamber door, and yeild the person of the said William Thomson who wes violentlie detained by them from coming to the Counsell this day to elect a new Counsell as one of the members of the said toun Counsell, who all of them refused so to doe Quhairupon the said provest protested against them as refuiseing to give obedience to her Majesties authoritie and the authoritie of the Magistrats of this Burgh contrair to their burges oath and allegiance, and thairupon took instruments in presence of Master Zacharias Gemmill of Boigsyde William Crawfurd and Hugh Buckle officers.

Irving 25 September 1702 years:—

List of the new Counsellours chosen for the said burgh for the year to come untill Michaelmes 1703 years in conjunction with Master Alexander Cunynghame present provest, William Stevinson baillie, William M'Taggart Dean of Gild and John Catherwood Theasaurer standing Counsellours by the sett by vertue of their offices:—

   The Right Honorable My Lord Montgomery.
   Master William Cunynghame late provest.
   John Thomsone, late baillie.

George Monro.	William Brown.
John Marschell.	Samuel Duncan.
Alexander Dyett.	John Caldwell.
Robert Haistie.	*ffor Trades—*
John Thomsone, Candlemaker.	John Thomson, Shoemaker.
William Martine, Skipper.	Andrew Henderson, Weaver.
William Caldwell, Maltman.	Michael Glasgow.
William Davidson.	William Thomson.

Irving, September 1702 years:—

Votes for new Counsellours of this burgh for the year to come untill Michaelmes 1703. In conjunction with

Master Alexander Cunynghame, provest.
William Stevinson, baillie.
William M'Taggart, Dean of Gild.   My Lord Montgomery ||||
John Catherwood Theasaurer.
Master William Cunynghame late provest |||| William Martine ||||
John Thomsone late baillie |||| William Caldwell ||||
Robert Haistie |||| William Davidsoun |||| Jo" Cultoun
Alexander Dyett |||| John Thomsone Shoemaker ||||
John Marschell |||| Andrew Henderson ||||
George Monro ||||
John Thomsone Candlemaker ||||

72. Inventory of Goods seized by the Collector of Irvine, and publicly burned, with minutes thereof.—6th and 7th April 1704.

Irving 6th Apryll 1704.

INVENTAR of the goods belonging to James Spottswood merchant traveller, and informed of and seized upon by Mr Alexander Cunynghame of Collellan Collecter of Irving upon the 4th instant and cognosced upon by John Marschell and George Monro present baillies of the burgh of Irving And this day sentenced by the saids Magistrats to be publicklie burnt att the Mercatt Crosse of the said burgh betwixt 11 and 12 hours in the forenoon to-morrow the 7th of Apryle instant And thereafter cognosced again by the saids Baillies and by Major James Cunynghame of Aikett and Mr Alexander Crawfurd of Fergushill tuo of the Commissioners of Supply within the Shirefdome of Air, as being called and desyred by the saids Magistrats of Irving for that effect, and thereafter inventared and valued by them as followeth :

Imprimis, ffyve pieces of green Say containing ane hundreth elnes att tuentie shilling Scotts per elne Inde ane hundreth pounds Scotts	100 00 0
Item sixtein elnes of black Cloath att ffyve pounds Scotts per elne Inde flourscore pounds Scotts . . .	080 00 0
Item Tuelve elnes of Cloath of a buff colour valued att three pounds Scotts per elne Inde threttie six pounds Scotts .	036 00 0
Item A remnant of Damis mixed or floured stuff, of four elnes, att tuentie shilling Scotts Inde flour pounds Scotts money	004 00 0
Item Tuo pair of new Stockings and tuo pair of worne Stockings which tuo pair of worne Stockings the Magistrats and Justices forsaid ordaine to be restored back to the owner in respect worne The saids tuo pair new Stockings valued att three pounds Scotts per pair Inde six pounds Scotts	006 00 0
Summa totalis of the said Goods att value forsaid is	226 00 0

Irving, the said sixth day of Apryle j^m vij^c and four years :—

The Inventar of goods forsaid imported from Ireland seized upon, cognosced and sentenced to be burnt ut supra Subscryved date forsaid by

J. CUNINGHAME.
J. MARSHALL, *Baillie.*
GEO. MONRO, *Balye.*
ALEX^R CRAUFURD.

Irving, seventh day of Apryle 1704 years :—

That the above written goods imported, cognosced upon, and sentenced to be burned ut supra, were accordingly burnt to ashes publicklie att the Mercatt Crosse tyme forsaid is attested by

J. CUNINGHAME.
ALEX^R CRAUFURD.
J. MARSHELL, *Baillie.*
GEO. MONRO, *Bailyie.*

Irving, 7th Apryle 1704 years :—

The quhilk day in presence of John Marschell and George Monro Baillies of the said burgh of Irving, the Boat called the Margaret of Combray sentenced by the saids Magistrats their decreet and sentence past upon the sixth day of Apryle instant, to be publicklie roped, and the pryce thereof to be divyded conforme to law, ffor importing of Irish Cloath, Seyes and Stockings from Ireland, is after publick ropeing, and burning of the candle, roped and sold to John Birshane of Bishoptoun younger ffor payment to be made to Mr Alexander Cunynghame of Collellan late provest of Irving and present Collector of Her Majesties customes thereat, for himself and others concerned in the division of the pryce of the said Boat of the soume of six pounds Sterling money of England, of the one half quhairof there is present satisfaction made, and for the other half thereof belonging to Her Majestie there is security given Whereupon both the saids persons, viz., Bishoptoun younger and Provest Cunynghame asked and took instruments.

Jo^N MARSHELL, *Baillie.*
GEO. MONRO, *Bailyie.*

73. *Roup of the Market and Bridge Customs of Irvine.—*
1st November 1705.

ATT Irving the first day of November j^m vij^c and ffyve years : The quhilk day the Impositione granted to this Burgh by Act of Parliament of ffourtie pennies Scotts over and above the 8^d of petty dewes for the peeks or weights and together therewith, making in all ffour shilling Scotts upon every sack of Meill, Corne, Beir, Pease, Beans, and all other graine quhatsomever that shall be brought into the weekly mercatts of this Burgh, and tuo shilling Scotts upon every sack of meill, and one shilling Scotts upon every sack of corne, beir, peise beans and other grains quhich shall be imported into the harbour of this Burgh by quhatsomevir person or persons and shall be sold within the samen Burgh, (excepting the Victuall to be imported by sea within this Burgh or harbour therof by burgesses inhabitants, quhich is only to pay the one half of these dewes, and als excepting farme victuall quhich is altogether exempted) are after touck of Drumm, publick ropeing and running of the sand glasse as use is, Sett to Robert Haistie merchant burges of Irving, ffor the years space following viz., From this Hallowday j^m vij^c and fyve years to Hallowday next j^m vij^c and six years ffor the soume of ane hundreth and one pounds Scotts money, payable quarterly att ffour termes in the year be equall portions viz., The first 4th pairt of the said soume att Candlemes next 1706 years : The second 4th pairt of the said soume att Mayday therafter : The third 4th pairt therof att Lambmes therafter : And the last 4th pairt therof and in compleat payment of the said tack dewtie att Hallowday next 1706 years : For payment quherof proportionallie att the saids respective termes of payment to the Theasurer of this Burgh the said Robert Haistie as principall and Samuel Duncan merchant burges of Irving as cautioner for him, be thir presents bind and obleidge themselves their aires executors successors and intromettors etc., conjunctlie and severallie, and hee to releive his said cautioner. In wittnes quhairof they have subscryved thir presents date forsaid before thir wittnesses John Hamilton clerk of Irving wryter hereof and Richard Cunynghame and Allan Francis wryters in Irving.

                                        ROBERT HASTIE.

Ri^{ch} Cunyghame, *wittness.*   SAMUELL DUNCAN.
Joⁿ Hamilton, *wittnes.*
All. Francis, *wittnes.*

Irving, the said 1st November j^m vij^c and ffyve years:—

The quhilk day the Bridge Customes of this Burgh, and als the petty customes therof, excepting the dewes upon the pecks or meill mercatt weights, are after beating of the Drumm, publick ropeing, and running of the sand glasse as use is, Sett to James Muir, tayleor, burges of Irving, ffor the year following, viz., From Hallowday 1705 to Hallowday next 1706 years ffor the soume of threttie six pounds Scotts money payable quarterly and proportionallie att and upon the first dayes of Februarij May August and November next to come j^m vij^c and six years: ffor payment quhairof to the Theasaurers of this Burgh att the saids respective termes of payment the said James Muir as principall and James Nevin merchant burges of Irving as cautioner for him hereby obleidge themselves their aires executors successors and tutors etc. conjunctlie and severallie, and hee to releive his said cautioner In wittnes quhairof they have subscryved thir presents date forsaid before thir wittnesses John Hamilton clerk of Irving wryter hereof, and Allan Francis and Richard Cunynghame wryters there.

JAMES MURE.
JAMES NIVINE.

Jo^n Hamilton, *wittnes*.
Ric^h Cunynghame, *witness*.
All. Francis, *wittnes*.

Memorandum The weights, beams and pecks following are to be enquyred after, viz.—

    ffourtein beams
    ffourtein bucketts
    ffourtein Broads
    Fourtein stand of ropes

Tuelve stand of lead weights, quhairof 12 half stones 12 quarters.

There are also sixtein pecks Irving measure, one quhairof is the Standart.

There are lykewayes   pecks of Linlithgow measure in the Counsell-house.

    ffirelocks
    Picks

Tuo Stand of Colours all belonging to the Toun.

74. *Act of Privy Council for a general Contribution for repairing the Harbour of Irvine.*—12*th February* 1706.

ATT Edinburgh the twelth day of ffebruary j^m vij^c and six years Anent the Petition given in and presented to the Lords of Her Majesties Privie Councill by the Magistrats of Irvine shewing that the toun of Irvine by reason of its Harbour hes bein a place of great trade and these many years bygone especially in transporting coalls to Ireland and returneing mony. The Harbour where the ships and boats lye and the entrie therto is invironed by sandie hills upon the south north and pairt of the east quarters so that as the wind blowes from the severall airts there aryses shelves and banks in the river which hinder the incomeing and outgoeing of ships: For removeing wherof the neighbours and inhabitants of Irvine have laboured with their hands and expended of the comon good and privat fortunes till they are overpowered and not able to master the work and these who were in use to come with their ships have severall times represented their dificultie and hardship to the Magistrats by being hindered to come in and goe off att the seasonable times by reason of these banks and shelves that have arisen and dayly aryse And the Magistrats not being able to undergo such a work by themselves unles assisted by the contribution of others who are all concerned in so good a work and of so universall concerne Therfore humbly Craveing to the effect aftermentioned as the said petition bears The Lords of Her Majesties Privie Councill haveing considered the above petition given in to them by the Magistrats of Irvine and the samin being read in their presence The saids Lords doe herby Grant to the petitioners ane voluntar Contribution to be collected within all the paroch Churches of this Kingdome upon such dayes as the petitioners shall appoynt after intimation at the paroch Churches the Sabath day before collecting therof, aither at the Church doors of the respective paroches or in such other maner as shall be concerted and agreed upon by the petitioners and that for repairing the Harbour belonging to the said toune removeing the shelves and banks and maintaining the harbour when cleared : And appoyntis the said collection to be payed in to William Cunninghame late provost of Irvine and John Marshall late Baillie there In respect that before extracting heirof they have given bond and found sufficient caution to the end forsaid and that at the sight and by the direction allwayes of the petitioners.

Extracted by me,   Ro^t Forbes, *Cls. Sti. Cons.*

75. *Roup of the Petty Customs of the Market, Bridge, and Anchorage of Irvine.—1st November 1706.*

Att Irving the first day of November j^m vij^c and six years: THE quhilk day the Imposition granted to this Burgh by Act of Parliament of flourtie pennies Scots over and above the eight penny Scots of pety dewes for the pecks or weights, and together therewith makeing in all flour shilling Scots upon every sack of meal corn bear peis beans and all other grains whatsomevir that shall be brought into the weekly mercat of this Burgh and two shilling Scots upon every sack of meil and one shilling Scots upon every sack of corn bear peas beans and other grains which shall be imported into the Harbour of this Burgh by whatever person or persons and shall be sold within the samen Burgh (excepting the Victuall to be imported by sea within this Burgh or harbour therof by burgesses inhabitants which is only to pay the one half of these dewes and als excepting farm Victuall quhich is altogether exempted) are after touck of Drum publick roping and runing of the sand glass as use is Sett to Robert Hastie merchant burges of Irving ffor the years space following viz. ffrom this Hallowday j^m vij^c and six years to Hallowday next j^m vij^c and sevin years ffor the soume of nyntie two pound good and usuall Scots money payable quarterly att four terms in the year be equall portions viz. The first fourth part of the said soume at Candlemes next j^m vij^c and sevin years The second fourth part of the said soume at Mayday thereafter The third fourth part at Lambmes therafter And the last fourth part therof and in compleat payment of the said tack dutie att Hallowday next j^m vij^c and sevin years For payment quherof proportionally at the saids respective termes to the theasurer of this Burgh the said Robert Hastie as principall and Samuel Duncan merchant burges of the said Burgh as cautioner for him be thir presents bind and obleidge themselves conjunctlie and severallie their airs executors successors and intromettars with their goods and geir whatsomevir And the said Robert Hastie principall to releive his said cautioner of all coast and damnage he or his forsaids can sustain therethrow in any sort In wittnes quhairof they have subseryved thir presents day month place and year above writtin before thir wittnessis Hugh Stevinsone wryter in Irvine and Allan Francis there and [writer] hereof.   Ro^tt Hastie.
                              Samuell Duncan.

Hugh Stevinson, *witnes.*

Att Irving the ffirst day of November one thousand seven
hundreth and six years :—

The whilk day the Bridge Customs of this Burgh and als the petty customs therof excepting the dewes upon the pecks or meal mercatt weights are after touck of Drum publick ropeing and runing of the sand glass as use is Sett to Samuell Duncan merchant in Irving for the year following viz. From Hallowday instant j^m vij^c and six to Hallowday next j^m vij^c and sevin ffor the soume of threttie pound Scots money payable quarterly and proportionally at and upon the first dayes of February, May, August, and November next to come all in the year j^m vij^c and sevin For payment quherof to the thesaurers at the saids respective terms the said Samuell Duncan as principal and Robert Hastie merchant in Irving as cautioner and souertie with and for him hereby obleidge themselves conjunctlie and severallie their airs and successors and he to releive his said cautioner. In witnes quhairof they have subseryved thir presents day month place and year above writtin before these witnesses Alexander Broun late Baillie and Allan Francis wryter in Irving and hereof.   SAMUELL DUNCAN.
       RO^{TT} HASTIE.

Alex^r Broun, *wittnes*.

Att Irving the first day of November j^m vij^c and six years :—

The whilk day the Water baillieship and Anchorage of this Burgh are after publick ropeing *ut supra* Sett to William Broun skipper in Irving ffor the space of ane year following viz. From the first day of November instant to the first of November next 1707 for the soume of sixtie ffour pound good and usuall Scotts mony For payment quhairof to the thesaurer of this Burgh the said William Broun principall and John Hay merchant in Irving as cautioner for him equally at Mayday and Hallowday they bind and obleidge them conjunctlie and severallie and successors And als to uphold the Pearches sufficiently dureing the forsaid space and to keep and place the turning pearches and other pearches in their due and propper places And to keep up and place the three ballast pearches where veshells are to cast out their ballast at the sight and advice of the Magistrats and Counsell. [And als not to suffer any coaches or carts to go alongst the Bridge without the Magistrats speciall allowance And if any shall doe in the contrairy that they shall bring the contraveener to the Magistrats.[1]] And it is hereby declaired that the said tacksman or partners are not to have liberty to buy or broke any herrings killings or other fishes more then for the use of their oun familie to the prejudice of the inhabitants under such penaltie and pains as the Magistrats and Counsell shall think fitt And the said William Broun principall obleidges him for the releiff of his said cautioner. In witnes quhairof they have subseryved thir presents day month place and year of God above writtin before thir witnessis Alexander Broun late Baillie and Allan Francis wryter in Irving and herof Declaring hereby that in case the Scots coalls shall dureing the said space be prohibite then the said tacksman is to be free of this present rope from the time the said prohibition shall take effect they paying for what time they shall have possest or bruiked before the said prohibitione effeiring to the said tack dutie.

WILLIAM BROUN.
JOHN HAY.

Alex^r Broun, *witnes*.

76. *Report by [Allan] Francis, Clerk of the Burgh of Irvine, to on the Council of the Burgh, and form of election of its Office-bearers.*—29th *June* 1710.[2]

THEIR councill consists of fifteen merchants, including the provost, two baillies, dean of gild, and treasurer, and two trades, making in all seventeen. They elect their magistrats, viz., the provost and two baillies, yearly, the first Munday after Michalmass; and the Friday preceeding they leit the magistrats, and do put two on the leit to the old provost and four to the two old baillies, and the Friday preceeding that they elect their new councill, and on the Friday after the election of the magistrats they choose their dean of gild, treasurer, clerk, fiscall, officers, visitors of mercats, birlamen, etc., and are obliged yearly to change two merchants and two trades. And the provost and two baillies are not to continue above two years. Which is attested by me this twenty ninth of June one thousand seven hundred and ten years.

Sic Subscribitur : A. FRANCIS, *Clerk*.

[1] This clause is cancelled in the original.
[2] *Misc. Scot. Burgh Records*, p. 195.

77. *Act of the Town Council of Irvine authorising the production of their Charter of Replegiation before the Justices at Ayr.*—29th October 1711.

ATT the Burgh of Irving the tuentie nynth day of October j^m vij^c and elevin years: The quhilk day the Magistrates and Couneill of the said Burgh understanding that there are severall of the Burgesses inhabitants of the said Burgh cited to compear before the Justices of the Peace att Air the morrow being the thrittieth instant Doe hereby authorise and impower Mr William Cunynghame present provest, and William M'Taggart ane of the present Baillies of the said Burgh to go over to Air the said day and there in their names to exhibite and produce the Burgh of Irving's Charter of Confirmation containing a power of Replegiation dated the sevinteenth day of November j^m vj^c ffourtie ane years (which is judicially delyvered to them) and to crave that such of the saids Burgesses as are summoned may be repledged and brought back to be judged by the Magistrates of Irving who by the said Charter are propper Justices within themselves. Extracted ffurth of the Records of council be me,   ALL. FFRANCIS, Cls.

78. *Bond by Residenters in Ayrshire for payment of stakes for the Prize to be shot for yearly at Irvine.*—1721.

WEE subscrivers oblidge us dureing life and residence within the Shire of Ayr conform to our subscriptions to give in half ane Crown to the Thesaurer of Irvine of each stake for the Pryse of Irvine to be shott for with gunns at the said Burgh the second Teusday of August yearly which Pryse was first sett out by Hugh Montgomery of Hartfield, he having generously complimented the said Burgh with the same All which stakes are to be applyed for the Pryse the subsequent years Consenting to the registration hereof in the Books of Council and Session or any others competent that letters of horning and other executorialls needful on six days' charge and other executorialls needfull in form as effeirs may pass hereon And thereto constitutes   our Procurators, etc.
In witnes whereof (written on stampt paper by James Marshell servitor to George and Hugh Monros wryters in Irvine) wee have subseryvit thir

presents at Irvine and   the   day of
and   day of   j^c vij^c and twenty one years.

Will. Cunninghame for one   Saml Adames one
William Simson for one   James Smith one
Ja. Smith for on   James Louttit for one
Bish. James Ramsay for one Henry Cuninghame one
John Crawfurd for one   Robert Hastie one
Alex^r Baillie for one   John Smith for one
John Brown for one   John Bryson for ane
Ja. Boyle for one   Hugh M'Cliesh for on
Pat^k Montgomerie for one   John M'Cleish for one
Will. Marshall for one   William Brown one
Tho. Biggar for one   Ja. Robertson for one
James Gray for one   Geo^r Norris
John Gemmill for one   William Cuningham for one
J. Harper p^t for one   Hugh Monro for two
Arthur Martine for one   John Holmes for one
Arch. Cuninghame for one   Alex^r Cuninghame for two
Jo. M'Kerrell for one   Zach. Gemmill for two
Charles Shedden for one   Edward Ker for one
Wm Montgomerie for one   Thos Boyd for one
Jo^n Thompson for one   Wm Gordan for one
James Cranfurd for one   Alex^r Barkly for one
Ja. Marshall for one   Robert Bryson for on
Ro. Crawfurd for one   Char. Boyle for one
Da^d Jack for one   James Cuninghame for one
Arch^d Lang for one   W. M'Taggart for one
Ro^t Montgomerie on   Robert Craig when at hom one
John Glasgow for one   Da. Muire one
           Matthew Montgomerie for one

79. *Act of the Town Council of Irvine erecting the Barbers of the Burgh into an Incorporation.—30th September 1723.*

ATT the Burgh of Irvine the thirty day of September one thousand seven hundred and twenty three years: The which day in presence of the Magistrats and Council of the Burgh of Irvine anent the Petition given into them by Robert Mitchell James White Robert Hastie James Spark Charles Rob Hugh Niven and Benjamin Mitchell barbers and wigmakers within the said burgh for themselves and others of that imployement who shall join with them hereafter Mentioning that where the saids petitioners being increased to a considerable number equall to if not beyond some of the trades and having for some years bygone join'd in an Society amongst themselves and rais'd a publick fond for pious and charitable uses they humbly address'd their Honours for an Act of Council in their favours establishing them in an distinct Incorporation by themselves conform to the practice of many other burghs in the Kingdome with power to them to elect yearly a Deacon amongst themselves with such other priviledges in relation to their trade as their Honours should find reasonable to conferr upon them in manner therin mentioned With the report made by William M'Taggart Provost James Nisbet Bayllie Mr William Cunningham late Provost John Holms and Robert Rodger appointed by the Magistrats and Council upon the twinty day of September instant to consider the said petition and make report thereof finding that by the laws of the Kingdome the Magistrats and Council of burghs are impowered to erect all trades into incorporations with power to them to elect Deacons yearly And thinking it just and reasonable that the barbers and wigmakers be erected into an incorporation and recomending the same to the Magistrats and Council And the said petition and report being read in presence of the saids Magistrats and Council upon the twinty seventh day of the said month of September instant the answering thereto and determination therof was continued to this day that the Magistrats and Council might be fully advis'd theranent And the said petition and report being this day judicially read in presence of the saids Magistrats and Council and having at length heard seen and considered the same and being therewith well and ripely advised The saids Magistrats and Council did and hereby do establish and erect the saids barbers and wigmakers within the Burgh of Irvine and their successors barbers and wigmakers within the said burgh into an distinct Incorporation and hereby grants power to them to elect an Deacon yearly amongst themselves and make laws and rules in relation to the said Incorporation and trade the saids laws and rules being always subject to the regulation of the Magistrats and Council of the said burgh present and for the time being. Extracted furth of the records of the Burgh of Irvine upon the twinty eight day of October j^{m} vij^{c} and twinty three years by me,

JA. MARSHALL, *Clerk*.

80. *Roup of the Customs of Irvine.*—1st November 1732.

CONDITIONS of the Roup of the Mealmercat Customs Anchoradge Petty and Bridge Customs to be rouped separately as follows viz.—

Imprimis The Customs of the Mealmercat are to be sett by way of publick roup for the year to come viz.—From Hallowday j^{m} vij^{c} and thirty two to Hallowday j^{m} vij^{c} and thirty three And the same to be uplifted conform to use and wont.

Item Anchoradges year forsaid the Town being oblidged to keep up the parches upon their own expences.

Item Petty and Bridge Customs, the Town being oblidged to allow ten shillings sterling for a weight house and for encouradgement publick intimation is to be made that all persons who have Butter and Cheese and others to sell to come to the Trone and not to dispose of them privately under the pain of confiscation of saids goods.

Item The Bod Penny to be fourty shilling Scots for each.

Item Half a crown of Dead Earnest for each.

The persons in whose hands the Roup shall fall are oblidged to find sufficient caution for payment of the respective prices (as the same shall be required) quarterly And the person in whose hands the Anchoradge shall fall is oblidged to keep the parches at the sight of the Magistrats the expences of upholding the same being upon the Touns accompt.

Irvine 1st November 1732.

The which day in presence of John Marshall of Greenhead provost and John M'Cleish bailly of Irvine the Customs of the Meal Mercat after publick roup and running of the glass fell in the hands of John Fetter, merchant in Irvine, at the price of thirteen pound sterling For payment quhairof quarterly he and James Templeton residenter in Irvine as cautioner for him bind and oblidge themselves conjunctly and severally and the said John Fetter oblidges him for relief of his said cautioner In witness whereof they have judicially subscribed thir presents att Irvine the said first day of November j^m vij^c and thirty two years.

    The Magistrates interpone their authority.   JN. FETTER.

Jo. Marshall.   JAMES + his + mark TEMPLETON.
Jo. M'Cleish.

                                                      Irvine, 1st November 1732.

The which day in presence of John Marshall of Greenhead provost and John M'Cleish bailly of Irvine the Anchoradges after public rouping and running of the glass fell in the hands of Robert Brown in Gouthries at the price of twenty three pound sterling money for payment whereof quarterly he and John Gray late bailly of Irvine as cautioner for him bind and oblidge themselves conjunctly and severally and the said Robert Brown oblidges himself for relieff of his said cautioner In witness quhairof they have judicially subscrived thir presents day and date foresaid.

    The Magistrates interpone their authority.   JOHN GRAY.
                                                                           ROBERT BROUN.
Jo. Marshall.
Jo. M'Cleish.

                                                      Irvine, 1st November 1732.

The which day in presence of John Marshall of Greenhead provost and John M'Cleish baillie of Irvine the Petty and Bridge Customs after publick roup and running of the glass fell in the hands of William Malcom carrier in Irvine at the price of twelve pound five shilling sterling for payment quhairof quarterly he and John Borland shipmaster in Irvine as cautioner for him bind and oblidge them conjunctly and severally and the said William Malcom oblidges himself for relieff of his said cautioner. In witnes quhairof they have subscrived thir presents judicially day and date forsaid.

    The Magistrates interpone their authority.   WILLIAM MALCOM.
                                                                      JOHN BORLAND.
Jno. Marshall.
Jo. M'Cleish.

81. *Contract between the Magistrates of Irvine and Thomas Brown, Mason, for building the Bridge anew.*—*15th January* 1748.

Att Irvine the fifteenth day of January one thousand seven hundred and fourty eight years It is contracted aggreed and ended betwixt John Dunlop and Robert Craig present baillies of the Burgh of Irvine and Thomas Bigger present Dean of Guild of Irvine for themselves and as haveing power and commission from the Town Councill of Irvine and as representing the community of the said burgh by their Act of Councill of date the ninth day of January j^m vij^c and fourty eight years to the effect after mentioned of the one part and Thomas Brown masson burgess of Irvine of the other part in manner following That is to say the said Thomas Brown by these presents binds and obliges him his heirs and executors as early in this Spring as the season will permit to pull down the Bridge of Irvine to the foundation and sufficiently to build a new Bridge in the place where the old one stands of the same number of arches and pillars, the pen of each arch of twenty seven inches deep, and each stone of the ring pen of the same number of twenty seven inches deep, of the same wideness or breadth of the present Bridge, with parapats or ledges from one end to the other of both sides of the Bridge three foot high above the causway, with one foot and an half of deed sand laid betwixt the pen and the causway And to make two square places one on each side in the middle of the Bridge of five foot wide and twelve foot long if they can be got of that size for men and horse goeing into when horse and carts are passing To raise the causway at the middle of the Bridge so as to make the water run to each end with ease without any gutters That he shall make the arches and pillars of any hight not exceeding of those of the present Bridge, the pillars of the same dimension as to the thickness with those of the present, conform to a plain to be delivered to the said Thomas Brown within six weeks after the date hereof, and to raise the two ends of the Bridge conform to the said plan And that he shall carrie on the building of said Bridge so constantly and expeditiously this Spring and Summer as to have it fitt for receiveing carriages in the month of October next with the ledges compleat so as to render passengers and carriages safe And to finish the causway of said Bridge for the weightyest carriages against the month of December j^m vij^c and fourty eight years And that in the month of March or Aprile j^m vij^c

and fourty nine the whole of the said Bridge shall be visited and inspected by two knowing tradesmen to be mutually chosen by both parties and in case of differences betwixt them then the said Bridge is to be visited by William Fullartoun of Fullartoun Esquire as umpire or oversman who is hereby appointed to determine the condition of said Bridge with respect to the sufficiency or insufficiency to whose determination both parties oblige themselves to stand and acquiess That he shall do the whole surface and ledges of said Bridge of sufficient hewn free stone of proper and sufficient sizes for such work and furnish lay down and pay the whole materials and men's wages Further the said Thomas Brown binds and obliges him to procure and find to the Magistrates of Irvine sufficient caution for his performance of the premisses before he draw the first partial payment of the sum after mentioned For which causes and on the other part the said John Dunlop Robert Craig and Thomas Bigger bind and oblige themselves and their said constituents the present Magistrats and Town Councill of Irvine and their successors in office as representing the whole body and community of the said burgh to make good and thankfull payment to the said Thomas Brown his heirs executors or assigneys of the sum of three hundred and fifty pound sterling as the adequat and aggreed price for building said Bridge sufficiently as aforesaid including all the materials to be furnished and that at the times and in the proportions following To witt Fifty pound sterling thereof on the first day of March next other fifty pound sterling at Whitsunday next a third fifty pound sterling on the first of July next another fifty pound sterling at Lambas next and the last flifty pound sterling in compleat payment of the said Bridge at the term of Whittsunday j^m vij^c and ffourty nine and that by and attour all the materials of the old Bridge which he may find to be usefull in building the new one And further they allow the said Thomas Brown and his servants to be employed in building said Bridge to cut turves for Dams to the said building upon any part of the Town's property that may be most convenient without any consideration therefor And both parties bind and oblidge them and their foresaids to observe perform and fulfill the premisses to each other hinc inde under the penalty of twenty pound sterling money to be paid by the party failzieing to the other observing or willing to observe their part attour performance Consenting to the registration hereof in the books of Councill and Session or any other Judges books that letters of horning on six days' charge and other executorialls needfull in form as effeirs may pass hereon they constitute their procurators. etc. In witness quhereof these presents consisting of this and the two preceeding pages with the marginall note upon the second page (written upon stampt paper by James Gemmill servitor to Robert Crawfurd, writer in Irvine) are subscribed by both parties place day month and year aforesaid before these witnesses the saids Robert Crawfurd and James Gemmill.

John Dunlop.
Robt Craig.

Ro. Crawfurd, *witnes*.   Tho. Bigger.
Jas. Gemmill, *witness*.   Tho. Brown.

[*On the back.*]

I the within designed Thomas Brown in regard the Magistrats and Town Council of Irvine have at sundry times implemented their part of the within contract by paying to me the sum contracted for building the Bridge of Irvine for which I gave receipts to their Treasurer therefore I discharge them of the within contract and whole effect thereof In witness whereof these presents (written by Robert Crawford wryter in Irvine) are subscribed by me at Irvin the twenty first day of Apryle seventeen hundred and fifty three years before these witnesses Thomas Bigger one of the late baillies of the said burgh John Innes wryter in Irvine and the said Robert Crawfurd It is declared that my receipts which lye in the Treasurers hands shall not import double payments of the sum hereby discharged. Tho. Brown.

Tho. Bigger, *witnes*.
Joⁿ Innes, *witness*.
Ro. Crawfurd, *witnes*.

[*Paper enclosed in preceeding.*]

We under subscribers being mutually chosen by the Magistrates of the Burgh of Irvine and Thomas Brown mason, to visite the Bridge of Irvine latly built by the said Mr. Brown, as to the suficiancy or insuficiancy thereof, to the best of our skill and judgment so far as it outwardlay appears to us, that the four arches of the said bridge are apparently strong, and that the leges being mostlay of the same old stones of the former leges, with a mixture of new, and are as strong as formerlay And our judgment upon the whole, so far as appears to us, as the Casy is diplay laid over with sand can pas no judgment one same. As witness our hands this twentyeth day of May one thousand seven hundred and forty nine years.

THOMAS ANDERSON.
PATRICK SMITH.

82. *Commission to James Gemmell, Writer, to be Fiscal of the Admiralty of Irvine.*—13*th November* 1752.

WEE James Boyle of Montgomeriestoune Provost James Campbell and James Hill bailies of the Burgh of Irvine Deput Admirals appointed by the Earle of Finlater over the whole Port of Irvine from Troon point to Kelly bridge conform to commission granted by his Lordship to us being well satisfied with the abilitys and qualifications of James Gemmill wryter in Irvine for exerceing the office of Procurator Fiscal of the said Admiralty Do therefore by virtue of the power granted to us by our said commission Nominat constitute and appoint the said James Gemmill wryter in Irvine to be our procurator fiscal of the said Admiralty with power to him to prosecute all criminals and offenders within the saids bounds of our Admiralty to levy collect and uplift all fynes amerciaments mulcts waifes and wracks within the aforesaid bounds and generally all and every other thing to do and execute that any other procurator fiscall of any other admiralty may lawfully do or cause to be done He alwayes accounting to us for the saids fines amerciaments waifes and wracks he may uplift and intromitt with in virtue hereof when desired Promissing to hold firm and stable all and whatsoever things the said James Gemmill in the exercise of the aforesaid office shall lawfully do or cause to be done And this our commission to endure dureing our pleasure. And that these presents may be insert and registrat in the books of Council and Session Court books of the said Admiralty or any other Judges books for preservation we constitute   our procurators In witness whereof these presents (written upon stamp'd paper by Robert Crawfurd wryter in Irvine) are subscribed by us att Irvine the thirteenth day of November new style one thousand seven hundred and fifty two years before these witnesses, William Laurie wright in Irvine and the said Robert Crawfurd.

JA. BOYLE.
William Lowiry, *witnes.*   JAMES CAMPBELL.
Ro. Crawfurd, *witnes.*   JAMES HILL.

83. *Attestation of the date of the Seal of Cause.*—*24th February* 1757.

At Irvine the twenty fourth day of February seventeen hundred and flifty seven years :—

THE which day We David Burns present Deacon Conveener of the Trades of Irvine and James Kennedy late Deacon Conveener of the Trades there and in presence of me Nottary Publick subscribing, the principall Seal of Cause granted by the Magistrates of the Burgh of Irvine in favours of the Incorporated Trades of the said Burgh being read and perused by us Do certifie that the said Seal of Cause bears date the third day of July one thousand six hundred and ffourty six years And that the Cooper trade is therein incorporate with the same priviledges as any other of the incorporated trades therein mentioned Given under our hands at Irvine the day and date above mentioned in presence of John Boyd apprentice to James Gemmill wryter in Irvine and John M'Fie merchant there.

DAVID BURNS.
JAMES KENNEDY.

Præmissa esse vera attestor.

JO^s INNES, *N. P.*

John M'fie, *witness.*
John Boyd, *witness.*

84. *Proposed Address by the Freeholders of Ayr to the King in regard to Arming the Inhabitants for Defence of the Coast.*—3d October 1759. [Print.]

Ayr 3d October 1759 :

CONVEENED the Noblemen and Gentlemen following, viz. The E. of Eglingtoun, the E. of Lowdoun, Alexr. Boswell Lord Auchinleck, Sir Adam Fergusson of Kilkerran, Mr. Wm. Duff sherriff depute of Ayr, Allan Whitefoord of Ballochmile, Wm. Ramsay of Montfold, Archibald Crawford of Ardmilland, Alexr. Crawford of New-wark, Rob. Hamiltoun of Bourtreehill, Andrew Hunter of Park, Jas. Whitefoord of Dinduff, Adam Crawford Newale of Polquharne, Wm. Logan of Castlemains, John Hamiltoun of Montgomriestoun, Alexr. Campble of Drumgrange, the Provost of Air, Mr. George Reid Minr. of the Gospel at St. Evox, Mr. John Cunningham of Bridgehous Minr. of the Gospel at Dalmellingtoun. The above Noblemen and Gentlemen having conveened this day in consequence of a concert of the freeholders met at Michalmas head Court yesterday, made choice of Lord Auchinleck for Preses, and were unanimously of opinion

That a humble address be presented to his Majesty by the Nobility, Gentry, and Clergy of the shire of Ayr, congratulating his Majesty on the success of his Arms by Sea and Land:

Thanking him for his care and vigilance which hath hitherto given us the quiet enjoyment of our estates amidst the alarm of war to which other nations have been exposed.

Expressing our desire to contribute what is in our power to assist his Majesty in carrying on his salutary schemes for the liberty of Europe and the safety of his dominions:

To represent, that notwithstanding our zeal for these great things, we find that the want and disuse of Arms renders us at present in a manner incapable to be of any use to ourselves or the public should the French make a descent on these Islands.

To propose, that in order to render the people of more effectual service to the public, as well as to enable them to defend themselves should the enemy land, where the regular troops are at a distance, that his Majesty may be graciously pleased to order the Sheriff, according to the old laws of North Britain still in force, to appoint Officers to train the fencible men in each parish and to order one thousand stand of Arms to be delivered over to the Sheriff, to be by him distributed among the Officers by him to be appointed, who are to be answerable to him for the same. And this method it is hoped will have the effect to train a considerable number of men who may be depended on in case of necessity:

Proposed, that the Heritors of the county shall contribute conform to their valuations for purchasing ammunition to the extent of two or three hundred pounds sterl. and this to be distributed by the Sheriff in the same way as the Arms are, viz. conform to the number of inhabitants in the parish. As also, that the Chelsea men must assist in training the men. The county must be at the expence of paying them sixpence per day when employed. And further, that an adjutant for each district shall be employed, and payed at the rate of two shillings and sixpence per day when employed:

Proposed, that the two royal Burghs of Ayr and Irvine shall each address seperatly to the same effect, praying Arms for their Burgesses, and their addresses shall go up along with that from the county.

The meeting ordered the above proposals to be printed, and copies of them to be transmitted to the whole Noblemen and Gentlemen Heretors of the county, and Ministers of each parish, with a letter from the Preses desiring their attendance at Ayr further to deliberate on the subject matter of the proposals, on Friday the 12th of October current.

ALEX. BOSWEL.

GENTLEMEN—By appointment of the meeting of the Freeholders, there is herein transmitted certain proposals on a subject of the last consequence to the county and to the kingdom. They were such as the meeting this day unanimously approved of and wish earnestly that the meeting on Friday the 12th may be as frequent as possible, and hope that you will attend, or if you be by any accident prevented, that you will signify your mind upon the proposals by a letter. I am your most humble servant,

ALEXANDER BOSWEL.

[*Addressed*]

To the honourable
    The Magistrates of Irvine.

85. *Letter to the Magistrates of Irvine in reference to an Address by them and the Magistrates of Ayr, to the King, regarding the Arming of the Inhabitants.*—15*th October* 1759.

SIR—Agreeable to your desire on Saturday I by this advise you that our Magistrates after converseing the inhabitants and finding them willing to be instructed in the use of and to bear arms in caice of any ffrench partie landing on this coast and to co-operate with their neighbours and the forces if any should be got in defending against such partie, this day in Council agreed to address his Majesty in the terms annexed, which address is to be signed by our provest and sent to Lord Auchinleck to be forwarded with the address from the county, as our Member is not at present at Court, and which method I suppose you will also follow by sending yours to Lord Auchinleck some time on Wednesday. Our provest is to write his Lordship to hint to the Secretary of State that wee might imploy 300 stand of Arms. I told you before that you should vary as far as you please the form of the Address that at least they may not appear to be the same draught. Make my compliments acceptable to Provist Hamiltoun. Forgive my being hurried.—I am, Sir, your most humble servant,

JA. FERGUSSON.

Ayr 15th October 1759.

[Addressed]

To Mr. James Allison present dean of Gild of Irvine.

[Address referred to in preceding Letter and on same sheet.]

To the Kings most Excellent Majesty. The Most humble Address of the Magistrates and Town Councill of the Burgh of Ayr in Council assembled. We Your Majesties most dutiful and loyall subjects beg liberty, with the most profound humility, to congratulate your Majesty on the glorious success of your Arms by Sea and Land, whereby the pernicious designs of our enemies have been hitherto baffled, our Commerce protected, and the peaceable possession of the fruits of our industry secured to us.

Being sensible of these inestimable blessings enjoyed by us under your Majesties most auspicious Government, we are ready to hazard our lives and fortunes in defence of your sacred Person and of our Country, now threatned with an invasion from a prefidious enemy rendered desperate by repeated losses and disappointments.

As your Majesties troops are at present necessarily employed at a distance from us, we and our fellow Burgesses are very desirious of being put in a condition of making all the defence in our power and of co-operating with the regular forces against the enemy should they attempt to land on our coast or to destroy the shipping in our harbour. But the want of Arms and ammunition renders us unable to accomplish these good purposes.

Allow us further, with the greatest submission, to lay before your Majesty the defenceless state of the whole Firth of Clyde, in the trade whereof many thousands of your faithful subjects are interested, and to pray in the most humble manner that your Majesty will be pleased to give such orders for defence of the said Firth against our enemies, as the exigence of the times will admitt; and also for putting the inhabitants of this burgh in such posture of defence as your Majesty in your great wisdom shall judge proper.

That Your Majesty may have continued success against your enemies, and long reign over a free and happy people, and there may never be wanting of your royal line, inheriting your princely virtues, to sit upon the throne of these Realms, is and shall be the constant prayer of your Majesties most faithful subjects the Magistrates and Council of your Burgh of Ayr.

Signed by our Præses in our presence and by our appointment.

86. *Papers in process between the Magistrates of Irvine and Mr. Kemp, Teacher of English, etc.*—1755-1759.

MINUTS the Magistrates and Councill of the BURGH of IRVINE against Mr. JAMES KEMPT, Schoolmaster of the English School in the said Burgh.—*Actor* Millar—*Alter* Hamilton Gordon.

MILLAR repeated in his charges ane Act of the Toun Councill of Irvine of the date the twenty eight of December j^m vij^c and fiftie four electing and nominateing William Henderson precentor of the Church of Irvine for one year commencing at Whitsunday j^m vij^c and fiftie fyve, and ane other Act of the seventh of May j^m vij^c and fiftie fyve, whereby it is declared that it was the intention of the Councill that the Suspender was not to gett ane sellary as English Schoolmaster at Irvine after the comeing Whitsunday and craved the letters may be found orderly proceeded.

HAMILTON GORDON repeated his Reasons of Suspension, and alleged that by ane advertisement at the publick Newspapers the 6th of April 1747 the Magistrats of the burgh gave notice that the Schoolmaster who then taught English was to leave the place and that the vacancie was to be supplyed by the first of June thereafter And for the encouragement of a person suiteably qualifyed for teaching English after the modern way that the yearly sellary or profites would amount to upwards of threttie pounds sterling per annum besides two pounds ten shillings yearly as precenter of the Church which the former Schoolmaster did not enjoy That in consequence of this advertisement the Suspender appeared as a candidate for the office and tryall being taken by a skilled person of the Suspender's abilities and qualifications for teaching English and writing And tryal being likeways taken of his precenting and the Magistrats and Councill weell satisfyed therewith they did unanimously elect nominat and choose the Suspender to be teacher of English in the burgh after the modern way and precentor of the Church giveing him the whole emoluments of marriages and baptisms by their act of the date the twenty sixth of May 1747 That albeit the Act of Councill bears his election to have been for one year after the date thereof, yet the Suspender being assured . . . at limitation of . . . was only to pre . . . the form of the . . . commissions . . . to the School . . . and as . . . there was no instance of a Schoolmaster being removed he brought up his family from Aberdeen and continued in the exercise of his offices for eight years, and contended that the Suspender being thus established in the office and no objection made either to his morall characther or fitness for the office he cannot be removed arbitrarly therefrom, from the nature of the office as weell as in good policie were such a practice . . . indulged it behoved to be a very great disadvantage to the education of youth And with respect to the office of precentor the pouer of disposall thereof was not in the Magistrats and Councill but in the Kirk Session And the Suspender accordingly holds that office by ane Act of the Kirk Session of the nynteenth of July 1747 That these proceedings of the Magistrats and Councill did not proceed from anie just exception that could have been made against the Suspender either from anie thing in his morall conduct or for any incapacitie for teaching, but merely by the influence of some of the Councill with a view to serve a friend or favourite of their own And the injustice of their proceedings appears the more remarkable that the Act by which they would deprive him of the sallary as Schoolmaster bears date on the 7th of May and the deprivation was to take place at the Whitsunday thereafter And that the Suspender's characther is unexceptionable appears from a certificate from the Minister and Elders and the greater part of the most considerable inhabitants of the burgh Notwithstanding whereof the Suspender is willing to subject both his characther and capacity to the strictest tryall And therefor the acts complained of fall to be suspended.

MILLAR answered That the teacher of ane English School in the Burgh of Irvine has not his office by anie publick law nor any legall establishment but meerly a voluntary act of the inhabitants, and as the Suspender was nominated to the office for one year only on the expirie of the year his office ceased That the Suspender was in no ways in the case of a School-

master of . . . or anie such office which hath its establishment
. That the Magistrats and Councill did remove the Suspender
. . give place to a person of greater merit And it is . .
Suspender to object to the Councells power of . . . . especially as
it was in virtue of their act he was admitted to the office and only in
consequence thereof continued the office for the interim till a question
which then subsisted between the Councill and Kirk Session with respect
to the power of electing the precentor should be determined From all
which it is evident the Suspender was removeable at pleasure and the act
electing Mr. Henderson into the office of precentor is dated in December
And his entry was not . . . till the Whitsunday thereafter . . . .
the act of the 7th of May was only an explanation of the Magistrats intention by the Act in December occasioned by some . . . of the Suspender's
that notwithstanding the said act he would claime right to the salery
which had been on his nomination agreed to be payed him by the .
Schoolmaster.

HAMILTON GORDON replyed That tho' the Suspender was only elected
for one year, yet haveing continued in the office for eight years his election
can at no rate be worse then his commission had been dureing pleasure
And in that case the Suspender could not be arbitrarly removed but upon
reasonable grounds as was found in a case betuixt the Magistrats of
Edinburgh and Mr. Massie a regent of their College and a latter case
between the Magistrats of Montrose and . . .

MILLAR duplyed That the case of a regent of a College and the present
are in no ways similar, and in the case of the toun of Montrose the Schoolmaster . . . . without mentioning anie time . . . . dureing
pleasure That the . . . . character founded on which bears date
. . . by the Suspender with a view as he pretended to service in
another place That the Magistrats could give a reas . . . cause for what
they did if it were necessary But as they apprehend the Suspender had no
title to continue in the office if another was chosen into it they would
rather for the Suspender's sake avoid entering into the . . . But if
this is found necessary they will be at . . . . descend upon the strong-
est reasons for turning   out of this office and electing a fitter
person in . . . .

[This paper is much wasted by damp.

Having advised the foregoing debate Finds that the Suspender having in consequence of the advertisement mentioned in the debate offered himself as a candidate for the office of Teacher of the English School at Irvine and Precentor and after tryall of his qualifications been admitted to that office and had been continued in it for severall years altho' he was originally elected only for one year that he could not be removed from the said office by the Magistrats arbitrarly and without just cause, such as incapacity immorality or malversation and therefore suspends the letters simpliciter and decerns. ROBERT PRINGLE.

1st August 1755.

Dear Sir—I have read Provost Campbell's letter of the 5th of August and I think the Magistrates may stop the payment of Mr. Kempt's sallary and of the ffees of Baptisms and Marriages in the meantime till the discussion of the Suspension. I am also of opinion that there is no occasion for entring upon a proof of Mr. Kempt's unfittnes or incapacity for the office And that the Act of Council dismissing him from his office will be reported independent of any such proof And I hope the Lord Ordinary will alter his Interloquitor, or if he does not I think the cause may be carried to the Inner House with probability of success.—I am, Sir, your humble servant,

THO. MILLER.

8th August 1755.

Mr. Peter Spark, Writer in Edinburgh.

8th August 1755.

Unto the Right Honourable the Lord Edgefielde The REPRESENTATION of the Magistrates and Councill of the BURGH of IRVINE

Humbly Sheweth—That in the process of Suspension at the instance of Mr. James Kempt late Teacher of English after the modern manner and Precentor of the Kirk within our burgh your Lordship 1st August 1755 having advised the debate 'finds that the Suspender having in conse-
' quence of the advertisement mentioned in the debate offered himself as
' a candidate for the office of Teacher of the English Schooll of Irvine and
' precentor and after tryal of his qualifications been admitted to that office
' and continued to serve in it for severall years altho' he was originally
' elected only for one year that he could not be removed from the said office
' by the Magistrates arbitrarly and without just cause such as incapacity

'immorality or malversation and therefore suspends the letters simpliciter
' and decerns.'

The Magistrates and Councill beg leave to [offer] a few considerations to your Lordship in hope of [some] alteration of the above interloquitor. And in the first place It appears from the Extract of Suspender's admission, dated 26 May 1747, ' that he was appointed Teacher of English after the
' modern manner and Precentor of the Church of Irvine for one year after
' the date with a sallary of £8 for teaching and £2 : 10 sh. for precenting in
' terms of the prop[osal] published in the Newspapers, providing that the
' Emoluments of Baptisms and Marriages thereby granted to Mr. Kempt
' should be accounted for and implied in part payment of the said sallary.'

These are the words of the Suspender's commission, and with regard to his office of Precentor the Chargers cannott conceive upon what ground it is that the precenter of this burgh should hold his office upon any other terms than his predecessors and the precenters of all the burghs in Scotland have always held this office. It cannott be disputed that the precentors of the churches of Edinburgh, Glasgow, and in all the burghs of the kingdome are in the absolute disposall of the Magistrates and Councill who may turn out their precentors and appoint others in their place at pleasure without assigning any reason for their choice. And the Chargers cannott find any reason why they should not have the same power in disposing of this office within their burgh as the Magistrates and Councill of other burghs have. The terms of the Charger's commission do not surely alter the nature of his office so as to make him independent of the pleasure of the Magistrates, at least after the expiry of one year. The Suspender was pleased to lay hold of a dispute which sometime subsisted between the Magistrates and Councill and Kirk Session touching the right of appointing the precentor and he was pleased to take the side of the Kirk Session and to plead that they only and not the Magistrates and Councill could turn him out of that office.

But in answer to this the Chargers again referred to the Suspender's Act of Admission, from which it appears that he derived his office from the Magistrates and cannott therefore challenge their right. It is true he also obtained an act of the Kirk Session approving of his election to the office of precentor.

But your Lordship will please know that this act is likewise recalled by the Kirk Session, as Mr. Henderson is now appointed to that office by the joint acts of the Magistrates and Councill and Kirk Session.

2dly, As to his other office of Teacher of English after the modern way the Chargers are equally at a loss to conceive upon what ground their Act of Councill dismissing the Suspender from that office should be suspended.

Your Lordship will please observe that the office is not established in the burgh by any law or publick foundation which can oblige the Magistrates and Councill to continue it longer than they think proper. It was sett up not many years ago when teaching of English after what is called the modern manner first came in vogue rather by way of experiment than with an intention to establish a perpetual office in the burgh, and therefore independant of every other consideration. The Chargers would willingly know from the Suspender upon what ground in law the Magistrates and Councill can be decerned to continue such an office in the burgh and to pay a yearly sallary therefor any longer than they think proper.

The Magistrates and Councill after tryall a good many years have found this modern manner of teaching English a mere farce and have therefore put an end to the office and to the sallary bestowed upon it, and have left it to the Parochial Schoolmaster or other private Teachers of English in the place to follow what method of teaching they think most proper. And they cannott conceive that it is in the power of any Court to decern them to continue the office and sallary of a Teacher of English after the modern way for the behoof of this Suspender unless he can show some publick Law or Act of the burgh which obliges them to keep up such a Teacher.

At the same time the Chargers admitt that if there is any obligation upon them whether expresst or implied in the Suspender's Act of Election whereby he can claim to be continued in this office or in the sallary therewith given for any continuance beyond their pleasure the same must be effectuall against the Chargers.

But instead of any such obligation in the Suspender's Act of Admission your Lordship will please observe that he is elected to the office of Teacher of English and Precentor of the Church for one year after the date, which is long since expired, and consequently he must be removeable at the absolute will and pleasure of the Magistrates and Councill.

Where indeed the publick law has fixed the endurance of any office to be ad vitam aut culpam, such as the offices of all the Supreme Judges, Masters of Universitys, Ministers and Parochial Schoolmasters, the Chargers will admitt that the Commission or Act of Admission to these offices ought to be always so explained as to import the endurance which the law has given them, but your Lordship will observe that the office in question does not fall under the above description.

It was lately introduced, and the Magistrates and Councill are under no obligation either by law or from their own deed to continue the office longer than they find it to be for the advantage of the burgh, and therefore they must beg leave to insist upon the rule of law that where a person accepts of a private office or employment either from a Corporation or private person for the continuation of one year expressed in his Commission he cannott of right claim to be continued in the office after the expiry of that year, but for thereafter must depend upon the absolute will and pleasure of his employers; the obligation upon them is limited to one year, after that expires they are at entire freedom to continue the person in their employment or not.

If the Chargers had appointed a law agent for the affairs of the burgh for the space of one year or more years express'd in their Commission, or should appoint a jaylor, town officer, or teacher of French, or of Navigation and Book-keeping, with a sallary for the space of one year it would be extraordinary to mentain that when the obligation ceased by the expiry of the year, and because the Magistrates and Councill voluntarily kept any of these persons in their office and [employment] for some years after, that thereby they became entitled to hold these employments and sallarys for life, so that the Magistrates and Councill would be oblidged to continue them in the office and sallary unless they would bring prooff before your lordship of some incapacity immorality or malversation which disqualifyed these persons for holding such offices: With great submission these cases are entirely parallell to the present, for the Chargers can perceive no difference betwixt a Teacher of English after the modern way, which is not an office established by law, and a Teacher of French, a Dancing Master, or a Mistress of Sewing, all these are entirely dependant upon the pleasure of the Magistrates and Councill except in so far as they have bound themselves down by their own act. The Suspender was pleased in the debate to quote two decisions: The first in the case of a Professor in the University of Edinburgh and the other of a Schoolmaster in the Burgh of Montrose. The Chargers' procurator has not been able to discover the first of these decisions. And at no rate can the parralel lye betwixt a Professor of an University which is a publick office importing continuance for life and the present case of a private office and employment which has no establishment either by law or by any act of the burgh, and for the same reason the decision of Montrose will as little apply to the present case where the question was concerning the office of Schoolmaster of the burgh, which is also a publick office established by law and which the Magistrates and Councill are oblidged to keep up. And such a Schoolmaster the Chargers do also support within their burgh entirely distinct from the office which this Suspender lately enjoyed.

And 2*dly*, It appears from the decision in this case of Montrose, as collected in the Dictionary, *voce* publick officer, page 292, that the Act of Election of the Schoollmaster of Montrose was in generall terms, neither bearing ad vitam or during pleasure, which therefore cannott apply to the present case where the Act of Admission expressly limits the endurance to the space of one year. And it seems . . . absurd to mentain that when the obligation expired at the end of the year that it should become perpetuall by the continuance of the Suspender in the office for sometime longer.

The Chargers will still avoid entering upon the reasons which determined them to remove this Suspender founded upon his unfittness and incapacity in many respects for doing the business and duty of his office.

The whole inhabitants were so sensible of this that they had taken their children from him and put them to other schoolls so that for some time his schooll . . . only attended by a few poor schollars educated by the charity of the Kirk Session. So that the Chargers submitt it to your lordship if it was consistent with the duty of the Magistrates and Councill to continue a sallary payable by the burgh to a person who could do so little for it.

> May it therefore please your Lordship to alter your former Interloquitor, and in respect of what is above sett furth to fliud the letters orderly proceeded.
>
> According to Justice, etc. THOMAS MILLER.

9th August 1755.—Allows this representation to be seen and answered, and in the meantime stops extracting.   RO. PRINGLE.

ANSWERS for Mr. JAMES KEMPT, Schoolmaster of the English
Schooll of the BURGH of IRVINE, to the REPRESENTATION of
the MAGISTRATES of the BURGH of IRVINE.

The Interlocutor of which the Magistrates complain was pronounced by your Lordship upon hearing parties at great length and advising Minutes of Debate containing in substance every thing that seems to be material in the Representation.

The Suspender was invited by a publick advertisement [1] in the two Edinburgh publick papers to offer himself to tryall for supplying a vacancy occasioned in the office of English Schoolmaster by the resignation of Mr. Baillie who then had it.

Upon a proper tryal the Respondent was found duely qualifyed and elected into the office of Schoolmaster by Act of Councill for the space of one year after the date of the Act,[2] whereby the Councill also gave him all the right they had to the emoluments of Baptisms and Marriages which Mr. William Dickie had that day resigned, provisionally that the Respondent should be accountable in so far as these should happen to exceed the sallary of eight pounds sterling which was then provided to him as Schoolmaster. He was also elected Precentor at a yearly sallary of £2 : 10s. sterling ; and

It was declared ' That if the emoluments did not fully pay up both ' these sums to Mr. Kempt yearly the Treasurer should pay up the ballance ' out of the Town's revenue, and this to be the rule of his payment untill ' the difference betwixt the Magistrates and Councill and Kirk Session be ' determined by the arbiters.'

These are the words of the Act of Councill, and for understanding the nature of the difference therein referred to the Respondent begs leave to appeal to two Extracts of the Minutes of the Kirk Session of Irvine lying in process and marked No. 12. The one is dated the 12th and the other 19th July 1747. By the first the Minister reported to the Session a proposall of the Town Councill for supplying a vacancy of English Schoolmaster Precentor and Session Clerk, and for ending amicably pro hac vice a dispute that had arisen between the Magistrates and Session concerning the right of presentation to the two offices last named. The particulars the Respondent has avoided, as your Lordship will no doubt think proper to read the

[1] April 6, 1747. [2] May 26, 1747.

Acts themselves, only by the last dated 19th July, it's agreed Mr. Kempt should present and officiate as Session Clerk till the right of presenting be ended by the arbitration. The Respondent was therefore invested in both offices.

The Magistrates and Town Councill took upon themselves to elect him into both; but the Respondent's right to the office of Precentor and Session Clerk did not rest upon the authority of the Act of Councill, he was elected by the Kirk Session; and whether they or the Councill have the legall title it is immaterial in the present question, as it cannott be denyed but that the Kirk Session were and have been time immemorial in the possession and consequently as in possession fell to be preferred, that is, during the dependance of the arbitration, or till such time as the Magistrates shall declare the right of patronage in this Court.

If it was proper or necessary to prove the possession, the Respondent is willing to undertake the proof by the Records of the Session, tho' he can hardly think the Magistrates will call it in question, as the Acts of Councill show these offices were not possessed by Mr. Baillie the former Schoolmaster, upon whose resignation the Respondent was elected.

It may suffice to notice that he continued to exerce the offices to the general satisfaction of the Magistrates Town Councill and Inhabitants and also with the approbation of the Session from his admission in May 1747 to December 1754, that upon these revolutions which occurr in the government of these little Burrows the Provost and the Schoolmaster of the Grammar Schooll had a freind of their own to provide, and this appeared to be a proper occasion for voting a demission per saltem of the Respondent from these three offices so as to make way for their own freind.

The apparent hardships of such an attack upon the Respondent, who had left Aberdeen upon the publick faith, who had been unanimously elected into all the three, who had continued for 8 years to discharge his duty without any complaint, and had endeavoured to avoid every ground of offence, induced many of the Councill to differ in sentiments from the Provost, so that the demission was carryed in the Councill only by a single vote.

The Motion was first moved in Councill[1] upon the Petition of Mr. William Cunninghame, the Teacher of the Grammar Schooll, to have a favourite of his own, Mr. William Henderson, appointed Precentor of the

[1] December 28, 1754.

Church of Irvine, which the Act of Council of that date bears, the Council by a majority of votes complyed with.

The next step was by another act of this date[1] to declare that it was and is their intention that Mr. Kempt is not to get any sallary as English Schoolmaster here after Whitsunday ensuing, and this they ordained to be notifyed by one of the officers leaving a copy of it at his dwelling-house.

Then about 8 days before Whitsunday the Respondent had notice given him to provide for himself and family, tho' the former Act of the 28th December related singly to the office of Precentor, whereof the sallary was no more than £2 : 10s., the sallary of the Schoolmaster being by agreement £8 sterling. And as to this office he had no notice given of the Magistrates' pleasure except as abovesaid 8 days before the term of his removall.

The Respondent having thus stated the form and manner of his election, with the Acts of Councill appointing his deprivation, he apprehends it will greatly shorten his answers to the grounds of the Representation.

The first argument is founded upon the Act of Councill in May 1747, and from them the Chargers are pleased to affect a great difficulty to conceive upon what grounds the Precentor should hold his office independant of the pleasure of the Magistrates after expiration of the year limited by the Act of admission.

To this the answer is obvious, unless the Petitioners are resolved to doubt if two and three make five. The Session have in the nature of the thing the right to elect the Session Clerk. They have also the same right in law to chuse a Precentor; his sallary is paid out of those emoluments that pertain to the Session. The Magistrates had no earthly connection with the perquisites that are paid at Baptisms or Marriages as a recompence to the persons who are concerned in making the proclamations or providing for the Baptisms, but be it sic aut sieut it is in virtue of the Kirk Session's election the Respondent entered upon and enjoyed the Precentor's office, and of consequence he could not be legally dispossess'd by the Act of the Councill without previously having the right declared to obviate this objection.

The Representers talk of an Act of the Kirk Session appointing Mr. Henderson to that office. The Respondent's doers, as they are not informed of the fact, need only observe till they have an opportunity of hearing

[1] May 7, 1755.

from their client, that is no sort of evidence yet produced in support of the alleadgance and therefore they cannott agree to hold it upon the Chargers' word.

They have also been pleased to form another doubt with respect to the Respondents being entitled to suspend the Act of Councill depriving him of his other office of Teacher of English. And in illustration of their doubt they compare the office to that of a Dancing Master, Writing or ffrench Master, a Teacher of Navigation, and at length descend to the Mistress of a Sewing Schooll, or even to the jaylor's office, and then ask if they could insist to be continued longer than the Magistrates shall please to allow.

It is answered There is no occasion to argue from imaginary cases to explain the present. Here is no new creation of an office, for there has been for near a century past a Grammar Schooll and an English School in the Burgh and parish of Irvine, and the Respondent's procurators will be forgiven to doubt whether it would not be more conducive to the publick good to suppress the Grammar Schooll rather than the other, for without the help of Grammatical learning the Countrey may be supplyed with good manufacturers farmers or tradesmen, and those for whose children the learned languages may be fitting and proper can be under no great difficulty to give them that education tho' the Irvine Schooll should be suppressed. But the Respondent has no occasion to carry the argument so far. Here is a very ancient establishment which was judged always proper and the present Magistrates do not mean so much to suppress as to transferr the office to a greater favourite, and the question is if they have that power arbitrarily without assigning or being able to prove what the law calls a bene placitum rationale. In the first place as to argument drawn from the stile of the Commission. The Respondent apprehends there is nothing in it, for that it is only a consequence of the old maxim Nolumus leges Scoticanas mutare. But the effect and explanation must be gathered from the practise, and the Respondent believes the Commission to the Grammar Schoolmaster runs precisely in the same stile and yet the Magistrates do not pretend a power to turn him out without a better reason than to make way for another.

2*dly*, Tho' it should be supposed the Magistrates have a power to turn out the Schoolmaster at the end of the first year, it will not follow that the same liberty subsists during the remaining years of his incumbency.

What he intends is, the first year may be understood as a seasonable time for the Magistrates or these interested to judge of his qualifications, but the year being expired and no objections, his office must be understood according to the nature of the thing to continue ad vitam aut culpam. My Lord Fountainhall in reporting the case of the Town of Montrose against Strachan states the argument upon this head in its proper light as taken from the prejudice it must be to the nation to allow a diversity of Schoolmasters upon the whim of one sett of Baillies who have all of them freinds to provide. He says such a diversity of Masters and way of teaching will ruin any school. And that in the case of Mr. Andrew Massie, the Regent whom the Magistrates of Edinburgh had deposed, his Gift not bearing ad vitam, the Lords reponed him, as the Magistrates could show no good cause to remove him and appealed to the authority of Bartolas, That where offices stand upon the foot of pleasure even that must be a bene placitum rationale. The Magistrates in the case of Montrose insisted they were bound to give no reason, as the office wholly depends both as to sallary and admission upon the Town, and states the case, What if a Baron establish a Schoolmaster to serve within the bounds of his barony, will he pretend to sitt against his master's will? and a Burgh Royall cannott have less power. They also affirmed the Town had suffered exceedingly by the continuance of Strachan, as in place of 100 scholars they had not twenty now. But notwithstanding of all this reasoning the Lords ordained the Town to condescend on some rational grounds of their dissatisfaction either from immoralities, insufficiency, malversations, or unsuccessfulness in his way of teaching or discipline, and to give some evidence or instruction thereof that the Lords might consider whether they merited deprivation or not.

The Respondent has stated the case at greater length to satisfy the Lord Ordinary that the same chain of reasoning which the Chargers now make use of was found insufficient in that instance.

It's true the Magistrates of Irvine pretend to make a difference betwixt this office and the office of a Regent or Parochial School, as partys are always willing to admitt distinctions and differences which they think don't hurt them. But where is the law or reason for the distinction? The reason against an arbitrary deposition is the prejudice and ruin to schoolls and scholars from a diversity of masters and the manner of teaching. And tho' the Magistrates cannot suppress a parochial school or a colledge yet what is that to say upon the generall point of deposing or admitting masters ad libitum.

But 3dly, The stile of the Commission supports the Respondent's argument and shows it was not meant to limite his continuance to a year.

It has been already noticed the Respondent's sallary was proposed to be paid out of the emoluments of Baptisms and Marriages, and that there was then a subsisting difference betwixt the Magistrates and Councill and Kirk Session as to the right for naming the Precentor.

The Commission referring to these particulars appoints ' That if these ' emoluments do not fully pay up both these sums to Mr. Kempt yearly ' that the Treasurer shall pay up the ballance out of the Town's revenues ' and this to be the rule of his payment untill the difference betwixt the ' Magistrates and Councill and Kirk Session be determined by the ' Arbiters.' Comparing this with the advertisement it is impossible to doubt of the terms of Mr. Kempt's election, or that it was not understood he should hold the office quam diu bene gesserit.

The provision respects a future period, namely, till the issue of the Arbitration, and that period is not yet come.

Upon the whole the Respondent hopes he has fully obviated what appears material in the Representation that there is no sort of affinity betwixt this and any of the supposed cases that are therein putt. He does not deny he may be turned out for such malversations as are referred to in the Interloquitor in the case of Montrose nor will he object to allow the Magistrates a prooff of such as soon as they shall be pleased to give in a pointed condescendance.

In respect whereof, etc.

CHA. HAMILTON GORDON.

Edinburgh, 13*th June* 1759.—The Lords having advised this Petition with the Answers thereto Replies and Duplies, Find that the Magistrates and Town Councill of Irvine with concurrance of the Kirk Session have properly removed Mr. James Kempt from the office of Precentor in the year 1755 and Decern. But find that Mr. Kempt is entitled to the bygone sallaries of said office till this date in respect of his having continued to officiate. But quoad the office of teacher of the English School they adhere to the Lord Ordinary's Interloquitor in respect the Councill for the Magistrates have produced no authority for insisting in a Reclaiming Petition as to that point.   ROB^T CRAIGIE, *I.P.D.*

Unto the Honourable Magistrates and Councillors of the Burgh of Irvine

The PETITION and COMPLAINT of Mr. WILLIAM CUNINGHAM, Master of the Grammar School of Irvine,

Humbly Sheweth—That I was chosen Master of the Grammar School about 36 years ago by the Magistrates and Councillors at the time, and have ever since continued in the exercise of that office to the satisfaction of the best judges without any competitor, untill of late that one Reid, a stranger from the North of Scotland, came here and had the assurance without so much as producing testificates or demanding your consent to incroach upon my office as the established master of the Grammar School by setting up a School within the town and teaching Latine and other parts of education, and to impose upon the inhabitants by exacting extravagant prices for teaching as appears from his discharged accounts.

That tho' this stranger soon deserted his school yet it has been continued and kept up by Mr. Kempt a teacher of English, who daily taught Latine and other branches of knowledge, which I conceive are my proper province. And again one Lesly, another stranger, is lately come to town, pretending to take up and teach in the said school notwithstanding of the Provost's order to the contrary, whereby divisions and animosities amongst the inhabitants (which are so destructive of the trade and prosperity of the burrow) may arise, and I who have an assistant approved of by the Council and likewise another helper suffer great prejudice.

That I conceive Mr. Kempt's acting such a part is the more inexcusable that he is only intitled to teach English, and has no authority to teach any other language, and yet seems to arrogate to himself the liberty of teaching what he pleases in defiance of the Magistrates and Councill against whom he has been so litigious as to maintain a law plea before the Lords of Session at Edinburgh for some years with respect to his continuance in the offices of Teacher of English and Precentor in the Church, which is at last finally determined against him by an Interloquitor of the 13th of June last.

> May it therefore please the honourable Magistrates and Council to give me such relief in the premisses and such security against future incroachments as you shall find just, according to Justice.
>
> WILL. CUNINGHAM.

Irvine 16th October 1759 :—

Mr. George Leslie proposed before Baillie Reid one of the present Magistrates of this burgh to teach in Mary M'Kelvie her house, Greek, Latin, French, Arithmetic, Writing, Book-keeping, Navigation, and most other practical parts of the Mathematics, in order to the Registration of the same in books competent, in terms of an Act of Parliament in the 19 of his present Majesty's reign.   GEO. LESLIE.

Though formerly qualifyed, yet not having a proper certificate of the same is now willing to qualify afresh.   GEO. LESLIE.

ACCOUNT. MR. CLERK.	Dr.
To teaching Latin and French to Mr. William Pond	7 sh.
To teaching Latin to Mathew Roberts . .	5
	12 sh.

Received the above and the same is discharged this 10th September 1759, at Irvine, by   JA. REID.

Mr. Leslie's compliments to the Provost of Irvine and begs to know where he should wait of him to satisfy him in everything requisite.
     Irvine 18th October 1759.

Mr. Leslie's compliments to Provost Hamilton and the other Magistrates of Irvine, as his credentials and certificates for teaching here have not been called for in the forenoon he thinks it discreet to let them know he begins to teach this afternoon and they may at any time see them upon sending him notice.
     Irvine 18th October 1759.

The Provost of Irvine's message to Mr. Leslie, the stranger who wants to sett up Schooll here, to tell him that his proposal to Baillie Reid in my absence was communicated to me yesternight when I came home and that I will take advice about it, and that in the meantime I discharge him upon his perill to teach in any Schooll in Town untill the Magistrates and Councill know better what he is and give their consent.
     18th October 1759.

87. *Commission by Archibald Earl of Eglinton, Deputy Vice-Admiral of Irvine, to Anthony M'Harg, Town Clerk, as his Substitute—15th November 1777.*

I ARCHIBALD EARL OF EGLINTOUNE Deputy Vice Admiral within the limits of the port of Irvine in virtue of a Commission of Admiralty granted to me by the Right Honourable John Earl of Breadalbane Vice Admiral of Scotland bearing date the thirtieth day of November one thousand seven hundred and seventy six years and registred in the books of the High Court of Admiralty in Scotland the third day of December thereafter whereby I am impowered to appoint substitutes And being well assured of the fidelity ability and loyalty of Mr. Anthony M'Harg Town Clerk of Irvine and of his skill in maritime affairs Do therefore hereby nominate constitute and appoint him the said Anthony M'Harg to be my substitute and Factor during my pleasure only within the limits of the port of Irvine from Kelly Bridge to the Troon Point in the shire of Air including the whole Islands and Rivers lying within these bounds With power to him to make and appoint officers, clerks, procurators, and other necessary members of Court for whom he shall be answerable And also with power to him to sett affix affirm hold and continue Admiral Courts within any part of the said bounds over all the limits thereof most commodious for that effect And there to administer and do justice in all matters and causes civil and criminall that shall be intended and pursued before him conform to the laws of Scotland Also to make decreets and Sentences to pronounce and the same to due and lawfull execution cause be put And to call and require all his Majesties leiges within the said bounds to put his decreets to due and lawfull execution And generally with power to the said Anthony M'Harg to use and exerce bruik and enjoy during my pleasure only the foresaid office within the foresaid bounds And to exact intromitt with uplift and receive the whole fees duties casualties and profits thereof during the continuance of this my commission to him And to act and do all things requisite and necessary thereanent as fully and freely as any other substitute Admiral and Factor within the said bounds did or might have done in any time bygone or may do in time coming Reserving always to the high Court of Admiralty in Scotland the sole power of cognoscing and determining in all Prizes and in Piracies and

other capitall crimes and in all other causes and actions which shall be
intented and pursued before the said High Court of Admiralty against
any person or persons within the said bounds And I likewise hereby
give full power and commission to the said Anthony M'Harg during my
pleasure only and within the bounds before mentioned for me and in my
name by himself and others to be employed by him to save and preserve
to the utmost of his and their power all stranded Ships Barges Boats and
other Vessels with their guns sails cables anchors and all other furniture
and apparelling thereof and all manner of goods aboard the same And also
to secure in their custody and keeping all manner of wreckt ships boats
goods royal fishes whales and others which shall happen to be wrecked
cast in or recovered upon any part within the bounds foresaid Providing
always that the said Anthony M'Harg be accountable as by acceptation
hereof he Binds and obliges himself his heirs executors and successors to
make faithful compt reckoning and payment to me or any having my
warrant for that effect of all the requisites duties and casualties arising
from the said office of Substitute and Factor hereby granted And of the
ships boats goods royal ffishes whales and others which shall happen to be
wrecked cast in or recovered as said is within the bounds before mentioned
after deduction and retention to him of so much of the same as shall defray
the necessary expences to be incurred by him in discharging the foresaid
office with a suitable gratification for his own pains But with and under
this express condition That the said Anthony M'Harg shall deliver or
transmitt to me or to any having my order for that effect regular just
and true accounts from time to time of all salvages to be recovered by
him And of all wrecks strays and other perquisites of Admiralty which
shall happen at any time to be in his possession And also his accounts of
Charges concerning the premisses duely instructed within the space of three
months after salvage or recovery Wherein if he the said Anthony M'Harg
faill he in that case by his acceptation hereof renounces the foresaid right
of retention But without prejudice always to his afterwards recovering
the Charges disbursed by him upon his producing proper vouchers of the
same And in order to render these presents the more effectual I consent
that the same be registred in the books of the High Court of Admiralty
in Scotland therein to remain for preservation And thereto constitute
                          my procurators etc., for that purpose In witnes whereof
these presents are written upon this and the two preceeding pages of

stampt paper by Robert Smith Clerk to John Wauchope Writer to the Signet and subscribed by me att Fairlie the fifteenth day of November one thousand seven hundred and seventy seven years before these witnesses Alexander Fairlie Esquire of Fairlie and John Allan his servant.

Eglintoune

Alex.' Fairlie, *witness*.
John Allan, *witness*.

88. *Memorial and Queries for the Magistrates of Irvine, in reference to the use of the Bridge.*—12th *August* 1783.

MEMORIAL and QUÆRIES for the MAGISTRATES and COUNCIL of the BURGH of IRVINE.

THE Harbour of Irvine is situated upon the Water of Irvine about half a mile from the Burgh It is within the Royalty and under the direction of the Memorialists.

Many years ago the Memorialists' predecessors erected a Bridge over the Water of Irvine in order to form a communication betwixt the town and harbour.

In the neighbourhood of Irvine there are a number of Coal mines from whence a considerable quantity of Coal is exported.

In going from these Coal pits to the harbour it is necessary to cross the water, which was done at a ford below the Bridge, where there is easy access; but the Coal carriages either in carts or on horses' back were not allowed to pass the Bridge, on which posts was put up to prevent them.

In 1748 the Bridge was rebuilt at the sole expence of the Town, and since that time Coals have been allowed to be carried along the Bridge and until lately they were of no great detriment to it.

For sometime bypast the exportation of Coal and the heavy carriages for transporting it to the harbour have greatly increased, and the Bridge is thereby much damaged which occasions a heavy expence to the Memorialists to keep it in repair while the Coal carriers refuse bearing any proportion thereof. It is material for the Memorialists either to put a stop to the practice altogether, or to fall on some means for making the Carters bear a proportion of the expence of the Bridge And therefore Quæritur

1mo Is it in the power of the Memorialists to prevent coals from being carried along the Bridge as was the case previous to the 1748, by erecting posts and otherways defending the avenues of the Bridge from Coals being carried along the same; or

2do Is it in the power of the Memorialists to levy a voluntary Toll on the Bridge to assist them in repairing the same It was mentioned that the place they formerly crossed the water was att a ford below the Bridge The Memorialists do not propose shutting up the ford and forcing the carriers to go by the Bridge, but in case they or any of them chose rather to go by the Bridge than the ford, could not the Memorialists exact a duty for that liberty without incurring any blame?

Edinburgh 12th August 1783:

These are the queries referred to in my Opinion.   J. C.

II.—COUNCIL BOOK OF IRVINE.

IRVING COUNCELL BOOK BEGYNNING THE SEXT OF DECEMBER 1664

WITH

SEDERUNT AND ACTS ON THE UTHER SYD.

At the Brugh of Irving the sext day of December 1664:—

THE quhilk day being conveinit in the Councelhous Robert Cunynghame provest Henry Lyne baillie John Broune thesaurer Andro Calderwood William Lin George Lyndsay, James Wricht David Speir and James Gemill concellours of the said burgh They all unanimouslie electit nominat and choose Arthur Hamiltone baillie clerk of Cunynghame to be clerk of this bruch dureing his lyftyme conforme to the comissione grantit be tham to him for that effect quha compeirand personallie acceptit the said office in and upon him and gave his aith de fideli administratione as use is. Admissione Hamilton.

At the Brugh of Irving the nynt day of December 1664:—

THE quhilk day being convenit in the Concelhous

Robert Cunynghame proveist

Henry Lyne baillie	George Lyndsay
John Broune thesaurer	James Wricht
Andro Calderwood	David Speir
Williame Lyne	James Gemill

THE quhilk day Robert Murchie (upon his awin confessione of his casting of ane staine of the steeple quhairwith ane child wes hurt in the lip to the effusion of his blood in greit quantite is unlawit in the soume of fourtie shilling Scotts and to remaine in prisone quhill the samen be payit. Unlaw Robert Murchie.

At Irving the threttin day of December 1664 yeirs :—being convenit in the Councelhous

  Robert Cunynghame provest   Henry Lyne baillie
  Andro Caldirwood   David Speir
  Williame Lin   George Lyndsay

Admissione of Archibald Muir to be burges.   The quhilk day Archibald Muir merchand in Irving quha is maried with Jonet Dunlop dochter to Robert Dunlop, smyth, burges and gild brother of the said brugh, is created and admitted burges of this brugh, quha gave his aith as use is, and referit the quantitie of his fyne and compositione therfoire to the magistratis ther modificatione ; ffor payment of quhich fyne the said Robert Dunlop became cautioner and souirtie for the said Archibald Muir his sone-in-law. And the said Archibald Muir acted himselff to releive his said cautioner. Sic subscribitur : Robert Dunlop Archibald Muir.

At Irving the threttin day of January 1665 yeirs :—

Sederunt

  Robert Cunynghame, proveist   Henry Lyne, baillie
  Andro Calderwood   George Lyndsay
  Williame Lin, conccellours   James Broun, conccellours

Thesaurer James Woodsyd.   The quhilk day the saids Magistrats and Councell elects nominats and chooses James Woodsyd, merchand burges of this brugh, to be common thesaurer therof, fra Michaelmas last bypast untill Michaelmas nixtocum ; quha compeirand in presens of the said Councell acceptit the said office in and upon him and gave his aith de fideli administratione as use is.

Procuratour fischall James Johnstoune.   The quhilk day James Johnstoune, couper, is created and admitted be the saidis Magistratis and Councell procuratour fischall of this brugh, quhill the next electione ; quha compeirand personallie acceptit the said office in and upon him, and gave his aith de fideli administratione, as use is.

Liquidation of Meill and Malt.   The quhilk day the Magistrats and Councell of this brugh liquidats and taxes ilk boll meill and malt payabill to this brugh be ther tenneuts and multurers, for this half yeirs payment imediatlie preceiding, ovirheid to the soume of thrie pund threttine schilling foure pennyes money.

THE quhilk day the said Magistrats and Counsell nominats and appoynts Hew Cunynghame lait proveist, James Fullertoun lait baillie, and Gilbert Wyllie merchand, to revise James Blaire lait baillie his thesaurer accompts for that yeir quherin he wes thesaurer of this brugh, upon the said James Blaire his owin supplicatioun given in befoire thame for that effect, and to report to thame betuixt and the secund day of Februar nixtocome.

Anent James Blaire his thesaurer accompt.

At Irving the threttin day of Januarij 1665 :—

Sederunt.

Robert Cunynghame, proveist.   James Woodsyd
John Broun, lait thesaurer   Henry Lyne, baillie
David Speir   William Lyne
James Wricht   Andro Caldirwood
            James Jonstoun

THE quhilk day the Magistrats and Councell of this brugh grantis commissione to the said Henry Lyne baillie, for himselff and in name of the proveist, bailyeis, councell and comunitie of this brugh, to ressave resignatione fra John Chalmer of Gaitgirth, and his procuratours in his name, of the landis of Knodgerhill Newmure, and thrie quarters of the Spittell meadow halden of them be the said John Chalmers in feu, in favours and for new infeftment thereof to be given and granted to James Fullertoun of that ilk, his aires and assignayes, conforme to the dispositione maid be the said John Chalmer to the said James Fullertoune thereof, procuratorie of resignatioune therein contenit, and chartour grantit be the said Magistratis and Councell thereupon ; and to give new seasing thereof to the said James Fullertoun of that ilk or his actornay in his name, eftir the forme and tennor therof and ordour of brugh useit in the lyk caices, reservand to them the feu deutyes and uthers contenit in the said Chartour.

Comissione in favours of the Laird of Corsbie.

At Irving the tuentie day of Januarij 1665 :—

Sederunt.

Robert Cunynghame, proveist

James Woodsyd   Henry Lyne, baillie
Andro Caldirwood James Jonstoune
Williame Lyne   David Speir
James Wricht   John Broun.

THE quhilk day Williame Thompsone tailyeor sone to Peter Thomsone

168   MUNIMENTS OF THE BURGH OF IRVINE.

Admissione of burges Williame Thompsone.

tailyeor and burges of this brugh, is created and admitted burges of this brugh, as eldest lawfull sone to his said deceist father, burges and gild-brother of the samen, quha gave his aith of fidelitie as use is, and referit the quantitie of his burges fyne to the modicatioune of the Magistrats, to be payet to the thesaurer of this brugh upon demand; ffor payment quherof Hew Thompsone flescheor became cautioner, and the said Williame Thompsone actit himselff for his releiff. Sic subscribitur : Hew Thompsone William Thompsone.

At Irving the secund day of March 1665 yeirs :—

Ropeing watter baillieschip and teind of the watter to James Johnstoun.

THE quhilk day the watter baillieschip and teind of the watter (except the teind of the cobbles), eftir publict ropeing, is sett to James Johnestoune, couper, burges of this brugh, for the space of ane yeir nixt ensewing : viz. fra the secund day of March instant to the secund day of March nixtocome in the yeir of God j^m vj^c sextie sex yeirs, ffor the soume of ffourty pundis Scotis, to be payet be him to the thesaurer of this brugh at the ordinar terme of payment : ffor payment quherof Williame Thompsone armourer is become actit as cautioner and souirtie for the said James Johnstoune, and the said James acted himselff to releive his cautioner. Sic subscribitur : Williame Thompsone   James Johnestoune.

Brig penny custom ropeal.

THE quhilk day the brig penny custome eftir publict ropeing is sett to the said James Johnstoun, for the space of ane yeir nixt ensewing, viz. fra the secund day of March instant to the secund day of March nixt ensewing in the yeir of God j^m vj^c thrie scoire sex yeirs forsaid, ffor the soume of twenty tua punds Scotts, to be payet be him to the thesaurer of this brugh at the ordinar terme ffor payment ; quherof the said Williame Thompsone is become actit as cautioner and souirtie for the said James Johnstoune and the said James Johnston acted himselff to releive his cautioner. Sic subscribitur : Williame Thomson   James Johnestoun.

At Irving the ellevint day of Apryll 1665 yeirs :—

Roping of the gras of the grein.

THE quhilk day eftir publict ropeing the gras of the grein is sett to Charles Broun, tanner, for this ensewing yeir, ffor the soume of ffyftie sex merks, to be payet to the thesaurer of this brugh at the ordinar tyme ffor payment ; quherof James Broun tanner acted himselff as cautioner for the said Charles, and the said Charles acted himselff for his releiff. Sic subscribitur : James Broun   Charles Broun.

THE quhilk day eftir publict ropeing the rottin bog under the clerk's aiker is sett to John Henry, carrier, for the ensewing yeir, ffor the soume of fyve merks sex schillings eight pennyes to the thesaurer of this brughe, at the ordinarie tyme ffor payment; quherof John Broun cordoner is become enacted as cautioner and souirtie for the said John Henry, and the said John Henry acted himselff to releive his cautioner. Sic subscribitur: J. H. Johne Broune, cautioner. *Roping of the rotten boig*

THE quhilk day eftir publict ropeing the teind of the Cobills is sett to Robert Cunynghame, proveist, for the ensewing yeir, ffor the soume of sextein pundis Scotts, to be payet be him to the thesaurer of this brugh at the ordinar tyme ffor payment quherof Williame Thomsone armourer is become acted as cautioner and souirtie for the said Robert Cunynghame, and the said Robert Cunynghame acted himselff to releive his cautioner. Sic subscribitur: Robert Cunynghame Williame Thomsone, cautioner. *and teind of the cobbills.*

At Irving the nynt day of Maij 1665 yeirs:—

Sederunt.

Robert Cunynghame, proveist	Henry Lyne, baillie
James Wodsyd, thesaurer	Andro Caldirwood
James Johnstoun	David Speir

THE quhilk day Robert Gardiner merchand is admitted and created burges of this [brugh], quha gave his aith as use is, and referit his burges fyne to the modificatioun of the Magistratis; and Alexander Dyet merchand became actit as cautioner and souirtie for the said Robert, ffor payment of the said burges fyne, eftir modificatioun therof, to the thesaurer of this brugh; and the said Robert Gardner acted himselff to releive his cautioner. Sic subscribitur: Robert Gairdner Alex' Dyett. *Robert Gardiner's admission as burges*

THE quhilk day Robert Hopkin weivar is admitted and created burges of this brugh, quha gave his aith as use is, and referrit the quantitie of his burges fyne to the modificatione of the Magistratis: Lykas Archibald Borland weivar became acted as cautioner for him for payment therof to the thesaurer eftir modificatioun therof; and the said Robert Hopkin acted himselff to releive his said cautioner. Sic subscribitur: Robert Hopkin Ar. Hamiltone, Clerk, at comand of the said Archibald Borland. *Admissione of burges Robert Hopkin.*

170   MUNIMENTS OF THE BURGH OF IRVINE.

Dischairge against Pinkeane and utheris to exerce frie trade quhill they be admitted burges.

THE quhilk day the Magistratis and Counsell of this brugh inhibites and dischairges James Porter, and Robert Nesmyth merchand, James Weir, sailler, and James Pinkeane weivar, fra useing of any frie trade or occupatione quhatsumevir incumbent to ane frie man and burges of this brugh, ay and quhill they be admitted burgess and pay ther burges fynes: ilkane off them under the paine of ten pundis Scotts, *toties quoties*, and that in respect they wer all lawfullie wairned be ane ordinar officer of this brugh, verified in Counsell, to have compeirit this day and admittit themselvis burgess and friemen of this brugh, and to have payet the burges fynes, and had nocht compeirit for that effect.

At Irving the tuenty sext day of Maij 1665:—

Sederunt.

Robert Cunynghame, proveist   Henry Lyne, baillie
John Broun   Andro Caldirwood
George Lyndsay   James Gemill
James Wricht   David Speir, consellours
Williame Lyne, consellours   James Johnstoun, procuratour fischall

Act anent the cutting of the dock.

THE quhilk day the Magistratis and Counsell of this brugh taking to ther serious considderatioun the great prejudice this brugh hes formerlie sustenit throw decay of ther harberie, and the Watter of Irving changeing its channell, quherby nether schips nor barks can repaire neir this brugh, and that ther is ane contract maid betuixt the said brugh and the lairds of Dundonald and Sewaltoun, quherby ther is libertie granted to the said brugh to cutt throw the lands of Marreis at that place callit the docke, for making of ane harberie at ane neir cutt: Have therfoire unanimouslie resolved and concludeit that the saidis landis sall be cutt throw at the place foirsaid, ffor changeing of the channell of the said watter, and that the Inhabitantis of this brugh goe out by quarters ilk day for cutting therof, the first quarter beginning at John Francis his hous, and James Gemmill his hous to be first wairned upon touk of drum, as the Magistratis sall think fitt, and ilk quarter in order eftirward as they sall be wairned be the drum, and unlawis ilk persone that sall absent themselvis fra the works in the soume of tuelf shilling Scottis for ilk day absence, *toties quoties* unforgiven. Sic subscribitur: Robert Cunynghame, proveist. Henry Lyne, baillie John Broun, counselour James Wricht, counseler James Johnstoun, procurator fischall Andro Catherwood, counseler George Lyndsay, counsellour William Lyne, counsellour David Speir, counselour Ar. Hamiltone, clerk, at comand of James Gemill.

The quhilk day James Weir sailler is created and admitted burges of this brugh, quha gave his aith as use is and referit the quantitie of his burges fyne to the modificatione of the Magistratis; ffor payment quherof to the thesaurer of the brugh eftir modificatione thereof; Archibald Hopkin sailler became acted as cautioner and souertie for the said James Weir, and the said James Weir acted himselff to releive his said cautioner. Sic subscribitur: Ar. Hamiltone, clerk, at comand of the said Archibald Hopkin James Weir. *Admissione of James Weir as burges.*

The quhilk day James Porter merchand is created and admitted burges of this brugh, as eldest lawfull sone to Hew Porter in Lochderne in Ireland quha wes burges of the said brugh, Lykas the said James Porter gave his aith as use is, and referit the modificatione of his burges fyne to the Magistrats modificatioun: ffor payment quherof to the thesaurer of this brugh eftir modificatioune therof James Kyll cooper acted himselff as cautioner and souirtie for the said James Porter, and the said James acted himselff to releive his said cautioner. Sic subscribitur: James Porter James Kyll. *Admissione of James Porter as burges.*

At Irving the tuentie eight day of June 1665 :—

Sederunt.

Robert Cunynghame, proveist   Henry Lyne, baillie
Robert Hamiltoun   James Wright
George Lyndsay   James Gemill
        James Johnstoun, procurator fischall

The Magistrats and Councell of this brugh taking to ther considderatioun the benefit that may redound to the inhabitants therof be setling ane common weeklie foot post for procureing of Intelligence from abroad, for keiping up commerce and traid, Have therfoire unanimouslie maid choise of Alexander Wintun to be common post of this brugh, quha is weeklie to depart this brugh towardis Edinburgh upon the Tuesday morneing, and to returne therto upon the Saturday following; ffor quhich the Magistrats *Anent the toune post.*

and Councell allowes to the said Alexander the soume of ten punds quarterlie dureing his service, to be payet be the thesaurer of this brugh, and to be allowit in the first end of the thesaurer accompts; and that the first quarters payment sall be payet to him presentlie be way of advance, and Siclyk allowes to the post tua schilling Scotts for ilk letre that he caries to Edinburgh for the inhabitants and burgesses of this brugh, and four schilling for ilk landwardis mans letre, and appoyntis ane badge to be maid to him with the tounes armes, for quhich he is to be ansuerabill. Sic subscribitur: Robert Cunynghame   Henry Lyne, baillie   Ro. Hamiltone   James Wricht, counsellour   George Lyndsay, counsellour   Ar. Hamiltone, at comand of the rest of the counsellouris presentt.

Act in favoris of Mr. Robert Tron anent the school.

THE quhilk day anent the complaint given in to the saidis Magistratis and Counsell be Maisteris Robert Tron schoolmaister of this brugh, and James Hay, doctor, againes severall persouns that keips schooles in the brugh, to the utter wraick and decay of the comone schooll therof, quhilk is the occasione of much confusione and decay of learning and educatione of youth, and contraire to the former Actis of this brugh maid thairanent: Quhilk being seriouslie considderit be thame, The saidis Magistratis and (*Sic.*) Councell ffor remedie therof, that no persone or persons quhatsumevir keip any schooll within this brugh at ther awin hand without consent of the Magistraties and Counsell therof under the paine of tuenty pundis Scottis, to be payet be the keiper of anie such schooll *toties quoties* (except for learning and educatioun of such children as hes nott atteinit the age of sex yeirs): And that the parent of the child keipit at the saidis schooles, nocht allowit as said is, sall be lyabill in the lyk fyne *toties quoties*, and ratifies all former Actis maid theranent.

Admissione of burges for Alexander Henry.

THE quhilk day Alexander Henry maessone is admittit and created burges of this brugh, quha gave his aith as said is, and referrs the modificatioun of the quantitie of the fyne for his burgeship to the Magistratis; ffor payment quherof eftir modificatioun of the samen James Johnstoun couper becomes cautioner actit in the Councell books of this brugh, and the said Alexander Hendrie actit himselff to releive his cautioner.   Sic subscribitur: James Johnestoun   A. Hamiltone, at comand of Alexander Henry.

At Irving the tuentie fyfth day of July 1665 :—

Sederunt.

Robert Cunynghame, proveist.

Henry Lyne, baillie	James Johnstoun, procuratour fischall
William Lyne	Andro Caldirwood
David Speir	George Lyndsay
John Broune, conscllors	James Wricht, conscllours

THE quhilk day the Magistratis and Counsell of this brughe conforme to the Iustructions sent to them be [the] lait Conventione of Borrowes, have nominat and appoynted the said Robert Cunynghame Comissioner for this brugh ffor attending the conventione of the estates of this kingdome presentlie appoynted to conveine by his Majesties appoyntment, togidder with the Conventione of the Borrowes of the said kingdome quha are presentlie also to conveine at Edinburgh, and that dureing the tyme of the sitting and meiting of the saidis tua Conventiones of Estates and Borrowes respective, and ay and quhill the dissolutione therof, conforme to the Comissione and Instructiones given to him for that effect apairt.

Comissione to Robert Cunynghame proveist.

At Irving the tuenty sext day of September 1665 :—

Sederunt.

Robert Cunynghame, proveist.

James Woodsyd, thesaurer	James Johnstoun, procuratour fischall
John Broune, lait thesaurer	Williame Lyne
David Speir	James Wricht
Andro Caldirwood, counsellors	James Gemill, counsellors

THE quhilk day the said Proveist and Councell having this day mett anent the electione of the Councell for the yeir ensewing, have all of them in ane voice nominat electit and chosen John Reid, younger, merchand, James Woodsyd thesaurer, Williame Slos, Archibald Mur, John Ros, Robert Francis, Robert Woodsyd, Hugh Kilpatrick, Andro Caldirwood, Adame Fullertoun, Alexander Dyet, David Dunlop, Robert Allane, and Allane Cunynghame, younger, merchands, Williame Dyet smyth and John M'Gill tailyeor, to be Counsellors of this brugh for the yeir to come, And ordenis them to be wairned be the officers to compeir befoire the proveist

Nominatione of counselleris.

baillies and Councell upon the tuenty nynt day of September instant to accept the said office in and upon thame and to give ther aithes de fideli administratione as use is. Sic subscribitur: Robert Cunynghame, proveist James Woodsyd Johne Broun Andro Catherwood James Wricht Williame Lyne David Speir James Johnstoun Ar. Hamiltone at comand of James Gemill.

At Irving the tuenty nynt day of September 1665:—

Sederunt.

Robert Cunynghame, provest   Henry Lyne, baillie
Andro Caldirwood   James Gemill, counsellours
James Wricht, counsellour

Admissione of councellours. THE quhilk day in presens of the saidis Magistratis and Councell conveinit, Comperit personallie the above nameit John Reid, Robert Francis, Robert Allane, David Dunlop, Robert Woodsyd and Archibald Muir, quha acceptit the office of Counsellours in and upon thame for the yeir to come and gave ther aithes de fideli administratione as use is: The saidis Williame Slos, Alexander Dyet, Adame Fullertoune, and John M'Gill being also present desyred the nixt day of the meiting of the Councell to advyse, quhilk wes granted and they wairned *apud acta* to compeir that day. The absentis of the above nameit Counsellours to be wairned to compeir and accept the thrid day of October nixtocome, and appoyntis the lites and election of the Magistratis to be maid that day. Sic subscribitur: Ro^{rt} Francis Johne Reid Archibald Muir Ro^t Woodsyd David Dunlop Ar. Hamiltone at command of Robert Allane.

Admissione of David Dunlop to be burges. THE quhilk day David Dunlop, sone to Robert Dunlop smyth is maid burges of this brugh, quha gave his aith as use is, and referit the quantitie of his burges fyne to the modificatione of the Magistratis, ffor payment quherof eftir modificatione of the samen, James Wricht, smyth is become cautioner for the said David, and the said David is become enacted for his releiff. Sic subscribitur: David Dunlop James Wright.

THE quhilk day Robert Allane merchand is maid burges of this brugh, quha gave his aith as use is, and referrit the quantitie of his fyne to the Magistratis modificatioun, ffor payment quherof eftir modificatioun of the samen, James Gemill flescher is become acted as cautioner and souirtie for the said Robert Allane, and the said Robert acted himselff for to releive his cautioner. Sic subscribitur: Ar. Hamiltone, at command of the saids Robert Allane and James Gemill.

At Irving the thrid day of October 1665:—

Sederunt

Robert Cunynghame, proveist	Henry Lyne baillie
James Gemill	Andro Caldirwood
Robert Francis	Robert Allane
Archibald Muir	David Dunlop
George Lyndsay	John Reid
James Wricht	Alexander Dyett
Williame Slos	John M'Gill
Robert Woodsyd	James Johnstoun
David Speir, counsellours	Hew Kilpatrick, counsellours

THE quhilk day the said Hew Kilpatrick is admittit burges of this brugh, quha gave his aith as use is, and referrit the quantitie of his burges fyne to the Magistratis modificatione, ffor payment quherof to the thesaurer eftir modificatione of the samen Alexander Dyet merchand is become cautioner and the said Hugh acted and obleist himself for his releiff. Sic subscribitur: Hugh Kilpatrick   Alex^r Dyett, cationer. *Admissione of Hugh Kilpatrick to be burges.*

THE quhilk day John Edward sailler is admittit burges of this brugh quha gave his aith as use is and referrit the quantitie of his burges fyne to the magistratis modificatione, ffor payment quherof eftir modificatione of the samen Johne Reid younger merchand became cautioner, and the said John Edward acted himselff to releive his cautioner. Sic subscribitur: Johne Edward   John Reid, cationer. *Admissione of John Edward as burges.*

THE quhilk day eftir leiting and voyting therupon Robert Cunynghame be pluralitie of voices is nominat and electit to be proveist of this brugh for the yeir to come, quha being present acceptit the said office in and upon him, and gave his aith de fideli administratione as use is. *Admissione and Election of Robert Cunynghame to be proveist.*

THE quhilk day eftir leiting and voyting therupon, as the manner is, Allane Cuming, lait baillie of this brugh, and Henry Lyne present baillie therof, *Electione of Allane Cuming and Henry Lyne to be baillies.*

Admissione of the said Henry Lyne. be pluralitie of voices are nominat and electit to be baillies of this brugh for the ensewing yeir; and the said Henry Lyne being present acceptit the said office in and upon him and gave his aith de fideli administratione as use is.

Electione of John Gray thesaurer. THE quhilk day John Gray merchand is nominat and electit to be thesaurer of this brugh for the yeir to come, quha being present refuised to accept the said office.

Election and admissione of James Johnstoun to be procuratour fischall. THE quhilk day the said James Johnstoune is be pluralitie of voices electit and chosen procurator fischall of this brugh for the yeir to come, quha being present gave his aith de fideli administratione as use is.

At Irving the tent day of October 1665:—
Sederunt.

Robert Cunynghame, proveist	Henry Lyne, baillie
Robert Frances	John Reid
Robert Woodsyd	Archibald Muir
Robert Allane	David Dunlop
Andro Caldirwood, Counsellours	James Johnstoun, Counsellouris

Anent absents fra the Counsell. THE quhilk day the Magistratis and Counsell taking to ther considderatioun that severall persons members of the counsell neglects to attend the meiting of the samen, quherthrow many matters of concernement tending to the weill of the brugh are neglected, Have therfoire ordanit and enacted that ilk member of Counsell quha sall nocht attend the meiting therof at the ringing of the bell, they being lawfullie wairned of befoir be the officer, and yit neglects to attend sall pay for ilk absence ten pund Scotts, *toties quoties*, except that they can schow ane reasonabill excuse for ther said absence as said is.

Anent Counsellours that hes nocht as yit acceptit. THE quhilk day the Magistratis and Counsell ordeins John Gray and Adame Fullertoune to remaine in prisone within the tollbuith of Irving, quher they presentlie are, ay and quhill they and ether of them accept the electione of thesaurer and councellour respective, And siclyk ordenis the officers of this brugh to apprehend the persons of the saidis Hugh Kilpatrick, John Ros, and John M'Gill, and William Slos, and to incarcerat them within the said tollbuith therin to remaine ay and quhill they and ether of them accept of ther said electiones as counsellouris, and give ther aithes as use is, and ordenis the said William Dyet to be wairned to the threttine day of October instant to accept of his said electione.

Irving the threttine day of October 1665 :—
Sederunt.

Robert Cunynghame, proveist	Henry Lyne, baillie
Robert Francis	Robert Allane
Andro Caldirwood	Archibald Muir
Robert Woodsyd, Counsellours	John Reid, Counsellours

James Johnstoune, procuratour fischall

THE quhilk day compeirit the said John Gray and acceptit the said office of thesaurer of this brugh for the yeir to come in and upon him and gave his aith de fideli administratione as use is. *Admissione of the Thesaurer.*

THE quhilk day compeirit in presens of the saids Magistratis and Counsell the saidis Adame Fullertoune John Ros and William Dyet quha all of them acceptit of the said office as counsellers of this brugh for the yeir to come, conforme to the foirsaid electione, and gave ther aithes de fideli administratione, as use is. *Admissione of Counsellours.*

THE quhilk day the Magistratis and Counsell having conveinit Robert Broun lait clerk of this brugh for exhibitione and productione befoire them of the recordis and registers of this brugh with the haill grundis and warrandis therof, Eftir severall desyres maid to him for that effect of befoire, quherof nochtwithstanding of his promeissis maid theranent hes still as yit neglectit or purposelie delayet to doe the samen, Have therfore ordenit him to compeir befoire thame upon the twenty day of this instant, and ther to exhibit produce and delyver up to thame the haill registers and recordis of this brugh with the haill grundis and warrandis therof upon aith with certificatione, etc. *Anent productioune of the towne recordis.*

THE quhilk day the Magistrats and Counsell of this brugh unlawis and amerciatis Hugh Kilpatrik and William Slos ilkane of them in the sowme of ffoure pund Scotts, for ther contumacie in nocht appeiring befoire thame this day and place to have acceptit of ther respective electiones as Counsellors of this brugh, conforme to the said electione, they being lawfully wairned for that effect, and siclyk ordenis them to be wairned to attend the Councell the tuentie day of October instant. *Anent Kilpaterik and Slos.*

178   MUNIMENTS OF THE BURGH OF IRVINE.

Anent the election of Stentmaister.

THE quhilk day the Magistrats and Councell of this brugh being chairged be vertew of letres of horneing flor payment to Sir John Weymis of Bogie, and Mr. William Scharp keipar of his Majesties signet, to mak payment to them of the soume of eight hundreth merks Scots quhilk is the said brugh of Irving's proportione of the soume of fourescoire thousand merkis, agreit upon to have bein advanceit be the royall borrowes of this kingdome in Anno 1650 yeirs, towardis the defraying of his Majesties personall chairges and utheris specifeit in the acts of parliament, acts of conventione of borrowes, and uther actis and warrands direct furth thairanent, Have for the moire speedie uplyfting thairof nominat and appoyntit Thomas Biggart, Niniane Holmes, Adame Cunynghame, elder, Lawrence Blaire, John Hunter, Alexander Dyet, Gilbert Wyllie, Alexander Orr, John Porter, John Reid, elder, David Broun, William Porter, William Gardner, Alexander Cochrane, and Andro Gemill, To be stent maisters flor imposeing of the said stent equallie upon the haill inhabitantis of this brugh, and utheris lyable in payment thairof, And for that effect ordenis them to be wairnit be ane officer to compeir befoire them upon Tuesday nixt, to give thair aithes of fidelitie, as use is.

Admissione of Robert Broun to be officer.

THE quhilk day the Magistrats and Councell of this brugh creats and admitts Robert Broun, smyth, to be ane of the ordinar officers of this brugh, quha being present and suorne, acceptit the said office in and upon him, and gave his aith de fideli administratione, as use is.

Irving the sevintein day of October 1665 yeirs:—

Sederunt.

Robert Cunynghame, proveist	Henry Lyne, baillie
Robert Francis	John Reid
Robert Allane	Andro Caldirwood
Archibald Muir	John M'Gill
William Dyet, counsellors	Robert Woodsyd, counsellours

James Johnstoun, procuratour fischall

Kilpatrick.

THE quhilk day Hugh Kilpatrick compeirand in face of Councell refuised to accept the office of ane Counccllor upon him, quhairupon the Magistratis and Councell ordaines him to remaine in prisone untill he accept.

THE quhilk day compeirit the said Williame Slos and acceptit of the said office of ane Councellor in and upon him, and gave his aith de fideli administratione as use is.

THE quhilk day Thomas Biggart, Laurence Blaire, John Hunter, Alexander Dyet, Gilbert Wyllie, Alexander Orr, John Porter, Williame Porter, Williame Gardner, Andro Gemill, and John Reid, elder, quha wer nominat be the Magistratis and Counsell to be stent maisters for imposeing of foure moneth ces and ane half, ffor payment of the said eight hundreth merks, upon ilk person according to there landis, means, and traid, within brugh, conforme to the former act, compeirit in presens of the said Councell and acceptit the said nominatione, and gave ther aithes of fidelitie, quhairupon the Magistratis and Councell ordeinit ilk ane of them to meitt within the Councell hous punctuallie at the ringing of the bell, ilk persone under the paine of ten pundis, *toties quoties*, and to be apprehendit and incarcerat quhill the said penaltie be payet.

THE quhilk day the Magistratis and Councell ordeinis John Reid lait thesaurer of this brugh To produce his dischairge of his intromissione with the tounes revenew that yeir quhairin he was thesaurer of this brugh, upon Fryday nixt with certificatioun.

Anent John Reidis thesaurarie.

THE quhilk day compeirit Alexander Orr merchand, quha declaired that in anno 1656 yeirs he gott fyve pund sterling consignit in his hand that wes given for the use of the Toun be the English for some quarterings, quhilk soum wes given up and delyverit be him to John Guthrie lait provest.

Declarationе Alexander Orr anent fyve pund sterling.

THE quhilk day anent the supplicatioun given in be James Porter indweller in this brugh, mentioneing that the said brugh is destitut for the present of any persone for instructing of youth in the airt of arithmethik, ciphering, and reetificing of thare hand wreitts, and tharefoire desyring libertie fra the Magistrats and Councell of the said brugh to exerce the samen, as the said supplicationne at maire lenth beirs: Quhilk being hard rein and considderit be the saids Magistratis and Councell, They al in one voice declaired that the supplicant may teach youth the airt of arithmetik, ciphering, singing of musick, and learning youth to rectifie thare wreitings, provyding he doe not prejudge the grammar schooll in teaching of youth to read or learne Scotts or latine or wreitt or doe ony uther thing quhilk the maisters of the grammar schooll wer in use to doe.

Act anent James Porter.

Irving the Tuenty day of October 1665 :—

Sederunt.

Robert Cunynghame, provcist　　Henry Lyne, baillie
John Reid　　　　　　　　　　　Robert Francis
Williame Slos　　　　　　　　　Robert Woodsyd
Robert Allane　　　　　　　　　David Dunlop
Archibald Muir　　　　　　　　Andro Caldirwood
John M'Gill, counsellors　　　Williame Dyet councellors
　　James Johnstoun, procuratour fischall　　John Ros

Kilpatrick. THE quhilk day compeirit the said Hugh Kilpatrick quha as of befoir refuised to accept the office of ane councellour in and upon him quhairupon the Magistratis and Councell ordeinis him as of befoire to remaine in prisone untill he accept.

Reid. THE quhilk day compeirit John Reid lait thesaurer quha in obedience of the former act produceit ane dischairge of his thesaurer compt under the hand of Niniane Ros quha succeidit him in the office of thesaurer daited the flyft day of Aprill 1648 yeirs, and as for the teind the Magistratis and Councell appoyntis John Porter and Alexander Dyet to audit his accomptis of the said teind upon Tuesday nixtocome, and to report to the Councell the tuenty sevint day of October instant.

Ros. THE Magistratis and Councell ordeinis Niniane Ros to be cited befoire thame to give ane accompt of his thesaurarie the nixt Councell day.

Robert Broun. THE quhilk day compeirit Robert Broun lait Clerk of Irving quha produceit tua old Court books the on thairof quhen umquhill Williame Cauldwell wes clerk, and the uther at the said Robert Broun his entrie to the clerkschip; The Magistratis and Councell ordeinis him to produce the rest of the tounes registers, and warrands thairof, upon the tuenty sevint day of October instant.

Burges Williame Wallace. THE quhilk day Williame Wallace messenger is admittit burges of this brugh be the saids Magistratis and Councell, quha gave his aith as use is, and referrit the quantitie of his burges fyne to the modificatioun of the Magistratis: Lykas James Johnstoune couper actit himself as cautioner for the said Williame Wallace for payment thairof and the said Williame Wallace acted himself to relieve his cautioner. Sic subscribitur: James Johnstoun　Williame Wallace.

COUNCIL BOOK. 181

Irving the tuenty sevint day of October 1665 :—

Sederunt.

Robert Cunynghame, proveist   Henry Lyne, baillie
John Reid   Robert Francis
Williame Slos   Robert Woodsyd
Robert Allane   David Dunlop
Archibald Muir   Andro Caldirwood
John M'Gill   Williame Dyet

James Johnstoune, procuratour fischall

The quhilk day compeirit the said John Reid lait thesaurer quha reported Reid. no diligence anent the auditing of his accompt of the teind, quhairupon The Magistratis and Councell ordeins him to remaine in prisone ay and quhill he mak payment to the Thesaurer of the said brugh of the haill teind conteinit in his book extending to   Reservand actione (Sic.) to him against thes lyabill in payment of the said teind.

The Magistratis and Councell continowes Niniane Ros untill the thrid day of November nixtocome quhilk day he undertook to cleir his accompts.

The Magistratis and Councell liquidats and taxes the boll teind meill dew Liquidatioun of to this brugh for the crop 1664 yeirs to foure pound Scots ilk boll. Teind.

The quhilk day compeirit the said Robert Broun quha produceit tua Robert Broun. Register books of bands and decreits, and tua Councell books, and declaired that he could produce no farder quhill he revised his presses for ane space, quhairupon the Magistratis and Councell continowes the act anent the productione of ony farder books records or warrandis untill the last Fryday of November nixtocome.

Compeirit John Guthrie lait proveist, quha confest the ressaving of some Guthrie. money fra Alexander Orre, but wes nocht cleir quhether it was ffyve pund sterling or nocht, and desyred that the Magistratis and Councell wold delay all procciding thairintill untill the returne of James Blaire lait baillie fra the fisching quhilk wes grantit.

The quhilk day the Magistratis and Councell ordeins Hew Wallace Against Wallace chapman, Robert Barnes, John Miller in Morrayes, James Buckill thair, and uthers. Williame Craufurde in brigend, and Hew Wallace thair, to be apprehendit and incarcerat within the tolbuith of Irving for useing of frie traid within the said brugh and liberties thairof, they being unfrie persons.

FOLLOWES the LIST of the ROLL given in to James Woodsyd, Thesaurer for the Toune Rent and Teind for the yeir 1664: Togidder with that yeirs Feu duty.

TEIND.

The rig sumtyme belonging to Walter Kid and now to ——	00 02 00
Williame Dyet for his rig	00 02 00
Jonet Armour for her tua rigis	00 13 04
James Blaire for his rigs	00 02 00
Item maire be him for Lochwairds ane boll nyne pecks and the fyft pairt of thrie pecks with the rest of his land pryce of the boll foure punds Inde	06 08 00
Robert Stewart for his tua rigs	00 13 04
Charles Broun for his rig	00 05 04
Williame Gardner for his rig	00 05 04
Robert Broun for his rigs	01 05 04
Item maire be him for his tua halff aikers of land at touneheid ane firlot ait teind meill at foure pund the boll	01 00 00
Adame Cunynghame for his rigs	00 05 00
Andrew Hendirsone for his rig	00 05 00
John Reid sumetyme proveist for his rig	00 04 00
Alexander Smyth in Kilwining for John Young his rig	00 08 00
Henrie Dyet for his tua rigs	00 13 00
Williame Craufurd his rig	00 05 04
David Walker his rig belonging now to Hew Thomsone	00 05 04
William M'Lurg his rig now belonging to ——	00 05 04
Peebles rig belonging to Corsbie	00 05 04
Item mair be him for his lands of Roddings ane boll teind meill, and for the Spittell meidow nyne pecks and the fyft pairt of thrie pecks of meill pryce foirsaid Inde	06 08 00
George Garven for his rig	00 05 04
John Muire for his rig	00 05 04
Clonbeith for his rig	00 05 04
Item maire be him for the landis sumtyme pertening to Archibald Howie	01 12 00
Alexander Craig for his rig	00 05 04
Henry Sommer for Thomas Weir's tua tailing rigs	00 10 08
Stephen Quhyt for his tua rigs	00 08 00

Bryce Muir for Giffertlandis rigs .	00	08	00
Hew Brown for Hew Houstoun's rigs . .	00	08	00
James Kyll and John Spirling in Hill for thair rig	00	08	00
Hew Broune for his awin rig . .	00	08	00
Maire be him for Peebles rig . .	00	04	00
Item maire be him for his pairt of Braidmeidow . .	04	16	00
Item maire be him for his chapel land thrie pecks teind ait meill and the fyft pairt of fyve pecks meill pryce forsaid Inde . . .	01	00	00
Thomas Reid his rig possest be Alexander Henry	00	08	00
Williame Fullertoun his rig .	00	08	00
Elizabeth Cauldwell for hir tua rigs . .	00	16	00
Thomas Spark and James Johnstoune for thair rig	00	08	00
Robert Portars relict for her rig .	00	08	00
John Porter for his rig . .	00	08	00
John Thompsone for his rig . .	00	08	00
Mr. Robert Barclay his rig nocht valued.			
Jonet Blaire relict of umquhill John Broun for her Sandierig	00	02	00
Niniane Ros for his tua rigs . . .	00	16	00
Garseaddane land now belonging to ——— tua bollis halff boll and the fyft pairt of halff ane boll teind ait meill pryce of the boll foirsaid	00	08	00
Garseaddanes rig belonging to ———	00	08	00
Thomas Biggart for his rig .	00	08	00
Robert Hammill for his thrie rigs .	00	17	04
John Cuming for his rig . .	00	06	08
James Gemil flescheor his rig .	00	06	00
Robert Gairdner for his tua rigs .	00	08	00
Hew Montgomerie for his foure rigs	01	02	06
Williame Henries relict for his rig	00	06	00
Henrie Lin for his rig . .	00	12	00
John Guthrie for his rig	00	03	04
Adame Fullertoun for Patrick Cunynghame's aiker of land at the Touneheid and halff aiker that wes Mr. Hew Trans and for his thrie ruid of land and Temple rig that followes the borne sevin peckis teind ait meill pryce of the boll foirsaid Inde	01	15	00

Item for his rig that followes his house		00 04 09
Item for his rig at the stackyaird .		00 01 00
Andro Calderwoods rig .		00 04 00
Robert Cunynghames rig .		00 05 00
Item maire be him for Weirsholme eight pecks tua pairt peck teind ait meill pryce foirsaid Inde		02 03 04
James Ros for his tua rigs		00 08 00
James Fullertoun for his lands in Gallowhill sex pecks and the fyft pairt of tua pecks teind ait meill pryce of the boll foirsaid Inde		01 12 00
Item for his tua rigs		00 16 00
Jonet Greir for his rig		00 08 00
James Galt for his rig		00 06 08
Umquhile David Dickie's rig belonging to		00 08 00
Williame Francis in staine for his fauld sex pecks and the fyft pairt of tuo pecks teind meill. Item for his tua aikers of land at the toune heid half ane boll meill. Item for his Temple lands foure pecks meill and for his tua rigs at the bornes the fyft pairt of ane firlot of meill price of the boll foirsaid Inde of all		04 16 00
William Francis afoirsaid for his rig formerlie belonging to		00 05 04
Robert Dunlop for his landis thrie pecks teind ait meill and ffyft pairt of thrie pecks pryce of the boll foirsaid Inde .		00 10 00
Item for his tua tail rigs .		00 16 08
Margaret Campbell relict of umquhill Robert Tailyeour for 3^{lib} 4 schillingis, and for thair pairt of the Gallowhill and rig at the Touneheid 40s. Inde .		05 04 00
John Dein for his tua rigs		01 06 08
James Kyll for Pennymoir's rig		00 08 00
Robert Henrie's rigs		00 11 00
John Steiles rig .		00 05 04
Margaret Georges rig		00 05 04
James Kyll for his rig		00 03 04
Hew Thompsone for his thrie rigs		00 10 00
David Francis for his rig		00 03 04

COUNCIL BOOK.

Niniane Holmes for his pairt 16s. 8d. of the Wod meidow	01	06	00
For umquhill Margaret Campbell elder her land now perteining to ——	00	19	04
Mr. Robert Barclay for his lands tua bolls and the fyft pairt of ane firlot teind ait meill pryce of the boll foirsaid Inde	08	04	00
James Neilson's land tua pecks and the ffyft pairt of ane peck teind ait meill maire for the rest of his lands thrie pecks and fyft pairt of thrie pecks teind ait meill pryce of the boll foirsaid Inde . . .	01	09	00
Hew Cunynghame for his lands tuelff pecks ffyft pairt of ane peck teind ait meill pryce of the boll foirsaid Inde	03	01	00
Item maire be him for his tailrig	00	06	08
Maister William Cunynghame for his pairt of the Seg medow	02	00	00
Jonet Tran for her tua rigs	00	16	00
Item maire be her for her landis in Gallowhill tua pecks and the ffyft pairt of tua pecks teind meill pryce of the boll foirsaid Inde	00	12	00
Robert Hamiltone for Dalrymple's wairds and Braidmedow tua bolls teind meill pryce of the boll foirsaid Inde .	08	00	00
Robert Woodsyd for his pairt of the Spittel meidow ane firlott and the fyft pairt of ane firlott teind meill pryce of the boll foirsaid	01	04	00
James Brownes land about the Touneheid . .	00	12	00
Item maire be him for the lands that wes David Barclayes ane firlot and the fyft pairt of ane firlott teind ait meill pryce foirsaid Inde	01	04	00
John Blaire for his tua rigs	00	16	00
John Harperis land the ffyft pairt of thrie firlots meill pryce of the boll foirsaid Inde . . .	00	12	00
John Guthrie for the lands of Hiemyre and boll teind meill pryce foirsaid Inde	04	00	00
SUMMA of the haill teind	113	13	09

VOL. II 2 B

Followes the TOUNELAND ROLL for the Thesaurer

Maister Robert Barclay thrie aikers at fourtein merks the aiker is	28 00 00
Hew Cunynghame fyve aikers at fourtein merks ilk aiker Item ane uther aiker at threttine merks Item uther thrie aikers roped for threttie pund sex schilling eight pennyes Inde	84 06 08
James Blaire thrie aikers at fourtein merks ilk aiker Inde	28 00 00
Robert Stewart thrie aikers of ropeit land for . .	35 00 00
John Thompsone thrie aikers halff aiker of land at fourtein merks ilk aiker and ane uther aiker at threttine merks Inde	41 06 08
Hew Thompsone thrie aikers of land at fourtein merks ilk aiker	28 00 00
Robert Brown ane aiker halff aiker land at fourtein merks ilk aiker	14 00 00
Hew Montgomerie for ane aiker halff aiker land at that rait	14 00 00
George Garven ane aiker halff aiker land at that same rait	14 00 00
Williame Wischerts relict for tua aikers of land at fourtein merks the aiker and ane uther aiker at threttin merks Inde	27 06 08
Williame Fullertown and Thomas Gardner equallie betwixt thame tua aikers of land at fourtein merks the aiker and ane uther aiker at threttine merks Inde . .	27 06 08
John Muire thrie aikers of land at ffourtein merks the aiker	28 00 00
Williame Dyet thrie aikers of land at ffourteen merks the aiker	28 00 00
Henry Dyet thrie aikers of land at the same rait Inde	28 00 00
Robert Dunlop thrie aikers of land at the said rait	28 00 00
James Galt smyth thrie aikers of land at the said rait	28 00 00
Williame Ros thrie aikers of land at the said rait .	28 00 00
Williame Porter tua aikers of land at fourtein merks and ane uther aiker at threttine merks Inde .	27 06 08
James Brown thrie aikers at that same rait .	27 06 08
Robert Francis thrie aikers at the said rait .	27 06 08
Thomas Spark younger thrie aikers at the said rait	27 06 08

COUNCIL BOOK.   187

Robert Wallace thrie aiker at the same rait Inde	27	06	08
James Spark thrie aikers at fourtein merks the aiker .	28	00	00
David Speir thrie aikers tua at fourtein merks and ane uther at threttine merks Inde . . .	27	06	08
David Speir and umquhill Williame Nevin thrie aikers at the said rait	27	06	08
Summa of the rent of the foirsaid seventie eight aikers	726	13	04

Followes the uther TOWNE LANDIS FISCHINGS TEINDS and uthers not in aikers.

The Gooslone sett to James Broun foir . . .	50	13	04
Rotten boig under the Knodgerhill set to Thomas Biggart for	04	10	00
Rotten boig besyd the Gleeb aiker sett to John Henry for	03	06	08
Reidburne sett to John Biggart's relict for . .	02	13	04
Rent at the Crocefurd sett to John Kidd for . .	13	06	08
The pasturage at the Boig syd sett to Allane Cuming for .	05	06	08
The Toune land in marreis sett to Hew Montgomerie and Charles Brown cautioner for . . .	07	00	00
The gras of the Grein sett to Charles Brown for . .	37	06	08
Teind of the Watter and Cobbiles set and ropeit to Robert Cunynghame, proveist for . . .	16	00	00
Earle of Eglintoun's factor for the Girnell booth .	03	06	08
Robert Steinsone for his booth . . .	6	13	04
Alexander Dyet for his booth . . .	11	00	00
John Clerk for the pettie customes fra Mertimes 1664 to Mertimes 1665	79	06	08
Brig custom sett to James Johnstown for . .	22	00	00
John Reid lait proveist his rigs ropeit to Williame Lyne for the use of the sessione John Henrie cautioner for .	03	13	04
John M'Gill for his booth . . .	1	00	00
Summa	267	03	04

FEW DEUTYES.

Alexander Blaire of Giffartland for his landis of Barow landis and uthers perteining to him	18	04	02

The Laird of Corsbie for Knodgerhill 4^{lib} 18s. for Newmuir 4^{lib} 18s. and for his pairt of Spittelmeidow thretty nyne schilling Inde	11	15	00
James Blaire for Loch waird	01	01	08
Robert Hamiltone for Dalrymple's waird	01	01	08
Item for the said Robert his pairt of the Rood meidow	00	09	08
Niniane Holmes for his pairt of the samen	00	09	08
Mr. Robert Barclay for Scottswaird	02	00	08
Robert Woodsyde for his pairt of the Spittellmeidow	00	09	08
Charles Brown for Gullicland	01	00	00
John Gottray for Hiemyre	01	05	00
William Frances for his tua faulds	01	08	00
Item for his rig in the Smiddie bar	00	00	04
The aires and successors of Hew Thompsone in Garscaddan for St. James laud	00	06	08
Clonbeith for his Loch landis and Gallowmuir	02	10	00
Hew Brown for Chapel land	02	00	00
The successors of Robert Tailyeor for the Rood meidow	00	10	00
Robert Brown for his Gallowmuir	01	12	08
James Kyll for his hous in Seasgait	00	03	00
Jonet Hepburne spous to John Muir for her Sandie rig	00	00	04
The Laird of Hunterstown for the Chappell	00	06	08
David Brown for his hous	00	01	00
Hew Montgomerie for his pairt of the Reddinghill	00	01	00
Item for his hous under the Councell hous	00	03	04
James Brown for George Hamulls hous	00	01	00
Item for M'Unsarts hill	00	05	00
The Laird of Skelmorlie for Ormescheoch quhilk is long awand	00	16	08
The Laird of Adamehill for Reddinghill 8s. 4d., for Hoil hous 8s. 4d., Freirsmylne 40s. Inde of all	02	16	08
Dunlop for Cowper's land	00	05	00
Mr. William Cunynghame for his pairt of the Roodmeidow	01	03	04
Hew Thompsone, Walker, for his hous	00	05	00
SUMMA of the foirsaid few deutyes	52	19	8

COUNCIL BOOK.

MYLNE RENT.

Item fra Williame Thompsone for the mylnes fra the first day of Maij 1665 to the first day of November the said yeir being tua quarters payment of the tak deuty thairin specifeit ffourtie tua bolls victuall halff meill halff malt pryce of the boll ovirheid four pund sex schilling eight pennyes Inde 184 03 04

BURGES FYNES

Archibald Muir . .	04 00 00
Williame Thompsone tailyeor	02 00 00
Robert Gairdner merchand	04 00 00
Robert Hopkin weivar . .	04 00 00
James Weir sailler .	08 00 00
James Porter . . .	04 00 00
Alexander Henrie macsson gratis . .	00 00 00
David Dunlop . . .	04 00 00
Robert Allane . . .	08 00 00
Hugh Kilpatrick . . .	04 00 00
SUMMA of the Fynes . . .	42 00 00

Summa of the haill thesaurer his chairge fra Michaelmas 1664 to Michaelmas 1665 . . . . . 1386 13 4

Ther is addit to this chairge Tuentie rex dollors for James Fullertons fyne and tuentie rex dollors for Charles Brown's fyne and sex pund for Hugh Thompsone his fyne This thesaurer's chairge will amount to 1508-13-04

Irving the thrid day of November 1665 :—

Sederunt.

Robert Cunynghame, proveist	Henry Lyne, baillie
John Reid	Robert Francis
Robert Allane	John Ros
Andro Caldirwood	Robert Woodsyd
Williame Slos	John Gray, Counsellors
John M'Gill, counsellors	James Johnstoune, procurator fischall

THE quhilk day Allane Cunynghame merchand quha formerlie wes nominat

Councellor Allane Cunynghame.	ane Councellor of this brugh compeirit in presens of the saids Magistratis and Councell and gave his aith as use is.
Act against Fullertoun.	THE quhilk day the Magistratis and Councell ordeinis Adame Fullertoun to be wairned to compeir befoire them the tent day of November instant to produce ane band granted to the Magistratis and Counsell of this brugh be James Fullertoun lait baillie of this brughe conteining the soume of principall with penaltie and annualrentis that the thesaurer may be chairged with the bygane annualrentis therof.
Liquidatioun of victuall.	THE quhilk day the Magistratis and Councell liquidats and taxes the pryce of the fourtie tua bolls halff boll victuall half malt halff meill dew be the multerers and fermorers of thair mylnes for the rent therof fra the first day of Maij last bypast to the first day of November now last bypast 1665 ilk boll therof ovirheid to ffoure pund sex shilling eight pennyes and ordeinis James Woodsyd lait thesaurer to be chairged thairwith.
Act and Commissione anent Ros.	THE quhilk day the Magistratis and Councell nominats Mr. Robert Barclay Allane Dunlop and Hew Cunynghame lait proveists of this brugh John Porter and Alexander Dyet merchands or ony thrie of them to audite Niniane Ros his thesaurer accompts and to report to the Councell under ther handis the tent of November instant.
Act Cunynghame.	THE quhilk day ordeins the officers of this brugh or ony ane of them to wairne Hew Cunynghame lait thesaurer to compeir befoire the tent day of November instant to give in his dischairge of his thesaurer [accompts] fra Michaelmes 1647 to Michaelmes 1649 yeirs.
	THE Magistrates and Councell modifies the pryce of ilk pund Candle to be sold within this brugh eftir the dait heirof to ffoure schilling Scots money in respect of the tallow and that under the paine of ffoure pundis Scots to be payet be the seller contraveiner heirof.
Anent middingis and back yaird dykes.	THE quhilk day the Magistratis and Councell of this brugh ordeins all middings to be removed off the hie streits thairof betuixt and Tuesday nixtocome under the paine of ten punds to be payet be the contraveiner owner of the saidis middings and that ilk persone concernit repaire ther back dyks for keiping good neighbourheid on with another within foure moneths eftir the dait heirof ilk persone interessed under the paine of ffourtie pundis money.

The quhilk day the Magistratis and Councell of this brugh hes admittit Hew Wallace merchand ane burges of this brugh quha gave aith as use is and referit the quantitie of his fyne to the Magistratis ther modificatioun ffor payment quherof to the thesaurers of this brugh David Dunlop maltman became cautioner and souirtie and the said Hew acted himself to releive his cautioner. Sic subscribitur: David Dunlop, cationer Hew Wallace.

Admissione of Hew Wallace ane burges.

The quhilk day ther being complaint given in befoire the Magistratis and Councell at the instance of James Johnstoune procuratour fischall against Williame Fullertoun wright ffor that upon the tuenty fourt day of October last bypast he fell upon Hew Garven and beat and bruised him in the dwelling hous of John Frew wright under darkness and cloud of night quhilk being verefied be the depositions of divers famous witness The Magistratis and Councell therupon ordeins Williame Fullertoun being personallie present to remaine in prisone within the tolbuith of the said brugh ay and quhill he mak payment of the soume of ten pundis Scots quherin he wes formerlie unlawit be the Magistratis of this burghe upon the sextein day of December last bypast and to find cawtioun for his apperance in caice Hew Garven depairt this mortall lyff be reassone of the strokes given to him be the said Williame Fullertoune and for his peaceable deportment heireftir.

Act anent Williame Fullertoune.

The quhilk day anent the supplicatioun given in befoire the saids Magistratis and Councell be James Broun tanner burges of this brugh againes John Guthrie lait proveist mentioning that quher in sommer last the petitioner having gathered togidder ane certain considderable quantitie of stones for building within this brugh and having caused heap the samen at the foot of the staine calsay Trew it is and of veritie that the said John Guthrie be himself and uthers in his name at his comand and directione and for his awin behove hes caused transport the saidis stones fra the place quher they had bein heaped be the petitioner to his awin yaird dyks without libertie fra the petitioner intending to apply the samen to his awin use And therfoire desyring warrand fra the saidis Magistrates and Councell to mak use of the saidis stones for his building Quhilk supplicatioune being hard sein and considderit be the saidis Magistratis and Councell upon the tuentie day of October last bypast They appoynted the said John Guthrie to be lawfullie wairned be ane ordinar officer to compeir befoire them to anser to the said complaint, and the said John Guthrie being accordinglie wairned be Hew Parker officer deuly certefied in Councell and nocht compeirand the Magistratis and Councell eftir exact tryall taken be them of the said supplicatioune ffand that the saidis stones did belong to the petitioner being gathered and heiped be him and uthers in his name for his use in manner contenit in the said supplicatioune and therfoire grants warrand to the petitioner to intromett with and leid away the samen to his awin use for his building The petitioner alwayes leiding als mony stones for the use of the said John Guthrie to the samen place quher the saidis stones now ly fra ony place quher the said John Guthrie sall keip the samen being at no greater distance nor the stones intromettit with be the said John Guthrie wes the tyme of his intromissione therwith. Sic subscribitur: Robert Cunyngheme, provist.

Irving the threttine day of November 1665 yeirs:—

Burgess.
E. Rothes, lord Comissioner

Qvo die Robertus Cunynghame prepositus dicti burgi de Irving Henricus Lyne unus ballivorum ejusdem cum avisamento et consensu consiliariorum dicti burgi insimul et frequenter judicialiter congregatorum in pretorio ejusdem burgi admiserunt et creaverunt nobilem et prepotentem comitem Joannem Comitem de Rothes dominum Leslie et Bellinbreigh supremum Comissionarium huius regni Scotie burgensem fratrem que gilde dicti burgi et hoc pro suo auxilio et benemerito dicto burgo et reipublicæ ejusdem impenso que desuper petiit instrumenta.

Lord Ogilvie.

Item admiserunt et creaverunt Jacobum dominum Ogilvie burgensem fratremque gilde dicti burgi et hoc pro suo benemerito et auxilio dicto burgo et reipublice ejusdem impenso, etc.

Lord Cathcart.

Item admiserunt et creaverunt Allanum dominum Cathcart burgensem fratremque gilde dicti burgi et hoc pro suo benemerito et auxilio dicto burgo prestito et impenso etc.

Lord Forrester.

Item Jacobum dominum Forrester burgensem fratremque gilde dicti burgi et hoc pro suo auxilio et benemerito dicto burgo impenso, etc.

Mungo Murray.

Item Quintigernum Murray fratrem germanum Comitis de Atholl burgensem fratremque gilde dicti burgi et hoc pro suo auxilio et benemerito dicto burgo impenso.

John Naper.

Item Joannem Naper fratrem germanum Domini Naper burgensem, etc. [as above].

L. Buchannie.

Item Jacobum Lumsdaill de Buchannie, etc.

Item Adamum Urquhart de Meldrum etc — L. Meldrum.
Item Gulielmum Arnott etc. — William Arnot.
Item Joannem Boill juniorem de Kelburne etc. — L. Kelburne.
Item Henricum Mackie servitorem Comitis de Rothes etc. — Henrie Mackie.
Item Capitanum Andream Patersone burgensem etc. — Capt. Andrew Patersone.
Item Capitanum Thomam Hamiltoun etc. — Capt. Thos. Hamilton.
Item Majorem Georgium Grant gubernatorem de Dumbartane deputatum etc. — Major Grant.
Item Capitanum Andream Dick etc. — Captaine Dick.
Item Robertum Chalmer fratrem germanum Joannis Chalmer de Gaitgirth etc. — Robert Chalmer.
Item Thomam Ogilvie servitorem domini Ogilvie etc. — Thomas Ogilvie.
Item Capitanum Joannem Binning etc. — Captain Binning.
Item Jacobum Ogilvie fratrem germanum domini Davidis Ogilvie de Innerqularitie militis, burgensem etc. — James Ogilvie.
Item Jacobum Gilbert servitorem Comitis de Rothes, burgensem etc. — James Gilbert.
Item Joannem Gordoun servitorem Comitis de Linlythgow. — Jo^n Gordoun.
Item Walterum Abercrombie, burgensem etc. — Walter Abercrombie.
Item Joannem Scott chirurgium Comitis de Rothes burgensem etc. — Jo^n Scott.
Item admiserunt et creaverunt Thomam Cristmas servitorem Comitis de Rothes burgensem fratremque gilde dicti burgi et hoc pro favore dicti sui Magistri. — Thomas Christmas.
Item Robertum Lundie servitorem dicti Comitis de Rothes burgensem fratremque gilde dicti burgi et hoc pro favore dicti sui magistri. — Ro^t Lundie.
Item —— Cumming servitorem dicti Comitis de Rothes burgensem fratremque gilde dicti burgi et hoc pro favore sui magistri etc. — Cuming.
Item Joannem Forbes servitorem dicti Comitis de Rothes et hoc etc. — Jo^n Forbes.
Item Joannem Houlatsone servitorem dicti nobilis Comitis . et hoc etc. — Jo^n Houlatsone.
Item Joannem Bell servitorem dicti Comitis . . . et hoc etc. — Jo^n Bell.
Item Jacobum Houlatsone servitorem dicti Comitis de Rothes etc. — James Houlatsone.
Item Jacobum Dausone servitorem dicti Comitis etc. — James Dausone.
Item Joannem Colvill servitorem dicti Comitis etc. — Jo^n Colvill.
Item Joannem Buchannane servitorem dicti Comitis etc. — Jo^n Buchannane.
Item Alexandrum Douglas servitorem dicti Comitis etc. — Alex^r Douglas.
Item Willielmum Adame servitorem dicti Comitis etc. — William Adame.

Jo{n} Done.	Item Joannem Done servitorem dicti Comitis etc.
Archibald Robertsone.	Item Archibaldum Robertsone servitorem dicti Comitis de Rothes etc.
Wm Robertsone.	Item Willielmum Robertsone servitorem dicti Comitis etc.
David Arnot.	Item Davidem Arnot servitorem dicti Comitis etc.
Wm Murray.	Item Gullielmum Murray servitorem dicti Comitis de Rothes etc.
Alexr Blair.	Item Alexandrum Blaire servitorem Comitis de Eglintoun . . et hoc pro favore etc.
Jo{n} Park.	Item Joannem Park de Dubbis servitorem dicti Comitis de Eglintoun . . et hoc etc.
Patrik Houstoun.	Item Patricium Houstoun servitorem dicti Comitis de Eglintoun etc.
Robert Maldsone.	Item Robertum Maldsone servitorem dicti Comitis de Eglintoun etc.
Jo{n} Kello.	Item Joannem Kello servitorem dicti Comitis etc.
James Nairne.	Item Jacobum Nairne servitorem dicti Comitis etc.
Jo{n} Smyth.	Item Joannem Smyth servitorem dicti Comitis de Eglintoun etc.
Jo{n} Steill.	Item Joannem Steill servitorem dicti Comitis etc.
Jo{n} Quhyt.	Item Joannem Quhyt servitorem dicti Comitis de Eglintoun.
James Ker.	Item Jacobum Ker servitorem dicti Comitis etc.
Jo{n} Eglintoun.	Item Joannem Eglintoun servitorem dicti Comitis.
Andrew Fischer.	Item Andream Fischer servitorem Comitis de Loudoun . . . et hoc etc.
George Hay.	Item Georgium Hay servitorem Domini Montgomerie burgensem fratremque gilde . . et hoc pro favore dicti sui Magistri.
Adam Davidson.	Item Adamum Davidsone servitorem Domini de Cathcart etc.
Wm M'Lurg.	Item Willielmum M'Lurge servitorem dicti Domini de Cathcart etc.
David Cunyngham.	Item Davidem Cunynghame servitorem dicti Domini etc.
James Rae.	Item Jacobum Rae servitorem dicti Domini etc.
William Muir.	Item Willielmum Muire servitorem Majoris Hugonis Bunteiu etc.
James Leslies.	Item Jacobum Leslies servitorem Henrici Mackie etc.
James Maghie.	Item Jacobum Maghie servitorem Willielmi Arnot burgensem etc. . et hoc pro favore dicti sui Magistri.
Thomas Schort.	Item Thomam Schort servitorem Quintigerni Murray etc.
Jo{n} Urquhart.	Item Joannem Urquhart servitorem Adami Urquhard de Meldrum etc.
David Walker.	Item Davidem Walker servitorem Joannis Boill Junioris de Kelburne etc.
George Abercrombie.	Item Georgium Abercrombie servitorem Comitis de Rothes etc.
Alexr Montgomerie.	Item ——— Alexandrum Montgomerie servitorem Montgomerie de Hesilheid etc.

Item Alexandrum Tailyeor servitorem Capitani Andree Dick etc. Alex' Tailyeor.
Item Jacobum Buchannane servitorem Jacobi Domini Forrester. James Buchannane.
Item Hugonem Lin in Corshill servitorem dicti Comitis de Eglintoun Hugh Lin.
etc.

Item Davidem Biggert mercatorem burgensem burgi de Edinburgh bur- David Biggart.
gensem fratremque gilde dicti burgi et hoc tanquam filio legittimo quondam
Thome Biggart mercatoris burgensis et fratris gilde dicti burgi qui solutus
est muletum et prestitit juramentum fidelitatis more solito qui desuper
petiit instrumenta.

Item Robertum Bar mercatorem in Kilwining burgensem dicti burgi de Bar.
Irving qui solutus est muletum et prestitit juramentum fidelitatis more
solito qui, etc.

Irving the flourtein day of November 1665:—

THE quhilk day the pettie customes of this brugh according to use and wont Pettie Customes.
eftir publict roping are sett to Robert Stewart merchand burges of this
brugh for ane yeir to come, viz. fra Mertimes 1665 yeirs untill Mertimes nixtocome 1666 yeirs ffor the soume of sevinscoire ane merks Scots ffor payment
quhairof the said Robert Stewart as principall and with him John Smaillie
meillman as cautioner and souirtie for him band and obleist them conjunctlie
and severallie to mak payment to the thesaurer of this brugh at the termes
useit and wont under the paine of ane thrid penny mare threttine schilling
foure pennyes being given in earnest and in pairt of payment of the samen
Sic subscribitur: Robert Stewart. Ar. Hamiltone, at comand of John
Smaillie. Gilbert Wyllie, *witnes*; John Porter, *witnes*.

THE quhilk day the Magistratis with consent of the maist pairt of the Porter burges.
Councell frequentlie conveined admitted and created Johne Porter tailyeor
burges of this brugh quha gave his aith of fidelitie as use is and referrit the
quantitie of his fyne to the modificatioun of the Magistrat and Johne Porter
merchand becomes cautioner for payment thairof to the thesaurer and he to
releive his cautioner. Sic subscribitur: John Porter: Johne Porter,
cautioner.

Irving the twenty fourth day of November 1665:—

Sederunt.

Robert Cunynghame, proveist
Allane Cunynghame
Adame Fullertoun
William Slos
Robert Allane, councellours

Henry Lyne baillie
Robert Francis
John Ros
Andro Calderwood
John M'Gill, consellours

James Jonstoune, pro^r fischal

Ros.

THE quhilk day continowes the making of Niniane Ros and Hew Cunynghame ther thesaurer accompts untill the nixt councell day.

Anent James Fullertoun his band.

THE quhilk the said Adame Fullertoun produceit in the presens of the saids Magistratis and Councell ane band granted to this brugh be James Fullertoun lait baillie conteining the soume of twelff hundreth merks Scots principall soume with penaltie and annualrent daited the sextein day of December 1663 yeirs quhilk is laid up in the chartor kist. The Magistratis and Councell ordeins John Gray present thesaurer to be chairged with tua yeirs annualrent thairof, viz. fra Mertimes 1663 to Mertimes last.

Anent the brig.

THE quhilk day the Magistratis and Councell of this brugh taking to thair considderatione the ruinous conditione of ther brig situat over the watter of Irving being schrunk in the pillers and decayet in the pen therof sua that the samen is lyklie presentlie to become unpassible to man or beast and sua useles and of ther present inhabilitie to re-edifie and repair the samen have therfoire unanimouslie granted Comissione to the said Robert Cunynghame proveist to repaire to Edinburgh upon the twenty eight day of November instant and to attend ther upon the comoun chairges of the brugh ffor supplicateing his Magesties most honorabill Comissioner and privie Councell for supply towardis the repairing and re-edificing of the said brig.

Anent money den to the proveist and clearing of accompts with him previding that tytue.

THE quhilk day the Magistratis and Councell grants warrand and comissione to John Broun James Wodsyd or any uther thesaurer quha hes any of the tounes money in ther hands to pay to the said Robert Cunynghame proveist the soume of ane hundreth threttie pundis nyne schilling four pennyes Scottis deburst be him for the Toune affaires in Julij and August last and for officers cloathes conforme to the particular accompt produceit in presens of the Councell unanimouslie approven and quhilk is to be allowed to the thesaurer payer therof in his thesaurer accompt.

Irving the 15th December 1665 :—
Sederunt.

Henry Lyne, baillie
William Slos
Robert Allane
Andro Calderwood
David Dunlop

John Reid
Robert Francis
Allane Cunynghame
Archibald Marr
John M'Gill

THE quhilk day the baillie and Councell ordeins the tua yeirs annualrent of the foirsaid tuelff hundreth merks to be uplifted fra the said James Fullertoun betuixt and Monday nixt that the samen may be sent to Edinburgh to Robert Cunynghame proveist for helping the defraying of his chairges ther in attending the tounes affaires and appoyntis Wm. Dyet and Adame Fullertoune lait thesaurers to advance to that effect twenty foure pundis Scots equallie betuix them quhilk is to be allowet to them in ther accomptis quhilk with the annualrent will extend unto ane hundreth and twenty pundis Scots. _{Anent money to be sent to the proveist.}

THE quhilk day ordeins Niniane Ros to produce the report of his thesaurer accompt under the handis of the foirsaidis auditors the nixt Councell day. _{Ros his thesaurer accompt.}

THE quhilk day ordeins John Gray present thesaurer to furnisch to the guard quha are to keip watch in the tolbuith durcing Captaine Thompsone and his pairtie ther aboid in this brugh daylie ane load of coalles and half ane pund of candle to be allowet to him in his thesaurer accompt. _{Coall and candle to the guard.}

Irving the 22nd December 1665 :—
Sederunt.

Henry Lyne, baillie
Allane Cunynghame
Archibald Muir
Robert Allane
John M'Gill

John Reid
Williame Slos
Andro Calderwood
James Jonstoune, procuratour fischall
Robert Francis

THE quhilk day the Magistratis and Councell of this brugh being perfytlie informeit of the manifold fornicationes or adulteries comitted be Jonet

Muir quha hes already brocht furth tua children in fornicatione or adulterie and is presentlie with child not knowing perfytlie to quhom and of her unchast cariage have therfoire ordeinit her to be banisched furth of this brugh betuixt and the first day of January nixtocome and nevir to returne againe under the paine of most severe punischement and sicklyk dischairges all the inhabitants of this brugh and everie ane of them to ressait harbor or intertein her in ther houss or to sett ony hous or chamber to her eftir the said day under the paine of ffourty pundis Scots to be payet be ilk persone contraveiner toties quoties.

Anent Collectors. The quhilk day ordeins Allane Cunynghame, John Gray, James Jonstoun, Adam Cunynghame younger, James Gemill, Niniane Holmes, George Erskine, Robert Nesmyth, Williame Slos, Thomas Galt, Andrew Gemill, to mak accompt of ther collectioune and intromissione with the stentis imposed upon this brugh the tyme of ther being collectors upon Tuesday nixt in presens of Johne Gottray lait proveist James Blaire lait baillie Alexander Dyet and John Porter or ony thrie of them quha are nominat auditors for that effect and to report to the Councell the nixt Councell day and ordaines the officers to wairne all of them for that effect.

Niniane Ros. Item ordeins Niniane Ros to report his thesaurer accompt under the auditors handis the nixt Councell day.

Anent quarter-maisters. Item nominats Alexr. Cochrane, William Gardner, John Porter, Hugh Thompsone weivar, James Jonstoun, Adame Cunynghame younger, Laurence Blaire . . . . . to be quartermaisters of this brugh for equalizing the soldier quarters dureing ther aboile and the assistant quartermaisters for coall candle and bedding.

Irving the secund day of Februarij 1666 :—
Sederunt.

Robert Cunynghame, proveist	Henry Lyne, baillie
Robert Francis	William Dyet
Robert Woodsyd	Robert Allane
John Gray	Archibald Muir
David Dunlop	John M'Gill
Andro Caldirwood, councellors	John Reid

William Slos, consellors

Act against Ros. The quhilk day the Magistratis and Councell considdering the severall delayes maid be Niniane Ros anent the cleiring of his thesaurer accompt doe therfoire ordaine the officers of this brugh to apprehend the persone of the said Niniane Ros and to incarcerat him within the tolbuith of the said brugh therin to remaine upon his awin expenss ay and quhill the said thesaurer accomptis be cleired.

Item ordeins James Blaire lait bailyie to be wairned to the nixt Counccll to cleir his thesaurer accompt.

Irving the sextein day of February 1666 :—

Sederunt.

Robert Cunynghame, proveist	Henry Lyne, baillie
John Reid	Robert Francis
James Woodsyd	Robert Woodsyd
Williame Slos	Robert Allane
John Gray	John M'Gill
Williame Dyet	Andro Caldirwood
Allane Cunynghame, counsellors	Archibald Muir, counsellors

James Jonstoun, pro' fischall

THE quhilk day Robert Woodsyd merchand enacts and obleiss himselff to satisfie and pay to the thesaurers of this brugh the haill bygane feu-deuty and teind that wes restand unpayet of his landis of Spittellmeidow with threttie eight shilling eight pennyes Scots of compositione for his entrie to the saids landis and that upon demand. Sic subscribitur : Robert Woodsyd. *Act Woodsyd.*

THE quhilk day John Gib officer as procurator for Mr. Alexander Tran sone lawfull to umquhill Mr. Robert Tran minster having resignit in the handis of the said proveist for himselff and in name of the Councell and communitie of the said brugh the landis of Spittellmeidow belonging to the said Alexander Tran in favoris and for new infeftment therof to be maid and grantit to Robert Woodsyd of the samen The said baillie and Councell grantis hereby comissione to the said Robert Cunynghame to give stait and seasing therof to said Robert Woodsyd and his spous conforme to the chartour subscribit be them in all poyntis. *Comissione for Woodsyd.*

THE quhilk day ordeins John Gottray lait proveist to be ci[ted] . . . befoir them the nixt Councell day anent the fyve pund sterling . . be him fra Alexr. Orr. *[Part of leaf torn away.]*

200   MUNIMENTS OF THE BURGH OF IRVINE.

Item ordeinis James Blaire lait bailyie to be cited and wairned to appeir befoire them the nixt Councell day for cleiring ther thesaurer accompts.

Anent Stent-maisters.

THE quhilk day the Magistratis and Councell nominats and appoynts James Woodsyd, Allane Cunynghame, Robert Woodsyd, Robert Allane, John Gray, Robert Francis, Alexander Cochrane, Thomas Biggart, Hew Thompsone, flescher, Niniane Holmes, James Blaire lait baillie, James Kyll, Andro Hendersone, Hew Thompsone younger weivar, and John Porter merchand stentmaisters ffor imposeing of the soume of tuenty pund sterling ffor upmaking of the inlaik of the soume of eight hundreth merks chairged upon this brugh for ther proportione of the soume of ffourscoire thousand merks appoynted be Act of Parliament to be imployed for defraying of his Majesties personall chairges in anno 1650 yeirs In regaird the soume now to be imposed wes imployed for payment of the rests deu to Bogie and Smyth upon the accompt of singular successors and for releiff of quartering.

M'Cleane burges.

THE quhilk day the Magistratis and Councell creatis John M'Cleane merchand burges of this brugh quha gave his aith as use is and referrit the modificatioune of his fyne to the Magistratis for payment quharof to the thesaurer James Jonstoune couper becomes cautioner and he to releive his cautioner. Sic subscribitur: Jo. M'Cleane   James Jonstoun.

At Irving the secund day of March 1666 :—

Ancorage and teind.

THE quhilk day the watter baillieschip haill ancorage and teind of the Watter of Irving (the teind of the cobbles being except) is sett to Robert Cunynghame present provest for the space of ane yeir nixt ensewing the dait heirof, viz. fra the secund day of March instant to the secund day of March nixtocome in anno j^m vj^c sextie sevin yeirs ffor the soume of thriescoire fyve pund Scotts money to be payett be him to the thesaurer of this brugh at the ordinar terme of payment ffor payment quherof Allane Cunyngham younger merchand is become actit as cautioner and souirtie for the said Robert Cunynghame and the said Robert Cunynghame acted and obleist himselff to releive the said cautioner. Sic subscribitur: Robert Cunynghame   Allane Cunynghame.

COUNCIL BOOK.

Irving the ffirst day of May 1666:—

THE quhilk day eftir publict ropeing the gras of the Grein of this brugh is sett to Bryce Muire messenger for the ensewing seasone ffor the soume of ffourty foure pund sex shilling eyght pennyes Scotts to be payet be him to the thesaurer at the ordinar tyme of payment ffor payment quherof Hew Montgomerie merchand actit himselff as cautioner and the said Bryce Muir acted himselff to releive his said cautioner. Sic subscribitur: Bryce Muire Hew Montgomerie. *Gras of the Grein.*

THE quhilk day eftir publict ropeing the gras of the Rotten boige of the said brugh is sett to Robert Cunynghame present proveist for the nixt ensewing seasone for the soume of ffyve merks Scotts to be payet be him to the thesaurer of the said brugh at the ordinar tyme of payment ffor payment quherof James Woodsyd merchand actit himselff cautioner and the said Robert Cunynghame actit himselff to releive his cautioner. Sic subscribitur: Robert Cunynghame   James Woodsyd. *Rotten boige.*

Irving the seventein day of Maij 1666:—

THE quhilk day eftir publict ropeing the teind of the Cobles is sett to Robert Cunnynghame proveist for the ensewing yeir for the soume of nyne pound Scotts to be payet be him to the thesaurer of this brugh at the ordinar tyme of payment ffor payment quherof John Ros merchand becomes actit as cautioner and sourtie for the said Robert Cunynghame and the said Robert Cunynghame acted himselff to releive his cautioner. Sic subscribitur: Johne Ros, cationer   Robert Cunynghame. *Teind of the Cobbills.*

Irving the sevint day of June 1666:—

THE quhilk day the chop beneath the Tolbuith staire is sett to George Erskine tailyeor for the yeir to come for nyne merks Scotts money quherof tuelff shilling payet to be payet to the thesaurer of this brugh at the ordinar terme of payment ffor payment quherof Archibald Muir merchand becomes cautioner and the said George obleiss him to releive his cautioner. Sic subscribitur: Archibald Muir   George Askine. *Chop beneath the tolbuith staire.*

THE quhilk day the new and old custome of the Brig is sett to Archibald Muire merchand for the ensewing yeir for the soume of ane hundreth sex *Custome of the brig.*

pundis Scotts to be payet to the thesaurer of this brugh at the ordinar terme of payment ffor payment quherof James Woodsyd merchand is become cautioner and the said Archibald is obleist to releive his cautioner and tuelff pence given in earnest. Sic subscribitur: James Woodsyd Archibald Muir.

Irving the 15th day of June 1666 :—
Sederunt.

Robert Cunynghame, proveist	Henry Lyne, baillie
James Woodsyd	Robert Francis
Robert Woodsyd	Williame Slos
Allane Cunynghame	Andro Calderwood
Wm. Dyet	Ro{t} Allane
Jo{n} Ros, consellours	Jo{n} M'Gill, counsellours

Unlaw Fullertoun and Gray. THE quhilk day unlawis Adame Fullertoune and John Gray ilkane of tham in the soume of threttie schilling Scots for absenting themselves fra the councell.

Anent the stent, 1666, for the taxatioune payments. THE quhilk day ordeins foure moneths assesment to be presentlie uplyfted conforme to the stent roll imposed upon this brucht for on moneth and sett doune be the foirsaid stentmaisters for satisfeing the said brughs taxatioune grantit to his Maiestie in August 1665 yeirs for the first termes payment thairof being the Witsunday terme 1666 yeirs And for satisfieing of sextein pund Sterling payet out at Ayr upon the tuenty fyft day of November last bypast for the singular successors to Sir John Weymis of Bogie and his deputes and for quarterings and for Williame Chalmers his service to the brught.

Anent the brig. THE quhilk day nominats James Blaire lait baillie and Thomas Biggart merchand burgessis of this brucht Commissioners for the brugh for agreing with quarriers for winneing of stanes for reparatioun of the brig and for leiding therof And ordeins and appoyntis James Woodsyd lait thesaurer to advance quhat money is necessar for that effect and for satisfeing of the saidis Commissioneris for ther paines and travell.

Unlawis Reids. THE quhilk unlawis Mr. John Reid marchand traveller in tuenty rex-dollours for selling of ane parcell of meill to John Reid eldar, merchand, imported be the said Mr. John Reid to this harborie and brugh of Irving and sold be him to the said John Reid eftir he wes prohibit be the Magistratis to mak venditioun therof, and notwithstanding of the said bargaine (In respect of the prohibitione foirsaid) ordeins the meill to be sold to the inhabitants of this brugh at eight shilling sex pennyes Scotts the peck being the pryce for quhich the said Mr. John Reid offerit the samen to the Magistratis for the use of the brugh and that for the space of twenty day eftir the dait heirof The pryce foirsaid to be payet in be the buyer to the said Mr. John Reid Item amerciatis and unlawis the said John Reid elder in ten rex dollours for his miscariage in face of councell and both pairtyes to remaine in prisone quhill the fynes be payet.

Irving 26 June 1666 :—
Sederunt.

Robert Cunynghame, proveist   Henry Lyne, baillie
Andro Calderwood   Robert Allane
John M'Gill, counsellouris

THE quhilk day unlawis and amerciatis James Sampsone in Dundonald flescheor in fyftie eight shilling Scotis ffor his bringing to the publict mercat of this brugh unsufficient blowne muttoune for making venditioune therof and ordains him to remaine in prison quhill it be payet.

Irving the threttin day of Julij 1666 :—

THE quhilk day Henry Lyne baillie with consent of the maist pairt of the Councell of this brugh nominats and creatts Williame Dickie wricht burges of this brugh quha gave his aith of fidelitie as use and referit the fyne to the said baillie his modificaicoune for payment of quhich fyne to the Toun thesaurer of this brugh George Garven is becom cautioner sourtie and the said Wiliame Dickie to releive his cautioner. Sic subscribitur: G. Garven Williame Dickie.   *For Wm Slos his roll for the 1667 Burges Dickie.*

Fourtein July 1666 :—

THE said baillie with consent of the Councell creatts and admits Robert Steinsone wricht burges of this brugh quha gave his aith as use is and referit his fyne to the baillie. Laurence Speir cautioner therfoir.   *Burges Steinsone.*

Irving the 24th Julij 1666 :—

Irving to Cunyngham.

THE quhilk day in presens of Henric Lyne baillie compeirit James Irving who sold to Robert Cuninghame proveist ane gray meir ringeyed one the farsyd and ane duck one the face one the sam syde with ane quhyt cloud under the sadle the said syde of the aige of ffyve yeares befoire thir witnessis William Fullertoune wright and William Fullertoune younger his sone and the said Henric Lyne baillie. James Irving Henric Lyne, *witnes*; Wilame Fulartown, *witnes*; Wilaume Fullarton, *witnes*.

Irving to Thompsone.

EODEM die ane mous broune colloured horse short rumped without any quhyt spot with ane sore place upone the top of the shoudher of the aige of sex yeares sold be the said James Irving to Williame Thompsone sword slypper burgess of the said brugh before thir witnesses William Fullertoune wright in Irving and William Fullertoune younger his sone and Henric Lyne, baillie. James Irving Henric Lyn, *witnes*; Wilame Fularttown, *witnes*; Willaum Fularton, *witnes*.

Irving the tuentie ane day of August 1666 :—

Sederunt.

Ro' Cunynghame, proveist	Henry Lyne, baillie
Allane Cunynghame	Robert Woodsyd
Jo⁰ Gray	Ro' Allane
Ro' Francis	Andro Calderwood
Archibald Muire	Williame Slos
Jo⁰ M'Gill, counsellouris	James Woodsyd, counsellouris

Exemption fra the custome of the brig. E. Eglintoun.

THE quhilk day the Magistrats and Counsell aforsaid taking to ther considderatioun the manifold gratitudes and good deids done and performit to this brughe be ane noble and potent Earle Hugh Earl of Eglintoune lord Montgomerie and Kilwining tending to the weill and comodite of the said brugh and especiallie the procureing be his lordships moyane of ane Act of his Maiesties Privie Councell in favors of the said brughe quhairby ther is ane custome granted to them of passengers and goods transportit ovir the Brig of Irving for nyntein yeirs Have therfoire exeemed the said noble Earle his servandis and familie fra payment of the said custome during the space foirsaid of the said Act for ther passing or repassing ovir the said brig with goods or utherwayes. Sic subscribitur: Robert Cunynghame, proveist Henry Lyne, baillie Wm. Slos, councellour Andro Calderwood, councellour Joʰ Gray, thesaurer Robert Francis, councellour Joʰ M'Gill James Woodsyd, councellour Allane Cunynghame, councellour Robert Woodsyd, councellour Robert Allane.

Irving the nyntein day of September 1666 :—

THE quhilk day Andrew Cultoun indwellar within this brugh is admittit and created be the said proveist baillie and ane great pairt of the Councell burges of the brugh quha gave his aith of fidelitie as use is and referrit the fyne to the modificatioun of the Magistrats. Burges Cultoun.

Irving the tuentie eight day of September 1666 :—

Sederunt.

Robert Cunynghame, proveist   Henry Lyne, baillie
Robert Francis   John Reid
Williame Slos   Robert Allane
Andro Calderwood   Archibald Muir
David Dunlop   Williame Dyet
John M'Gill—counsellours

THE quhilk day be pluralitie of votes the saidis proveist baillie Robert Francis Johne Reid Andrew Calderwood David Dunlop and Allane Cunynghame merchand Robert Allane John Ros James Woodsyd Adame Fullertoun Hew Thompsone Laurence Blaire Alexander Cochrane and James Kyll merchandis John Steill tailyeor and William Suantoun saidler to be Counsellours of this brugh for the yeir to com. Nominatioun of Councellours.

Be pluralitie of voites the persons eftirnameit are leeted for proveist for the yeir to come, viz.—

Robert Cunynghame, present proveist   Mr. Robert Barclay
Allane Dunlop of Craig

Leeted for Baillies.

Henry Lyne, present baillie   Allane Cunyng[hame]
James Blaire   Robert Wallace
James Fullertoun   Laurence Blaire

Irving the secund day of October 1666 :—

Electione of Counsellours.

THE quhilk day convenit within the Councell hous Robert Cunynghame proveist Henry Lyne baillie The saidis Robert Francis John Reid David Dunlop Robert Allane Andro Calderwood John Ros Hugh Thompson James Kyll John Steill and Williame Suantoune quha being solemnly suorne acceptit the office of councellour upon thame and for faithfull administratione therof during the yeir to come The saidis Adame Fullertoun Allane Cunynghame Alexander Cochrane James Woodsyd and Laurence Blaire being for the present abscnt are appoynted to accept at thair returne.

THE quhilk day convenit for electione of the Magistratis the new admitted councellors above nameit with the old councellours following to wit Williame Slos George Lyndsay Gilbert Wyllie Williame Dyet Archibald Muir John M'Gill and James Wricht quha being suorne for fidelitie as use is electit the persones following to be Magistratis for the yeir to come, viz.—

                Robert Cunynghame, proveist
        Henry Lyne   Laurence Blaire, baillies

Proveist, baillies acceptationes.

THE quhilk day the saidis Robert Cunyngham and Henry Lyne compeirand as said is, acceptit the saidis offices in and upon thame and gave thair aithes of fidelitie as use is And the said Laurence Blaire is ordered to accept and give his aith at his returne.

Thesaurer.

THE quhilk day the saidis Magistratis and Councell elected and nominat Williame Slos merchand to be thesaurer of this brugh for the yeir to come quha compeirand personallie acceptit the samen in and upon him and gave his aith of fidelitie as use is.

Procurator fischall.

THE quhilk day Williame Thompsone armorer is electit procurator fischall of this brugh for the yeir to come quha being present acceptit the said office in and upon him and gave his aith of fidelitie as use is.

Comissione Cunynghame.

THE quhilk day grantis comissione to Robert Cunynghame proveist to infeft and seasing Thomas Boyd in Kilmarnok and Jeane Tailycor his spous in the landis apprysed be thame fra James Tailycor sone to Robert Tailycor cowper conforme to the decreet of apprysing, quhilk are halden of the Toune in ordinar feu.

Irving the 12th day of October 1666 :—
Sederunt.

Robert Cunynghame, proveist	Henry Lyne, baillie
Robert Allane	James Kyll
John Ros	Hugh Thompsone
John Steill counsellours	Williame Suuntoun, counsellours

William Slos thesaurer

The Magistrats and Councell ordeins the officers of this brugh to wairne Laurence Blaire elect bailyie Adame Fullertoun and Alexander Cochrane counsellours to compeir before thame upon the sextein day of October instant to accept of ther respective offices ilk person under the paine of tuenty punds money.

The quhilk day the Magistrats and Councell creats and admittis John Henderson cordeinner burges of this brugh quha gave his aith of fidelitie as use is and referrit his fyne to the Magistrats modificatione and for payment quhairof James Hendersone wricht became cautioner and he obleiss himselff to releive his cautioner. Sic subscribitur : James Hendersone A. Hamiltone at command of John Hendersone. *Burges Hendersone.*

The quhilk day Robert Bar merchand in Kilwining being maid burges of this brugh be the proveist bailyie and counsell of the samen upon the threttine day of November last bypast acted and obleist himselff to pay to the saidis Magistrats or ther thesaurere for the tyme his burges fyne the quantitie quhairof he referrit to the saidis Magistrats thair modificatione And siclyk in caice that he used any frie traid of merchandicing within the said brughe or liberties tharof that he sould be lyabill in payment of the publict burdeingis to be imposed upon the said brugh conform to his traid. Robert Bar. *Act Robert Bar.*

Irving the threttine day of November 1666 :—

The quhilk day the pettie customes of this brugh is sett for the yeir to come, viz. fra Mertimes 1666 To Mertimes 1667 yeirs to Williame Thompsone armorer burges of this brugh for the soume of thriescoire ellevin pundis Scotts money to be payd to the Magistrats of this brugh and thar thesaurer at the termes useit and wont for payment quhairof Johne Snaillie meilman in Irving became cautioner and souirtie under the paine of ane thrid penny moire and the said Williame Thompsone to releive *Pettie customes.*

his cautioner. Tuelff shilling given in earnest. Sic subscribitur: William Thompsone   Ar. Hamiltone at comand of Johne Smaillie cautioner.

Irving the sextein day of November 1666:—
Sederunt.

Robert Cunynghame, proveist	Henry Lyne, baillie
John Reid	Williame Slos, thesaurer
Andro Calderwood	Hugh Thompsone
John Ros	Robert Allane
Williame Suantoun	John Speir

William Thompsone, procurator fischall

Precept for the Minister. THE quhilk day the Magistrats and Councell ordeins ane precept to be drawne upon Johne Quhyt in Holme mylne and Johne Boill in Loch mylne to pay to Mr. Alexander Neisbit minister tua chalders victuall half meill half beir quhilk is restand to him be the toune of stipend the cropt 1665 yeirs and uther bill or precept to be drawne upon William Thompsone armorer of fourty pundis Scotis to be payet to the said minister of housemaill preceiding Witsunday last and the said victuall and money sall be allowit in the first end of the accompts they produce and the minister's dischairge conforme to the saids preceptis.

Citatione of Councellours. ITEM ordeins Laurence Blaire Alexander Cochrane and Adame Fullerton to be wairned be the officers to appeir befoire tham the nixt Councell day to accept thar offices according to thar electioun with certificatioun.

Candle. ITEM ordeins and appoynts ilk pund candle to be sold at the rait of thrie
Bread. schilling foure pennyes for this seasone and ilk loaff of quheit to be tuelff ounce weight of sufficient bread and to be sold at tuelff pennyes Scotis and the contravenar to pay fyve pund *toties quoties*.

Irving the tuentie eight of December 1666:—
Sederunt.

Robert Cunynghame, proveist	Henry Lyne, baillie
Robert Allane	Andrew Calderwood
Robert Frances	John Ros
John Steill	Williame Suantoun

Acceptatioun of Councellours. THE quhilk day compeirit the saids Alexander Cochrane James Woodsyd and Allane Cunynghame quha wes nominat Councellours the tyme of the electione maid at Michaelmes last for the yeir to come and acceptit the said office in and upon thame and gave ther aithes of fidelitie as use is.

THE quhilk day nominats and appoynts Johne Porter Alexander Dyet and the clerk to audit the lait thesaurers and collectors of stents thair accomptis and to conveine tham befoire themselvis fra tyme to tyme and to report ther procedure thairintill to the Councell quha are to tak present course for compelling the deficients to pay ther deus eftir compt to be maid. *Commissioners for auditing accomptis.*

THE quhilk day finds that Andro Calderwood Archbald Muir Robert Allane and Hugh Garven youngair quha wer appoynted Collectours for uplyfting of the stent imposed upon this brugh upon the sevintein day of October 1665 yeirs for payment of the eight hundreth merks Scotis being the Townes proportione of the soume of Foure scoire thousand merks quhilk the royall borrowes of this kingdome were be Act of Parliament appoyntit to advance for payment of his Majestie's personall chairges in anno 1650 hes satisfiet the said stent and siclyk that Alexander Dyet Williame M'Tagart Johne Huntere and Hugh Kilpatrick quha wer appoynted Collectors for ingathering of the stent imposed upon this brugh upon the tuelff day of June last bypast for payment of the Witsunday termes taxatioun 1666 yeirs being the first termes taxatioun grantit to his Majestie in August 1665 yeirs and the remanent of Bogie's ces and quarterings hes also satisfiet the said stent And therfoire in regard the saidis burdeings are satisfiet with the saidis Stentis the Magistrate and Councell exoners and dischairges the saidis Collectors therof in tyme comeing conforme to the dischairges grantit to them be the proveist and bailyie therof. *Exoneratione of Collectors.*

THE quhilk day nominats Robert Cunynghame proveist to be Commissioner for the brugh for attending the ensewing conventione of Estates quhilk is appoyntit be his Majestie to be halden at Edinburgh the nynt day of Januarij nixtocome and that ane Comissione be drawin up theranent. *Ro: Cunynghame Commissioner.*

THE quhilk day creats and admits David Craufurd cordonner burges of this brugh quha gave his aith as use is and referrit his fyne to the modificatioun of the Magistrats for payment quhairof William Galt meillar is become cautioner and he acted himselff to releive his said cautioner. Sic subscribitur: Ar. Hamiltone, at comand of Wm. Galt. David Craufurd. *Craufurd burges.*

210   MUNIMENTS OF THE BURGH OF IRVINE.

Irving the fourt day of Januarij 1667 yeirs :—

Sederunt.

Robert Cunynghame, proveist	Henry Lyne, baillie
James Woodsyd	Williame Slos
Alex^r Cochrane	Andro Calderwood
Robert Francis	Robert Allane
Allane Cunynghame	John Ros
William Suantoun	Johne Steill

Precept for the Minister's Stipend. THE Magistrats and Councell ordeins William Thompson armorer Johne Quhyt and John Boill to lay in to Mr Alexander Nisbit minister tua chalders meill for the Stipend deu be the brugh to him for the cropt 1666 yeirs and the samen with his dischairge sall be allowit to tham in the first end of the accompts.

Liquidatione of the Multurs. Item liquidats ilk boll beir and malt restand be the multerers of ther mylnes since November 1665 yeirs untill Candlemas nixtocome to fyve pund threttine schilling foure pennyes Scotis ilk boll ovirheid.

Impositione of ane Stent. THE quhilk day nominats James Blaire John Porter James Woodsyd Alexander Cochrane Thomas Biggart Robert Stewart and James Kyll to impose and equalize amongst the Inhabitantis ane moneths assesment That the Magistrats and Councell may impose als much as sall satisfie the localitie of quarterings the preceiding winter and to sett doune upon Tuesday or Wednesday nixt.

Irving the eight day of Januarij 1667 yeirs :—

Sederunt.

Henry Lyne, baillie

Allane Cunynghame	Robert Francis
Alexander Cochrane	David Dunlop
Hugh Thompsone	James Kyll
James Woodsyd	Robert Allane

THE baillie and Councell considdering the severall good deids done and performed to this brugh and inhabitants of the samen be ane noble and potent lord Alexander lord Montgomerie and his lordships predicessors in tyme bygane and that throw the said noble lord his moyan and meanis the said brugh and inhabitants therof are greatlie eased of the burdeing of quartereing under quhich the neighbour townes doe ly burdened Have in consideracione therof appoynted Robert Francis ane of ther number to mak offer to the said noble lord of ane hundreth rex dollors or fyve hundreth merks as ane token of ther respect to the said noble lord Requesting the said noble lord to accept of the samen to be payet within eight or ten dayes eftir the dait heirof Allane Cunighame councellor Henry Lyne, baillie James Kyll Robert Allan Hew Thamson William Suintone David Dinlop counseller Ro^{tt} Francis, counsler A. C. James Woodsyd, consler.

THEREFTIR the said baillie and Councill afoirsaid ordaines the offer of ane hundreth rex dollors or fyve hundreth merks to be augmented to the soume of fyftie pund Sterling and the last foure hundreth merkis to be payet betuixt and the first of Maij nixtocome in consideratione of the foirsaidis good deids performeit be the said noble lord to the said brugh. Henry Lyne, baillie David Dinlop, counseller Ro^{tt} Francis, counselr Hew Thamson William Suintone Allane Cunigham James Woodsyd A. C. Robert Allan James Kyll

Irving the 18th Januarij 1667 :—

Sederunt.

Henry Lyne, baillie	Allane Cunynghame
Robert Allane	John Ros
James Kyll	Hugh Thompsone
Andrew Calderwood	David Dunlop
Alexander Cochrane	Johne Steill
Robert Francis	James Woodsyd

THE quhilk day the baillie and Councell grantis commissione to James Johnstoune couper to sie that the staines that are win at the craig for the use of the Brig to be rightlie loaden upon the carts and that ther be no unsufficient staines brocht fra the craig for quhich the said James is to have payment both for his paines and chairges. *Commissione to James Johnstoun.*

THE quhilk day the baillie and Councell considdering that the persones formerlie appoynted to impose ane monethis assesment towardis the payment of the former yeirs localitie hes neglected the imposing therof Thairfoire the said baillie and Councell of new nominats and appoynts *Stentmaisters for the localitie, 1666.*

John Porter Alexander Cochrane Alexander Dyet Williame Thompsone James Woodsyd James Kyll and Thomas Bigger stentmaisters for imposing of the said stent and for equalizing the present quarterings And appoynts tham to meitt and convein quhensoevir they are requyred be the Magistrats under the paine of fyve pund Scotts to be payet be ilk contraveiner *toties quoties.*

Unlaw Semple. THE quhilk day unlawis Margaret Semple weidow in the soume of fyve pundis money for her trangressing of the act maid be the Magistratis and Councell anent the pryce of the candle at Michalemas last shee having compeirit and confessit herselff guiltie.

Irving the tuentie tua day of Januarij 1667 :—

Sederunt.

Henry Lyne, baillie
Alexander Cochrane
James Woodsyd
David Dunlop
Williame Swantone, counsellors

William Slos, thesaurer
Allane Cunynghame
James Kyll
Andrew Calderwood, councellors

Unlaw Thompsone. THE quhilk day unlawis and amerciats Hugh Thompsone flescheour in the soume of sex pundis money for his beatting and stryking of John Edgelie litster within the dwelling hous of Johne Thompsone flescheour his father upon the nyntein day of Januarij instant according as the samen wes verefied in presens of the said baillie and Councell be the deposition of diverse famous witnessis ressaveit suorne and examined in the said matter eftir that the said Hugh Thompsone had compeirit and denyet the indytment given in thairanent.

Irving the tuenty fyft day of Januarij 1667 :—

Burges Hugh Garven. THE quhilk day Hugh Garven younger wricht is created and admitted burges of this brugh quha gave his aith of fidelitie as use is and referrit his fyne to the modificatione of the Magistrats for payment quhairof Hugh Garven elder wricht became cautioner and the said Hugh to relieve his cautioner. Sic subscribitur: Ar. Hamiltone at command of Hugh Garven, elder Hew Garven.

THE quhilk day Thomas Craufurd wright is admittit and created burges of this brugh quha gave his aith of fidelitie as use is and referrit his fyne to the Magistrats modificatione for payment thairof John Ros merchand became cautioner and he to relieve his cautioner. Sic subscribitur: John Ross   Thomas Craufurd.

Burges Tho. Craufurd

Irving the eight day of Februarij 1667 :—

Sederunt.

Robert Cunynghame, proveist	Henry Lyne, baillie
Alexander Cochrane	Adame Fullertoun
James Woodsyd	Allane Cunynghame
Andro Caldirwood	Robert Allane
John Ross	Williame Suantoun
Hugh Thompsone	Williame Slos
James Kyll	

THE quhilk day compeirit Adame Fullertoun merchand quha wes nominat ane counceller for this yeir and acceptit the said office in and upon him and gave his aith of fidelitie as use is.

Counceller Fullertoun.

THE quhilk day the Magistrats and Councell nominats and appoyntis Allane Cuming James Blaire lait baillies Adame Fullertoun Allane Cunighame John Reid younger merchand William Slos John Porter Robert Allane Gilbert Wyllie Niniane Holmes William M'Taggart Robert Nesmyth elder Hugh Thompsone tailyeor Williame Gardner and John Macgie stentmaisters for imposing of thrie monethis assesment being the first thrie moneths supplie grantit to his Majestie be the Conventione of Estates in Januarij last quhilk is to be payet betuixt and the fyftein day of Apryll nixtocome.

Nominatione of Stentmaisters.

THE quhilk day the Magistrats and Councell Ratifies and approves the dischairge grantit be Henry Lyne baillie to George Erskin and Robert Nesmyth collectors of the stent imposed upon the tent day of May 1665 yeirs for payment of the inlaik of ane yeirs excyse fra May 1664 to May 1665, and for tua yeirs maintenance of tua poor boyes in the manufactory of Ayre alias Montgomeriestoun and for foure seamen outreiked for his Majesties service in Februarij 1665 quhilk dischairge beirs dait the

Ratificatione of George Erskine and Robert Nesmyth their discharge.

214   MUNIMENTS OF THE BURGH OF IRVINE.

tuentie nynt day of Januarij 1667 and conteinis tua hundreth threttie tua pundis fourtein shillings eight pennyes to be ressaveit in the haill heids and claussis thairof.

Irving the fyft day of March 1667 :—

Watter baillieschip teind of the watter and ancorage.

THE quhilk day eftir publict ropeing the watter baillieschip with ancorage and teind of the watter (except the teind of the cobbills) is sett to Robert Cunynghame proveist for the ensewing yeir viz. fra the secund day of March instant to the secund day of March nixtocome 1668 for the soume of fyftie fyve punds Scotts money to be payet to the thesaurer of this brugh at the termes useit and wont for payment quhairof John Ros merchand became cautioner and the said Robert Cunynghame to relieve his cautioner and ane tuelff pence given in of earnest. Sic subscribitur : Robert Cunynghame   Joⁿ Ross.

Irving the tent day of Aprill 1667 :—

Sederunt.

Robert Cunynghame, proveist   Henry Lyne, baillie
Adame Fullertoun   Allane Cunynghame
Robert Francis   Alexander Cochrane
James Kyll   Hugh Thompsone
Williame Suantoun   John Steill

Comissione for infefting Sir Laurence Scot in the landis of Knodgerhill and uthers.

THE quhilk day the Magistrats and Councell grants commissione to   to infeft and seis Sir Laurence Scot of Clerkingtoun Knicht in the landis of Knodgerhill Newmuir and Spittellmeidow apprysed be the deceist Sir Williame Dick fra the aires of umquhile ——— Peebles quhairunto the said Sir Laurence Scot hes right be dispositione assignatione or apprysing fra the said Sir Williame Dick conforme to the Chartour to be subscribit be tham thairanent To be halden of the proveist baillies Councell and communitie of the said brugh of Irving siclyk and in the samen forme and manner as the said umquhill Sir Williame Dick or his authors held the samen The said Sir Laurence payand the double of the feu deuty in caice Sir William Dick his imediat author wes infeft and gif the said umquhill Sir William Dick wes not infeft the said Sir Laurence is to be in the Tounes will for ane yeirs rent.

Irving the nyntein day of Aprill 1667 :—

Sederunt.

Robert Cunynghame, proveist	Henry Lyne, baillie
Robert Francis	Allane Cunynghame
Williame Slos	James Kyll
Alexander Cochrane	James Woodsyd
David Dunlop	Robert Allane
Hugh Thompsone	Adame Fullertoun
Williame Suantoun	John Reid

The quhilk day the Magistrats and Councell appoynts Robert Francis Adame Fullertoun Williame Thompsone Robert Allane and Alexander Dyet To consider the stent roll imposed for the localitie and to impose als much stent upon thes that wer frie of quartering thes tua yeirs last bypast according to the said roll as will furnisch nyne beddis with blanketts and scheits quhilk is appoynted to be delyverit to the garrisone quhilk is to be setled in the hous of Deane besyd Kilmornok. *Anent localitie.*

The quhilk day deliverit to Johne Gray lait thesaurer his thesaurer book for the yeir 1665 quhilk comprehends the teind for the yeir 1665 quhilk extend to (in money) Ane hundreth threttie on pund sextein shilling the rent of the Toun land for the cropt 1666 in respect the samen sould be still payet be way of advance extends to sevin hundreth tuentie sex pund threttine shilling foure pennyes The few deutyes for the yeir 1665 quhilk extends to fourtie tua pund nyntein shilling eight pennyes The roped landis and customes for the yeir 1665 yeirs extending unto thrie hundreth threttie ane pund tua shilling four pennyes And the burges fynes preceiding Michalmes 1666 extending to threttie tua pund quhilk soumes extendis in haill to 1263^{lb} 16/ 5^d. *Ane not of John Gray his thesaurer book.*

The quhilk day the Magistratis and Councell nominats and appoynts James Galt younger smyth to dress the Toune knok for ane yeir to come and to ring the Tolbuith bell according to the ancient custome tuice ilk day during the said space (except upon the sabbath day) viz. at fyve hours in the morneing and ten hours at night and to ring the secund bell ilk sabbath conforme to old use and wont for quhich he is allowed to have the fies formerlie allowed to thes that dischairged this imployment lykas the said *Ringing of the bell and dressing of the knok.*

James Galt being present acceptit the said chairge and referrit to the Magistrats will quhat farder allowance they will bestow upon him for the said imployment moire nor the old fies and thairupon thair wes delyuerit to him ane shilling in earnest.

Burgis Craufurd. THE quhilk day John Craufurd natural sone to umquhill John Craufurd of Catsburne is be the Magistrats and Counsell created and admittit burges of this brugh and that for his service done thairto in goeing out for the said brugh to his Maiesties navall service against the Dutch in Februarij 1665 as ane seaman quha gave his aith of fidelitie as wse is.

Secundo Maij 1667 :—

Burgessis. Laird Craigie. SIR Thomas Wallace of Craigie knicht is maid burges and gildbrother of this brugh be the proveist and bailyie with consent of the Councill pro auxilio et benemerito.

Laird Gaitgirth. Johne Chalmer of Gaitgirth is also maid burgis and gildbrother.
Wallace. James Wallace wreittar in Edinburgh is also maid burges and gildbrother.
Dick. Thomas Dick servitor to the said Sir Thomas is also maid burges and gildbrother pro favore magistri.

Thrid day of Maij 1667 :—

Gras of the Rottin boig. THE gras of the Rotten boig besyd the clerk's aiker sett to John Broun cordoner for this ensewing seasone 1667 for the soume of fyve merks Scotts to be payet to the thesaurer of this brugh at the tyme useit and wont for payment quhairof John Reid elder merchand is became cautioner and John Broune acted himselff to releive his cautioner sexpence given in earnest. Sic subscribitur : Jo^n Browne   Jo^n Reid.

Eodem die :—

Gras of the Greene. THE gras of the Greene for the said seasone is eftir rope[ing sett to] John Smaillie meilman for the soume of Threttie pund sex eight pennyes Scots to be payet be him to the thesaurer at the tyme useit and wont for payment quhairof Johne Reid elder merchand acted himselff as cautioner and Johne Smaillie to releive his cautioner. Sic subscribitur : Jo^n Reid. Ar. Hamiltone, at comand of Jo^n Smaillie.

Teind of the Cobbills. THE teind of the Cobbills for the ensewing seasone is sett to Robert Cunynghame proveist eftir publict ropeing for the soume of ten pundis Scotts money to be payet be him to the thesaurer at the ordinar tyme of payment, for payment quhairof George Erskine tailyeor becomes cautioner and the said Robert Cunynghame acted himselff to releive his said cautioner. Sic subscribitur: Robert Cunynghame, proveist. George Erskeine.

Irving the threttine day of Maij 1667:—

THE quhilk day Robert Cunynghame proveist Henry Lyne baillie with consent of the maist pairt of the Counsell frequentlie convenit addmitted and creatit James Cleland lait proveist of Bangour within the countie of Doune and kingdome of Ireland burges of this brugh and that for his service and help done and performeit to the brugh quha gave his aith of fidelitie as use is and took instruments.

<small>Burges Cleland.</small>

Irving the fourtein day of Maij 1667:—

Sederunt.

Robert Cunynghame, proveist	Henry Lyne, baillie
William Slos	John Reid
Alexander Cochrane	James Kyll
Robert Allane	Hugh Thompsone
Andro Caldirwood	Robert Francis
Williame Suantoun	Johne Steill
David Dunlop	

The quhilk day the Magistrats and Councell ordeins the haill thesaurers (except John Gray) to be presentlie incarcerat within the tolbuith quhill they mak thair thesaurers accomptis that quhat money is in thair hands belonging to the toune may be advanced for repairing of the Brig quhilk is now fallen doun.

<small>Anent thesaurers Comptis.</small>

Item comissionats Williame Thompsone armorer to buy timber and dailles and imploy workmen for making ane passage over the broken pen of the Brig to the people quhill it be repaired quha is to be payet for his debursementis and paines conforme to the accompt to be given in be him.

<small>Comissione to Wm Thompsone.</small>

THE quhilk day the Magistrats and Councell grants comissione to the proveist or baillie or any ane of thame to ressave resignatione of that aiker of land halden of the proveist baillies councell and communitie of the said brugh callit the Rood meidow fra Robert Hamiltone merchand burges of this brugh heretour thairof and Sara Ritchard his spous and to grant new

<small>Comissione for infefting James Fullertoun in the Rood meidow.</small>

218   MUNIMENTS OF THE BURGH OF IRVINE.

infeftment thairof to James Fullertoun merchand burges of the said brugh conforme to the dispositione maid and grantit be thame to the said James Fullertoun and procuratorie of resignatione thairin conteinit daited the   day of   instant quhairanent thir presents is to be ane sufficient warrand the said James Fullertoune paying and cleiring all bygane few deutyes and teinds and payand the double of the feu deuty for his entres in name of compositione.

Irving the tuenty fourt day of Maij 1667 :—
Sederunt.

Robert Cunynghame, proveist	Henry Lyne, baillie
Williame Slos	Robert Francis
Allane Cunynghame	David Dunlop
Johne Steill	Hugh Thompsone
Adame Fullertoun	James Kyll
Williame Swintoun	Andro Caldirwood
Robert Allane	Alexander Cochrane

Anent the brig. THE quhilk day the Magistrats and Councell now convenit Ratifies approves and confirmes the agriement maid with John Symth macssoune in Kilmauris anent the re-edificing of the broken arch or bow of the Brig with the tua pillars quhairupon the samen is foundit on each syd thairof quhairby the Toune is obleist to pay unto the said John Symth ane thousand punds Scots monethlie quhill it be all payet And to furnisch foure hundreth stones togidder with ane shuiff for upholding of the said arch quhill it be compleitit and to dame the watter as occasion and necessitie requyres For quhich caussis the said John is obleist to re-edifie and sufficientlie repaire the said arch and tuo pillars and to furnisch lyme sand and quhat farder stones beis neidfull. Subscribit be the saids Magistrats and Councell. Sic subscribitur: Robert Cunynghame, proveist Henry Lyne, baillie   Williame Slos, thesaurer   Robert Francis, counsellor Allane Cunynhame   David Dunlop, councellor   Williame Suintoun, counsellor   Hew Thompsone, councellor   Adame Fullertoun, councellor   Andro Caldirwood, counseller   James Kyll, councellor   Robert Allane, counseller Johne Steill—*J. S.* his mark   Alexander Cochrane—*A. C.* his mark.

Anent Stent maisters. THE quhilk day the Magistrats and Counsell nominats Robert Francis Robert M'Kerrell James Woodsyd Hew Thompsone John Gray John Porter

Alexander Orr Williame Thompsone and Williame Porter stentmaisters for imposeing of the secund thrie moneths supply granted to his Maiestie in Januarij 1667 viz. Aprill Maij and June and uther tua moneth ordinar assesment for payment of the kings Majesties taxatione for the Witsunday terme 1667 yeirs granted to his Majestie in August 1665 being the secund terme thairof.

Irving the last day of Maij 1667 :—

THE proveist baillie with consent of the maist pairt of the Councell frequentlie convenit in the Councell creats and admits Robert Bryssone merchand in Kilwinning burges of this brugh quha gave his aith of fidelite as use is and referrit his fyne to the Magistrats modification for payment Thomas Bigger merchand becomes cautioner and he to relieve his cautioner. Sic subscribitur: Robert Brysone Thomas Bigger.

Burges Bryssone.

Irving the tuentie ane day of June 1667 :—

THE quhilk day Robert Cunynghame proveist with consent of the Councell frequentlie convenit created and admitted Robert Nesmyth sone to Robert Nesmyth wricht burges of this brugh quha gave his aith of fidelite as use is and referrit his fyne to the Magistrates modificatione for payment quhairof Alexander Cochrane merchand becomes cautioner and he to releive his cautioner. Sic subscribitur: Robert Nesmyth. A. C.

Burges Nesmyth.

Irving the fourtein day of September 1667 :—

THE quhilk day Henry Lyne baillie with consent of the Councell frequentlie convenit created and admitted Williame Broune sailler indweller in Irving burges of this brugh quha gave his aith of fidelitie as use is and referrit his fyne to the modificatione of the Magistrats for payment quhairof David Broune walker became cautioner and he to releive his cautioner. Sic subscribitur: David Broune Williame Broune.

Burges Wm Broun.

THE quhilk day Charles Broune sone naturall to James Broune tanner is be the said baillie with consent of the baillie created burges of this brugh quha referrit his fyne to the modificatione of the Magistratis for payment quhairof the said Henry Lyne became cautioner and he acted himselff to releive his cautioner. Sic subscribitur: C. B. Henrie Lyne.

Burges Charles Broun.

220   MUNIMENTS OF THE BURGH OF IRVINE.

Exemptione of the twa Brounes fra payment of thair burges fynes.

THE quhilk day the said Henry Lyne taking to considderatione the severall services done to the brugh of Irving and inhabitants thairof be the saidis William and Charles Brounes and for increaseing of trad and policie within the samen remitts and dischairges the foirsaidis burges fynes to have bein exacted fra thame be vertew of thair severall actis of admissione above wreittin. Sic subscribitur: Henry Lyne, baillie Johne Broune, *witnes*; David Broune, *witnes*.

Irving the twenty sevint day of September 1667:—

Sederunt.

Robert Cunynghame, provest   Henry Lyne, baillie
Williame Slos   Adame Fullertoun
Robert Francis   Robert Allane
James Woodsyd   Alexander Cochrane
David Dunlop   Hugh Thompsone
James Kyll   John Steill
Andro Caldirwood   Johne MacGill — and

Gilbert Wyllie, councelloris

Nominatione of Councellors.

THE quhilk day the Magistratis and Councell nominats Williame Slos Niniane Holmes John Reid youngar John Ros James Woodsyd Alexander Dyet Alexander Or Andro Caldirwood Alexander Cochran Robert Allane Robert Nesmyth Robert Francis James Kyll Andrew Hendirsone and George Erskine to be councellors of this brugh for the yeir to come.

Leits for the provest.

THE quhilk day be pluralitie of voices Robert Cunynghame present provest Mr. Robert Barclay lait provest and Allane Dunlop of Craig ar voited for the leit of the provest for the yeir to come.

Leits for baillies.

THE quhilk day be pluralitie of voices Henry Lyne Laurence Blaire William Slos John Reid elder John Reid youngar and Robert M'Kerrill are be pluralitie of voices voited to be upon the leit for baillies for the yeir to come.

Leits for thesaurer.

THE quhilk day Williame Slos Robert Woodsyd and Charles Broune are voited to be upon the leit for thesaurers for the yeir to come.

Leit for fischall.

THE quhilk day William Thompsone Thomas Galt and James Johnstoun are be pluralitie of voices lited to be fischall for the yeir to come.

COUNCIL BOOK.   221

Irving the first day of October 1667 being Tuesday :—
          Sederunt.

Robert Cunynghame, proveist   Henry Lyne, baillie
Alexander Cochrane   Robert Francis
John Reid   Andro Caldirwood
David Dunlop   James Woodsyd
James Kyll   Robert Allane
Hugh Thompson   Allane Cunynghame
William Suantone   Johne Steill
      William Gardiner for Andro Henderson quha wes absent
   Gilbert Wyllie for Alexander Dyet   John Dyksone for William Slos
   George Lyndsay for Adame Fullertoun   Thomas Bigger for John Ros

THE quhilk day Niniane Holmes Alexander Or Robert Nesmyth and George   Admissione of
Erskine quha wer nocht formerlie councellors compeirit and acceptit and   Councellors.
gave their aithes of fidelitie as use is.

THE quhilk day Alexander Cochrane John Reid youngar James Woodsyd   Admissione of
Andrew Caldirwood Robert Allane Robert Francis and James Kyll   Councellors.
compeirit and acceptit and gave their aithes of fidelitie as use is.

THE quhilk day the saidis William Gardiner Gilbert Wyllie John Dicksone
Thomas Biggar and George Lyndsay compeirand for above nameit persones
quha wer absent gave their aithes of fidelitie as far as they wer concernit in
the electione conforme to the custome of this brugh   Alexander Dyet and
Andrew Hendirsone to accept the nixt meiting.

THE quhilk day be pluralitie of voices Robert Cunynghame is electit proveist   Cunynghame
of this brugh for the yeir to come quha compeirand acceptit the said office   Proveist.
in and upon him and gave his aith of fidelitie as use is.

THE quhilk day Henry Lyne and Laurence Blaire are be pluralitie of voices   Lyne and Blaire
electit baillies for the yeir to come   The said Henry Lyne compeirand [etc.   Baillies.
in common form as above] and Laurence to accept the nixt meiting.

THE quhilk day be pluralitie of voices Robert Woodsyd is electit Thesaurer   Woodsyd
of this brugh for the yeir to come, quha, etc.   Thesaurer.

Galt proˡ fischall.	THE quhilk day be pluralitie of voices Thomas Galt is electit procuratour fischall of this brugh quha compeirand, etc.

Irving the fourt day of October 1667 :—

Sederunt.

Robert Cunynghame, provest	Henry Lyne, baillie
Robert Francis	James Woodsyd
Robert Allane	Ninian Holmes
Alexander Or	Robert Nesmyth
Andro Caldirwood	Alexander Cochrane
John Reid	James Kyll
	Robert Woodsyd

Acceptatione Slos and Ros to be councellors.	THE quhilk day John Ros and William Slos compeirand acceptit the office of councellor, etc.
	Alexander Dyet compeirand refuises to accept and is thairfore ordered to remaine in prisone Continowes Laurence Blaire his acceptatione untill the nixt meiting of the Councell.
Anent the repairing of the kirk dyk.	Appoynts Robert Francis and Alexander Cochrane to commune with the minister anent the repaireing of the Kirk dyk for keeping beasts furth thairof and to report the nixt meiting.
Pryce of candle.	Ordeins the pund of candle to be sold for foure shilling Scots for the yeir to come and the contraveinar to pay fyve pund *toties quoties*.
Visitatione of flesch.	Ordeins and appoynts Williame Thompsone and James Johnstoune to visit all flesch that is brocht or sett furth to be sold in this mercat that the samen be sufficient quha are to be warned to accept.
Pryce of quheat bread.	Ordeins ilk loafe of quheat bread to consist of tuelff ounces of good and sufficient stuff and to be sold for tuelff pennyes Scots and the contraveinar to pay fyve pund *toties quoties*.
Visitatione of meill.	Ordeins John Porter meilman and Edward Armor youngar to visit the meill brocht to be sold within this brugh that the samen be sufficient quha are to be wairned to accept.
Comission to Allan.	Ordeins Robert Allane to goe to Kilmornok to tak ane accompt of the beddis furnished be the Inhabitants of this brugh to the garrison of Dein and to have allowance for his chairges.
Anent the Ingathering of the supplie.	THE quhilk day in respect of ane complaint given in to the Councell be the collectors of the last thrie moneths supply that severall of the Inhabitants

refuiss to pay their respective proportions thairof the Magistratis and Councell ordeins the deficients to be incarcerat within the Tolbuith of this brugh quhill they mak payment to the collectors of ther proportions of the saidis thrie moneths supplie. And als declaires the deficients to be lyabill for all quartering that sall be maid for deficiencie.

Irving the fyftein day of October 1667 :—

Sederunt.

Robert Cunynghame, proveist	Henry Lyne, baillie
John Reid	Robert Francis
Robert Woodsyd	Robert Nesmyth
Alexander Or	Andro Caldirwood
James Kyll	Johne Ros
Niniane Holmes	George Erskine, Councellors

The quhilk day compeirit Laurence Blaire quha acceptit the office of baillie in and upon him and gave his aith of fidelitie as use is.

The quhilk day nominats James Blaire John Porter John Gray Thomas Bigger Alexander Or Robert Nesmyth Alexander Dyet William Gardiner and William Hendirsone weivar stentmaisters for imposing the last foure moneths supplie. — Stentmaisters.

The quhilk day John Smyth maessone in Kilmars Johne Cowane maesson in Stevinstone Thomas Wilson maessone thair Mathew Allasone maessone thair and John Young maessone thair are be the saids proveist baillies and Councell created burgessis of this brugh for their good and faithfull service done thairto in repairing and building up the pen of the Brig that wes fallen and the pillars that wer shrunk, quha gave their aithes of fidelitie as use is. — Burgesses of Maessones.

Irving the threttine day of November 1667 yeirs :—

The quhilk day the pettie customes of this brugh eftir publict roping are sett to Henry Lyne baillie for the yeir to come viz. fra Mertimes 1667 to Mertimes 1668 for fyftie fyve pundis Scotts to be payet to the magistrats and their thesaurer at the tymes useit and wont for payment quhairof Laurence Blaire baillie becomes cautioner and the said Henry Lyne to releive his cautioner tuelff schilling given in earnest. Sic subscribitur : Henrie Lyne Law. Blair, cationer. — Pettie customes.

Irving the tuentie tua day of November 1667 :—

Burges Robert Speir.

THE quhilk day Robert Cunynghame proveist and Henry Lyne baillie with consent of the maist pairt of the Counsell frequentlie convenit created and admitted Robert Speir tailyeor burges of this brugh quha gave his aith of fidelitie as use is and referrit his fyne, etc. Laurence Speir, tailyeor cautioner. Sic subscribitur: Lawrance Speir, caur^r Robert Speir.

Burges Hugh Boyd.

THE quhilk day the said proveist and bailyie with consent as said is creats and admitts Hugh Boyd tailyeor burges of this brugh quha gave his aith, etc. [ut supra] William M'Tagart tailyeor cautioner. Sic subscribitur: W M T : Hugh Boyd.

THE quhilk day the said proveist and bailyie with consent foirsaid creats and admitis Robert Speir John Steinsone weivar burges of this brugh quha gave his aith of fidelitie as use is [etc. as above] John Makgie weivar cautioner Sic subscribitur : John Mackgie, cau'.   Joⁿ Steinsone.

Irving the sevint day of December 1667 :—

Sederunt.

Robert Cunynghame, proveist	Alex^r Cochrane
Robert Woodsyd, thesaurer	Robert Francis
Williame A. Slos	John Ross
Robert Nesmyth	Niniane Holmes
Alexander Or	James Kyll
Andro Caldirwood	George Erskine

Procurator fischall against Robert Allane.

THE quhilk day the Magistratis and Councell unlawis and amerciats Robert Allane merchand in the soume of ten rex dollors for his beatting stryking and abusing of Thomas Galt procurator fischall of this brugh conforme to the Indytment given in thairanent quhilk wes cleirlie verefied and proven in presens of the said proveist and Councell and declaires the said Robert Allane uncapable of any publict trust within this brugh at ony tyme heireftir. The fyne wes thaireftir modified to tuentie pundis Scotis and band given thairfoire.

Lawborrowes Galt to Allane.

THE quhilk John M'Kie schipwright becomes acted as cautioner and sourtie for Thomas Galt afoirsaid that Robert Allane merchand his wyf bairnes men tennents and servandis and all uthers his majesties leidges sall be harmeles and skaithles in thair bodies landis heretages taks steadings rowmes possessiones and on nawayes troubled nor molested thairintill be the said Thomas nor be na uthers of his causing sending hounding out comand ressait assistance or ratihabitione quhom he may stop or lett directlie nor indirectlie utherwayes nor be ordour of law and justice in tyme comeing under the paine of fyve hundreth merks money, and he to releive his cautioner. Sic subscribitur: Ja. Hunter, notarius de mandato dicti Joannis M'Kie Thomeque Galt.

The quhilk day Adame Fullertoun sailler becomes acted in the borrow court bookis of this brugh as cautioner and souirtie for the said Robert Allane [in similar terms and under same penalty as the foregoing]. Sic subscribitur: Adame Fullertoun Robert Allane. Lawborrowes Allane to Galt.

Irving the threttine day of December 1667 :—

The quhilk day Robert Cunynghame proveist Henry Lyne and Lawrence Blaire bailyeis with consent of the maist pairt of the Councell . . . . created and admitted James Galt smyth burges of this brugh quha gave his aith [etc. in common form] James Wricht dagmaker cautioner. Sic subscribitur: James Wright James Galt. Burges Ja. Galt.

The quhilk day the saids proveist and bailyeis with consent foirsaid created and admitted David Buchannane smyth burges of this brugh quha gave aith [etc. as above] Williame Suantoun saidler cautioner. Sic subscribitur: William Swintoun. David Buchannan. Burges David Buchannan.

Irving the sevintein day of Januarij 1668 :—

Sederunt.

Robert Cunynghame, proveist

Henry Lyne	Laurence Blaire, baillies
James Woodsyd	Robert Woodsyd
James Kyll	John Ros
Alexander Cochrane	Alexander Or

Andro Caldirwood, counsellors

The quhilk day the Magistrats and Councell ordeins the touneland to be measured and roped betuixt and Candlemas nixt and declaires that no persone is to have the benefit of the saidis landis quhill they satisfie quhat Roping of toune land.

is deu be thame to the thesaurers and ordeins the timber of the brig to be roped.

Proc Fischall agt Alexr Armour.

THE quhilk day Alexander Armour couper being fund guiltie be the saidis bailyeis and Counsell of abusing of Robert Cunynghame proveist of this brugh upon the sextein day of Januarij instant in the publict hie streit out of his drunkennes he demanding ane order for arreisting of the persone of Alexander Forman quhilk wes grantit did notwithstanding thairof oppinlie exclame against the said proveist saying the devill tak you and your justice both in hie contempt of authoritie is amerciat and unlawed be the saidis bailyeis and Counsell in the soume of tuentie pundis Scotis and to remaine in prisone quhill Monday nixt the tuentie day of Januarij instant and than to be taken out of prisone betuixt ten and tuelff hours befoire noone and sett up in ane pillorie with ane paper on his face and thaireftir his burges tickett to be publictlie lacerat and riven be tuik of drum The fyne wes delyverit to Lawrence Blaire bailyie and Allan Cuming lait baillie and John Ros merchand acted thamselvis to produce the persone of the said Alexander upon the   day of Januarij instant within the tolbuith of Irving thairin to remaine quhill he fulfill the foirsaid decreit under the paine of tuentie rex dollors—quhilk act is daited the tuentie day of Januarij 1668 yeirs.

Irving the sevint day of Februarij 1668 :—

Burges Jor Burnes All proceiding given in chairge to Woodsyd for burgess.

THE quhilk day John Burnes tailyeor sone to umquhill Peter Burnes cordoner is be the saids proveist and bailyeis with consent . . admitted and created burges of this brugh quha gave his aith [etc. in common form] Hugh Garven elder wricht, cautioner.

Irving the eightein day of Februarij 1668 :—

Sederunt.

Robert Cunynghame, proveist	Laurence Blaire, baillie
Robert Francis	Alexander Cochrane
James Woodsyd	Robert Woodsyd
John Ros	James Kyll
Niniane Holmes	Robert Nesmyth
Alexander Or	Andro Caldirwood

George Erskine, counsellors

Toun Lands.

THE quhilk day the Magistrats and Counsell appoynts the Toune land to be given out for sevin yeirs beginning the cropt 1668 at the rent that the samen wes sett for the last sevin yeirs according to lotts and that non be admitted to have any pairt thairof quhill they satisfie the thesaurers of quhat they are deu for byganes And the inhabitantis to be wairned by touk of drum for that effect And sielyk appoynts the Bushlandis and uther landis useit to be roped the fourt day of March nixtocome.

THE quhilk day the Magistrats and Councell nominats Robert Cunynghame proveist to attend the nixt conventione of borrowes quhilk is to be halden at Edinburgh upon the thrid day of March nixtocome and appoynts the thesaurer to pay his chairges conforme to use and wont. Comissioner for borrowes.

Followes the just double of the COMMISSIONE quhilk wes subscribit be the baillies and Counsell :— Commissione

At Irving the tuentie ane day of Februarij j^m vj^c sextie eight yeirs :—

THE quhilk day the proveist baillies and councell of the brugh of Irving in ordour to ane missive direct to them be the right honorabill the proveist baillies and counsell of the brugh of Edinburgh beirand dait the sext day of December last bypast intimating that thair wes ane generall conventione of the royall borrowes of this Kingdome appoynted be the particular conventione of the borrowes holden at Edinburgh in December last To meit at Edinburgh the thrid day of March nixtocome Anent the setling of ane stapill port The fyftie souze imposed upon the tun of French wyne The tuelff pounds imposed upon ilk bow of forraine salt The fynes and penalties exacted be David Weymes and his deputs anent the braidth of linnen and anent linnen yairn And anent severall uther particulars quhilks concerns the welfare of the royall borrowes of this kingdome And therfoire desyring thame to send ane comissioner sufficientlie authorized Have unanimouslie nominat and appoynted Robert Cunynghame proveist of the said brugh of Irving their comissioner to the effect foirsaid with full and ample power to him to consult treat and conclud with the rest of the commissioners of the royall borrowes of this kingdome anent the premissis particularlie and generallie abovewritten and ony uther particular that does or may concerne the welfare of the royall borrowes of this kingdome sielyk and als frielie in everie respect as any uther comissioner of ony royall brugh of this kingdome may doe in the premissis promittand to hald firme and stable all and quhatsumevir thingis their said comissioner for thame and in their names in the premissis lawfully does. In witnes quhairof thir presentis are subscribit be the bailyeis and commoun Counsell of the said brugh and their clerk day yeir and place respective foirsaidis.

Ane LIST of the TOUNE LANDIS as the samen wes given out to the Inhabitants be lott for the ensewing sevin yeirs at the rait the samen wes sett at the preceiding sevin yeirs and quhat ilk persone payes thairof Ther being tuentie sex lotts in all quhairwith Robert Wood is to be chairged.

1. Mr Robert Barclay lait proveist ane aiker of infield land for his first lott being the tuentie tua aiker ane aiker nixt the Clerks aiker for his secund lott being the sexteint aiker and ane aiker in Hayes Holme last possest be John Thompsone in Cruikit aiker being the tuentie secund aiker the first tua aiker at fourtein merk and the last at threttine merks quhilk is 27 : 06 : 08.

2. Thomas Bigger and William Dyet ane aiker of infeild land being the threttint aiker for their first lott their secund lott is the sevint aiker on the south syd foranent the Gushett aiker the 25 aiker begining towardis the Duntoun Know last possest be David Speir for their thrid lott quhairof tua aiker at fourtein merkis the aiker and the thrid aiker at the said rait Inde of all 27 : 06 : 08.

3. Hugh Montgomerie merchand ane aiker inland being the fyft aiker ane aiker last possest be John Francis carrier being the eighteen aiker for his secund lott The tuenttieth aiker last possest be Laurence Wilsone southward for his thrid lott tua aikers at fourtein merks the aiker and the thrid aiker at threttine merks 27 : 06 : 08.

4. Robert Broune clerk and Charles Broune   for their first lott the secund aiker of infeild land for their secund lott the tuentie sext aiker last possest be John Thompsone elder and for their thrid lott the fyft aiker last possest be Hugh Thompsone pryce of tua aikers thairof fourtein merks ilk aiker and the thrid at the samen rait   Inde 28 : 00 : 00.

5. Charles Broune for his first lott the tuentieth on aiker of the infeild land for his thrid lot the tuentie fourt aiker last possest be John Thompsone and for his uther lott being his secund lott the tuentieth aiker last possest be William Ros carrier ilk aiker of tua aiker at fourtein merks and the thrid at threttine merks 27 : 06 : 08.

6. David Speir walker for his first lott the eight aiker of infeild land for his secund lott the nynt aiker last possest be Thomas Gardiner and for his thrid lott the threttine aiker fra the Dunton Know last possest be William Gardiner and William Porter ilk aiker of tua at fourtein merks and the thrid at the same rait   Inde 28 : 00 : 00.

7. John Gray merchand for his first lott the sext aiker of infeild land for his secund lot the 24th aiker last possest be Robert Broune clerk for his thrid lot the sextein aiker last possest be John Francis nixt the burne on the south ilk aiker of tua at fourtein merks and the thrid aiker thairof at   Inde 27 : 06 : 08.

8. John Porter meilman for his first lott the sexteinth aiker of infeild land the 2jth nixt the burne last possest be John Steinsone for his secund lott and for his thrid lott the fourt aiker possest be Robert Dunlop ilk aiker of tua thairof at fourtein merks and the thrid at the same rait Inde 28 : 00 : 00.

9. John Thompsone flescheor for his first lott the tent aiker of infeild for his secund the eight aiker nixt the Guschett and the sext aiker last possest be John Muir tailyeor for the thrid lott ilk aiker of tua thairof at fourtein merks and the thrid at the same rait   Inde 28 : 00 : 00.

10. Hugh Thompsone flescheor for his first lott the 20th aiker of infeild for his secund lot the thrid aiker last possest be Adame Cunynghame elder and for his thrid lott the sevint aiker westward last possest be John Muir ilk aiker of tua thairof at fourtein merks and the thrid aiker thairof at the samen rait Inde 28 : 00 : 00.

11. John Henry carrier for his first lott the 25th aiker of infeild last possest be David Speir for his secund lott the sevinteinth aiker on the south syd of the gait last possest be David Cauldwell and for his thrid lott the nynt aiker from the Duntoun Know, last possest be Williame Ros carrier ilk aiker of tua aiker at fourtein merks and the thrid at the samen rait   Inde 28 : 00 : 00.

12. David Auld and John Gibsone younger for their first lott the fourteinth aiker of infeild for their secund the tent aiker last possest be Robert Dunlop and for his thrid the sevinteinth aiker fra the Duntoun Know possest be William Fullertoun callit the Ducathoill ilk aiker of tua thairof at fourtein merks and the thrid aiker at threttine merks   Inde 27 : 06 : 08.

13. James Fullertoun lait baillie for his first lott the sevint aiker of

infeild for his secund lott the 15th aiker last possest be Hugh Thompsone flescheor and for his thrid the fourteinth aiker last possest be George Garven ilk aiker thairof at fourtein merks ilk aiker 28 : 00 : 00.

14. George Garven and Henry Dyet the 19 aiker of infeild for their first lott for ther secund the 22d aiker nixt to John Porter meilman his aiker westward last possest be James Spark couper and for ther thrid lott the tent aiker callit the Smiddie aiker last possest be David Speir at fourtein merks the aiker Inde 28 : 00 : 00.

15. Allane Cuming lait baillie the 26 aiker of infeild land, last possest be William Gardiner and William Porter for his first lot for his secund the 19th aiker last possest be William Gardiner and William Porter and for his thrid the thrid aiker fra the Dunton Know last possest be James Blaire at fourtein merks ilk aiker 28 : 00 : 00.

16. Robert Woodsyd merchand the 24th aiker of infeild last possest be Hugh Montgomerie and John Thomson for his first lott The fourtein aiker last possest be John Porter for his secund lot the fyftein aiker fra the Duntoun Know last possest be Hugh Walker for his thrid lot at fourtein merkis ilk aiker Inde 28 : 00 : 00.

17. Adame Fullertoun sailler and William Ros carrier for ther first lott the thrid aiker of enfeild for ther secund the 23 aiker last possest be the said William Ros and for ther thrid the tuentie sext aiker fra the Duntoun Know callit the Poddock holme ilk aiker of tua at fourtein merks and the other at threttin merks Inde 27 : 06 : 08.

18. Robert Francis and James Woodsyd for ther first lott the 15th aiker of infeild for ther secund lot the Hip aiker and for ther thrid lot that aiker last possest be Adame Cunynghame elder nearest to Mr. Robert Barclay his Caukit aiker tua aiker therof at fourtein merks ilk aiker and the thrid at threttine merks Inde 27 : 06 : 08.

19. Hew Broun and Thomas Spark for ther first lot the nynt aiker of infeild for their secund lott the threttint aiker last possest be John Davie and for ther thrid the tuelf aiker possest be David Auld nixt the Bushland ilk aiker of tua therof at fourtein merkis and the thrid at threttine merks Inde 27 : 06 : 08.

20. John Broune cordoner for his first lott the sevintein aiker of infeild for his first lott the fourt aiker possest be Edward Armour elder for his secund lott and for the thrid the ellevint aiker nixt the Bushland last possest be John Davie James Spark is joynit with him ilk aiker of tua

therof at fourtein merk and the thrid aiker at threttine merk Inde of all 27 : 06 : 08.

21. John Muir elder for his first lott the tuelt aiker of infeild for his secund the fyft aiker last possest be John Henry and the nynteinth aiker last possest be Laurence Wilsone for his thrid lott ilk aiker of tua therof at fourtein merkis and the thrid at threttine merkis Inde 27 : 06 : 08.

22. Robert Dunlop smyth for his first lott the ellevint aiker of the infeild The tuelt aiker callit Bolton's aiker and for his thrid the tuentieth on aiker fra the Duntoun Know nixt to Hugh Montgomerie's aiker ther on the west ilk aiker of tua aiker therof at fourtein merkis and the thrid aiker at threttine merks Inde 27 : 06 : 08.

23. Thomas Spark maltman the first aiker on the south of the infeild for his first lott The sext aiker callit the Guschett aiker for his secund lott And the eight aiker nixt the Quarrell hoill possest be James Spark for his thrid lott at fourtein merk the aiker therof Inde 28 : 00 : 00.

24. Robert Cunynghame proveist the fourt aiker of infeild land for his first lott, for his secund the elevint aiker on the north last possest be David Brown and the secund aiker fra the Duntoune Know last possest be William Dyet for his thrid lott at fourtein merkis the aiker is 28 : 00 : 00.

25. Henry Lyne baillie the eight aiker of infeild for his first lott and for his secund the tuentie fyft aiker possest be Henry Dyet and for his thrid the first aiker fra the Duntone Know possest be John Thompsone flescheor ilk aiker of tua therof at fourtein merkis the thrid at the samin rait Inde 28 : 00 : 00.

26. James Blaire lait baillie the 23th aiker of infeild callit Quarrell hoill for his first lott the secund aiker callit Schort Boylets for his secund and for his thrid the eightein aiker alongst the burne in Halyes ilk aiker of tua at fourtein merks and the thrid aiker at threttin merks is 27 : 06 : 08.

> Summa of the haill aikers is 78 and the rent is 726 : 13 : 4, and quhilk is already payet in to Robert Woodsyd thesaurer be way of advance for the yeir 1668.

Irving the fourt day of March 1668 :—

THE Buschland (reservand the innermost aiker to James Hunter) is sett to Henry Lyne baillie for the ensewing sevin yeirs for fyftie pundis Scots to be payet per annum to the thesaurer at the ordinar tyme of payment for

Buschland

payment quhairof James Fullertoun of Bartancholme becomes cautioner the said Henry acted himselff to releive his cautioner. Sic subscribitur: J. Fullertoun, cautioner   Henry Lyne.

Rotten boig. THE Rotten boig under the Knodgerhill eftir ropeing is sett to James Fullertoune lait baillie for the ensewing sevin yeirs for eight merks Scots per annum [etc. ut supra] Henry Lyne baillie, cautioner.

Rotten boig. THE Rotten boig besyd the Clerks aiker is sett to James Fullertoun fer . . . sevin yeirs, for thrie pund threttine shilling four pennyes yeirlie [etc. as before] Henry Lyne baillie, cautioner.

Marcis. THE quhilk day the Marreisland is sett to John Broune cordoner for the ensewing sevin yeir nixtocome for fourtein merks Scots yeirlie to the thesaurer [etc. as before] Robert Stewart merchand cautioner.

Boigsyd. THE land at the Boigsyd is sett to Thomas Bigger merchand for . . . . sevin yeirs for payment of fyve pund threttine shilling four pennyes yeirlie [etc. as before] Hugh Thompsone flescheor cautioner.

Rigs at the seagait. THE tua rigs at the Seagait acquyrit fra Proveist Reid is sett to John Broun cordoner for . . sevin yeirs for thrie pund Scots yeirlie [etc.] Robert Stewart merchand cautioner.

Burges John Dicke THE quhilk day Henry Lyne and Laurence Blaire bailyeis with consent . . created and admitted John Dickie wright burges of this brugh quha gave his aith [etc. in common form] James Fullertoun of Bartancholme cautioner.

ROPING OF THE TIMBER OF THE BRIG.

Roping of the brig timber.
The tua halff schaves lyand at the watter syd at the back of David Brounes yeard is sold to William Thompsone efter publict ropeing thereof for 14 06 08

The broken halff sheaff lyand nixt to the toune hous is sold to bailyie Henry Lyne eftir roping for   .   .   .   03 00 00

The nixt halff scheaff lyand nixt therto sold to the said Henry Lyne for 05 06 08

The broken halff scheaff lyand nixt therto is sold to James

Kyll couper for four merkis Scotis and the stoill besyd the
samen is sold to the said James Kyll for thrie pund threttine
shilling four pennyes eftir publict roping Inde . . 06 06 08
   The halff sheaf lyand nixt to the foot of the Grein is sold
to Hugh Thompsone for 06 03 04
   The halff sheaff lyand at the Tinhous burne nixt the toune
is sold to the said Hugh Thompsone for . . . 06 03 04
   The halff sheaff beyond the burne is sold to James
Hendirsone wright for 05 16 08
   The sawen trie lyand at the Tinehous burne is sold to
William Thompsone for 01 13 04
   The tua short tries lyand on the brig is sold to John
Porter merchand for 04 06 08
   The meikle mast lyand on the north syd of the brig is
sold to James Blaire for 12 00 00
   The uther mast lyand on the south syd is sold to William
Thompsone for 10 06 08
   The tries lyand betuixt the Croce and the Tolbuith is sold
to George Erskine for 01 04 00
                       Summa   77 03 08

Irving the fyft day of March 1668 :—

The quhilk day the watter baillyieschip and teind of the Watter of Irving   *Watter baillieschip.*
is sett to George Erskine tailyeor for the soume of fyftie four pundis for
the ensewing yeir, viz. fra the secund of March instant to the secund day of
March 1669 yeirs to be payet to the thesaurer at the accustomed tymes of
payment, etc. David Dunlop, cautioner.

Irving the sext day of March 1668 :—

The quhilk day Henry Lyne and Laurence Blaire bailyeis with consent
. . . admitted and created Johne Andersone merchand burges of   *Jo. Andersone*
Glesgow brother to William Andersone lait proveist therof and Henry   *burges.*
Cunynghame merchand burges of Ayr burgessis and gildbrethren of this
brugh quha gave their aithes as use is, and that for their services, etc. to
this brugh.

Irving the sevintein day of March 1668 :—

Sederunt.

Robert Cunynghame, proveist.

Henry Lyne	Laurence Blaire, bailyeis
John Ros	Williame Slos
Alexander Cochrane	Andro Caldirwood
Alixander Or	Robert Francis
James Kyl	George Erskin, counsellors

Anent harbouring of strangers beggers. THE quhilk day the Magistrats and Counsell taking to ther serious consideratioun the great oppressione committed within this brugh throw the recepting and harbouring of strangers without testimonialls and throw the harbouring vagaboundis beggers and uthers Doe therfoire inhibit and dischairge all the inhabitants of this brugh to lodge and harbour any stranger within the samen without sufficient testimoniall or harbour any vagabound beggers or uthers of that kind without acquenting the Magistrats therwith under the paine of fyve pund Scots to be payet be ilk contraveiner *toties quoties* And that ilk inhabitant keip uthers skaithles in ther handis under the alyk penaltie *toties quoties* And that proclamatione be maid heirof that non pretend ignorance.

Stentmaister for ane drummer. THE quhilk day the Magistrats and Counsell nominats and appoyntis Alexander Cochrane John Porter John Gray Williame Thompsone and Alexander Orr stentmaisters for imposeing of foure schilling Scots equallie amongst the inhabitants of this brugh for ilk dayes maintenance of the ordinar drummer and sett doune ane stent roll therof.

Irving the tuentie eight day of Aprill 1668 :—

Gras of the Grein. THE gras of the Grein for this seasone eftir publict roping is sett to George Garven wreittar for the soume of fyftie sevin marks Scots to be payet be him to the thesaurer of this brugh at the terme useit and wont for payment quhairof James Hunter wreittar becomes cautioner and the said George to releive his cautioner. Sic subscribitur: G. Garven   Ja. Hunter.

Irving the secund day of May 1668 :—

THE quhilk day James Picken weivar is admitted and created burges of this brugh be Robert Cunynghame proveist and Henry Lyne baillie with consent . . quha gave his aith [etc. in common form], Andro Henderson weivar cautioner. *Pickin burges.*

THE quhilk day William Ros carrier is admitted and created burges etc. Williame Thompsone armourer cautioner. *Ros burges.*

Irving the eight day of Maii 1668 yeirs :—

Sederunt.

Robert Cunynghame, proveist.

Henry Lyne	Laurence Blaire, bailyeis
Robert Francis	Robert Nesmyth
Niniane Holmes	Alexander Or
Andro Caldirwood	James Kyll
James Woodsyd	Williame Slos

George Erskine — counsellors

THE quhilk day in presens of the proveist bailyeis and Counsell of this brugh compeirit personallie James Woodsyd quha wes thesaurer of this brugh fra Michaelmes 1664 untill Michaelmas 1665 yeirs, quha conforme to ane Act of the Magistrats and counsell of this brugh beirand dait the tuentie eight day of December 1666 yeirs quhairby the saidis Magistrats and Counsell nominat John Porter Alexander Dyet and the clerk to audit the lait thesaurers accompts and for that effect to convein the saidis thesaurers befoire thame fra tyme to tyme and to report ther proceidure thairintill to the Counsell produceit ane report under the handis of the saidis thrie auditors beirand the said James Woodsyd to have chairged himselff with the particulars following quhilk wes conteinit in the chairge given to him of the tounes rents and casualities fra Michaelmas 1664 untill Michaelmas 1665 yeirs, viz. In the first for *James Woodsyd his thesaurer compt and his exoneration.*

Small teind	110 02 01
Toune land	726 13 04
Roped land	276 03 04
Mylne rent	184 03 04

Burges fynes	046 00 00
Feu duty	043 01 10
Fynes and unlawis	122 00 00
SUMMA of the said chairge is ane thousand fyve hundreth eight pundis thrie shilling ellevin pennyes	1508 03 11

DISCHAIRGE.

Payet out be the compter be ticketts and warrands under the magistrats handis	1407 16 10
Item defeasit to him for Skelmorlie's feu deuty	0000 16 08
Item for the laird of Adametoun	0002 16 08
Item for the compter's fie	0008 13 04
SUMMA of the dischairge is ane thousand foure hundreth Tuentie pund 3s. 6d.	1420 03 06
Sua chairge and dischairge being compared togedder the compter rests unto the Toune	0088 00 05

James Woodsyd thesaurer accompt.

In respect qubairof and that the said James Woodsyd had farder payet out for the Toune to James Galt wheelwright tuelff shilling Scots and to the clerk at comand of the magistratis fyve pund sextein shilling and off ane band granted be him to Robert Woodsyd present thesaurer of the said brugh of the soume of fourescoire ane pund tuelff shilling Scots quhilk compleits the said soume of eightie eight pundis money foirsaid and with quhich the said Robert Woodsyd is to be chairged in his thesaurer accompt Thairfoire the saidis Magistrats and Councell ordeins ane dischairge to be granted to the said James Woodsyd of his thesaurer accompt the tyme above written and of his intromissione with the toune's rent and casualities during the said space conforme to his chairge. Sic subscribitur: Robert Cunynghame, provost Henry Lyne, baillie, Law: Blaire, baillie, Robert Francis, counsellor, James Kyll, counsellour William Slos, counsellor Robert Nesmyth, counsellor Niniane Holmes, counsellor George Erskine, counsellor A oz C. Andro Caldirwood, counsellour.

Comissione for thesaurer accomptis.

THE quhilk day the Magistrats and Counsell continowes the Comissione grantet to John Porter Alexander Dyet and the clerk for auditing trying and exameining of the lait thesaurers their accompts and addes Robert Nesmyth youngar to thame and ratifies approves and confirmes the said former comissione given to the saidis John Porter Alexander Dyet and the clerk with all reports to be given thairof in tyme coming.

The Magistrats and Counsell liquidats the pryce of the boll teind meill for the cropt 1667 last bypast to eight merks Scots and the mylne rent at that rent. Liquidations of teind.

Item the Magistratis and Counsell modifies to James Galt wheelwright the soume of fyftie merkis Scots money for ringing of the Bell and keiping of the Knok for the yeir to come and modifies to him ten merks for the last yeir by and attour quhat he has ressaved. Modifications of James Galt's bcall for ringing of the bell.

The quhilk day in presens of the saidis proveist bailyeis and Counsell of the said brught compeirit personallie John Gray lait thesaurer of the said brugh To wit fra Michaelmas 1665 yeirs untill Michaelmas 1666 yeirs quha conforme to the Act [cited above] produceit ane Report under the hands of the auditors beirand the said John Gray to have chairged himselff with the hail tounes rent teindis casualities roped lands customes fynes and utheris conteinit in his chairge given to him for the said space The totall of quhich chairge extentis unto ane thousand fyve hundreth nyntein pund 4s. 5 penneyes . . 1519 04 05 John Gray his thesaurer accompt.

Dischairge.

Of quhich soume ther is payet out be the compter conforme to the precepts and warrants under the Magistrats hands the soume of (in words) 1313 13 06
Item defeasit to him of John Reid his band quhilk he hes not ressaved and quhairwith Robert Woodsyd present thesaurer is to be chairged 0032 18 00
Item William Wallace messenger his burges fyne quhilk the magistratis forgave . . . 0004 00 00
Item Adametouns feu deuty 0002 16 08
Item Skelmorlie's feu deuty 0000 16 08
Item the compter's fie . 0008 13 04

Summa of the dischairge   1362 16 10

Sua chairge and dischairge being compared the compter rests to
the Toune . . . 0156 07 07

Item, sensyne ther is foure pund Scots given doun be the magistrats
of John Edwardis burges fyne conteinit in the said John Gray his chairge
sua yit rests 0152 07 07

In respect quhairof and of fyftie eight shilling Scots being ane rex
dollor payet out be him to the clerk . . . . and of ane band granted be
him to Robert Woodsyd present thesaurer of the said brugh conteining the
soume of 149 pund 9s. 7d. quhairwith the said Robert Woodsyd is to be
chairged . . . . Thairfoire the saidis Magistrats and Counsell ordeins ane
dischairge to be granted to the said John Gray. [In form and with same
signatures as the preceding.]

III.—EXCERPTS FROM BURGH ACCOUNTS

1. *Burgh Account.*—1600-1601.

JOHNNE RUSSALL's thesaurar fra Witsonday 1600 to Witsonday 1601 Compt maid the 29 Julii 1601. His cherge according to the uther tiket extendis to vj^{c}lvijli xixṡ ijd.

Exoneratioun as followis:—

Item to Stein Hog . .	xṡ	w:[1]
Item to Robert Peblis . . .	vjṡ	w:
Item to Johnne Russallis selff . .	vijli xvṡ xd	w:
Item to Johnne Mur for Mr. Patrik Galloway .	xijli	w:
Item to Jonet Peblis	iiijli	w:
Item to a cripill for horse . .	xxṡ	w:
Item another compt to Johnne Russall .	lvṡ	w:
Item to Robert Bawre . . .	ij merk	w:
Item to Johnne Wilsoun messinger .	iiijli	w:
Item for horses to William Scot and Johnne Quhytfurd xiijṡ iiijd		w:
Item to by a schert to a pure man	xṡ	w:
Item to Allane Skeoch . .	iijli xiijṡ iiijd	w:
Item to Johnne Auld . . .	xlṡ	w:
Item to Gilbert Gerven for copeis .	xxvjṡ viijd	w:
Item to pure Johnne Lope . .	xxṡ	w:
Item the offeceris claythis .	vijli vjṡ viijd	w:
Item for hiring . . .	xxli xṡ	w:
Item to Johnne Wilsoune messinger .	xli	w:
Item fiftie ane ṡ iiijd . .	liṡ iiijd	w:
Item to Jonet Cunyghame .	iiijli iiijṡ	w:
Item to James Birrell . .	xijli xiijṡ iiijd	w:
Mr. William Wallace . .	xxli	w:
Item to Mr. William Wallace	xli	w:

[1] w stands for *warrant*.

Item to William Symsoun knokkeipper	xijs vjd	w:
Item to Jonet Cunyghame	vli tnas viijd	w:
Item for wyne to Robertland	iiijli xvs	w:
Item to Oliver Broun	xxs	w:
Item Johnne Russallis selff	ij merk	w:
Item to Johnne Mur	xxxs	w:
Item to Johnne Mur	vli viijs	w:
Item to Niniane Barcley	lli	w:
Item James Birrell	xli	w:
Johnne Peblis provest fie	iiijli	w:
Item send to Edinburgh	iiij^xx xiijli vjs viijd	w:
Item to Jonet Cunyghame	xxiijli xs viijd	w:
Item to Jonet Cunyghame	vli vjs	w:
Item to the gudman of Garrich	lxvli	w:
Item to knokman	xviijs xd	w:
SUMMA	iiij^c jli xixs ijd	
His charge exceidis his discharge	ij^c lvjli	

(Sic.) In pretorio 4 Septembris 1601 Johnne Russill hes maid his compt of his depursingis sen his last compt maid the xxix of Julii last quhairin he wes awand ij^c lvjli.

Item first to Lowrence Scott	w:	xli
Item to Niniane Barclay	w:	lxxli
Item to William Scott and to furneis the chergis of the workmen that come to work the clayth be the burrowis	w:	xixli xijs

In pretorio 16 October 1601. Compt maid be Johnne Russall of his last rest as followes:—

Item to Laurence Scott	xxxli	w:
Item to Laurence Scott	xlli	w:
Item to Thomas Tempiltoun	xls	w:
Item to Niniane Barcley	lxxxli	w:
Item to William Scot and to send to Edinburgh	xixli xijs	w:
Item tane af him of the quarter merk feis	xxxvli and xiijli xs	
SUMMA	xlviijli xs	
Item mair tane af him for ane aikir of land	xxvjs viijd	
Item for the baillie William Pervuis baillie fie	xls	

EXCERPTS FROM BURGH ACCOUNTS.

Item tau af him Hew Tranis unlaw .	.	xlli
Item taue of Johnne Barnis burges fyne seing he mareit a fremanis dochter	.	iijli
Item the lay silver of David Dempster	.	xxxv merk
Item for the Hoilhous . .	.	viijs iiijd
Laurence Scot for the gallowns	.	xxxijs vijd
Item Allane Steinston buith maill	.	iiij merk
Item his fie allowit .	.	xls

SUMMA   ijᶜlxxxxvjli ixs vijd iiijᶜjli xixs ijd.

Indorsed: Johnne Russallis compt 1600 flittit.

2. *Burgh Accounts.*—1601-1602.

CHAIRGE to NANIANE INGLIS of the casualities of this burgh fra Witsonday 1601 to Witsonday 1602 dureing his thesaurarie.

~~Item Niniane Inglis unlaw and Johnne Russall his cationer for offending the proveist . . . .~~	~~xli~~ *Sic*
Item the superplus of the pettie custom fra James Brydeine	v merk xld
Item Patrik Tran and Thomas Cuming for the wattir fischeing	x merk
Archibald Howies burges fyne . .	xls
Jonet Bukillis unlaw for resaveing of sturdie beggeris	xli
Johnne Brydenes unlaw for takand his firlot to the coist syde to missour the unfriemenis salt and lossing of his salt thair againes the tounes actis	jᶜli
Item the brig penny to Gilbert Watt Johnne Tueid his cationer	xxli xs
Item fra Gilbert Watt for his bygaine brig pennie	xx merk
Johnne Wilsoun in Gaillis burges fyne Johnne Wilsoun skippar cationer	xli
Blak Johnne Dunlop in Saltcottis burges fyne	viijli
Hew Jones in Saltcottis burges fyne	viijli
Johnne M'Gibbonn his burges fyne	xli
Johnne Boyd in Saltcottis burges fyne	viijli
William Wilsoun travellour in Ireland Johnne Tueid his cationer burges fyne . . .	iiijli
David Stewart burges fyne	xli
Waltir Stewart burges fyne	x merk
Johnne Huntar in Blook burges fyne	x merk
Gilbert Huntar in Monkgrenane burges fyne	v merk

	James Robesoun in Saltcottis burges fyne	x merk
	Johnne Quhyte in Saltcottis burges fyne	x merk
	Alister Gastoun in Saltcottis his burges fyne	x merk
	Hew M'Kie in Saltcottis his burges fyne	x merk
	Johnne Braidschaw in Saltcottis his burges fyne	viijłi
iuj"li	Thomas Harbert in Saltcottis his burges fyne	viijłi
	Robert Blak in Saltcottis his burges fyne	v merkis
	Johne Blak thair his burges fyne	viij merk
	Thomas Dunlope thair his burges fyne	viij merk
	Thomas Rannaldis blude unlaw	xlš
	David Dempsteris peis and quheit silwir	xxxv merk
	Item Allane Steinstounes buithe maill of Johnne Russallis thesaurarie	iiij merk
	James Broun in Saltcottis burges fyne	xłi
	Robert Fultoun burges fyne	xłi
	Item the unlaw of Robert Steill in Dalgrey for tuilzeing	v merk
	John Thomsoun flescheouris burges fyne	vłi
	Johnne Spark burges fyne	vłi
	Robert Tailyeour in Kilmernokis burges fyne	xłi
	Archibald Gillespie in Kilmernok his burges fyne	xłi
	Margaret Tranis unlaw xłi with ane new disobedience	
	Patrik Atkin in Fairlie burges fyne	xłi
	Johnne Forrester	xłi
	Johnne Or	xłi
	George Boyd	xłi
	Robert Forrester	xłi
	Item Marteine Baillies unlaw for his brydell	vłi
	Johnne Steinstounes Brydell unlaw	vłi
Sic.	~~And Johnne Young kirk bellman for Theophulus Sinclaires brydell unlaw~~	vłi
	Hew Parker and Johnne Steinstounes two unlawis ilk ane xlš	iiijłi
	David Mulingis burges fyne	iiijłi
	James Connellis burges fyne	xłi
	Johnne Aitkin	x merk
	Edwerd Hemphill in Fynnik burges fyne	xłi
	Item Kilmernokis protestatioun silwir	viijłi
	Johnne Robesoun in Saltcottis burges fyne	xłi
	Thomas Boyd cationer for Johnne Boyd his brother	xłi
	Johnne Auld blude silver resavit fra William Patoun	lxxxxviiłi
	Alexander Blakburne	j^e merk
	Peitter Howy in Saltcotis burges fyne	xłi

EXCERPTS FROM BURGH ACCOUNTS. 243

Allane Symontones wyfis unlaw .	x merk
Hew Cochranes burges fyne	vli
Neill M'Kinlayes burges fyne . .	xli
The gers of the grein . . .	xijli
Hew Henderson blude on Johnne Mur . .	vli

SUMMA of the casualiteis is seven hundreth xli vjs viijd ij⁷li vjs viijd

3. Compt of Borrowed Silver and Depursings when the Town went to Dumbarton.—Circa 1602.

COMPT of the BORROWIT SILVER and DEPURSINGIS as followes :— Item this is the first borrowit silver that Thomas Boyd intromettit with quhen the Toun yide to Dumbartane the particular followes :—

Payit be a w.	Item Stene Robesoun	v merk
Payit be a w.	Johnne Thomsoun .	v merk
Payit be a w.	Johnne Wilsoun .	v merk
Payit be a w.	Alexander Cunninghame	v merk
Payit be a w.	Edward Cawane .	v merk
Payit be w.	David Speir .	viij merk
Payit be a w.	James Bryding .	viij merk
Payit be a w.	Johnne Rannald .	v merk
Payit be a w.	Johnne Biggart .	v merk
Payit be a w.	Niniane Holmes .	v merk
Payit be a w.	William Or .	v merk
Payit be a w.	Cudbert Davie .	v merk
Payit be a w.	Thomas Huchesoune .	v merk
Payit be a w.	Johnne Mortoun	viij merk
Payit be a w.	Niniane Weir .	v merk
Payit be a w.	Alexander Lowrie .	v merk
Payit be a w.	Allane Ros .	v merk
Payit be a w.	David Walker .	v merk
Payit be a w.	Johnne Bogis . . .	1s.

SUMMA j'ij merk xs. money. This silver wes delyverit to Thomas Boyd in his ganging to Dumbarten and wes all depursed except xxxix merk delyverit to the Provest.

Payit be a w.	Item Robert Craig borrowit fra him .	viij merk
Payit be a w.	Item the Provest borrowit seusyne John Russall .	v merk
Payit be w.	Hew Quhyit . . .	v merk

Payit be w.	Alexander Montgomery	v merk
Payit be a w.	Johnne Mur skipper	v merk
Payit be a w.	Robert Cunninghame	viij merk
Payit be a w.	Andro Dunlope	viij merk
	Archibald Howie	viij merk
	Item the silver resavit fra Thomas Boyd	xxxix merk

SUMMA . . . lxxxiij merk

Item mair resaved fra Johnne Thomsone and Johnne Russall ilk ane of thame xxxli to mak out the soume to Lowrence Scott . lxli

SUMMA . . viij^{c}xiij merk

Item mair resaved William Wilsones burges fyne . . iiijli
Item mair resaved Gilbert Watis auld brig pennie . xx merk

SUMMA . ij^{c}xxvij merk

EXONERATIOUN OF PATRIK TRANES DEPURSINGIS.

Item first to Laurence Scott	j^{c}viijli xvs
Item to his boy of drink silver	vjs viijd
Item to my Lord Argyles man	xs
Item mair to Johnne Hart for careing the townes lettres to Edinburgh	xiijs iiijd
Item in Thomas Cumingis quhen the silvir wes borrowit	xiijs iiijd
Item send to Edinburgh with Alexander Montgomery to bring hame Suspensioun aganes Glencarne and than depursed	iiijli xld
Item with the Laird of Blair quhen we gatt our discharge subscryvit with the said Laird in Johnne Blares of our teindis iiij pyntis of wyne	xxvjs viijd
Item mair to the Maister of Paisley four pyntis of wyne and ane pund of almontis	xxxjs viijd
Item to Thomas Fairlie my Lord Glencarnes man j pynt wyne j breid	viijs
Mair for our disjoynes quhen we raid to Air about the Saltcoit boitis	xxxiijs iiijd
Item for our denneris that day we tuik the townes seasing the Lochmilne capoun nocht comptit	vjli vjs viijd
Item mair with Hew Glen at twyse	xxs
Item mair that day James Boyd brak warde	xxvjs viijd
Item with Aslos thairefter about James Boydis caus iij pyntis wyne	xxs

Item with Hew Glen the last tyme as he yeid throw the toun j pynt wyne	vjs viijd
Item to the Kirk a fourt pairt of salt	xxd
Item for the making of his sark	xijd
Item for tua chopynis of aill to him	ijs
Item that day to Laurence Scotis disjoyne he resaved his money	xls
Item depursed be me in Air with honest men of this toun in the provestis of Air and in Thomas Cumingis sensyne	lvjs
Item gevin to the boyes that day to by thair disjoynis we raid to Dumbartoun	xiijs iiijd
Mair with Johnne Michell quhen he trystit with us for the Saltcoitis ij pyntis wyne	xiijs iiijd
Item my awin horse to Dumbarten	xxvjs viijd
Item to William Houstoun for his wages	viijs
Item mair ane quart wyne in Thomas Cumingis foir seller quhen I resaved the remanent of the silvir frome Thomas Boyd	xiijs iiijd
Item to Thomas Lope for making the Frensche manes claithes	ixs
Item to Johnne Biggert for clayth to be the Frensche manes sark and claithes	iijlib ijs
Item for my provest fie fra Michelmes 1600 to Michelmes 160j	iiijlib
Item for four treis coft for Mathew Homill to be lewiris	xiijs iiijd
SUMMA	vij^{xx}vijli xijd
Supir expendit	9li xijd

4. Burgh Accounts.—1607-1608.

THE compt of JOHNNE NEILSOUN thesaurer of his comptis intromettit with of the dewties of Irwine and casualities fra Witsonday 1607 to Witsonday 1608 yeiris.

In the first the comptar is chargeit with the dewties of the Bogflattis extendding to lxxv aikiris j ruid xxiiij fallis at v merkis the aiker inde ij^{c}lilib vjs viijd . . . . . ij^{c}ljlib vjs viijd

Item the land with the Duncanhill	ixlib		
Item the Busland	xlij merkis	Inde	lijlib vjs viijd
Item the four buithis	xjli xiijs iiijd		
Item Johnne Kid for the Corsfurd	liijs jiijd		

Item with the haill few dewties extending yeirlie to xxxviijlib viijs iiijd Tua yeiris inde	lxxvjlib xvjs viijd
Item with the casualities the said yeir	xlib
SUMMA of his charge of the dewties and casualities abonewrittin	iij^{c}lxxxixli xs

Item he is chargit with tua restis of tua stentis viz. the first Trone stent and first king stent .	lxxixlib vjs viijd
Item he is chargeit with the sowme of fyve hundreth merkis money borrowit fra Johnne Neisbit .	iij^{c}xxxiijli vjs 8d

SUMMA Totalis   viij^{c}ijlib iijs iiijd

EXONERATIO PREMISSORUM.

In the first the comptar is exonerit with the comptis eftirspecefeit debursit be him in maner undirwrittin That is to say debursit be him to Robert Tran for ane cordell conforme to warrand . . . . vlib vjs iiijd

Item to Thomas Boyd provest conforme to warrand	xxixlib xs
Item to Agnes Moncreiff as the warrand beiris .	viijli
Item to William Cauldwell clerk debursit be him upon w./	xxjli viijs
Item to the said William delyverit be him to Laurence and Johnne Nisbit	iij^{xx}vjlib xiijs iiijd
Item to Thomas Boyd provest upone uthir warrand	xjlib ixs
Item to Mr. William Wallace upon warrand .	xllib
Item to Johne Harvie for jestis conforme to w./ .	iiij^{xx}ixlib xs
Item to Jonet Mure as the warrand beiris .	liijlib vjs viijd
Item to Laurence Scottis sone conforme to w./	iijlib xvjs
Item to James Birrell upon warrand .	xxijlib vjs

SUMMA Lateris   iij^{c}ljli vjs iiijd

Item to Robert Broun of Burrowland . .	vjlib
Item debursit be the comptar in small comptis of expenssis at divers tymes at the provest and ballies command in particular comptis for by the warrandis quhairwith he is exonerit . .	xvli xijs viijd
Item to Edward Duncane wricht upone warrand .	vijlib vjs viijd
Item to James Winrahame for Dunbartane stent as the w./ beiris	xxxiijli vjs
Item to Thomas Cuming ballie of borrowit money .	xxxiijli vjs 8d
Item to Johnne Mure herringman as the warrand beiris	viijli
Item to Williame Scott for his fie . .	xls
Item to Johnne Wilsoun messinger as the w./ beiris	xls
Item to Hew Thomesone for ganging to Edinburgh w./	xxxiijs iiijd
Item to Johne Bigart warkman w./ . .	vjli vjs viijd
Item to Jonet Wilsoun as the w./ beiris .	vli viijd
Item to Johne Young to pey ane glaswindo .	xlvjs viijd

EXCERPTS FROM BURGH ACCOUNTS.

Item to Laurence Lyn as the w./ beiris .	xli iijs viijd
Item to Johne Peblis elder . .	xviijlib
Item to William Mure w./ . .	iijli xvs iiijd
Item to Johne Ros npone warrand .	iijlib
Item to James Boyd couper . .	xxvjs viijd
Item to Johne Browne w./ . .	xld
Item to Williame Mure younger	xiiijli xld
Item to Johne Barclay w./ . .	ixli xiijs iiijd
Item to Margaret Ballie w./ . .	xxjli xiijs 4d
Mair includit in the said w./ . .	xxs
Item to Johne Wilsoun messinger upon w./	xls
Item to Rob Kyle . . .	xiijs iiijd
Item to Margaret Cunyngham uppone w./ .	xvili xviijs iiijd
Item to William Patoun w./ .	xijlib

Item the comptar is dischargit nyne lib xviijs ressavit be Margaret Cunyngham fra Robert Broun as ane part of the few dewties v merk for ane yeiris dewtie of William Steinstoun his buyth and tua merkis of burges fyne ressavit be hir fra Laurence Lyn Inde . xiiijli xjs 8d

Item to Thomas Boyd provest of borrowit silvir .	xxxiijli vjs viijd
Item to Alexander Cunynghame for tua buistis of confectis	xxiiijs
Item to the provest quhen he raid to Selkirk .	xxjli iijs iiijd
Item to Johnne Randell conforme to w./ . .	vli ijs xd
Item to James Galbraithis man .	xlviijli
Item to Johnne Dyett w./ . .	xxxiijs iiijd
Item to William Gemmell w./ .	vli vjs viijd
Item to Johne Mure cuik w./ .	liijs iiijd
Item to Thomas Boyd provest for his fie mid yeir .	iiijlib
Item to William Dyett upone warrand .	xiij merkis

Item he is dischargit with the rest of ane compt quhairin he is superexpendit of the King and Trones stentis as the compt beiris . . xijli vs iiijd

Summa Lateris .	iijᶜiiijˣˣxvlib xjs vjd
Item allowit to the comptar his thesaurer fie	iiijlib
Item for his fies in ingaddering the stentis	iiijlib
Summa Lateris	viijlib
Summa Totalis	vijᶜlvlib
Summa of the Charge .	viijᶜijli xld
Discharge .	vijᶜlvlib

Sua restis upoun the comptar xlvlib quhilk he is presentlie appointit to gif to Johne Hehous thesaurer and the said Johne Hehous ordinit to be chargit thairwith: Comptit the xxix day of Julii 1609. Subscrivit with thair handis

Thomas Boyd, provest	Robert Trane
William Scott	Johne Cwmmyng
Robert Kyle	David Tweydy, elder
Steine Robisone	R. Cauldwell, *clericus*

5. *Burgh Accounts.*—1608-1609.

In pretorio burgi de Irwin xiij Octobris 1609 :—

Presentes.

Thomas Boyd provest
Williame Mure ballie   Hew Scott ballie
William Scott   Robert Trane   John Bandell

Quo die ADAME GALT thesaurer hes maid his compt of his ressettis and debursingis intromittit with and casualities this last yeir fra Witsonday 1608 to Witsonday 1609.

In the first the comptar charges himselff with the dewties of the towne land extending to lxxv aikiris j rud xxiiij fallis extending the aikir to v merkis money Inde ij^{c}lib vjs 8d for ane yeir.

Item the land at the Duncanehill . . .	ixli
Item the Busland . . .	xxviijlib
Item the four buithis . . .	xjli xiijs iiijd
Item Johnn Kid for the Corsfuird . . .	liijs iiijd
Item with the haill few dewties the said yeir . .	xliiijli xiijs iiijd

Item the casualities the said yeir following :—

In the first fra Stevin Wilsoun in Lairgis	xxli
Item fra Johne Aikin thair . .	xxvjlib xiijs iiijd
Item fra David Aitkine . .	lli
Item Patrik Aikin thair . .	xxlib
Item fm Thomas Harbert .	xllib
Item fra Robert Forrester . .	iij^{xx}vjli xiijs iiijd
Item fra Johne Forrester . .	xxxlib
Item fra William Thomesone	xxxlib
Item fra Johne Or	xxlib
Item fra James Robesone .	liijli vjs viijd
Item fra Johnne Robesone .	xxvjlib xiijs iiijd

Item fra Moyses Irne	iijlib
Item resavit for the brig penney	xvijlib vjs viijd

SUMMA of the haill Charge within specefeit extendis to . vijᶜliñ ijs

DISCHARGE.

In the first the comptar is dischargeit with the comptis following, viz. To the provest to keip the pittie conventioun in Air . . xlib

Item to Mr. William Wallace upoun warrant	xiijli vjs viijd
Item to James Gray and Johnne Fallewisdaill w/	lxlib
Item to Johnne and Robert Thomesones w/	xxvjs viijd
Item to Johnne Ros youngar for wark	xiijs iiijd
Item to William Dunlope his servand for lyme	xvjs
Item to the provest to keip the generall conventioun	jᶜ merkis
Item to Mr. William Wallace upone w/	xxvjli xiijs iiijd
Item in small comptis upone w/	viiili iijs iiijd
Item to Thomas Boyd provest for small compt	vijli viijs iiijd
Item mair to him for the rest of his compt	xiijli xvs
Item to James Birrell upone w/	vlib
Item to William Scott for his fie	xls
Item to Margaret Ballie upone w/	xlib vjs viijd
Item to Gilbert upone w/	iiijlib
Item to Johnne Neisbit and Hew Thomson w/	jᶜijlib
Item to William Mure youngar upon w/	iijli xvjs viijd
Item to Mr. William Wallace upon w/	xllib
Item to Patrik Thome for hors corne	xvs
Item to Thomas Boyd provest for herring w/	xvjlib
Item to James Birrell w/	xiiijli xiijs iiijd
Item to Johnne Symsone Smyth for oyle	xs
Item to Thomas Boyd provest upon w/	xxlib
Item to Thomas Cuming of small comptis	xijli iijs iiijd
SUMMA Lateris . iiijᶜxllib	
Item to Hew Thomesone upone w/	xls
Item Litill Andersone messinger w/	xxvjs viijd
Item to James Birrell upone w/	xlib
Item to Quintine Mure upon w/	liijs iiijd
Item to Johnne Symsone for mending the knok	liijs iiijd
Item to Johnne Barclay ballie upone w/	iijli xs
Item in small comptis	xijli ixs viijd
Item to Jonet Cunyngham upone w/	xxviijs viijd

250   MUNIMENTS OF THE BURGH OF IRVINE.

Item to Petir Ged and for druik w/ .   iijli xvs
Item to Hew Thomesone w/   .   xvjs
Item in small comptis   .   .   xijli vjs iiijd
Item to William Cauldnell w/   .   xijlib
Item to James Birrell quhill Maii 1609   xlib
Item to certane personis in small comptis w/ .   vlib xiijs iiijd
Item to Johnne Mure in Fischmercat w/   .   liijs iiijd
Item to the minister for Witsonday last   .   lxvjli xiijs iiijd
Item to Thomas Boyd provest at the parliament   lilib
Item to Robert Trane upon w/   .   .   vlib vijs ijd
Item to James Browne skipper for the firlott .   vli
Item in small comptis w/ .   .   .   xxiiijli vijs ijd
Item to Thomas Boyd provest and William Mure ballie
for thair fies quhill Michaelmes 1609 .   .   vjli vjs viijd
Item to Thomas Boyd provest debursit be him w.   .   vjlib
            SUMMA Lateris   ij^cxlvijlib
            SUMMA Totalis   .   vj^ciiij^{xx}vijlib

Sua rests upoune the comptar lxiiijlib ijs quhairof tane aff his fe xls Item Barbara Jamesone hir disobedience xxxijs vijd Sua restis conforme to the account, lxlib ixs vd.

6. *The Toune's Compt auchtand to Margret Hamiltoun.*—1610.

	Lib.	s.	d.
Imprimis with the baillyeis and Archibald George with sindrie utheris in the toune quhen Stein Quhyte yeid to Peter Ged and drinking with Stein Hoig	0	33	0
Mair quhen the younkeiris of the toun went out to thair May play with provest and bailyeis in ane lawing	0	40	0
Item with the Kirk sklaitteres provest and baillyeis at the compt making	0	20	0
Item that day the burgessis wes maid Archibald George wes in ane choippen of wyne at	0	5	0
Item the proveist and baillyeis and sindrie utheris in the tounes effaires	0	22	0
Item with the erle of Eglintoun quhen the proveist baillyeis and clerk desyred the lane of his sklaittaris to the common wark of [*torn away*] in expenssis	vij	0	0
Mair with the proveist the Laird of Towcroce his brother and the clerk with sindrie utheris in ane lawing . . .	0	27	0

	Lib.	s.	d.
Mair be the provost bailyie and Archebald George with the lord of Lowdouns messinger of armes ane choippen of wyne and ane lang breid at	0	8	4
Mair for the communion wyne this same yeir 1610 is 9 quarttis at	9	0	0
Mair with Stevin Hog at the doun taking the ferry boit . .	0	xi	viij
SUMMA . . .	xxvij	iiij	0

Allane Ros thesaurer ye sall answer to Margaret Hamiltoun abonewrittin xxvij^{lib} iiij^s abone specifeit, quhilk sal be allowit to you from your comptis Subscrivit with our handis at Irvine the xxi day of September 1610.

D. CAULDWELL, *clericus*
The first of December subscrivit be us.

WILLIAM MUR, baillyie
HEW SCOTT, baillyie
JOHN DUNLOPE, baillie
ANDREW TRAN, baillie

7. *Towne's Compt.*—1611.

Item Imprimis That day my Lady Crawfurde came throw this Town thair wes twa quartis wyne ane buist of almoundis and twa quheit breid. 58^s 8^d

Mair ane Mounonday morneing with sum strangeris whom Mr. Hew Skot the minister present ane pynt of wyne. 10^s

Mair with the Laird of Montgrinnen ane pynt of wyne whom Mr. William Cawldwall present. 10^s

Mair that day Mr. David Barclay teichit he and Archibald George provest whom Mr. Robert Kyll present. 22^s

Mair that day the minister wes desyrit to the Tolboothe thaireftir the Provest Baillies with sum of the Counsell Minister and Skoolmaster that wes to thair denneris. 3lib. 2s.

Mair to the Laird of Carnell ane pynt uill half ane mutskein accavytie and ane quheit bread. 10s.

Item to me lord Bishope quhen he wes in this toun four quartis ane pynt of wyne ane schopen Accavytie ane quheit bread. 5lib. 13s. 4d.

Mair to the Provest of Glasgow and quart of wyne and ane quheit breid 23s. 4d.

Mair with the Laird of Blair that day the Provest wes absent. 58s. 8d.

SUMMA above wryttin Sevintein lib. awcht s.

Item that day the Maister and the Provest Archbald George wes agriit with the gudeman of the Ackens the gudeman of Garix Mr. William Wallace of Symytown thair lawing wes fyve merkis and thre pyntis of 12s. wine xxxvj sh.

SUMMA   5lib. 2s. 8d.

Item ane lawing with Stein Hog the first day we yed to the Troone 16s. and ane half mutskein accavytie 5s.

Mair ane uther day. fourtein s.

Mair that day the Laird of Corsbie wes at the Troone ane quart of wyne and ane qubeit breid xixs. 4d.

Mair that day the Baillie of Monetown wes thair and his folkis. xixs. 4d.

With the Laird of Montgrinen quhen we gatt his discharge. 32s.

Mair with the officer that scharget us for lawborrowis. 13s.

Summa Totalis . . 26lib. 18s. 4d.

Allane Ros lait thesaurer ye sall pey to Jeane Cuming abone specifeit the sowme of xxvjlib. xviijs. iiijd. money in satisfactioun of the soumes abone specifeit quhairnnent thir presentis salbe warand Subscrivit with our handis at Irwine the xiij day of July 1611. Archibald George, provest

Andrew Tran, bailie
William Mur

D. Cauldueli, *Clericus*

8. *Account for Refreshments to the Magistratts of Irvine, etc.—*
12th *January* 1648.

Extract of the Wyne gottin from Johne Wricht to the Toun's use.

	Lib.	s.	d.
Imprimis be Johne Dunlop ane of the bailyeis for the tyme to give to the bailie of Air 3 chopeins of wyne . .	0	18	0
with ane wheit breid . .	0	4	0
with ane glass	0	3	0
Mair half pound of candle quhen the Committie satt about quartering of the souldieris	0	3	4
Mair the baillies and clerk in our owin hous with Major Stewart ane pynt of wyne with ane schort breid			
Mair the tuo baillies with Captane Campbell ane chopein wyne with ane chopein of aill	0	7	0
Mair ten pyntis of wyne to the Tolbooth quhen Mr. David Heriott was maid burges . .	6	0	0
with sex wheitt breid .	0	24	0
with tuo pund candle .	0	0	16
with tuell unce of suggour	0	20	0
Mair a pund of candle to the Tolbooth when the syss was holdin on James Greir and ~~Robert Kyle~~ . . .	0	6	8
Mair upon the 9 day of October ane pynt of wyne with the proveist and baillie in our seller . .	0	12	0

Sic.

EXCERPTS FROM BURGH ACCOUNTS. 253

	Lib.	s.	d.
with ane schort breid	0	4	0
and ane candle	0	0	8
Mair ane pynt of wyne that the proveist gave Mr. David Heriott quhen he went away aff the Toun	0	12	0
Item bestowit be the baillies and clerk when they gat thair Toun seall fra John Kirkwood	0	36	0
Item another tym the baillies and clerk with Liwtenent Wilsoun who came for quartering about the browes Adam Lillie of Air and Girvan having cum here upoune the comitie being present .	0	xv	0
SUMMA . . .	xiiij	v	viij

Off the whilk sum of xiiijlib. vs. viijd. we ordain you Ninian Ros to mak payment to John Wricht and his wyiff and thir presentis sall be your warrand. Subscryveit at Irwing 12 Januar 1648. JOHN REID, proveist. RO^T BROUN.

9. *Account of Disbursements by John Dunlop, for the Burgh of Irvine.—Circa 1653.*

THE count of the moneys reseved be me JOHNE DUNLOPE from a boy quhilk was puttin in prisson bien on theiffe with stoune goods and brak prison the count of the munie extends to threte two dallors les or more as the note beris as I tuk it.

Depurst out beine to on wabster wyfe cal Tempiltoun that daualit at the tound ends in the dib hous 24s.

For on blanket sho boght from the theafe quhilk was givin bake to the just aunder presently.

Item to Johne Guttre bely when Johne Ride was capten five cros dallors to pay for mele to be brisket to the souldiors 13lib 15s.

Item when the souldiors was goin out pour crafts men when the war goin out souldiors to give to supplie ther wifes was delevirit betuix the cors and the tolbouth 12lib.

Item to Johne Heay to beat the druine 12s.

Item to Jeames Creag to goe to Glesgoue to sea quhat condition Glesgou was in when the souldiors was lyen at Boddel 24s.

Item to sume wimen that cam out of Minibol that was goen to Glesgou becaus the wisitetion was in Eare they wad not permit them to stay in the tound al night the bely John Gutre and I convoyit them by and geve them mete and drink quhilk I pait 12s.

To a drumer boy of Eare cam from Kilsyth quhilk was in John Hukter baksters al night I was disyrit to give him 12s.

Item more tual souldiors Colonel Howies and sume of Magore Boyds and soum of Capten Boys of them muthir nekit and had nothing the provist gairt me give them 9lib.

Item on souldior of the Yearil of Castil cam to John Clarkes of the toundhead pittifuly woundid and the provist callit Tobeas the surgen to pansim and to dres his wounds I geve to Tobeas and him 3lib.

Item when we went to Miutros at Boddel tual dallors 34lib. 16s.

Item in chergis in Glesgou Capten Heay and thes that went with us in Willem Houis hous and other pearts 9lib.

Thereftir Marget Brouns in Irvin with soum of our tounds foke with the magistrat of Eare for drink we bistouit ther wine and other things 49s.

         SUMMA . . is 86lib. 9s.

As for the wallat was takin away from the thife was tekin by the Inglisis that night with much more goods of my aun as wil apire.

As for the gray neag that had the spiven that was boght for the sociat Reade was almost stervid and I was desyerid to take him in and geve him mete sum aght dayes before the breck of Homilton and that Manouday the Ingleses cam in I had him sedilt and brydilt and that night they cam in being in my stebil they tocke him and when they went away with much moyion of Mestres Broune gat the horse agean bot nether sedil nor brydil nor horse culler and geve the horse smuth that tocke him tend shillin sterlin and eftir I went out of the tound I tuke him alongst to Carick in Gallova with me thereftir I sold him for nind and twenty pund I houp ye wil alou me for the kepin of him so longe.

Owand to John Dunlop by the towne at perusing of his accoompts .	62	7	8
Rebate for townland and teynd owand to John Porter .	17	11	8
Item owand to William Hendrie . .	30	05	4
Item owand to Gilbert Wyllie . .	00	05	4
Item to Robert Cochran .			

10. *Account by Bailie John Dunlop against the Burgh of Irvine.*—1653-57.

THE Count of the TOUND of IRVIN anne to me JOHNE DUNLOPE.

	Lib.	s.	
Item when Johne Ride baley and I was send to the Lerges with my lord Muntgumre when the wisitetion was in the Lerges to get five bots to goe about to Moule when Dayed Lesle was ther to Robert Muntgumre for ane horse hyre	0	20	0
Item to goe to Glesgoue the bely James Bleare and I to Alexander Grege for his horse hyre when the wisitetion was in Glesgoue	0	40	0

EXCERPTS FROM BURGH ACCOUNTS.

	Lib.	s.	d.
Item in chergis be a night in Pesley chergis my selfe and my horse	0	43	0
Item for on boy cam from the Seson of Steuerton hear and to cere on leter backe with him ther .	0	6	0
Item to on mesinger when Johne Ride and I was tuo byeles cherged for the ecksyes	0	12	0
Item for one horse hyer to goe up to my Lord Coheren to Johne Dunlop to befrind us at the comitte	0	6	0
Item for one man and wyfe and three childrin of supplie that cam out of one suspecke peart and wold not suffir them to remen I was disyerit to give them	0	12	0
Item for tuo yeares fiell being byelle	4	0	0
Item when I was sent to Stirline threttine dayes	26	0	0
More in gevin to the misser halfe of on dallor .	0	30	0
More givin to the clarke for extrek of the acke	3	0	0
SUMMA .	41	15	0
Riesevid of this when I went to Stirline	24	0	0
Remens of this count	17	15	0
Item I was sent to Eare before I went to Decith to sei quhat mendir of comission ther I was on night and day ther I pait for John Snodgarse horse of my aune chergis	0	46	0
Item that when I went away to Decith the causit me paye out that day .	0	5	0
Item I geve Johne Moure in Enbrogh then to agent our bisines anent our ses with one letter I gat from Loutennen-General Lambart	0	30	0
SUMMA 36lib. 1s. 21-16-			
Resevid of this or I went to Decith .	24	0	0
So rests of this count 19lib, 13s.			
July fifte thrie—The tound sent me ovir to the govirnor of Eare give he could help us anything anent our ses he sead he could not so thereftir I was sent ovir agen to sei give he wad wret a lettir to the Louttinen-General in our favores he thoght it not fite he sould and did refouse to giv it so cammine home Mr. Mathis being in this tound the provist and I did spake to him and he did undirteake to us give we wad send ovir agen he sould purches a letter from the govirnoure to us I was send ovir agen and did obtine the lettir so I pait Johne Snodgars for his horse	0	30	0
Item my aune chergis and the horse on night I was of the thrie I was ther .	0	34	0
Item when the Inglismen cam to proclaime the Justes of Eare Court I geve	0	12	0

	Lib.	s.	d.
Item when Cabten Givven in my hous with the provist and sume others fechit a chopin of wyne and eale and sume bride I geve out	0	15	0
Item when Johne Porter and I went to Nitton to trye quhat condition they war in when the wisitetion was ther cost me	0	6	0
Item I was sent ovir to Eare when Mr. Robert Darkle began to persheu the tound and to sei give he had callit so I spake for on to anser for us when we ar callid I was in chergis with him and my selfe and my horse that night	0	36	0
Item June fiftefour—I wassent oviragen when it was callid in chergis	0	20	0
Item Heu Cunigame went ovir thereftir I pait out	0	15	0
Item for John Snodgars horse hyer	0	12	0
Item for belly fie five year			
Item when I was sent last to Enbrogh I went upon the sext of Desember last and returnid hear agen the sevint of Jenuar quhilk mead threte on dayes at fourte s.	62	0	0
Item the purse stod beine the subscryvin of the book of the barons	0	12	0
Item thereftir when I went to give in supplication to the steats for the wretin of the supplication with Inglis hand	0	12	0
More on to the General I gave another	0	12	0
Ane supplicatio ovir agen to the steats ane other	0	12	0
More to the clarks man	0	5	0
More eftir I cam home I was sent ovir with the lettir to the govirnor about the bedes I was ther a night tomoro al day me horse mete was	0	8	0
My aune chergis was	0	19	0
The govirnor could not at then give no ansuar becaus he bot trye quhat came of the bedes			
Thereftir I was sent ovir for the ansuar agen of that lettir and was ther al night I pait Johne Snodgars for his horse hyer	0	12	0
For meat al night to the hors	0	8	0
And my aune chergis	0	13	0
SUMMA	89	14	0
Ressaveitt of this quhen I wantt to Edinburgh 30lib.			
So ther rests 59lib. 14s.			
Rests owand	44	15	0

Rebate off this compt which is 44lib. 15s. the sowme of twelve pound 8d. that hee is restand of the boyes money his receits and depursmentis being compared, with twentie uyn pund 6s. 8d. that hee gate for the horse ther will be resting owand him the sowme of twentie sevin shilling eight penies Scotts by the towne.

11. *Account of proportion due by the Burgh of Irvine to the Agent of the Royal Burghs.*—1653-4.

ACCOMPT dew by the BURGH of IRVING to the AGENT for the ROYALL BURROWES.

	Lib.	s.	d.
Ther proportione of 3778lib. 2s. dew by act of Burrowes in July 1653	34	00	2
Annual-rent thairof to this day and dait . . .	02	00	0
Ther proportione of 5510lib. dew by act of Burrowes in July instant	49	13	0
	85	13	2

Edinburgh 4 July 1654.—Received from James Boyll present provost of Irving the above wryttine accompt and dischairges him and the Burgh thairof.

JA: ELPHINSTONE.

12. *Account of Expenses incurred by the Magistrates of Irvine for Refreshments.*—29th August 1655.

THE TOWNIS COMPT.

	Lib.	s.	d.
The provest with some Inglishmen 2 pynts of aill and on breid—5s.	0	5	0
The provest and Hewgh Cuninghame with Pittlone ane pynt of aill half a muchken of aquavitie on breid . .	0	7	0
The provest Adam Cuninghame elder with the Magistratis of Aire 3 chapineis of wyne 4 unce of suger tobako and pypes about Macclatchie	1	13	0
The provest and John Dunlope Hewgh Cuninghame and the Clark with sundrie otheris of the Counsell and a minister that was imployed to pritch a pynt of wine 2 brid 2 pyntis of aill . .	0	18	8
SUMMA .	3	03	08

Alexander Dayet mack pyment too Aggnes Coninghame off the somme off thrie pund thrie shiling acht penneys Scottis conform too the particulars above expressid and thes shal bee your warant. Susberyvit with our hands Irvin Agust 29, 1655.

A. DUNLOP.
HEWGH CUNYNGHAME.

13. *The Compt of John Guthrie his Chairges and Depursinges for the Toun of Irwin in Edinburgh.*—[1656.]

	Lib.	s.	d.
Imprimis to William Purves clerk to the exchequer for production of the tounes chartour	5	16	0
Item for copieng of the chartour and redendo thairof for William Purves registeres	0	18	0
Item to William Purves for the extract of the tounes last eque .	5	16	0
Item to his man for looking the exchequer rollis and extracting of it	2	0	0
Item to Mr. Thomsoun his brother . . .	9	10	0
Item spent with him be John Cunynghame . .	2	3	0
Item to the dictator of the rollis of exchequer conform to ordour .	2	0	0
Item to the keiper of the exchequer doore . .	2	8	0
Item to the keiper of the register . .	3	12	0
Item for registration of the tounes band .	4	9	0
Item payed for the eque	88	0	0
Item for fyve suplicatiounes wryting to give the Lordes .	3	0	0
Item to Mr. John Eleis man for wryting his [torn]	0	12	0
Item to the keiper of the counsell doore .	1	16	0
Item for tua lether bages to keip the tounes wrytes .	0	6	0
Item for my horse hyre	5	10	8
Item for my awin and my horse chairges for the space of eightein dayes	36	0	0
Item with Captan Given and John Cunynghame .	1	0	0
	185	6	0
Advanced of this in money	120	0	0
Restis	65	6	0

Primo October 1656:—

This abonwrittin compt is producit hard red seine and considderit be the Magistrates and Counsell.   R. BROUN, *Cls.*

Received of his accoumpt for corn fyne	3	0	0
Item for butter fyne . .	2	18	0
Item that wes takin from the cheese . .	23	11	8
Item for advanced for him for thrie moneth mantanence Julie Agust September 1656 .	12	0	0
SUMMA . 41lib. 9s. 8d.	41	09	8

	Lib.	s.	d.
So Restis indew to the coumpter of this accoumpt to the toune	23	17	8
But prejudyce of any uther accoumpt that the coumpter hes to chardge the toune with or quhat the toune is to lay to his chardg.			
Item that ye ar dew in Wm. Henryes Role for the monthes of October November and December 1656, 4lb. 13s. 4d. per mensem	14	0	0
Item that ye received from Gilbert Wylly owt of the excyse mony	12	0	0
Item that ye are dew in Allen Cuningham and Alexander Or's Role for the monthes of January February and March 3lib. 15s. per mensem	11	5	0
Compt being made John Gutrie restis awand in this paiper	13	7	0

14. *Order for payment to William Morison "the Burgh's Post," for carrying a Letter.—4th November* 1656.

You William Hendrie lait thesaurer faill not to pay to William Morisonne the borrowes post for delyvering a letter to meit at a particullar conventioun at Edinburgh tuelfe shilling and this salbe your warrand. Subscryved the 4 of November 1656.

M. Ro^t BARCLEY, proveist.
H. CUNYNGHAME, bailye.

15. *Account of Disbursements and Losses sustained by John Dunlop, Bailie of Irvine.—Circa* 1656.

A TRUE accoumpt of the Debursements and Losses sustained by JOHN DUNLOP quhill hee was Magistrat of Irvine: 1. In tyme of Alaster Mackdonald: 2. In the tyme of the Sectaries prevailling, after the defeat at Hammiltoune.

First in the tyme of ALLASTER MACKDONALD.

	Lib.	s.	d.
Imprimis for my charges eght dayes in Kilmarnock quhill I was sumoned before the committie	005	00	00
Item my fyne which I payet by order of committie after much intercession of mitigation	053	06	08
Item for redemption of my goods taken by Captain Muir and his sojours quhill I was marched to Glasgowe	018	00	00
Item in chairges quhill I was sumondet before the comittie in Glasgow	006	00	00
Item for ane horse and man to come to me to Kirkubright quhill I was sumond to the comittie at Edinburgh	006	00	00

	Lib.	s.	d.
Item for ane horse which I was necessitat for to buy not finding any to hyr in a storme for my carying to Edinburgh and which diet by the way in my returne	055	00	00
Item being fyned in Edinburgh by the committie there in 500lb. which by the intercession of friends was past I was partlie in chairges partly to the clerk being in Edinburgh tuintie thrie dayes above	038	00	00
Item after my horse diet for a horse to carie me home and chairges	003	08	00
SUMMA	184	06	08

2. In the tyme of the SECTARIES after the break and defeat at Hammiltoune.

	Lib.	s.	d.
Imprimis ane fedder bed and its furnitour to the garisoune at Eglintoune which I never gate back	030	00	00
Item waired out on two sojours under the bloudie fluix and brought from the garisoune in Eglinton and laid on my wyfe in my absence and on Serjan Wilson that with others came evrie day to them and caused bring seck and sugar measses and other necessars	040	00	00
Item seven dossen of Irland bords als brod as dealls which thretie fyfe the night they wer quartered upon me tooke out of my celler	042	00	00
Item nyne dealls which they wailed from amongst the rest	006	00	00
Item thrie pair of new plaids at 16lb the pair which they tooke as ther onne	048	00	00
Item above 20 water bolls of salt lost by ther horses put in the celler wher it was and they had the kea with them eght dayes quhill they went to the garisoune of Eglintoune	100	00	00
Item nyn bolls meall in thrie hogsheads taken away by them and eaten up in ther quarters	090	00	00
Item four great barrells of buiter disposed on by them in lyk maner	100	00	00
Item two carashes of beaf newlie salted	024	00	00
Item threttie stone of Iron taken by them out of my celler	060	00	00
Item the Iron Standers out of my house on the hill valued to	012	00	00
Item twoll eiken jeasts quhilk thy tooke and made fyrwood to ther guard	036	00	00
Item four tries which cost	009	06	08
SUMMA	627	06	08
SUMMA Totalis	811	13	04

The particular debursments and losses above writtin I the above named John Dunlop sustained over and above other losses and chairges in my crop and other wayes common and incident to me with other inhabitants And which though promised long agoe to be refoundet according to the abilitie of the place in a tacit way wer never as yet taken in serious consideratione and which I should not now trouble the Counsell de novo with notwithstanding of all my losses and other straits wer it not, I humblie exspect they will without furder delay consider of the samin and give my former supplicatione a favourable answer.

Indorsed: Coumpt of John Dunlops debursements and losses.

16. *Account by Lawrence Blair against the Magistrates of Irvine for Refreshments.—28th April 1658.*

ACCOMPT for the TOWN to LAWRENCE BLAIR.

	Lib.	s.	d.
Imprimis for ane pynt of sack tobaco pyps and beir	02	12	4
For ane choppein seck by Baylyie Conynghame	01	0	0
For two choppeins seck by Craig and Baylyie Conyngham with Mr. James Scott	02	0	0
For 3 choppeins seck by Baylyie Conyngham and Craig with the Justeices and Governour of Ayr	03	0	0
For ane choppein of wyn by Craig and the clark with the Livetennent of the last troup	00	10	0
For beir breid tobaco and pyps by the proveist with the quartermaster	00	12	0
For beir tobaco and pyps by the proveist with the quartermaster	00	05	8
For ane pynt wyn and thrie pynts wyn with the proveist of Ayr by the proveist and bailyies with tobaco and pyps	03	18	0
For 3 pynts wyn with Conynghamheid and Renallan	02	14	0
	16	12	0

Robert Cocherane lait thesaurer yea shall pay at sight heirof to Lawrence Blair for this above writtin compt the somme of sixteine pund tuelfe shilling and it salbe allowed to you in your accoumpts. Subscryved thir presentis with our hand at Irwine the 23 of Apryle 1658.   M. RO^T BARCLAY, proveist.
H. CUNYNGHAME, bailye.

17. *Order for Payment for carriage of a Letter to Edinburgh.—14th April 1659.*

HEW Muntgomrie thesaurer ye sall not faile to give to David Caulderwood fourtie shilling Scotts for caricing a Leter to Edinburgh at the Magistrates desire at it salbe allowed in your compt. Subscrivit with our hands at Irvin the fourtine day of Aprile 1659.   M. RO^T BARCLY, proveist.
 2 0 0   WILLIAM WISHEART, baillie.

18. *The Provost's Account.—Circa* 1659.

Receaved by the Proveist DUNLOPE.

	Lib.	s.	d.
. . . Alan Cumming .	66	0	0
Item from Perstown paroch .	24	0	0
Item from Peirstoune .	26	0	0
Item from Beith paroch .	6	12	00
More from Beith for thrie monthes and a half localitie	292	6	6
Item from Thorntown and Craig .	20	17	6
Item from Georg Montgomerie	16	00	00
	429	4	0

Debursed of this by the PROVEIST.

	Lib.	s.	d.
First to Robert Stewart	71	14	0
Debursed by the Proveist to Girvand .	130	13	0
Lost of 12 ryellis .	4	16	0
Given to Jhone M^{ck}gill .	42	0	0
Given to Janet Grier .	12	12	0
	170	1	0

Sic.

So rests by the Provist . 259lib. 3s. 0d.

```
420  4  0         250 11  6          83 10  6
170  1  0          41 15  0          83 10  6
-------           --------           83 10  6
259  3  0         292  6  6         --------
                                    250 11  6
```

JHONE GUTHRIES Rent.

	Lib.	s.	d.
Anable Wallace hous	10	13	4
For the rig .	2	0	0
Hous in Kirkgat .	5	6	8
For a booth downe the gat	4	13	4
For Helen Dunschiths yard .	7	13	4
For the hous downe the gate	2	13	4
For a rig downe the gat .	2	8	0
For two yards in Seagat .	8	0	0
For a yard at the port	4	0	0
For the back hous	8	13	4
	56	1	4

Charg 66 01 8
12 rayes att 56

2 Kedeais at 20
4 rex dolors

19. *Account between Provost Craig and David Catherwood for the use of the latter's horse.*—11*th March* 1662.

11 March 1662 :—

COUNT betwixt Provist CRAIG and DAVID CATHERWOOD for his hors.

Ittem Imprimus my hors to Air to put the souldiers by this towne.

Ittem The meiting the gentillmen in Air.

Ittem Another tyme quhen yeu and the rest of the gentillmen in the Countrie was chairged to look how the works sto'd.

The meiting the oficers another tyme to put by the bagag hors by this towne.

Ittem Another tyme the meiting the governour and the gentillman.

Ittem Three tyme to Kilmarnock at the meiting of the Shyr.

Ittem Three tyme meiting the Earll of Eglintoune and the gentillmen of the Shyr.

Ittem a rod to the Parlement.

Ittem my hors out of Edinburgh from the Parlement againe.

Thes arr too testifie that ther is indew upon this account tuelf pund Scotts quhilk in equite I judge should bee payet. A. DUNLOP.

Irvin, Juni 20 1663.

20. *Account against the Magistrates of Irvine for Refreshments.*— 1661-1662.

ACCOMPT be TOWN since Michalmes 1661.

	Lib.	s.	d.
Imprymies 3 choppeins wyn 2 pynts aill breid tobaco and pyps with Sir Adam Blair .	01	09	04
Att the clusing of the Dean of Gild a pynt of wyn 4 pynts aill and 4 breid is in all .	01	17	00
With Thomas Garvan 3 choppeins wyn, 3 pynts aill, breid, tobaco and pyps .	01	14	00
For a pynt aill with William Chammers .	00	02	00
For 5 muchkeins wyn with Baylie Fergesoun and men of Air .	01	00	00
For a choppein wyn with Colonell James Montgomrie .	00	10	00
For 2 pynts wyn, 3 pynts aill, breid, tobaco and pyps, with the shereff [of] Nidsdaill .	02	14	00
For 3 choppeins wyn, 2 pynts aill, two breid, tobaco and pyps with my Lord Cocheran .	02	01	04
For ane pynt wyn tobaco and pyps with one Ca : Crafurd .	01	03	00
For a choppein wyn with the provest of Air .	00	10	00
For 3 choppeins wyn, a pynt beir, tobaco and pyps with the excismen .	01	14	00

	Lib.	s.	d.
For a choppein wyn with the Laird of Blair	00	10	00
For a quart of aill to the mill	00	04	00
For a choppein wyn with Blair and others	00	10	00
For a choppein wyn with ane Ingleis captain	00	10	00
For breid and aill to the stair bigging	00	06	00
For a choppein wyn and breid with my lord Cocheran	00	11	04
For 2 pynts wyn, tobaco and pyps with the Commissioners of Shyre	01	17	00
For 2 pynts aill with William Chamers and 2 sojours	00	04	00
For 4 choppeins and a muchkein [wyn], a pynt beir, tobaco and pyps with the shereff	02	02	00
For 5 choppein wyn, 2 pynts aill and breid with the provest of Air	02	07	04
For a pynt of aill and a muchkein of wyn with baylie Cocheran	00	06	00
For a choppein wyn with my Lord Montgomry	00	08	00
Rests when yow wer with James Galt	01	03	00
For 5 muchkeins wyn, a pynt beir and 2 pyps with James Mudie	01	03	02
For beir and wyn, tobaco and pyps with the customers	00	14	08
For a choppein wyn, tobaco and pyps with the collector of the shyr	00	09	02
For a choppein wyn with Williame Chameris and Charles Dalrimpl	00	08	00
For a choppein Seck and a choppein wyn, beir and breid with the mineisters	02	04	00
For 38 pynts of wyn to the Communion	24	06	00
For 5 pynts wyn, 7 pynts aill, 5 breid, tobacco and pyps with the Proveist of Air and others	05	14	08
For 2 pynts aill, tobaco and pyps	00	06	00
For a pynt wyn to Bedlan his hows	00	16	00
For a pynt wyn and a choppein seck, breid and aill with Colonell James Montgomry	02	05	04
For 3 pynts aill at the casting John Gibs rent	00	08	00
For 2 quarts aill, 5 quarts of aill, 3 quarts and a choppein wyn, two dozen of glesses att the bonfyrs	10	10	08
For a choppein wyn, beir and sewgor with my Lord Montgomrij	00	17	00
For 6 pynts beir and breid after Dunlops buriall	01	01	00
For 3 muchkeins wyn with George Montgomrij	00	12	00
For 5 choppeins wyn, 3 pynts beir, 4 pynts aill and pyps and biskett with my Lord Montgomrij my Lord Cocheran and others	02	18	00
For 2 pynts wyn, 2 pynts beir, and breid att the Proveist goeing to Edinburgh	02	00	08
For a pynt wyn, sewgor and breid with Major General Mongomrij	01	04	04
For 3 choppeins wyn, 2 pynts aill and breid with my Lord Egleinton	01	11	04

	Lib.	s.	d.
For 6 pynts and a choppein wyn, 3 pynts beir, 6 oz. of sewgor, 3 breid, 2 oz. tobaco, 1 dozen of pyps, with my Lord Cocheran and the Iugleis Knight	06	17	00
For a pynt wyn with CloberLill	00	16	00
For 3 choppeins wyn, tobaco and pyps with David Biggertt that was to carrij money to Edinburgh	01	05	08
For 4 pynts of aill, pyps and tobaco when my Lord Kingston was maid burges	00	10	08
For a muchkein seck with my Lord Wintons Chamberlan	00	12	00
SUMMA	lxxxxv	x	0

Off the whilk soume abonewrittin extending to the said soume of fourscoir fyftin lib. xs. contenit in the within and abonewrittin Compt we ordain yow Alexander Cochran Thesaurer to mak payment to Marione Pebls spous of Laurence Blair incontinent efter the sight heirof and the samin sall be allowit to yow in your Accompts keipand thir presents for your warrand. Subscryvit with our hands at Irwin the 26 day of September 1692.
A. DUNLOP, provest.
J. CUNYNGHAME, baily.
W. Broun.
ALLAN CWMING, baily.

Received the abonesaid Compt from Alexander Cocheran this 17th December 1662 be me.
LAUR. BLAIR.

21. *Account for Refreshments to the Magistrates and their Guests.*—1663.

The TOUN of IRVING'S Compt dew to GEORGE GARVEN.

	Lib.	s.	d.
Imprimis Provest Guthrie with the baillies and Provest Craig with the erles of Annandaill, Carnwarth, Drumlanerk and Dalziell fyve chappenis seck thrie quarteis pund sugger and tua braid wheit breid is	06	18	00
Item ane anker of seck conteinand ellevin pynts and ane chappein at tua merk and a half the pynt quhen the Lord Commissioner was heir is	19	03	04
Item upone the 6 January 1663 Provest Guthrie and remanent Magistrats with the erles of Eglintoun Wintoun and divers uthers nyn pynts new wyn thrie braid wheit breid half ane pund suger and ane unce of tolbacco and nyn pypps is	10	00	06
Item according to directioun givin to the said erles thair gentlemen ane chappein wyn and tua pynts aill	00	14	00

	Lib.	s.	d.
Item the proveist and sum uthers with Carnell and Undirwoode anent the tyrsting for payment of the money awand be thame to the toun ane chappein wyn ane braid breid and ane unce of tolbacco is .	00	14	00
SUMMA . .	37	09	10
Off the which accompt thair is to be deducit for twelff pynts claret wyn that was remaining unspent of the wyn that was gottin frae Williame Wischart when the comissioner was heir quhilk was sold to the said George at 10s. the pynt except ane mutchkein wyn the proveist was at the bargan making being 4s. Inde to be deducit .	5	16	0
So remains to be payit to the said George	31	13	10

Off the whilk soume of Threttie ane pund threttein schilling ten pennyis Scotts Alexander Cochrane lait thesaurer quho hes not as yit maid your accompts ye sall not faill to mak payment to the abonenamit George Garven and the samyn salbe allowit be us to you in your accompts keipand thir presentis for your warrand. Subscryvit at Irving the ffirst day of Apryll 1663.   JOHN GUTHRIE, proveist.

                                                          ALLAN CUMING, baily.

                                                          ALLANE CUNINGHAME, bally.

Receavit be me George Garven frae the abonenamit Alexander Cochrane the abonewrittyn soume contenit in the abonewrittyn ordour.

        31lib. 13s. 10d.   G. GARVEN.

22. *Account for Refreshments to the Magistrates.*—1663-1664.

The TOUNS Compt since the 2 of November 1663 awand to MARIOUN CUNYNGHAME.

	Lib.	s.	d.
To Lawrence Blairs hous the prowest Hew Cunynghame sent for ane pynt of wyn	00	16	00
Be William Makbein to Lawrence Blairs hous thrie pynts of wyn	02	08	00
The 9 of Desember to Lawrence Blairs hous with the prowest of Ayre four pynts of wyn . .	03	04	00
The 21 and 22 of March the prowost Hew Cunynghame the baylie Robert Wallace prowost Craig and the clark was with the Lion Herat and the men that was with them five chopins of sek .	05	00	00
At the sam tym for thrie pynts of ayll on broad brid tobaco and pyps	00	11	08
7 day of Apryll the prowost Hew Cuninghame James Blare and James Fullertone was with the prowost of Ayr ane quart of French wyn .	01	16	00

EXCERPTS FROM BURGH ACCOUNTS. 267

	Lib.	s.	d.
ii day of Apryll The prowost Hew Cunyngham and the clark Robert Broun was with Generall Major Robert Montgomrie ane pynt of wyn ane pynt of ayll and ane brod brid . . .	01	03	00
When Robert Cunyngham was maid prowost they drank thrie pynts of wyn thrie pynts of ayll and sex broad breid .	03	18	00
That day the grasse of the grein was roped ther was left unpyed	00	02	04
Given to the prowost Hew Cunyngham to give to the Lion Harat 4 dolleris is	11	12	00
Given to pay the post that brought the leter for the Convention of Borows	00	18	00
9 of May 1664 the prowest Robert Cunynghame the baylie James Fullertone and the clerk Robert Broun was with Enterkin five chopins of wyn 4 broad bread 5 chopins of ayll two pyes of ressins .	03	14	00
14 of May The prowost Robert Cunyngham the baylie James Fullertone Hew Cunyngham William Garner William Tomson was ane pynt of wyn is	00	18	00
17 of May To Lawrence Blairs hous to the prowost and the two men that brought the leter that the visitation was in Holland .	00	09	00
	36	10	00

Of the quhilk somme of threttie sex pund ten shilling awand be the Toun to the said Marioun Cunyngham for the caussis aforsaid we ordain you Adam Fullertoun lait tresaurer to mak payment to the said Marioun Cunyngham your spous and the samen sall be allowit be us to you in your compts keipand thir presentis for your warant. Subscryvit 27 Maij 1664.   ROBERT CUNYNGHAME, provist
                   JA: FULLARTON, baylie
                   HENRIE LYNE, baillie

23. *The Town's Account to Janet Barclay.*—1669-1670.

The TOWNS Acount due to JANET BARCKLY begining in October the 7th 1669.

	Lib.	s.	d.
7th October. Imprimus, the provest and the baliffs the minister and som others being their 2 chopins of wine 2 pynts of aile ½ a one of tobacco and 4 pyps	00	19	00
8th October. Mor the Magistratis and the rest of the Councell at the choising the Commissioner for the parliament 2 pynts of wyn 2 pynts of ail a short bread 1 one of tobacco 5 pyps	01	19	02
October. Mor on Thursday after they cam from the Sesion the Magistratis and minister with som otheris on pynt of wyn on chopin of aile	00	14	04

	Lib.	s.	d.
Mor that sam day eight days when they cam from the Sesion on chopin of wyn and on pynt of aile	00	08	08
Mor the nixt day after on chopin of seck was sent for to Balif Blairs the provest and som strangeris being there . . .	00	13	04
Mor with Balif Blair and Corprell Terbet and some other gentlmen 5 mutchkins of seck and on pynt of aile . . .	01	15	04
Mor on pynt of seck was sent for to the balifs when Captain Blair and som other gentlmen was there in company with the provist .	01	06	08
Mor within 2 days on pynt of seck that was sent for to Balif Blairs the provist and som of the Councell being their about som of the towns busines	01	06	08
December 17th. Mor the provist and the balifs and som of the Councell after a meting about som busines 5 chopins of new wyn and on pynt of aile	02	07	00
Mor the provist and the minister and provist Barckley with som others 2 chopins of wyn on chopin of aile on one of tobacco and 4 pyps	01	01	04
January 1670. Mor the provist and Alexander Dyet with som others of the Councell about som acountis on chopin of wyn 2 chopins of aile on one of tobacco and 4 pyps	00	14	04
Mor the nixt day the provist and som strangers on chopin of wyn	00	09	00
Mor given at the provist direction to men that was dresing the church 5 chopins of aile and 2 pynts of beer being all at sundry tims	00	10	04
February. Mor that time the stent masteris was in the tolboth 5 pynts of beer 2 pynts of aile and som candls was sent for to the tolboth	00	15	00
Mor that day provist Cuningham was buried that was sent for to Balif Blairs hous my Lord Eglinton being there and som otheris 2 pynt of seck	02	13	04
February 26. Mor sent for to the tolboth the provist and som with him on chopin of wyn and on pynt of aile . . .	00	11	00
March 10. Mor spent with James Boyl and som otheris when he fetch hom som papers to the town from Edenburgh 3 chopins of wyn 1 pynt of aile on one of tobacco and 4 pyps and for dyet and ail to a boy that fetch hom som mor papers 7s. 4d. . . .	01	19	00
May 18. Mor spent with Glenkairns brother Cornell Cuningham on chopin of wyn 2 chopins of aile ½ a one of tobacco and 4 pyps .	00	12	06
June 10. Mor the provist and provist Barckley and som of the rest of the Councell with Mr. Alexander Crafford 4 mutchkins of wyn 1 pynt of aile ½ a one of tobacco and 4 pyps . . .	01	01	06
Jun 21. Mor the provist and balifs and clerk after som meiting of the town busines 1 chopin of wyn 1 pynt of aile ½ a one of tobacco and 3 pyps .	00	12	06

		Lib.	s.	d.
Jun 23. Mor the provist with som strangeris and the new Colector 1 chopin of sek on chopin of beer ½ a one of tobacco and 2 pyps	.	00	18	04
July 18th. Mor the provist and Balif with Adamtown and som otheris gentlmen on chopin of wyn on chopin of aile		00	10	00
Mor that was givin at the provist direction to the men that drest the scholars sait and for sent to the kirk at sevrall tims 5 pynts of aile		00	10	00
Mor sent for to the Casa layers 1 pynt of ail at the provist order		00	02	00
July 23. Mor with the Leard of Sesnock and som otheris gentlmen 2 chopins of wyn 2 pynts of aile on of them that went to the Casa layeris and a short bread		01	05	00
July 27. Mor the provist and the minister and sesuon 1 pynt of wyn 2 pynts of ail and a short bread . . .		01	05	00
Mor sent for that day by the provist order 1 pynt of aile		00	02	00
August 10. Mor that day Mr. Archbal Dickson chyld was buried being the 10 of August with the Leard of Perston and som otheris 5 chopins of wyn 2 pynts of ail on short bread on one of tobacco and 4 pyps		02	14	00
August 12. Mor the provist with the Leard of Dunlap and some others 3 mutchkins of wyn .		00	13	04
Mor by the provist order to the workers at the kirk dyk 1 pynt of aill		00	02	00
Agust 25. Mor with Mr. Hutchisons soun in law Mr. Dunbar 1 mutchkin of seck 3 chopins of aile .		00	12	00
Mor to the kirk dyk 1 pynt of aile at the provist order .		00	02	00
Mor at the closing of the papers concerning the Nether hill landis for wyn befor they went owt in the morning and for meat and drink afterwards—altogether couns to . . .		04	04	00
September 8. Mor sent for to George Garvans hows my Lord Eglinton being their 2 pynts of wyn		01	16	00
September 12. Mor the provist and balif with Mr. Gledstons and som other strangeris 1 chopin of wyn 1 chopin of seck 1 chopin of aile and 2 nackets		01	09	00
Mor that day with the Leard of Roberland on pynt of wyn on pynt of aile		01	00	00
Mor the nixt day sent for to Balif Blairs hous the provist and som strangeris being there 2 mutchkins of seck . .		00	18	00

James Kyle thesaurer yea sall pay unto Jonet Barclay the foirsaid accompt extending fourtie pund fyftein shilling eight pennyes Scotis And the samen sall be allowit to you in your thesaurer accompt Given at Irving the 23 September 1670 yeris.

JAMES BLAIR, proveist.
ALLAN CUMING, bailley
LAUR. BLAIR, baylie

270   MUNIMENTS OF THE BURGH OF IRVINE.

I Janet Barckley grants me to hav recavid from Jams Kyle treasurer the within wreitin acount extending to forty pounds fyftin shilling and eight penis Scots acording to the within writin precept and doth discharge him of the samin as wittnes my hand at Irwin this ninth of December on thousand six hundred and seavnty

JONETT BARCKLAY
D. BROUN, wittnes
HUGH KIRKPATRIK, wittnes.

24. *Accounts for Refreshments to the Magistrates, etc.*—1670.

ACCOMPT be the TOWN since the 15 May 1670.

	Lib.	s.	d.
Imprimis with Sir Adam Blair ane pynt wyn .	00	18	00
At the bonfyr 4 pynts beir	00	10	08
Mor att severall times ane gallown and half of aill with workmen and others	01	14	00
For a pynt wyn aill and breid at the choising the Commission	01	09	00
Mor att a consultation with Proveist Barklay 5 muchking wyn a pynt aill tobaco and pyps befoir the Proveist went to Edinburgh .	01	07	06
To Skipper Angus and his marchant when they com a shoir a pynt wyn and 3 pynts aill is	01	04	00
For a pynt wyn to the clarks hous befoir he went to Edinburgh .	00	18	00
Mor	01	04	00
For keiping the Militia hors 22 dayes for hay and corn .	08	16	00
For a pynt wyn and a pynt aill with the Baylie of Air .	01	00	00
For 2 pynts wyn 2 pynts beir and breid when the proveist com from the Conventione of Burrowes	02	02	10
For a pynt wyn and 2 pynts beir efter the Buriall of Mistris Alexander	01	03	04
For drink att severall tymes with workmen and others . .	00	16	00
For 4 pynts wyn and a pynt of aill and breid with Mr. John Tran and sum straingers	03	16	06
Spent att the Getting the chairg of horning with the Burrowes Agent	00	12	00
For ane pynt of wyn with the Bishop . . .	00	18	00
For aill at many severall tymes befoir the man was wounded and sine is marked and comes to	05	12	00
And for breid tobaco and pyps to the sam . .	01	04	00
For two half Muchkeins brandie att severall tymes and four pynts of aill is	00	16	00
Mor att the choysing the Magistrats 8 pynts of aill and ane pynt of brande and breid is	02	14	00

	Lib.	s.	d.
Mor with the Master of Roos and Robertland younger 4 pynts of aill and breid is	00	11	00
With the Quartermasters att the Billets maiking 5 pynts aill	00	10	00
Mor with Collonell Hurrie 8 pynts aill	00	16	00
Mor for meitt to men and hors	00	16	00
At the choissing the Thesaurer and compted	01	14	00
At the choissing the Dean of Gild and compted	01	09	00
Being choisin Magistrat for thrie year togidder	06	00	00
SUMMA is	50	05	10
Wherof receaved in exchang of the towns hors	14	08	00
	35	17	10

James Kyle couper lait Thesaurer pay unto Laurence Blaire lait Baillie the foirsaid accompt extending unto threttie fyve pund sevintein shilling ten pennyes Scots and the samen sall be allowed to you in your Thesaurer accompt Given at Irving the fourt day of November 1670

ffor JAMES KYLE   JAMES BLAIR, proveist
    lait Thesaurer   ALLAN CUMING, bailie
JA: HAMILTONE.   HENRIE LYN, baillie.

I doe acknowledg heawe receawed from James Kyll lait Thesaurer the wholl within written accompt extending to threttie fyve pond seventein shillings ten penneis Scotts witnes my hand this 21 Januarij 1671.   LAUR: BLAIR.

25. *Account for Refreshments.*—1670.

	Lib.	s.	d.
Item the provist June the 15 with Belligellie ane pynt of wine	00	18	00
Item Baylie Cuming with the clerk and Capten Leslie four chopings of wine tua chopings of beare tobacco and pyps the 22 June	01	02	08
Item the provist with the collectors James Fullartown and William Speir thrie chopings of aiell 30 June and a muchkin of wine	00	07	06
Item the said day the provist sent for to George Garvens house for a pynt of wyne when my Lord Eglintoun receaved the monie for the millitia horse	00	18	00
Item the said day the provist with baylie Cuming and the clerk and James Kyle met about the servants fies thrie muchkins off wine	00	13	06
Item the provist and the clerk when that they came from the Tolbooth the 1 July a muchkin of wine	00	04	06

	Lib.	s.	d.

Item the provist paying his way to Edinburgh the secownd of July tua chopings of wine 00 18 00

Item the 7 Julie Baylie Blaier with the ships companie and the skipers good ffather eight pynts of beare ane muchkin of brandie tobacco and pyps 01 13 04

Item for the accownt of the barr parch be directioue of the provist for drinke with fyve cast of double planstour naiels . . 04 08 06

SUMMA 11 04 00

19 July. Item the provist gave to the men that went to Aier to the buriall a pynt of beare 00 02 08

21 ditto. Item the provist with John Glasgow ffor stones to the bridge thrie chopings of beare and ane choping off wine with a glass that was broken 00 19 00

20 ditto. Item Baylie Cuming with the provist the skiper and marchant and some uthers tua muchkings of wine thrie chopings off beare and pyps 00 13 08

July 15. The provest with Mr. Hugh Craffourd ane pynt of wine 00 18 00

July 29. The provest with Carrlung two muchkins of wine . 00 09 00

August 2. The magistrats with Mr. Robert Trans some four mutcking of wine and ane chapin of beir and tobacco and pypes . 01 00 04

August 8. The provest with Alexander Cochrane and George Montgomrie and ane Glasgow anent the stones ffour mutchkines of wine and ane pynt of beir and tobacco and pyps . . 01 10 04

August 9. The provest Bailyie Cuming and the clerke with Munckurulin three chappins of wine and ane pynt of beir tobbacco and pypes 01 12 00

Upon the last Fryday of July the provest with some of the counsell ane pynt of wine three pynts of ail tobaco and pyps . . 01 06 00

SUMMA . 08 02 00

August 30. The provest the clerke and George Garven two mutchkings of wine and a chapin of ail 00 10 00

August 31. Item sent about to the provest house to give the provest of Innererrra two chappings of wine . . . 00 18 00

Item sent about to the provest house to give to strangeres at sevrail tymes nyne chapins of wine 04 10 00

September 7. The provest with Mr. Wallace procurator in Air ane mutchkin of wyne and a chapin of ail . . . 00 05 06

September 10. Baylie Cuming with Mr. Gladstaines three mutchkins of secke and ane chapin of ail . . . 01 08 00

EXCERPTS FROM BURGH ACCOUNTS.

	Lib.	s.	d.
September 14. The magistrates with provest Campbell of Glasgow togither with the baylie of Glasgow fyve chapins of secke ffour chapings and ane mutchking of wine six pyntes of ail two ounces of tobbacco twelve pypes	07	07	10
September 14. Item sent about to Lawrance Blaires to give the Presbiterian Ministers ane pynt of secke	01	16	00
September 15. The magistrats with proveist Campbell in Lawrance Blaires house two chapings of secke	01	16	00
September 16. The magistrats with the provest of Glasgow ane pynt of burned secke	02	00	00
More the said day sent about to Lawrance Blaires to give the Laird of Lamroghtoune and other gentlemen ane pynt of secke and eight chapins of wine and three knaires of brandie	05	14	00
More the said day in our laich seller to give my Lord Eglintounes men ane mutchking of secke and ane chaping and ane mutchking of wine	01	02	06
September 17. The magistrats with the clerke and James Huntar ffour chapings of wyne two pynts of ail ane ounce of cut and dry tobacco and three pyps	02	02	02
More that day sent about be the provest to the clerkes house ane chaping of secke	00	18	00
September 19. The Magistrats with Hunterstoune and Hew Huntar two mutchkings of wine and ane chaping of ail	00	10	00
More the said day the Magistrats and the clerk with the young Scholmaster two chapins of wine and two chapins of ail and tobacco and pyps	01	02	00
Item at sevral tymes in the laich salleres six pints of ail	00	12	00
SUMMA	32	03	00
SUMMA of the Total is	139	12	06

Irving the 23 September 1670 :—

Hugh Thompsone thesaurer pay unto Robert Francis the forsaid accompt extending unto ane hundreth threttie nyne pund tuelff schilling sex pennyes Scots and the samen sall be allowit to you in your thesaurer accompt.

JAMES BLAIR, proveist.
ALLAN CUMING, baillie.
LAUR: BLAIR, baylie.

Ro. HAMILTON   139lib. 12s. 6d.

1670: Irwin the 10 of October.—I aknowlege myself to be payet be Hew Tamsone of the sowme of an hundreth threttie nyne pownd tuelf sh. Scots six penyes

ROBT. FRANCIS.

274   MUNIMENTS OF THE BURGH OF IRVINE.

26. *Account for Refreshments.*—4th October 1676.

The Touns Account dew to George Garvens wyf 4 October 1676.

	Lib.	s.	d.
Imp. The Majestratis wit George Garven ane muchkin of seck and ane chopeing of aiell	00	11	00
Item The Majestratis with George Garven ane chopeing of wine tuo muchkings of seck thrie chopeings of aiell . . .	01	12	06
Item The Majestratis ane chopeing of wine tuo unce of sugger and ane pynt of aiell	00	12	00
Item The Majestratis ane chopeing of wine and tuo unce of sugger	00	10	00
Item The Majestratis the first night the Minister came .	01	02	00
Item The Majestratis the nixt night with the Minister .	01	00	08
Item The nixt night with the Minister . . .	00	17	00
Item The Majestratis with Ascock gentellman ane chopeing of wine tuo unce sugger thrie gills of brandie tuo unce of sugger and bread .	00	18	04
Item The Majestratis with George Garven when he came home with the Minister tuo chopeings of wine . . .	01	00	00
Item The Majestratis with Hewgh Brown and uther gentellmen thrie chopeings of wine ane pynt of [aill and] bread with ane muchkin of wine sent for to the provests house . . .	02	00	00
Item The Majestratis with Craigens ane chopeing of wine and ane pynt of aiell	00	11	08
Item The Majestratis with George Garven thrie muchkings wine .	00	15	00
Item The Majestratis with severall gentellmen tuo chopeing wine .	01	00	00
Item The Majestratis with severall gentellmen thrie chopeing of wine and four unce of sugger	01	13	04
Item The provist to his own house in sendeing lettiris to the Minister ane chopeing of wine	00	10	00
Item The Majestratis with Major Butting and uther gentellmen tuo pynts of wine and eight unces of sugger . . .	02	06	08
Item The Majestratis with some gentellmen thrie chopeings of hott wine and four unce of sugger	01	13	04
Item The Majestratis with the Ministeris women quhen that they came first ane chopeing of wine and tua unce of sugger and ane quart of aiell and ane short bread	00	18	04
Item The Majestratis the morow eftir with the Ministeris women ane chopeing of wine and sugger and bread . .	00	12	08
Item The Majestratis when they went to Monfoodis buriall half ane muchking of brandie	00	04	00

EXCERPTS FROM BURGH ACCOUNTS.   275

		Lib.	s.	d.
Item The Majestratis with my Leadie Eglintown chopeings of seck		03	00	00
Item The Majestratis with my Lord Montgomerie a pynt		02	00	00
Item The last tyme that the Minister came home .... chopeings of secke and sugger aiell and bread		04	16	00
		30	04	06
Item The Minister woman gat ane muchking of seck with George Garven		00	10	00
Item The Ministeris dayet first and last horse meat and servantis cowntted befor the provist and baylie Montgomrie		18	00	00
		18	10	00
		30	04	06
SUMMA of all is		48	14	06

The which soume fforesaid off ffourtie eight powndis fourtine shilling sex pennies Scotis I doe atest to be trew   MARGRAET MONTGOMERIE.

John Reid [lait] thresowrer ffaiele nocht upon sight heirof to paye to Margaret Montgomerie the above wryten accownt extending to fourtie eight pownds fourtine shillings six pennies Scotis monie [which] shall be allowed to you at your counpt makeing Given at Irvine the thrid day off Februar 1677.

JAMES BLAIR, proweist
HEW MONTGOMRY, baillie

27. *Account between the Burgh of Irvine and their Agent.—* 11th *June* 1677.

COMPTE deue by the BRUGHE of IRWIN at Edinbrugh 11 June 1677.

	Lib.	s.	d.
To William Brown Adjent ther proportiown of 8832li. 12s. of messive dewes conforme to ane Acte at Glasgowe in Jully 1675 at 18s. on ilk 100lib. Irwins proportiown is	080	0	0
The annual-rent thairof from Whitsundye 1675 to Whitsundye 1677 is	009	12	0
Item conform to ane Acte of Barrows at Edinbrugh in Jully 1676 Irwins proportiown of 2821lib. 12s. for messeivs is	25	7	0
The annual-rent thairof ane year is	1	10	6

	Lib.	s.	d.
Item conform to the messeive letter now sent to Irwin thair is debursed by William Brown since Julye 1676 quhilk extends aiftir calculatiown thairof to 4760lib. Irwins proportioun thairof is	33	13	4
Summa dew to William Brown adjent	150	02	10
Item to the Exchakirt for Irwins Eque	014	13	4
Item to Hew Browne himselfe for his paines	004	00	0
Summa	168	16	2

John Reid baillye and latte Theawssaurer who is not as yeit absolwed of your said accomptes ffealle not on sighte heirof to paye to Hew Broun student of the lawes at Edinbrugh who is to paye owt the samine for owr brughe at Edinbrugh as is abone wryttin and to return to us discharges conform the sowm of ane hundreth three score aughte pund sixtein shillings two pennis Scots quhilk sall be allowed to you at your compte makeing, takein his reseat thairof and keipeing these presens for your warren Geivin at Irwin the 11 June 1677.   JAMES BLAIR, proweist.

HEW MONTGOMRIE, baillie.

Receaved be me Hugh Broun the above said soume and I obleidge my selfe to imploy the said soumes ffor the uses above directed as witness my hand att Irwin the eleventh off Junij j^{m}vj^c and seventie and seven yeirs.   HUGH BROUN.

28. *Account for Refreshments.*—1679-1680.

ACCOUMPT due by the TOUNE of IRVING to JAMES FULLARTON Younger. Begun on the 11th March 1679.

	Lib.	s.	d.
Imprimis with Perstoun young and old the Magistrats being present three pynts of clairet wyne	03	00	0
Mor for 4 pynts of aill and 4 wheitt breid	00	11	0
March 12. Mor the Magistrats with the visitouris at the Bridge	00	12	6
9 December. Fetcht to Robert Francis house at the Magistrats direction with my Lord Loudoun and the provest of Ayr, 2 pynts of wyne	02	10	0
Mor the said day with my Lord Ross a pynt of wyne	01	00	0
Mor with the Master of Ross, 1 pynt of wyne	01	00	0
Mor fetcht be black Robert Francis when the host was heir 4 pynts of wyn	04	00	0
	12	03	6

EXCERPTS FROM BURGH ACCOUNTS. 277

	Lib.	s.	d.
23 January 1680. That day the Magistrats was chosen three chopins of wyne	01	10	0
24 January. The Magistrats with others casting the Locality 3 chopins of wyne one gill of brandy . . .	01	13	0
5 February. The Magistrats with the Magistrats of Ayr 5 pynts of wyne one quart of aill, tobacco and pyps 3s. 4d. in all .	08	07	4
Item befor the Buriell one pynt of wyne the sayd day Robert Murchland at the Magistrats comand . . .	01	00	0
9 February. The Magistrats with John Crauford of Ayr and uthers a chopin of wyne	00	10	0
10 February. The Magistrats with the fiscall and others upon the touns accompt 1 chopin wyne one pynt of aill . .	00	11	0
12 February. The Magistrats with the massons concerning the bridge 3 chopins of aill one gill of brandy . .	00	05	0
Dicto. The Magistrats with some of my Lord Humes troup, a chopin of seck	00	10	0
13. February. The Magistrats with my Lord Humes master of horse one pynt of seck and wheitt breid . . .	01	15	0
14. The Magistrats with the visitors fyve mutshins of seck with one choppin of aill	02	01	0
15. The Magistrats and others one choppin of seck . .	00	16	0
17. The Magistrats when they went to Carletouns buriall upon ane flitted coumpt	01	04	0
Dicto at night	00	11	0
18. When the Corps went out a mutskin of brandy . .	00	08	0
19. The Magistrats with severall other gentilmen 5 pynts of wyne tobaco and pyps	05	08	0
20. The Magistrats with gentilmen of my Lord Humes troup one pynt of seck	01	12	0
The Magistrats about the Locality one choppin of seck . .	00	16	0
Item when the milnes wer sett 3 chopins of wyne . .	01	10	0
Mor one pynt of seck	01	12	0
4 March. The Magistrats with the Quartermasters in a fitted accoumpt	01	18	0
Mor the sayd day 1 choppin of wyne . . .	00	10	0
	46	10	0
5 March 1680. The Magistrates with Stent Masters: 4 gils of brandy with 4 chopins of aill one mutskin of wyne . .	00	17	0
Dicto The Magistrats with the boatmen who broght the stones to the Bridge for aill and brandy . . .	00	08	0

		Lib.	s.	d.
6. The Magistrats with severall of the officers 2 pynts of wyne 2 pynts of aill tobacco and pypes		02	07	0
8. The Magistrats with ane Irish gentilman ane choppin of seck		00	16	0
11. The Magistrats with the shirif of Ayr and uthers 4 chopins of wyne 3 pynts of aill 1 gill of brandy, tobacco and pypes		02	10	0
In March flitted accompt		02	04	0
25 March. When the herd was hyred 1 chopin of seck 3 half mutskins of brandy		01	08	0
1 Aprill. The Magistrats with severall others one mutskin of seck		00	08	0
At tuo sevrall tymes the Magistrats sent to the Bridge 8 pynts of aill		00	16	0
1 May. The Magistrats with Captain Fleming 5 mutskins of seck 3 chopins of aill		02	03	0
4 dicto: the Magistrats with the provost of Ayr 3 pynts of wyne		03	00	0
Mor the sajd day. The Magistrats with James Weir and uthers about the buying of tymber a pynt of wyne		01	00	0
Mor to the Bridge 4 pynts of aill		00	08	0
Mor to John Barnes upon the Bridges accompt		00	02	0
7 May. Mor to the Bridge 5 pynts of aill		00	10	0
8 May. Mor the Magistrats with the Generall Major 3 chopins of wyne 1 chopin of aill		01	11	0
10 May. The Magistrats with some other gentilmen to witt Bayllie Ninian Anderson one choppin French wyne 3 choppins of seck one pynt of aill		01	16	0
11 May. Mor the Magistrats with the boatmen that broght in the stones 5 pynts of aill with 2d. worth of breid		00	12	0
Mor the said day Robert Murchland with the workers at the Bridge 2 pynts of aill half a mutskin of brandy		00	08	0
12 May. Bayllie Lin with the workers at the Bridge		00	01	0
13. The Magistrats with others to the Bridge 4 pynts of aill		00	08	0
18. To the Bridge 2 pynts of aill		00	04	0
19. The Magistrats with Bayllie Lin and others at the Bridge 2 chopins of aill 2 gils of brandy		00	07	0
21. The Magistrats with John Crafurd and some others of the men of Ayr 2 pynts of wyne		02	00	0
Dicto Robert Murchland with the massons 2 pynts of aill		00	04	0
		26	09	0
29 May 1680. The Magistrats nyne pynts one choppin of wyne		09	10	0
Dicto: Tuo pynts of seck		03	04	0
Dicto: Eight pynts of aill		00	16	0

	Lib.	s.	d.
31 May. With the Boatmen 3 pynts of aill and breid .	00	08	0
Dicto: With Bayllie Hunter of Ayr and others 4 pynts of wyne with a pynt of seck .	05	12	0
1 June. The Magistrats with the collector and other gentilmen a quart of wyne	02	00	0
2. The said day 1 choppin of aill .	00	01	0
4. The Magistrats with Hew Broun and uthers a pynt of wyne and choppin of aill .	01	01	0
5. The Magistrats with Eduart Wallace 1 choppin of seck with a pynt of aill	00	17	0
15 dicto. The Magistrats with a gentilman half a mutskin of seck	00	04	0
16. The Magistrats with some gentilmen 3 chopins of wyne with 1 once tobacco	01	11	0
18 Dicto. The Magistrats with the Massons 4 pynts of aill and half a mutskin of brandy	00	12	0
23 dicto. To the workers at the Bridge with Robert Murchland 2 pynts of ail a gill of brandy with herring	00	08	8
24 dicto. The Magistrats with Mr. Rainkin 3 pynts of wyne with a gill of brandy	03	02	0
25 dicto. The Magistrats with sevrall others 3 mutskins of wyne 1 gill of brandy a pynt of aill	00	19	0
The Magistrats after the sheaff setting up a choppin of seck	00	16	0
29 dicto. To the Bridge 4 pynts of aill	00	08	0
The sayd day the Magistrats with mor 3 pynts of wyne 2 gils of brandy tobacco and pypes	03	06	0
9 July. The Magistrats with Sir Robert Barclay and General Major in a fitted comupt for wyn and aill tobacco and pypes	03	10	0
12 dicto. The Magistrats with some young domines 7 mutskins of wyne with 2 pynts of aill	01	19	0
The sayd day to the Bridge 4 pynts of aill	00	08	0
17. The Magistrats with others 1 pynt of seck	01	12	0
24. The Magistrats with others 5 mutskins of wyne 2 gills of brandy	01	09	0
Mor the sayd day to the Bridg 6 pynts of aill	00	12	0
Mor the 28 day when the sheaf was taken doun a gallon ayll	00	16	0
Mor the sayd day drunken in the hous by the Magistrats for wyne aill tobacco and pypes	02	10	0
2 September 80. Mor the sayd day for 8 pynts of aill with the workers of the bridge	00	16	0
Mor by the Magistrats with the Magistrats and some gentilmen of Ayr three chopins of seck and 3 gils of brandy	02	14	0

23 September. Mor with the Magistrats 2 gils of brandy 1 pynt of aill			Lib. s. d. 00 06 0	
			50 17 0	
	SUMMA the three pages	To witt in the first .	046 10 0	
		Item in the second .	029 9 0	
		Item in the third page	050 17 0	
SUMMA what is due by the Magistrats			126 16 0	

Thir three pages is ffund to be shortt three pond sixttine shillings Scotts so itt is butt 123 17 06

        SUMMA is . 123 17 6

Robert Bryssone thesaurer faill not to pay to James Fullertoun and his wyfe this abovewrittin accompt of ane hundreth twentie thrie pounds seventein shillings sex pennies Scots and take ane recept thairof and the samyne salbe allowit to yow in your thesaurer compts. Given at Irvin the 27th December 1680 yeiris.

             HEW MONTGOMRIE.
             JO: MONTGOMERIE.

I James Fullarttoun grants me to be fullie satisfied conforme to the abovewrittin precept as wittnes my hand at Irving the 14 March 1681. JA: FULLARTTOUN.

  1 page 46 10 10
  2 page 26 09 00
  3 page 50 17 08
    ―――――
   123 17 06

29. *Account for Refreshments.*—[1678-1680.]

ACCOMPT of the Toune of Irvine due to ANDREW GEMMILL and his Spouse, as followeth :—

September 27 1678. Imprimis at the chusing of the new council, the Magistrats and Council spent 22s. 10d.	Lib. s. d. 01 02 10
Item October 1. Provest Cumming and Deane of Gill with ane gentlman brother to Mistris Stirling spent 13s. 6d. . . .	00 13 06
Item October 1. Spent be Provest James Blair and some gentlmen with him 9s.	00 09 00
Item October 1. At Bayliffe Mountgomries order sent to Robert Francis, quhair he was with some gentlmen a pynt of claret at 18s. .	00 18 00

	Lib.	s.	d.

Item Februar 11 1679. Spent be Provest Cuming, bayliffs Mountgomrie and Reid, Deane of Gill, Beoch, Alexander Cochrane, Robert Francis, Robert Murchland, Robert Nesmith, Robert Weir, and diverse others and William Francis they being anent the giving order to John Mountgomrie late theasurer the first two moneths and ane halfe cesse 14s. 10d. 00 14 10

Item Februar 20. Provest Cumine and all these persons mentioned in the forsaid account, anent laying donne a way to pay the Ministers stipend 5s. 00 05 00

Item October 16. Spent be Provest Cumine and others a pynt of ale 00 01 08

Item October 18. Spent be Provest Cumine, bayliffe Reid, and Deane of Gill with Captain Strachan and others, in seck, sugar, pypes, ale, tobacco, and bread 01 16 02

Item October 28. Spent be Provest Cummine and Captain Strachan with several others in ale and brandy 5s. 10d. . 00 05 10

Item October 29. Spent be Provest Cummine and the two baylies, Deane of Gill, and others being mett anent the calling of the community of the burgh togither for the regulating of the touns affairs, 9s. twa pennies 00 09 02

Item ane pynt of ale to the officers for warning the community to meitt 00 01 08

Item November 12. Bayliffe Mountgomrie, Alexander Dyett late fiscal and William Lyne that went with the bell for the petty customes spent 2s. 6d. 00 02 06

SUMMA Total of this accompt is 07 00 02

Januar 23 1680. The TOUNE of IRVINGS ACCOMPT due to ANDREW GEMMILL and his Wife, as followeth :—

Imprimis, Provest Boyl the Laird of Corshill and severall other gentlemen and Laurence Wallace three choppins of white wine, at 18s. per pynt 01 07 00

Item Januar 28. Provest Boyl with the Laird of Kelburn's man a mutchkine of white wyne 00 04 06

Item Januar 30. Beoch, bayliffe Mountgomrie, Provest Cuming, bayliffe Reid, William Francis and diverse others of the council, that night that he came from the committie of Air spent in ale and tobacco 6s. and 10d. 00 06 10

Item February 1. Provest Boyl Provest Cuming, Bayliffe Linnee and James Woodside and others, 3 mutchkins of white wine . 00 13 06

		Lib.	s.	d.

Item February 4. Provest Boyl with Mr. Hammiltoune, James Woodside, Robert Murchland, and diverse others, two pynts and ane chappine of white wine with halfe ane ounce of tobacco and 3 pypes . . 02 06 02

Item February 5. Being Granards sons buriall day provest Boyl with my Lord Mountgomrie, Lord Cathcart, Lairds of Blair and Corshill, the surveyer, the collectour, and Glengarnock, Sheoltoune and Doctor Wallace and others, eight pynts of claret wine two ounces of tobacco and eight pypes, is in all 8lib. 3s. 8d. . . . 08 03 08

Item that same night Provest Boyl, Beoch, Survayer, and the collectour with others ane chopine of claret wine, half a mutchkine of brandie with ane ounce of sugar 00 14 10

Item February 18. Being that night that Carlentouns corps came to the toune, the two bayliffes with several of the tounes folks that went out to meitt his corps, 7 pints of ale 4 bread ane ounce of tobacco and five pypes 00 19 10

Item February. Bayliffe John Mountgomrie sent for halfe a mutchkine of brandie to William Swintounes house . . . 00 04 00

Item March 3. John Mountgomrie bayliffe Robert Murchland, James Woodside Liftenant Dalyell and the ancient that is in Robert Murchelands with diverse others 6 pynts claret, 2 bread, and 2s. for tobacco and pipes 06 04 00

Item March 23. Bayliffe John Mountgomrie, William Francis, Robert Francis younger, John Hart and William Smith mason quhen they wer agreeing for building of the bridge . . . 00 11 00

Item May 25. Provests Boyl and Cummine, Generall Major Mountgomrie, Provest Campbell, Major White, the collector and diverse others ane pynt of claret wine 1lib. . . . 01 00 00

Item June 3. At Bayliffe Hew Mountgomries order to James Galt quhen he was dressing the clock a pynt of ale 2s. . 00 02 00

Item June 17. Bayliffe John Mountgomrie, Blair, Kilbirny, collectour and others 3 pynts Rhenish wine, 6 ounces sugar, 5 choppines of ale and a loafe 02 18 06

Item June 23, the Provest with my Lord Mountgomrie a pynt of Rhenish wine, and two ounces of sugar quhich is . . 00 15 06

Item July 19. Provest and Baylies with the Minister and Clerk and Thomas Forbes with diverse others, 3 chopins of claret wine at 20s. per pynt, a chopine seck 15s., two mutchkines Rhenish wine 7s., four chapins of ale 4s. 10d., two ounces of tobacco and eight pipes 3s. 4d., the officers a chapine of ale, is in all 3lib. 4d. . 03 00 04

August 13. Bayliffes John Mountgomrie and Hew, with William Crawford in Air, William Swintoune and others 6 chapins of claret wine and tobacco and pipes . . . 03 01 00

		Lib.	s.	d.
August 23. Bayliffe John Mountgomrie with Edward and Robert Wallaces and others, 9 mutchkins of claret wine is	.	02	05	00
Summa of this acompt is	. .	34	17	08
Item September 25. A pynt of ale to the officers by bayliffe Mountgomries orders	. . . .	00	02	00
Summa Totalis is		34	19	08
Summa of both these accompts is		41	19	10

Robert Bryssoune Thesaurer of the burgh of Irving pay upon sight heirof to Agnes Thompsonne spous to Androw Gemmill the withinwryten soume of Fourty ane pund nynteen shilling ten penyes Scotts money contenit in the two withinwryten pages and take hir ressait thairoff quhilk soume sall be allowed to you att the making of your thesaurer compts. Given att Irving the twelt of May 1681 yeires.

Hew Montgomrie, ballie.
Jo. Montgomerie, baillie.

Recived from Robert Bryson fourtey and an pund and nintin shilin and ten pennies Scotes conform to the abonwreten presep and discherges him of the samen at Irwin the tent day of Juley 1682. Andrew Gemll.

30. *Account for Candles for the use of the Guard.*—1678-1680.

The Tounes Compt for Candels to serve the Gaurd with.

	Lib.	s.	d.
First to the Tolbooth when the comitie was heir that came out of Air March 15 1678 two pound of candels .	00	09	04
1679 September 1 to the Dregounes ane pound of candels	00	05	00
Item September 2 & 3 & 4 being but half a pound in the night .	00	07	06
Item from September 5 to November 8 being sextie and four dayes they geting thrie quarters pound of candels evrie night is in all 48 pound at 5s. the pound	12	00	00
Item when the Dregonnes came back againe December 12 to December 25 being 13 nightes 12 unce a night is sex pound and 12 unce at 5s. the pound in all	01	13	09
In 1680 To the Foot Gaurd from March 1 to May 3 being sextie and thrie nights the first night they got but half a pound but all the rest they gote a pound evrie night at 4s. 8d. pound in all is sextie and two pound and half of candels	14	11	08

	Lib.	s.	d.

Item from May 3 to May 29 they gote half a pound evrie night being 26 nightes is thretine pound of caudls at 4s. 8d. pound . 03 00 08

SOMA . 32 07 11

Robert Bryson treasurer pay to John Gray merchant this above wretten accumpt of thrite tuo pound seven shilling eleven penies Scots munie in satisfactione of this and all other accumpts deu to him by the burch of Irvin preciding the deate hearof and take his receat therof and the same shall be alloued to you in your treasure accumpts. Given at Irvin the sixt of September one thousand six hundred eightie one years.

HEW MONTGOMRIE.
JO. MONTGOMERIE.

Grantes me to have reeived frome Robert Brysone satisfactione of the forsaid comept of therritie and tuo pound and seven shiling and ten penies Scotes Wittnis my hand at Irvine September 30 1681. JOHN GRAY.

31. *Account for Refreshments.*—1680.

The TOUNES Compt deu to MARGRAT MONTGOMRIE.

	Lib.	s.	d.
The 2 January 1680. John Montgomry of Beoch, Baillye Reid and some others with some gentlmen ane pynt of wyne . .	01	00	00
22 Janwar. The provest and baillies with Pearstoune, Bischopton, Kelburn, and some other gentlmen, 13 pynts claret wyn . .	12	00	00
Item Hugh Montgomrie with some gentlmen ane pynt of claret wyne . .	01	00	00
27 Janwary. The proveist and baillyes with some gentlmen fyve mutchins claret wyne ane pynt of aill and fourtein penyes for tobacco and pypes .	01	08	02
Item Beoch with some other gentlmen ane pynt of claret wyne .	01	00	00
2 Feberwary 1680. The proveist and baillyes with Mr. James Cuningham and sundrie other gentlmen, 10 mutchins claret wyn and tobacco and pypes	02	12	00
4 Feberwary. Item Beoch with some gentlmen ane chopin wyne .	00	10	00
Baillye Hugh with some gentlmen 3 chopins wyne	01	10	00
18 Feberwary. Item the said Baillye with some gentlmen of Glasgow ane mutchin seck and chopin of aill .	00	09	00
The said Baillye with the Baillyes of Glasgow two pynts and a chopin of seck and ane mutching of claret wyn and a chopin of aill .	04	06	00
16 March. The proveist and baillyes with the captaines and officers for two peices beaf and drink .	00	12	00

EXCERPTS FROM BURGH ACCOUNTS.

	Lib.	s.	d.
Item for stoves broth and kaill	00	12	00
For ane leg of veill	01	04	00
For Bread	00	12	00
For two henns and ane wyld fowll	00	18	00
For aill	00	16	00
For tobacco and pypes	00	03	00
For ane mutching of sack	00	08	00
For fyftein pynts of wyne	15	00	00
Baillye Hugh with some gentlmen fyve mutchins claret wyne two chopins of aill and sixtein penyes for tobacco and pypes	01	08	08
15 Apryll. The said baillye with some gentlmen two chopins claret wyne and ane mutchin of sack	01	08	00
28 Apryll: The baillyes with some others a mutchin sack	00	08	00
Item baillie Montgomrie with some gentlmen four mutchins seck quhen Carltons corps past by	01	12	00
Item Beoch and others with some gentlmen at twa tymes ane pynt and a mutchin whyt wyne, a pynt of claret and a chopin of seck	03	02	00
In the begining May 1680. The proveist with the Earle of Airlie Captain Inglish and others, 8 pynts seck 24 shilling for corn and straw	14	00	00
Baillye Hugh with some gentlmen ane chopin of seck	00	16	00
The proveist with the laird of Blair and Master Charles Fleming two pynts claret wyne	02	00	00
The baillies with Mr. Robert Selkrig and others two pynts claret	02	00	00
Item baillye Montgomrie with strangers and men of Air two chopins and a chopin of sack	02	16	00
The proveist with provest Campbell and others ane pynt of claret	01	00	00
Item baillye Hugh with some gentlmen ane chopin claret and mutchin of seck	00	18	00
29 May. Eight pynts claret wyne	08	00	00
The proveist with him who pretends to be laird of Luss two chopins sack	01	12	00
Baillye Hugh with some gentlmen ane chopin claret and ane chopen sack	01	06	00
The proveist with Pearstone, Cesnock and others 3 chopins claret ane chopin sack ane pynt of aill	02	08	00
Baillye Hugh with some gentlmen four chopins claret and ane mutchin seck	02	00	00
When the proveist was goeing to Edinburgh 4 chopins seck	03	04	00
Baillye Hew with Doctor Bell and other gentlmen thrie chopins claret wyn	01	10	00

	Lib.	s.	d.
Baillye John with Langshaw and other gentlmen ane chopin of seck	00	16	00
Baillye with some gentlmen 4 chopins claret	02	00	00
The provoist with the Minister and ane gentlman that came from my lord Granard two chopins of seck	01	12	00
Baillye Hugh with some gentlmen two chopins claret and a mutchin of seck	01	08	00
Item he with other gentlemen ane pynt of claret and a chopin of seck	01	16	00
The provoist and Beoch with Broych and others ane chopin seck and a pynt of aill and tobacco and pyps	00	19	08
Baillye Hugh with some gentlemen ane chopin claret and thrie mutchens of seck	01	14	00
The baillies with some Irland gentlmen 2 chopins seck	01	12	00
Hugh Baillie Montgomrie with some other gentlmen ane chopin seck	00	16	00
Baillie John with some gentlmen ane chopin and ane mutchin seck	01	04	00
Baillie Hugh with some others a chopin seck	00	16	00
SUMMA Totalis	112	10	06

	Lib.	s.	d.
Imprimis the Magistratts with some genttllmen six mutchkins of seck	02	08	08
Item the Magistratts with some genttllmen 2 mutchkins of seck	00	16	00
Item they wer with some genttllmen 3 chopins seck	02	08	00
Item att ane other tyme they wer	00	16	00
Item they wer with some genttllmen ane pyntt	01	12	00
Item att the burriell of the Ledie Gargonock they wer two pyntts of seck	03	04	00
Item ther wes with Blair and Kellburne that the Magistretts wes 2 pyntt of seck	03	04	00
Item att ane other tyme 3 chopins of seck	02	08	00
Item they wer with genttllmen att ane other tym 2 pyntts and ane mutchkine	03	12	00
Item the provistt sentt for to Robert Fransises housse to my Lord Cassells 5 pynts and 1 chapines	08	16	00
Item quhen Killbirnie wes borried the Magistrets with severall genttlmen 2 pyntts one chapine	04	00	00
Item the Magistretts one pyntt of wyne	01	00	00
Item the Magistrets with som genttllmen 1 pynt thrie mutchkins of seck	02	16	00

	Lib.	s.	d.
Item ane pyntt bruntt clearrett and ane muchkin of seck	01	08	00
SUMMA	38	08	08
SUMMA of the other page brought over	112	10	06
SUMMA Totallis of both pages	150	19	02

Robert Breisson Treasurer pay to Janet Garveen daughter to George Garveen Writer in Irvin this above writen soum extending to ane hundreth and fiftie punds nintene shillins two pennies Scots money in full satisfaction to her of all coumpts den by the toun preceeding the date heirof and take her receipt therof quhich shall be allowed to you in your treasurer accoumpts. Given at Irvin this 29 off December 1680 years. HEW MONTGOMRIE.
JO. MONTGOMERIE, bailie.

Grantts me to have receaved in name and behallf of Jannett Garrven my wyf this above written presept of ane hundreth and fiftie pand nynttin shillings two penies Scotts and dischairges the samine. As wittnes my hand att Irvin this first of June 1681. GEORG MOUNTTGOMRIE.

32. *Account for Iron Work, etc.*—*18th November* 1680.

COMPT of the naills for the Mill receved by JOHN M'MUREY for the use of the Burgh of Irvine November the 18th 1680.

	b. ster.	a. ster.	d. ster.	b. ster.	
Item inpremes for the sarking of the Mill five hunder dobell pllenshor att eightin pene a hunder	00	07	06	00	
Item mor a hunder dobell pllenshor	00	01	06	00	
Item two hunder dobell pllenshor	00	03	00	00	
Item for the stokes mending for yron and work	00	05	00	00	
Item for four pynts of beire to thes that caried them up and down	00	00	09	00	2t
Item for a hunder sellat naills for the reparing the tollbuth	00	01	01	00	2t
Item hallf a hunder singell pllenshor for the window brods for the mill	00	00	05	00	
Item five cast of singell pllenshor for the window bands for the mill	00	00	01	00	2t
Item four pound a hallf of tined work in gudgons and rings and eyes and strapes for a whill barow	00	01	06	00	
Item mor sewen pownd and thre quarters a pound for shoing the trinell of the whill barow	00	02	07	00	
SUMMA	01	03	06		

MUNIMENTS OF THE BURGH OF IRVINE.

COMPT of the nails for the sellating of the Mill receved by ROBERT WILLSON.

	lb. ster.	s. ster.	d. ster.	h. ster.	
Item inpremes a hunder dobell pllenshor	00	01	06	00	
Item two hunder sellat naills	00	02	02	10	4t
Item a hunder sellat naills	00	01	01	00	2t
Item hallf a hunder dobell pllenshor	00	00	09	00	
Item half a hunder singell pllenshor	00	00	05	00	
Item a hunder sellat naills	00	01	01	00	2t
Item a hunder sellat naills	00	01	01	00	2t
Item two hunder sellat naills	00	02	02	00	4t
Item hallf a hunder dobell pllenshor	00	00	09	00	
Item hallf a hunder singell pllenshor	00	00	05	00	
Item two hunder sellat naills	00	02	02	00	4t
Item a hunder sellat naills	00	01	01	00	2t
SOMA	00	15	00		2t

SOMA in all is one pound sterlling and eightine shillings sterlling and six pence sterlling and two turnours.

| Item mor for a hors and man to Gllesgow with Leftenent Doyells tronks when they marched. | 00 | 03 | 00 | 00 |
| Item mor for a hors with Baillef Montgomrie to convey Duk Hamelltone. | 00 | 00 | 06 | 00 |

Robert Bryesone treasurer pay to Airchbald Dunlop smith tuentie fyve pound Scotts four shilling Scotts in satisfactione of this within wryten accompt and take his receat therof whilk shall be aloud to you in your treasurer accompts. Given at Irvine the 2 day of August 1681.   HEW MONTGOMRIE.
                                                                                    JO. MONTGOMERIE, baillie.

I Archbald Dunlop smith indweller in Irvine grants me to have receved upon the just accompt of the above wrytin precept the just soume off tuinte five pound ffour shilling Scotts mony. As wittnes my hand at Irvin this 19 off Agust 1681 years.
                                                                                    ARCH. DULLAP.

33. *Account of John Dean, Cooper in Irvine, for making "New Pecks" for the Town.—March* 1681.

	Lib.	s.	d.
John Dean cuper in Irving hes made thrie new pecks ffor the toun off Irving usse the pryce off every peck is tuinty shiling Scots	03	00	00
Item ffor dressing furtine old pecks at 4s. per peice	02	16	00

Item to John Grander ffor lossing off the ruffes off five pecks and festing of thame againe and the pricks off thes peckes	01	00	00
Item to Alexander Shaw ffor waiting ffour dayes worke at the leist to sie the pecks righted and messured	01	04	00
Item to John Gardner ffor making new girthes to the thrie new pecks and briges and pricks to thame	03	00	00
Item ffor drink with the men now and then quhen they wer dressing now and then	00	13	00
This compt is in wholl altogither the sume is eleven pund thretine shilling Scots	11	13	00

Robert Bryssoun thesaurer faill not upon sight heirof to pey to James Porter merchand the forsaid compt extending to Elevin pund 13s. Scotts money, who is ordained to give the samyne to John Dean Alexander Shaw and John Gairner ilk ane of thame conform to their owne parts and the samyne sall be allowed in your thesaurer compts. Given att Irving the 26 March 1681.   HEW MONTGOMRIE.

James Porter merchant in Irvin grantes to have receaved from Robert Brysone present tresurer the above mentioned sume is ellevene pund and thretine shilling Scots as wittnes my hand at Irving tuinty six day off March one thousand and six hundreth eighty one yeir.   JAMES PORTER.

34. *Account for Refreshments.*—1680-1681.

ACCOMPT dew be the TOUNE of IRVINE to JOHN HUTCHESON Apothecarie ther.

	Lib.	s.	d.
21 Agust 1680. Imprimis 5 gallons of wyne for the Communione	040	00	00
Item Ane chopine of wyne the same day	00	10	00
Item For aill and brandie quhen the Sesse was payd	00	16	00
Item quhen Duck Hamilton was in Toune for whyt wyne claret and brandie	08	03	08
11 September. Item Of fixed accompt by the Magistratts with some gentlemen	06	18	00
13 Septemb. Item Spent by the Magistratts with gentlemen for wyne aill tobacco and pypps	07	16	08
24 Septemb. Item By the Magistratts with gentlemen for wyne and aill and brandie tobacco and pypps	01	18	04
1 October. Item 1 muchkine brandie and 2 pynts aill in the fornoon befor dinner quhen the Magistratts was elected	00	12	00

		Lib.	s.	d.
Item After the electione 2 muckius brandie and shugar		00	17	06
Item The tyme of dinner 1 muchkine of brandie		00	08	00
Item 15 pynts and 1 chopine of wyne		15	10	00
Item 16 pynts of aill above what was the tyme of dinner		01	12	00
Item Ane dinner to the Magistratts and Counssellors with ther atendants		07	00	00
Item 6 unce of tobacco and 20 pypps		00	09	04
2 October. Item 1 chopine of wyne and 3 chopins of aill		00	13	00
Item Quhen the Treasuerer was chossen for wyne aill bread and brandie		05	13	00
Item Quhen the Steiple was taken doune for wyne aill and brandie		01	16	00
11 October. Item By the Magistratts with my Lord Kilsyth and his attendants of wyne aill and brandie		13	04	10
14 October. Item By the Magistratts for aill and brandie quhen upon compts		00	15	00
15 October. Item By the Magistratts quhen Dindonald was heir of wyne and brandie		02	17	00
21 October. Item Quhen the Ladie Gargonock was buried of aill brandie and shugar		02	16	00
18 Novembri. Item Quhen Kilburnie was buried for aill and brandie		00	03	00
4 Decemberi. Item By the Magistratts with some gentlemen for wyne aill and brandie		01	16	04
1 Januarii 1681. Item By the Magistratts with gentlemen for wyne and aill		00	17	00
13 Januarii. Item At Gargonocks sons buriall for brandie and aill		00	12	00
Item That same day 1 muchkine of wyne		00	05	00
14 Januarii. Item The Magistratts quhen in Georg Garvens with gentlemen 1 pynt of wyne		01	00	00
15 Januarii. Item Be the Magistratts for aill and brandie		00	12	00
24. Item Be the Magistratts with gentlemen for wyne and aill tobacco and pyps		01	10	00
25. Item Be the Magistratts with gentlemen 2 pynts wyne		02	00	00
26. Item 1 pynt and 1 chopine wyne be the Magistratts		01	10	00
26. Item of fitted Accompt by the provist and baylies		02	00	10
4 Februarii. Item Be the Magistratts with gentlemen for aill and brandie		01	10	00
21. Item Be the Magistratts for aill and brandie		00	12	00
1 March. Item of fitted Accompt by the Magistratts		00	16	00

		Lib.	s.	d.
9 March. Item For brandie and shugar by the Magistratts with gentlemen		01	06	00
4 Apryl. Item 1 chopine of wyne by the Magistratts		00	10	00
13 Apryl. Item By the Magistratts with gentlemen 1 pynt wyne		01	00	00
4 May. Item For wyne and aill by the Magistratts		01	12	00
20 May. Item For wyne and aill by the Magistratts with gentlemen		02	17	00
23 May. Item For wyne and bear bread and tobacco and pyps by the Magistratts		02	10	00
25. Item For wyne tobacco and pyps and aill and bread		05	06	00
4 Junii. Item By Magistratts with gentlemen 2 pynts wyne		02	00	00
Item For wyne and aill		01	13	00
SUMMA		154	04	06

Robert Brysone Thesaurer Pay to John Hutcheson apothecar this within writtin sowme of ane hundreth fyftie four pounds four shillings sex pennies Scots in satisfactione to him of this within writtin accompt and all other accompts dew to him by the Toun of Irving preceeding the dait heirof and take his recept thairof and the same salbe allowit to you in your thesaurer accompts Given at Irving the nynt day of September 1681 yeirs. HEW MONTGOMRIE.
JO: MONTGOMERIE.

35. *Account for Refreshments.*—1681.

The Towns Compt dew be the Magistrats and Counsell to JAMES FULLARTONE and MARY PORTERFEILD spoussis begining on the 3 Janwary 1681.

	Lib.	s.	d.
3 Janwary 1681. Imprimis the Magistrates, dean of gild and counsell, ane pynt of brandy 8 ounce of suggar 6 pynts aill and 3 breid	03	15	00
Item Ane chopin of brandy and six pynts of aill, ane ounce of tobacco and six pypes to the stentmasters	01	10	00
Item The Magistrats and counsell with the men that brought the sklaits and uther company at severall tymes	04	00	00
21 Janwar. Item The Magistrats and dean of gild with the merchants and owners of that ship called the Henry of Londondarry ane pynt of brandy 8 ounce of suggar and 3 pynts aill	02	06	00
Item The Magistrats with the officers of Collonell Dowglass' regiment that were goeing to Irland ane pynt of brandy and 8 ounce of suggar	02	16	00

	Lib.	s.	d.
Item for four pynts of aill 4 half ounces of tobaco and 8 pypes	00	11	04
Item the Magistrats with the massons that put the riggin stan on the mylne eight chopins of aill and two mutchings brandy	00	16	00
Item on Paschmunday the Magistrats with proveist Muire and uthers ane mutchin brandy two ounce of suggar and two pynts of aill	01	12	00
12 Aprile. The dean of gild with some of his counsell at the setting upe of the pearches 5 pynts bear and a gill of brandy	00	19	08
18 Aprile. With the Magistrats of Ayr ane pynt of brandy with suggar	02	00	00
20 Aprile. The Magistrats with ane of the baillyes of Ayr and uthers thrie mutchens brandy with suggar	01	12	00
29 Aprile. The Magistrats with Captain Strachen and uthers ane pynt of brandy and a gill	01	14	00
Item the same day ane gallon of aill and ane chopin of brandy	01	12	00
Item ane mutchen of brandy	00	08	00
Summa	25	12	00

Robert Brysone theasaurer faill not to pay to James Fullartone and his wyfe the abov wryten compt of twenty fyve pounds twelve shelling Scots in satisfactione to them of all former accompts dew to them by the town preceiding this day and take thair recept thairof and the same shall be allowed to yow in your thesaurer compt Given at Irving the twentie seventh day of September j^m vj^c four score ane years

Hew Montgomrie, baillie
Jo. Montgomerie, Baillie

Received be me James Fullarttoun from Robert Bryson the within writtin precep as wittnes my hand at Irving the 30 of June 1682. Ja. Fullarttone.

36. Order for payment of quartering two Soldiers.—April 1681.

Robert Brysone payt out for quartering of two souldiers of Captain Strachins troup quhich came upon the toune on the 29 Apryl [16]81 2 marck and half a pound of candle 2s. 4d. quhich shall be allowd to him in his treasurer accompts.

Hew Montgomrie.

37. Order on the Treasurer to pay £19 to the Smith for dressing the Town Clock, etc.—18th April 1681.

Robert Brysone thesaurer faill not upon sight heirof to pay to David Buchanan smith the sowme off nynteinth pounds Scotts ffor his dressing and mending of the toun cloak efter William Weir went to Ireland and for furnisheing cords passes oyles

for ane certane space during the tyme off vacancie of Magistrats and for polishing mending and dressing of the officeris halberts and for ane hors lock to the stocks in the Tolbooth as also upon the accompt of his paines and expenssis in takeing doune of the steiple upon the tolbooth And take his recept thairof and the samyne salbe allowit to yow in your thesaurer accompts. Given at Irving the eighteinth day off Apryle 1681 yeiris. HEW MONTGOMERIE, baillie.
Jo: MONTGOMERIE, baillie.

I David Buchanan hemerman in Irwin grants me to have receved from Robert Bryson treserour the above writen sowme. As witnes my hand the twenty second of Aprill 1681. DAVID BWCHANAN.

38. *Order for Payment of various Town Charges.*—29th *April* 1681.

ROBERT BRYSONE thesaurer pay to Thomas Boyds man for the postage of ane letter fra the Proveist from Edinburgh to the toune sex shilling and to John Tasker of Darnest for calseying of the Bridge sex shilling and to William Meldrum two shilling for putting two begeris along the bridge Inle in haill ffourtein shillings Scotis and the samyne salbe allowit to yow in your thesaurer accompts. Given at Irvin the 29 Aprile 1681 yeiris. Jo: MONTGOMERIE, bailly.

39. *Order on the Treasurer of Irvine for the price of* 6000 "*Sklaitts.*"— 5th *May* 1681.

Irvine May 5th, 1681:—

ROBERTT BRYSONE thesaurer be pleised to pay to Adam Ker and Donald M'Coage fyve pound nyne shillings sterling and that for sax thousand sklaitts and the ffraught theroff ffor the usse off the toune and lykevayes give to Captaine Strahane eight Leg dollors and that ffor bygone Locallitie owne by the toune off Irvine condeschended upon by the Magistratts and this shall be your warrand.
J. BOYLE.

Irvine January 4, 1681:—

Receaved ffrom James Whyt colecttor off the cesse off Irvine fyve pound sterling and nyne shillings and that for six thousand sklaits and the ffraught thairoff ffor the usse off the toune. Wittness our hands at Irvine day and daite forsaid by usse underscrivers. ADAM KER.
DONALD M'COAG.

65	155 05 04
22 08	124 10 09
87 16	279 15 01

40. *Order for payment of Account for Calseying the Bridge.—7th May* 1681.

ROBERTT BRYSONE thesarer pay to John Tasker case layer nine pound Scotts in satisfaction of the casing of the new Bowe of the Bridg and for mending of seviall pices therof and tack his recatt and itt shall be alowed to yow in your Thesarer acompt. Given at Irving the seventh of Maij 1681.

           HEW MONTGOMRIE.
           Jo. MONTGOMERIE, baillie.

Receved be me John Tasceker the above written some of nine pounds Scotts from Robertt Brysone Theserer this the sevent of May 1681. ✝ T

41. *Order for payment of Salary to William Meldrum, the Town Marshal.—*16*th May* 1681.

ROBERT BRYSONE thesaurer pay to William Meldrum marshall ten merkes Scots to ane accompt of his bygane service to the toune and take his recept thairof quhilk salbe allowit in your thesaurer accompts. Given at Irvine the 16th May 1681 yeiris.

           HEW MONTGOMRIE.
           Jo: MONTGOMERIE, baillie.

Grants me to hav recevat from Robert Bresone ten markes.
           W. MELDRUM.

42. *Order for payment of drawing* 86 *draught of Stones for the Bridge Calsey.—*25*th May* 1681.

ROBERTT BRYSSOWN present Thressorer pay to James Watsown the sowme of fowr powndis sex shillingis Scotis and that for drawinge of fowr score and six drawght of stones for the casinge of the bridge in this present month of May and the samine shall be alowed to yow in your accomptis. As wittnes owr hand att Irvin the 25 of May j^m vj^c fowrscore and ane yeiris. HEW MONTGOMRIE.

Recived alow writn priset frome Robrt Bryson fowr pon sixth shilen Scots this day May 26^t 1681. ✝ W. [J. W.]

43. *Order for payment of the price of ten Trees.—*28*th May* 1681.

ROBERT BRYSSONE Thesaurer pay to John Montgomerie of Beoch sextie thrie pund eightein shilling Scotts money as the pryce of ten tries consisting of ane hundreth fourtie tua feetts bought and received for the use of the Lochmill from the said John Montgomrie and take his receitt therof and the same shall be allowed in your accompts. Given at Irving the 28 May 1681. HEW MONTGOMERIE, ballie.

Resaved fra Robert Brysone thesaurer this abowe writine precept subscrived with my hand at Irving the 28 May 1681. JO: MONTGOMERIE.

44. Order for payment of price of 10 Loads of Coals for a Bonfire.—30th May 1681.

ROBERT BRYSSOUN thesaurer pey upon sight heirof to Alexander Hamiltoun coall greve att Corshill heugh the soume of three pund three shilling four pennys Scotts money as being the pryce of ten leads of coalls furnished be him upon the publick acompt of this burgh quhilk were burnt upon the 29 May and the samyne sall be allowed in your thesaurer compts. Given att Irving the 30 May 1681.

HEW MONTGOMRIE.

Receavet from Robert Brysone toun thesarer the soume of thrie pund thrie shillings four penise Scoats conform to the above writen precepe.

A. HAMILTON.

45. Order for payment for Skins for the Town's Drum.—31st May 1681.

ROBERT BRYSSONE thesaurer faill not upone sight heirof to pay to Johne Walker twintie schilling Scotts for tua skinns of pairchement furneischit be him to be heids to the touns drum and the samyn salbe allowit to yow in your accompts keipand thir presentis for your warrand. Subscryvit at Irwing the last day of May 1681 yeiris.

JO: MONTGOMERIE.

Recived be me John Wlkr abow precap from Robrt Bryson twintie shilen Scots said May 1681. † W

46. Order for payment of Sand for the Kirk.—14th July 1681.

ROBERT BRYSSOWNE present Thresurer yee shall pay to Thomas Gibsowne eghtine shillings Scotis and that for twelf drawght of sand for poyntinge of the Kirk and the samine shall be alowed to yow in your thressurer compt. As wittnes our handis at Irvine the 14 of July 1681. HEW MONTGOMRIE.

47. Order for payment for Lime for the Kirk.—15th July 1681.

ROBERT BRYSSOWNE pressent Thressaurer yee shall pay to Thomas Blair for fowr lodis of lyme that hee hes browght for dressing of the Kirk the sowme of Thretie two shillings Scotis and the samine shall be alowed to yow in your Thressurer compt. As wittnes our hands att Irvin the 15 of July j^m vj^c fowrscore and ane yeiris.

HEW MONTGOMRIE.

I Thomas Blair recived abov writin cowmpt.

THOMAS BLAIR.

48. *Various Burgh Accounts.—August and September* 1681.

ROBERT BRYSONE theasaurer pay upon sight heirof to James Galt son to umquhill James Galt wheilwright the soume of Eight pounds Scotts for his attending upon the town Knock for half a year preceiding the fourtein of Junij last and the productione heirof shall be sufficient for allowing the samyne in your thesaurer compts. Given at Irving the sixtein day of August j^{m}vj^c eighty ane. HEW MONTGOMRIE.

JO. MONTGOMERIE.

Receaved be me James Galt from Robert Bryssoun this above wryten soume of eight pund this 16 August 1681. W. FRANCIS, nottar, at command of James Galt.

ROBERT BRYSSON thesaurer faill not upon sight heirof to pay to Robert Francis sailler, the soume of thrie pound sixtein shilling Scotts money being for some drink to witt thrie gallons of aill and a quart of acquavitie given at severall tymes to the layers in of the damm of Holm Mylne, and a quart of aill given at severall tymes to the men that took down the steiple And the samyne shall be allowed in your theasaurer compts. Given at Irving the nyntein day of August j^m vj^c four score ane yeares.

HEW MONTGOMRIE.

JO. MONTGOMERIE.

Received satisfaction of the above writtene sume thre pond sixtine shilling at Irving the 6 of September 1681. RO^T FRANCIS.

ROBERT BRYSONE treasaurer give to ane poor man James M'Tagart eightein shilling Scots and to another named George Craik sex shilling and the production of this sall gett it allowit in your accompts. Given at Irvin the 22 August 1681 yeiris.

JO. MONTGOMERIE.

ROBERT BRYSONE thesaurer delyver to Fergus Jonstoun post ffourtie shilling Scots for carying in of the Proveists horses to Edinburgh and the same sall be allowit to yow in your accompts. Given at Irving the 29th August 1681 yeiris.

JO. MONTGOMERIE.

ROBERT BRYSONE thesaurer pay upon sight heirof to William Meldrum marshell twentie merkis Scots to ane accompt of his fiallis dew by the toune of Irvine preceiding Lambmes last and take his recept therof and the same salbe allowit to you in your thesaurer accompts. Given at Irving the 27th August 1681 yeiris.

Jo. Montgomerie, baillie.
Hew Montgomrie.

Recived above writne priswp frome tresour Robrt Bryson twinti marks Scots mony last Agos 1681. Wilem Meldrum.

Robert Brysone thesaurer pay to William Meldrum marshell twentie four shillings Scots in pairt peyment of ten burdein of fog furnished and caried by him to the Kirk and this salbe your warrand. Subscrivit at Irvin the 17th September 1681 yeiris.

Jo. Montgomerie.

Recwed from Robert Bryson tresowr 17 September twinti fowr shilin Scots abow writu preswp. William Meldrum.

Robert Bryssoun thesaurer pey upon sight heirof to John Gairner smith the somme of three pund four shilling Scotts money for ffour hundreth of sklait nailles furnished be him to the dressing of the Kirk, quhilk sall be allowed in your thesaurer compts. Subscrivit att Irving the 24 of September 1681. Hew Montgomrie.
Jo. Montgomerie.

Grants me to be payed of the above wryten compt. John Gairner.

Robert Bryison treasuerer pay to William Meldroom thrie shilling sterling quhich with former tuo shillings compleatts him for cairieng 18 burden of fooge to the church this shall be aloued to you in your treasurer accompts. Given at Irvine the 24 September 1681. Hew Montgomrie.

Recwed abow writine preswp thrie shilen sterlin 26 September from Robert Bryson tresowr. Wilem Meldrume.

Robert Bryssoun thesaurer pay upon sight heirof to Robert Dook glessenwright the somme of eighteen punds Scotts money for twelve dayes working att the Kirk and sklaiting of the samyne in so ffarr as wes necessar, being for himself his man and his servitour. And quhilk somme sall be allowet in your thesaurer compts. Given att Irving the 24 September 1681. Hew Montgomrie.
Jo. Montgomerie.

Grants me Robert Dook to hawe recwed frome Robrt Bryson tresour the soum of eightyen pon Scots abowe writn priswp September twintie fowrt 1681.

Robert Dook.

49. *Account of the Treasurer's Disbursements.*—1681.

ANE Accompt of what ROBERT BRYSONE theasaurer hath depursed for which he hath no precept in the year 1681.

	Lib.	s.	d.
Imprimis 30 May. Given to Androw Caldwall at command of the proveist James Boyll	01	05	00
More to the men that wrought in the Duntan Know quarrall at the said proveists ordar for drink	00	04	00
August second. More for mixing of lime and sand to the Kirk at Beochs ordar	00	08	00
More at Baillye Hew Montgomries ordar to William Hay	00	04	00
More at Beochs ordar for a pair of pockets to put the money in that wes sent to Edinburgh belonging to the two cess	00	03	04
More 30 September. Given to Edward Hamiltone at the proveist and Beochs ordar quhen James Porter came with him	00	14	00
More given to Robert Muir for holding the Magistrats horses at Fergushills wyfes burriall at Killwining	00	02	00
More: 11 October 1681. At the proveists order for coal and candle to the tolbooth quhen my Lord Ross wes in town	00	16	00
More: 28 June 168 . Given at the proveists ordar	00	02	00
More: 3 July 1682. Given to James Galt at baillye Beochs ordar four fathom cordage	00	04	04
More to Alexander Dyett for oyll to the towne clok that James Galt receved upon the 22 of November 81	00	04	00
More to the said Alexander Dyett be James Galt for oyll to the clok that was geven upon the 29 of June 82 att balie Fwlartownes order	00	04	00
	04	10	08

Robert Brysone theasaurer pay the abovwryten compt extending to flour pound ten shilling eight pennyes Scottis and the samyne shall be allowed to you in your thesaurer compts. Given at Irving the   day of   1682 yeires.

50. *Order for payment to Hugh Montgomery of his Salary as Bailie, and other sums.*—19th August 1682.

ROBERT BRYSONE theasaurer pay upon sight heirof to Hugh Montgomerie lait baillye of Irving the somme of four pounds Scotis as being two yeirs cellarie dew to the said Hugh Montgomerie for the two last yeirs he was baillye of the said burgh to witt fra

Michalmess j^m vj^c sevintie nyne to Michalmass j^m vj^c eighty ane yeirs   Item pay to the said Hugh two shilling starling depursed be him to Robert Miller for casting the goat leading to the loch runing betwixt the taelling rigs and the town lands   As also pay to the said Hugh Montgomerie threttie shilling Scotis as the pryce of thrie cliff boards furnished be him to the Loch Mylne and received be Hugh M'Murray, and take the said Hugh Montgomerie his receipt therof and the samyne shall be allowed to you in your thesaurer compt   Givin at Irving the nyntein day off August j^m vj^c fourscore two yeirs
Jo. MONTGOMERIE, baillie
JA. FULLARTTOWN, baillie

	£	s.	d.
I Hew Mounttgomry lait ballie in Irving grantes to have receaved from Robert Brysoun the above mentioned precept the same is six pund fourtie shilling Scots. As wittnes my hand at Irving eight day off Septtember one thousand six hundreth and eightie two yeires HEW MONTGOMERIE.	1	4	0
	1	10	00
	6	14	00

51. *Order for payment on account of the Militia Horse for the Town of Irvine.*—12*th February* 1684.

William Rodger Towne Theasurer upon sight hereof pey to John Craufurd Burges of Irvine the soume of fflourty shillings sterling money upon the account of the Militia Horse and thir presents together with his recept of the samine shall obleidge us to allow the same to you in your Theasurer accompts.   Given and subscryved at Irvine the twelth day of February 1684.
Jo. MONTGOMERIE, bailie
Jo. BOYD, Bayllye

For William Rodger Towne Theasurer of Irvine.

Grants me to have recevel from William Rodger Treasorer the contents of the above written precept.   As wittnes my hand at Irwine the eight day of Aprill 1684.
JOHNE CRAFWRD.

52. *Account between James Boyll, late Provost, and the Burgh of Irvine.*—1679-1686.

ACCOMPT due be the BURGH of IRVINE to JAMES BOYLL since December j^m vj^c seventy nyne yeeris :—

May 1680.—The Toune was summonsd ffor irregular electione and the King's Councill ordered the old Magistrats to elect a new I being sent to compeer for the Toune.

	£	s.	d.
Imprimis To Hugh Stinstone seven rex dolloris	020	06	00
More To his servantis . .	001	08	00
Carry forward	021	14	00

		£	s.	d.
Brought forward	.	021	14	00
More To the Clerk with my Bill to the Councill	.	002	18	00
More To Kilmarnock with Beoch anent the localitie where wee stayed all night	.	005	18	00
More For extracting the Act of Electione		008	12	00
More To my charges in going to Edinburgh	.	034	16	00
		073	18	00
July 1680.—More To the Conventione of Burrowes to my propper expensses	.	034	14	00
More to tuo Equies (79) and (80) Thretty four pounds tuelve shilling	.	034	12	00
More To Hugh Wallace for Burrow dues as per recept	.	026	08	04
More To Burrow Servantis		002	18	00
More To tuo hundreth and six Deallis furnished to the Bridge		111	12	00
		210	04	04
June (81).—More When we were summoned before the Councill for not taking the Declaratione where the provoist and I was at Edinburgh	.	055	12	00
July (81).—More For my service to the Parliament being from the tuenty of July to the nynteen of September	.	200	00	00
More To the Register and his servant with my Commissione		017	16	00
		273	08	00
May (82).—More When the Toune was summoned for not taking the Test before the Councill It cost me in expensses 125lib. 16s. Whereof sixteen dolloris borrowed from James Hay	.	125	16	00
July (82).—More To my charges to the Conventione of Burrows		034	00	00
More To the Æquies (81) and (82) yeeris		034	10	00
More To the Burrow Dues per recept	.	040	13	00
More To Burrow Dues peyed at Irvine 25 September 1682		024	10	06
		259	09	06
July (83).—More For my expensses to the Burrows		034	00	00
More To the Equies		017	08	00
Carry forward		051	08	00

		£	s.	d.
Brought forward		051	08	00
More For tuo Linlithgow Meassouris to the Toune		008	04	00
		059	12	00

	£	s.	d.
July (84).—More To my expensses to the Burrows	034	16	00
More To the Burrow Agent for Burrow Dues 1683 and (84) yeeris	085	13	02
More To Craufardstoune ffor the Colledge of St. Andrews the halfe moneths Cess	054	00	00
More To Mr. Dunlop when wee were summoned for the Tounes Revenews	007	16	00
	182	05	02
SUMMA Tottalis	1058	17	00

	£	s.	d.
More To James Thomsone Quarter Master to Captaine Stewart ffor Localitie as per recept	015	00	00
More For seventy peece of free stones furnished to the Holme Milne	012	00	00
	027	00	00

To money receaved from the TOUNE to ballance by JAMES BOYLL.

	£	s.	d.
Imprimis From John Small tuelve bolls malt at 6lib. per boll	072	00	00
More Ane hundred pounds Scotts from him and Robert Weir	100	00	00
More From William Rodger late Theasaurer	200	00	00
More From Robert Bryssone alowed be the Proveist 60 rex dolloris	174	00	00
More From William Swintone late Theasaurer	100	00	00
	646	00	00

Nota.—That I never receaved anything for my attendance at two Justice Courtis at Air and meeting of the Shyre in my time.

Wee underscryvers being appointed be the Magistratis and Councill of the burgh of Irvine to state and peruse the Accomptis debursed be James Boyll laitt Proveist of the said Burgh upon the account of the samen burgh have perused and considered this above written accoumpt and wee find the samen extends in whole to the somme of one thousand fflourscore fyve pounds seventeen shilling Scots money And that the said James Boyll acknowledges his receaving six hundreth ffourty six pounds in part thereof and that wee have seen the equies and recepts of Burrow Dues and missives mentioned in the said accompt which are to be produced herewith and recoummends to the Magistratis and Councill of the said Burgh to order his peyment of the ballance of the forsaid accompt and to try if the said James Boyll hes receaved any more money upon account of the said Burgh then what he hes charged himselfe to have receaved As wittnes our hands att Irvine the tuenty nynt day of October j^{m}vj^{c} eighty six yeeris

Jo. MONTGOMERIE, Provost
JOHN BLAIR
JA. HAY

53. *Account due by the Town to Janet Garvan.*—1686.

ACCOMPT due be the TOUNE of IRVINE to JANET GARVEN beginning 23 January 1686.

	Lib.	s.	d.
23 January 1686. Imprimis The Magistratis and some of the Councill three pyntis of wine ane pynt of aill ane jill of brandy and 2s. 8d. for tobacco and pyps Inde	03	06	08
25 Item The Magistratis with some gentlemen of Air Three pyntis of wyne ane jill of brandy and ane pynt of aill	03	04	00
Item more the said day sent for be the Magistratis to Mr. Walter Edmonstouns 4 pyntis of wyne	04	00	00
26 Item The tuo Bailzies with another gentleman ane jill of brandy and ane pynt of aill	00	04	00
30 Item The Magistratis and Councill when they were subscry-ving the tackis betwixt my Lord Montgomrie and the toune ffour pyntis of wyne and for aill brandy tobacco and pyps 20s.	05	00	00
Februarij 1. Item The Magistratis with young Pearstoune, old Broomlands and Bryce Blair and the clerk and utheris ffyve pyntis of wyne and for tobacco and pyps and aill 9s. Inde	05	09	00
4. Item Some of the Councill being sent be the Magistratis to entertaine Mr. Wallace when he came to seek the coall that night when he came flor aill and brandy tobacco and pyps	00	11	00
5. Item The Magistratis with the said Mr. Wallace 6 pyntis of aill ffour jills of brandy and ten chapins and ane mutchkine of wyne	06	05	00
6. Item The Magistratis with him in the morning ane chapine of wyne ane pynt of aill and ane baick .	00	13	00
Item the said day in the afternoon the Magistratis lykwayes with him and some of the Councill and utheris 7 chapins of wyne and for aill tobacco and pyps 12s. 8d. Inde	04	02	08
7. Item with him in the morning ane chapine of aill	00	01	00
8. Item The Magistratis with Pearstoune Doctor Reid Langshaw and severall other gentlemen in the morning 3 chapins of wyne	01	10	00

EXCERPTS FROM BURGH ACCOUNTS. 303

	Lib. s. d.
Item In the afternoon with Pearstoune Proveist Boyll and severall utheris 4 chapins of wyne and 2s. for tobacco and pyps . .	02 02 00
10. Item The Magistratis, with the coal Ingineer in the morning and at night ffour pyntis of wyne tuo pyntis of aill ane jill of brandy and 2s. for tobacco and pyps Inde	04 08 00
11. Item The Magistratis with George Montgomrie apothecarie in Air ane pynt of wyne	01 00 00
12. Item The Magistratis and some of the Councill after they came from the councill three pyntis of wyne and ane Mainshott .	03 01 00
15. Item The Magistratis with William Smith meassone ane pynt of aill	00 02 00
Item The said day the Magistratis with Pearstouns elder and younger Doctor Reid and severall uther gentlmen ffyve pynts of wyne two pyntis of aill and 2s. for tobacco and pyps . .	05 06 00
SUMMA	50 06 04
16 February. Item The Magistratis with the said William Smith meassone ffour chapins of aill	00 04 00
Item The same day in the morning the Magistratis with an Air gentlman and some utheris ane pynt of wyne ane chapine of aill and two baiks	01 03 00
Item The same night the Magistratis and clerk with George Monro clerk and severall uther gentlmen tuo pyntis of wyne ane pynt of aill and 2s. for tobacco and pyps . . .	02 04 00
17. Item The Magistratis when they wer stateing Michael Glasgow his accomptis Portry being in company after the accomptis were stated tuo pyntis of wyne . . .	02 00 00
18. Item The Magistratis and clerk anent some of the touns affairs ffour mutchkins of wyne	01 00 00
23. Item The Magistratis with some gentlmen ane pynt of wyne and ane chapine of aill	01 01 00
24. Item That day that proveist Cuninghame in Air was buried William Suintoune with some uther Councellouris with the Coall Ingineir after they came home three mutchkins of wyne three pyntis of aill and ane ounce of tobacco and three pyps . .	01 02 10
25. Item The Magistratis and Clerk and severallis of the Councill with the coall Ingineir 4 pyntis of aill ane ounce of tobacco and 5 pyps	00 10 02
2 March. Item The Magistratis with ane gentleman a stranger ane chapine of wyne and ane pynt of aill . . .	00 12 00

	Lib.	s. d.

6. Item Sent for be the Magistratis to William Suintouns to David Buchannen three jills of brandy 00 06 00

Item That same day the Magistratis with William Smith measson three chapins of aill 00 03 00

10. Item Sent for be the Magistratis to John Broune shoemaker his house tuo pyntis of wyne 02 00 00

11. Item The Magistratis with David Buchannan and William Suintoune and utheris tuo jills of brandy . . . 00 04 00

12. Item The Magistratis and wholl Councill 4 pyntis of wyne 4 pyntis of aill and 4s. for bread . . . 04 12 00

13. Item The Magistratis with David Buchannan and William Suintoune ane chapine of wyne 00 10 00

Item the same day in the afternoon sent for be the Magistratis with David Buchannane to William Suintoun's house three chapins of aill and halfe mutchkine of brandy . . . 00 07 00

19. Item Sent for be the Proveist and Bailyie Boyll to Bailyie Boyd's hous ane pynt of wyne 01 00 00

20. Item The Magistratis with Pearstoune elder two pyntis of wyne and 4s. for aill and bread . . . 02 04 00

23. Item Bailyie Boyll with David Buchannan Burrowland and William Suintoune 3 jills of brandy and ane pynt of aill . 00 08 00

SUMMA 21 11 00

30 March. The Magistratis with David Buchannan and severall utheris eight chapins of aill and for tobacco and pyps 2s. . 00 10 00

1 Appryll. The Magistratis and Councill with David Buchannan anent the toune clock six pyntis and ane chapine of wyne tuo pynts of aill and 3s. for bread and 4s. for tobacco and pyps . 07 01 00

2. Item The Magistratis with David Buchannan three pyntis of wyne and 1s. 6d. for tobacco and pyps . . . 03 01 06

5. Item The Magistratis with young Pearstoune and utheris ane pynt wyne 01 00 00

6. Item The Magistratis with young Kelburne ffour chapins of wyne ane pynt of aill and ane baik . . . 02 03 00

7. Item The Magistratis with David Buchannan and severall utheris the day that he was to goe for Glasgow ane pynt of wyne ane pynt of aill and ane baik 01 03 00

9. Item The Magistratis with William Smith when they gave him ane precept for peyment of building the Church style 4 chapins of aill and halfe mutchkine of brandy . . . 00 08 00

EXCERPTS FROM BURGH ACCOUNTS.

	Lib.	s.	d.

13. Item The Magistratis with Pearstonne younger Mr. Dunbarr and Bailyie Oseburne in Air ffour pyntis of wyne ane pynt of aill and ane baik and 1s. 4d. for tobacco and pyps 04 04 04

14. Item The Magistratis with Mr. John Montgomrie and severall utheris three pyntis of wyne 03 00 00

15. Item The Magistratis with Gleneys and Mr. John Montgomrie and severall utheris ffour chapins of aill two jills of brandy and 2s. for tobacco and pyps 00 10 00

16. Item The Magistratis with Colsfeild Proveist Boyll and severall utheris the day after William M'Taggartis daughter was maried seven pyntis and ane chapine of wyne and for aill bread tobacco and pyps 20s. 8d. 08 00 08

16. Item The Magistratis with Glenayes and utheris ffor aill brandy tobacco and pyps 00 17 00

17. Item The Magistratis with severall gentlmen and William Suintoune and George Arskine in company tuo pyntis and ane chapine of wyne and 1s. 8d. ffor tobacco and pyps . . 02 11 08

20. Item The Magistratis with severallis of the Counceill and uther gentlmen ffour chapins of wyne and six chapins of aill . 02 06 00

22. Item The Magistratis with Mr. John Montgomrie the clerk and Hugh Hutchesone and utheris ane pynt of aill and halfe mutchkine of brandy 00 06 00

26 Item The Magistratis with Pearstone Corshill Tourlands and Busbie and severall utheris three pyntis and ane chapine of wyne 03 10 00

Item The Magistratis clerk William Suintoune and severall utheris tuo pyntis of wyne and for tobacco and pyps 2s. Inde . 02 02 00

1 May. Item The Magistratis with the Bailyie of Newmilnes ane chapine of wyne 00 10 00

SUMMA . 43 04 02

3 May. Item The Magistratis with old Broomlands and some uther gentlmen three mutchkins of wyne ane chapine of aill and for tobacco and pyps 1s. 4d. 00 17 04

5. Item The Magistratis with young Pearstonne and utheris tuo chapins wyne 01 00 00

7. Item The Magistratis with the Bailyie of Newmilnes and severall uther gentlmen three chapins of wyne . . 01 10 00

11. Item The Magistratis and Clerk with John Wallace colyier and ane Glasgow gentlman and severall utheris three chapins of wyne ane pynt of aill and 2s. for tobacco and pyps . 01 14 00

13. Item The Magistratis with Mr. Patrick Cumine and severall utheris two chapins and ane mutchkine wyne . . .	01 05 00
14. Item The Magistratis with the Bailyie of Newmilnes and utheris three mutchkins of wyne . . .	00 15 00
Item Mr. Wallace and his workeris at the heugh with Robert Weir and utheris at severall tymes when they came in from the heugh eleiven pyntis of aill . . .	01 02 00
15. Item The Magistratis with Bailyie Oseburne in Air and severall uther genthnen three pyntis of wyne . . .	03 00 00
17. Item The Magistratis with young Pearstone and utheris 3 chapins wyne . . .	01 10 00
22. Item The Magistratis with Mr. Wallace and severall utheris 4 mutchkins wyne . . .	01 00 00
24. Item The Magistratis with young Pearstone ane pynt of wyne	01 00 00
26. Item The Magistratis with Bailyie Biggart Mr. Wallace and utheris who were at the heugh ffour pyntis of aill ane ounce of tobacco and half ane duzon of pyps . . .	00 10 04
Item Mr. Wallace and his workeris at severall tymes when they came from the heugh ffour pyntis of aill . . .	00 08 00
28. Item The Magistratis with Thomas M'Gill at Edinburgh ane pynt wyne . . .	01 00 00
Item The hyred toune workeris at the heuch at severall tymes 14 pyntis aill . . .	01 08 00
Item The Magistratis with the Deacon conveener of Air with William Saintoune Hugh Montgomrie and severallis of the Councill ane pynt wyne . . .	01 00 00
29. Item The Magistratis and Councill for the solemnity 15 pyntis of wyne 12 pyntis of aill 2 ounces tobacco and on duzon of pyps Inde . . .	16 08 08
4 June. Item The Magistratis with Pearstoune and uther gentlmen ane pynt of wyne and for tobacco and pyps and bread 2s. 8d.	01 02 08
5. Item By Robert Weiris appointment given to the men who were casting turfs three pyntis of aill and ane farle of bread .	00 06 08
Item The same day the Magistratis with Thomas M'Gowne William Saintoune and utheris concerned for attending the Holme Milne ffyve mutchkins of wyne . . .	01 05 00
7. Item The day of beginning the casting of clay in setting doune the first shank for the heuch. Brought to the heuch for the workmen and drunken be the carieris 10 pyntis of aill and 2 kaikis of bread . . .	01 04 00

		Lib.	s.	d.
8. Item Furnished lykwayes to the workeris 12 pynts of aill and three kaiks of bread		01	10	00
SUMMA		40	16	08

9. Item Furnished lykwayes to the workeris 28 pyntis of aill and six kaiks of bread and for cheese 4s. and at night when they came from the heugh 4s. for tobacco and pyps. . . . 03 16 00

10. Item More furnished to the workeris 16 pyntis of aill and tuo kaikis bread 01 16 00

Item The said day the Magistratis with Pearstoune and some uther gentlmen ane pynt of wyne 01 00 00

11. Item Furnished to the heuch ane gallon of aill and four farles of bread 00 18 08

12. Item The Magistratis with Mr. Wallace and utheris after they came from the heuch it being Saturday 3 pyntis of wyne and given to the workeris at the Magistratis direction 4 pyntis of aill   Inde 03 08 00

Item more for tobacco and pyps at the same tyme . 00 02 00

16. Item The Magistratis with Mr. Wallace and Mr. Johnstonne and severall utheris after they came from the heuch ane pynt of wyne and ane pynt of aill. 01 02 00

17. The Magistratis with Mr. John Montgomrie Bailyie Fullartoune the clerk William Saintoune and utheris when Mr. John was going for Edinburgh three chapins of wyne . . 01 10 00

18. Item Sent for to the heuch to the workeris three pyntis of aill 00 06 00

17. Item Given to the workeris at the proveists directione after they came from the heuch 4 pyntis of aill . 00 08 00

18. Item The Magistratis with Bridgend ane pynt of wyne and ane pynt of aill 01 02 00

19. Item To the workeris at the heuch with Robert Weir 3 pyntis of aill 00 06 00

22. Item The Magistratis with severallis who were at the milne working three pyntis of aill and sent to the workeris at the heuch that night ane pynt of aill 00 08 00

24. Item To the workeris at the heuch three chapins of aill and ane pynt sent to the heuch at Robert Weiris direction . . 00 05 00

25. Item The Coalyieris ffyve pyntis of aill whereof ane in the morning and ane sent to the heuch and three in the afternoon when they came from the heuch and for tobacco and pyps 1s. . . 00 11 00

	Lib.	s. d.
26. Item The Magistratis with Mr. Wallace and the rest of the coalyieris ffour pyntis of aill ane chapine of wyne ane ounce of tobacco and halfe duzon of pyps	01	00 04
28. Item The Magistratis with Pearstone and severall uther gentlmen two pyntis of wyne	02	00 00
30. Item Given to the coalyieris at the Magistratis order ffour pyntis of aill	00	08 00
2 Julij. Item The Magistratis with sundrie gentlmen ane pynt of wyne and another of aill And given to the coalyieris at the same tyme three pyntis of aill Inde	01	08 00
5. Item The Magistratis with severall gentlmen ane chapine of wyne and ane pynt of aill	00	12 00
7. Item Given to the coalyieris ffour pyntis of aill	00	08 00
SUMMA .	22	15 00

8. Julij. Item Sent to the men who drew the water out of the heuch the tyme of the taking out the timber three chapins of aill at night and three chapings of aill in the morning And ane kaik of bread and four pyntis of aill to the remander of the workeris . .	00	16 00
12. Item The Magistratis with ane gentlman ane chapine of wyne and two pyntis of aill	00	14 00
Item The Magistratis with the clerk and severall utheris ane chapine of wyne upon the 10 day of July And given to the coalyieris the said day at the Magistratis desyre being the day of their entring to the second shank for the heuch ffour pyntis of aill Inde . .	00	18 00
12. Item The Magistratis with Pearstonne and severall uther gentlmen six pyntis of wyne and ane pynt of aill . .	06	02 00
16. Item The Magistratis with ane gentlman a strauger ane chapine of wyne and ane pynt of aill . .	00	12 00
Item The said day given to the coalyieris at the Magistratis directione ffour pyntis of aill	00	08 00
19. Item The Magistratis with some gentlmen ane double jill of brandy and ane pynt of aill	00	06 00
22. Item The Magistratis with some gentlmen two pyntis of aill and ane ounce of tobacco and ffour pyps . . .	00	06 00
24. Item Given to the coalyieris at the Magistratis directione three pyntis of aill	00	06 00
26. Item The Magistratis with John Wallace and utheris three chapins of aill and ane mutchkine of wyne	00	08 00

	Lib.	s.	d.
27. Item The Magistratis with young Pearstoune and severall uther gentlmen ffyve chapins of wyne	02	10	00
30. Item The Magistratis with some company ane jill of brandy	00	02	00
7 August. Item To the coalyieris at the Magistratis directioune tuo pyntis aill	00	04	00
8. Item The Magistratis with Mr. Wallace Mr. Johnstoune and utheris three chapins of aill and ane jill of brandy	00	05	00
Item Sent for be the Proveist to George Arskins house upon the fyfth day of August halfe ane mutchkine of brandy	00	04	00
Item The said 5th day Bailyie Boyll with ane Lergs man ane jill of brandy and ane chapine of aill	00	03	00
10. Item The Magistratis with Proveist Muir Bailyie Oseburne in Air and severall otheris ane chapine of cold wyne and two chapins of burnt wyne	01	13	04
11. Item The Magistratis with Bridgend Broomlands elder and otheris three chapins of aill ane jill of brandy halfe ounce of tobacco and three pyps	00	06	02
12. Item The Magistratis with Hugh Montgomrie at Eglishoune and severall otheris six chapins of aill and for tobacco and pyps 1s.	00	07	00
Item Given to the coalyieris at the Magistratis direction the same night two pyntis of aill	00	04	00
SUMMA	16	14	06
14 August. Item The Magistratis the tyme of their receaving their gloves from the Bailyie of Cuninghame three chapins of wyne and ane pynt of aill and ane pype	01	12	02
16. Item The Magistratis with Pearstone Kelburne and severall utheris ane pynt of wyne halfe ane mutchkine of brandy ffour pyntis of aill two ounces of sugar two wheat bread ane ounce of tobacco and six pyps	01	18	00
17. Item To the coalyieris at the Magistratis direction two pyntis of aill	00	04	00
21. Item Given to the coalyieris at the Magistratis directione when the Herds gott their supperis ffour pyntis of aill	00	08	00
23. Item The Magistratis with the Thesaurer and severall utheris when Robert M'Gleish was peying his burges fyne ffour pyntis of aill half ane mutchkine of brandy ane ounce of tobacco and halfe duzon of pyps	00	14	04
Item The said day sent for be the Magistratis to William Sunitounes aue mutchkine of brandy	00	08	00

	Lib.	s.	d.
7 September. Item Given to the coalyieris at the Magistratis directione when they gott the first coall ane gallon of aill . .	00	16	00
Item The Magistratis themselves at the same tyme halfe ane mutchkine of brandy and ane quart of aill	00	08	00
Item Given at the Magistratis direction to Bryce Stinstone and David Auld at severall tymes two pyntis of aill . . .	00	04	00
11. Item Given to the colyieris at the Magistratis directione ane quart aill	00	04	00
Item Sent for be the Magistratis to George Arskine his house ane mutchkine of brandie	00	08	00
15. Item The Magistratis and Councill when the second coall was gottin and the letter came from the Chancelour to the Magistratis ffyve pyntis of aill ane jill of brandy and 1s. 2d. for tobacco and pyps	00	13	02
Item Given to the coalyieris at the Magistratis directione at the same tyme flour pyntis of aill	00	08	00
Item More given to them at the Magistratis order since that tyme ane pynt of aill	00	02	00
24. Item The Magistratis and Councill for aill bread brandy tobacco and pyps	01	11	06
25. Item The Magistratis when peruseing the Thesaureris their accomptis ffor aill and brandy	00	15	00
Item The said day the Proveist with Proveist Boyll and severall utheris ane pynt of aill and two jills of brandy . . .	00	06	00
Item Given to the coalyieris that same night at the Magistratis directione ffour pyntis of aill	00	08	00
Item Sent for be the Magistratis to William Suintouns house three jills of brandy	00	06	00
Item Given to Thomas M'Gowne to give Mathew Frew when he was working at the Holme Milne . . .	00	04	00
1 October. Item The Magistratis three pyntis of aill half ane ounce of tobacco and two pyps . . .	00	07	00
9. Item Given to the coalyieris at the Magistratis directione ffour pyntis aill	00	08	00
Summa	12	13	02
14 October. Item The Magistratis and Councill and severall gentlmen the tyme of their solemnizeing the anniversarie thanksgiving in comemoration of his Majesties birth day ffyfty fyve pyntis of wyne with sugar at 18s. per pynt Inde . . .	49	10	00
Item at the same tyme three gallons and ane half of aill	02	16	00

	Lib.	s.	d
Item More the same tyme six ounces of tobacco and three duzon and ane halfe of pyps and six baikis and halfe aue pound of candle to the Kirk, Schooll and Tolbuith for the ringing of the Bells Inde	01	03	04
18. Item The Magistratis with Pearstone the collector and severall other gentlmen ffyve pynts of wyne	05	00	00
33. Item The Proveist when he came from Saltcoatis desired to give the coalyieris tuo pynts of aill	00	04	00
28. Item Given to them at the Proveists order when they gott the thickest coall ane gallon of aill	00	16	00
29. Item The Magistratis with Pearstoune the collector and severall uther gentlmen when the collector was admitted burges seven pynts of wyne And for aill, bread, brandy, tobacco, and pyps 16s. Inde	07	16	00
1 Novembris. Item Being the day when Proveist Montgomrie went for Edinburgh the Magistratis and Proveist Boyll and the collector and severall of the Councill three chapins of wyne six chapins of aill and for bread 1s.	01	17	00
8. Item The Magistratis with Pearstoune elder and the collector and Armillan and severall uther gentlmen 3 pyntis of wyne and for tobacco and pyps and utheris called for at the said tyme 15s.	03	15	00
14. Item The Magistratis with ane gentlman and William Swintoune present ane chapine of wyne	00	10	00
19. Item The Magistratis the night that the Proveist conveened the brewaris anent their excyse before he went to Edinburgh with some gentlmen ane pynt of wyne ane quart of aill half ane ounce of tobacco and two pyps	01	05	00
20. Item That day the Proveist went to Edinburgh he and the Bailyies and Pearstones son William and the Clerk and severall of the Councill ffyve chapins of wyne with sugar	02	18	04
6 Decembris. Item The Magistratis with Broomlands elder the Clerk and severall other gentlmen Bryce Blair and severall of the Councill ane chapine of wyne ane pynt of aill and ane jill of brandy	00	14	00
7. Item The Magistratis when they were putting the coalyieris to their work after they hade gotten ane new cord three pyntis and ane chapine of aill and Robert Weir and utheris splyceing the cord three pyntis of aill and ane farle of bread	00	13	08
10. Item The Magistratis and Councill after they hade come from the Councill house making some bargane with Robert Dickie anent the toune victuall ffour mutchkins of wyne eight chapins of aill and 2s. for tobacco and pyps	01	10	00

		Lib.	s.	d.
Item The Proveist Bailyie Boyll the clerk and utheris with Captain Hugh Montgomrie Colsfeild and severall other gentlmen with some things that was debursed be her for defraying of some charges for Robert Maxwellis buriall	.	04	06	00
SUMMA		84	14	04
Item ffor meat drink and horse meat furnished be her to John Wallace coalyier at severall tymes from the fourt of February to the tent of July 1686 conforme to ane particular accompt		27	06	00
SUMMA		27	06	00

WEE undersubscryveris who are appoynted be the Magistratis and Councill of the burgh of Irvine to state and peruse Jonnet Garvine relict of umquhill George Montgomerie hir taverne accompt dew to hir be the saidis Magistratis and Councill have considered and perused this above and within wryten accompt dew to the said Jonnet be the saidis Magistratis and Councill commensing from the twentie thrid of January last to this day and date consisting of nyne pages at the leist eight pages and one artickle wryten upon the nynt page And doe find that the said Jonnet hes trewlie and reallie furnished the samen by order of the Magistratis and Councill of this burgh conforme to hir oath and depositione given thairupon in our presencis and that the samen extends in the whole to the soume of Three hundreth and twintie punds ane shilling tuo pennies salvo justo calculo. As witness our hands att Irvine the eleventh day of December j^m vj^c eightie yeiris. Jo. MONTGOMERIE, provest.
PATRICK BOYLE, Ballie.
JOHN BLAIR.
JA. HAY.

Robert Weir thesaurer pay to Jonnet Garvine above named the soume of Three hundreth and twintie punds ane shilling tuo pennies Scottis money conforme to this above and foirewryten accompt and approbatione and act of Councill maid thairupon of this date and take hir recept thairof which salbe allowed to yow in the first end of the roll of the roped laudis milne rentis and utheris pertaining to this burgh delyvered to yow this day. Given att Irvine the twintie thrid day of December 1686.
Jo. MONTGOMERIE, provest.
PATRICK BOYLE, Ballie.

I Jonnet Garvine within designed grant me to have receaved from Robert Weir thesaurer of the burgh of Irvine the soume of Three hundreth and twintie punds ane shilling tuo pennies contained in the within writtin accompt and precept And therfor dischairgis the Magistratis and Councill of the burgh of Irvine and the said

Robert Weir and all utheris whom it effeiris of the samen. As witnes my hand att Irvine the eight day of January j^m vj^c eightie sevin yeiris befor thes witnesses James Whyte merchand in Irvine William Swintoune saidler thair and James Hay clerk of the said burgh wryter heirof.   JEANET GARVES.

    William Suintone, *wittnes.*
    James Whyt, *witnes.*
    Ja. Hay, *witnes.*

54. *Account for Refreshments.*—1686-1687.

ACCOMPT due by the BURGH of IRVINE to JANET GARVEN beginning the 23 of December j^{m}vj^c ffourscore six yeers being the day the last precept was subscryved for peyment of last accompt due be them to her

	Lib.	s.	d.
23 December 1686. Imprimis the Magistrats and Councill the said day ffyve mutchkins of wyne and for aill tobacco and pyps 15s. Inde	02	00	00
Item The Proveist Baillye Boyd and some of the Councill anent some of the touns affairs at which time David M'Clatchie and John Thomson in Dalry came in to them anent some particular affair ffyve mutchkins wyne	01	05	00
Item That day the Proveist subscryveit Adam Grayes precept for peyment to him of his cellarie for keeping the Knock and ringing the Bell ane pynt of aill and halfe mutchkine of brandie	00	06	00
Item The Magistrats upon some tounes affairs three mutchkins of wyne and was immediatly sent for to the Clerks chamber	00	15	00
31 December. Item The Magistrats being come out of Killwinning with Broomlands elder and younger John Hay and uther gentlemen ane pynt of wyne and for aill tobacco and pyps ffourteen shilling	01	14	00
Item The Magistrats with some gentlemen ane pynt of aill and halfe mutchkine of brandie	00	06	00
8 January 1687. Item The Magistrats and Theasaurer receaving some Milne rent from James Whyte ane pynt burnt wyne with sugar halfe mutchkine brandy and ane baick and ane pynt of aill	01	10	00
Item sent for be the Magistrats with some gentlemen of Air to William Suintone his house half mutchkine of brandie	00	04	00
14 January. Item The Magistrats with severalls of the Councill when the Proveist went to Glasgow ane pynt of aill and halfe mutchkine of brandy	00	06	00

	Lib. s. d.
Item The Magistrats and Councill when Alexander Montgomerie Sevenaikeris brother was admitted burges tuo pynts of wyne .	02 00 00
Item The Magistrats and utheris when Killwinning brewaris gave up ther entries ane pynt of wyne .	01 00 00
Item The Magistrats with severall gentlemen three pynts of wyne tuo pynts of aill ane gill of brandie and ane baick .	03 07 00
14 March. Item The Magistrats with some gentlemen Hugh Barckley being present ane pynt of wyne ane chapine of aill and ane baick .	01 02 00
20 March. Item The Magistrats and souldiers that came with ane letter to the toune for delyvering up of two prisoneris three chapins of wyne ffour chapins of aill and ane baick .	01 15 00
21 March. Item The Magistrats with some gentlemen (The Brewaris of Beith being conveened at Irvine) ffyve mutchkins of wyne	01 05 00
Item The Magistrats with some gentlemen of Air three pynts of wyne .	03 00 00
1 Appryll. Item The Magistrats with Robert Muir and Mr. John Montgomerie in Edinburgh and uthers tuo pynts of wyne .	02 00 00
7. Item The Magistrats Proveist Boyll and uthers ane pynt of wyne .	01 00 00
11. Item The Magistrats Proveist Boyll and some uthers of the Councill that day that Mr. Muir and Montgomerie were admitted burgesses ten pynts and ane chapine of wyne and tuo baiks .	10 12 00
	35 07 00

JEANET GARVEN

15 Appryll 1687. Item The Magistrats some Councellouris with James Millikine Andrew Spark and uthers three chapins of wyne and ane pynt of aill .	01 12 00
20. Item The Magistrats with Mr. Muir and uthers tuo pynts of wyne .	02 00 00
22. Item The Magistrats with Mr. William Rodgers Broomlands elder Francis Broddie and uthers three chapins of wyne and ane pynt of aill .	01 12 00
25. Item The Magistrats with James Gemill in Glasgow ane pynt of burnt claret wyne sugar chapine of aill and ane baick .	01 05 00
27. Item The Magistrats with severall gentlemen tuo pynts of wyne	02 00 00
29. Item. The Proveist with Edward and Laurence Wallaces and uthers ane pynt of wyne in posset and sugar and milk .	·01 04 00
5 May. Item The Magistrats and some of the Councill ane chapine of wyne ane chapine of aill ane gill of brandie and ane baick .	00 14 00

		Lib. s. d.	

Item Upon Wittsune Munday therafter the Magistrats with the souldieris who came to lift the Cess with some of the Councill three pynts of wyne and two pynts of aill with tobacco and pyps Inde   03 05 00

Item Upon the   day of May said yeer the said Magistrats with some of the Councell ffour mutchkins of wyne three pynts of aill and tuo baicks and for tobacco and pyps 2s. Inde   01 10 00

Item That day that ane express came from the Lordis of Councill anent ane Commissioner for the conventione of royall burrows the Magistrats with the said post who brought the advyce ffor liquor and uthers which was then immediatly compted   03 10 00

Item The Magistrats with the stent maisteris and the clerk anent taking accompt of the stent rollis ffor aill brandie tobacco and pyps   01 00 06

Item The Magistrats and Councill anent some of the tounes affairis for aill tobacco pyps and ane gill of brandie   00 14 06

Summa   20 07 08
The preceeding page   35 07 00
Inde in all   55 14 08

Jeanet Garven.

55. Account by John Murray, Wright, for work done in the Church and School of Irvine.—1697.

Compt dew by the Magestrats of Irvine to John Murray wright for work at the Church and School of Irvine 1697 as follows :—

	Lib. s. d.

Imprimis For raising the Magistrats loft for their part   12 00 00
Item For 15 foott of glass in the south syde of the church at 4s. per foott   03 00 00
Item 7 foott and ¾ in ane window in the south Isle pryce forsaid   01 11 00
Item For mending of two uther windows   01 04 00
Item 22 Lozens in windows in the Church   01 01 00
Item 200 double plensher for dressing the tables and forms at the Communione   02 00 00
Item 100 and ¾ single plensher to the same use   00 17 06
Item 200 and ½ door nailes for the use aforsaid at 8s. per 100 is   00 18 00
Item For thrie pound six unce iron work for bands and batts to the door wheir the elements stood at 4s. per pound is   00 13 06
Item Two pair jam bands thairto at 10s. per pair is   01 00 00
Item Eleven dails at 13s. 4d. per peece is   07 06 08
Item Six foott and a half new glass in the schoole pryce forsaid   01 06 00

316   MUNIMENTS OF THE BURGH OF IRVINE.

		Lib. s. d.
Item For ane window broad with ane iron band to one window in the schooll		00 03 00
Item For the tables making dressing and setting at the Communione and making ane closs roume in the Church to keep the elements		06 00 00
SUMMA		39 05 08

Wee undersubscryvers auditors nominat by the Magistrats and Counsell of the Burgh of Irving ffor perusing and auditeing the above writtin accompt doe make our report That the forsaid accompt is just and reasoneable amounting to threttie nyne pounds ffyve shillings 8d. Scotts and recommends the payment thairof to Magistrats and Counsell. As witnesseth thir presents subscryved by us att Irving this 23 Februarii 1698 years.

JA: NISBET   JA: DICKIE
JO^S HAMILTON   HUGH GARVEN

56. *Account between the Soldiers in the Companies of Captain Mosman and Captain Erskine, and certain Inhabitants of Irvine.*—1700.

ACCOMPT of what is dew by the SHOULDIERIS in Captain Mossmans Company to the persons after named INHABITANTS of IRVINE.

		Lib. s. d.		Lib. s. d.
Imprimis	By Alexander Caddall to Jannet Porter	0 4 0	}	00 07 0
Item	By him to James Nivein	0 3 0		
Item	By Corporall Seath to James Nivein	2 0 0	}	2 10 8
Item	By him to William Rasyde	0 10 8		
Item	By William Bruce to Martha Shedden	2 7 0	}	03 18 8
Item	By him to James Nivein	0 5 4		
Item	By him to Isabell Cunninghame	0 10 4		
Item	By him to George Watt	0 8 0		
Item	By him to Samuell Hunter	0 8 0		
Item	By Robert Watson to Jannet Bryden	0 7 2	}	04 04 4
Item	By Robert Watson to James Nivein	0 10 0		
Item	By him to Martha Shedden	2 10 0		
Item	By him to William Rawsyde	0 04 8		
Item	By him to Alexander Whyt	0 12 6		
Item	By William Leslie to James Nivein	1 02 0	}	03 04 04
Item	By him to Marion Muir	0 9 0		
Item	By him to Martha Shedden	0 4 0		
Item	By him to William Rawsyde	0 5 4		
Item	By him to Jannet Bryden	1 3 8		

EXCERPTS FROM BURGH ACCOUNTS.   317

		Lib.	s.	d.	Lib.	s.	d.
Item	By Mr. Maitland to Isobell Cuningham	1	2	0	02	06	0
Item	By him to David Tweed	1	4	0			
Item	By Charles Damster to William Crauford	0	14	0			
Item	By him Marion Muir	0	2	0	01	1	8
Item	By him to Martha Shedden	0	3	0			
Item	By him to Agnes Young	0	2	8			
Item	By John Stewart to Martha Shedden	0	01	8			
Item	By him to Marion Muir	0	05	0	0	10	8
Item	By him to William Rawsyde	0	04	0			
Item	By Duncan M'Calster to William Crawfourd	0	05	0			
Item	By him to Jannet Bryden	0	04	0	01	01	8
Item	By him to William Smaillie	0	13	8			
Item	By John Frazer to Margaret Dunlop	0	3	0			
Item	By him to Marion Muir	0	10	6	0	19	10
Item	By him to Jean Frances	0	6	4			
Item	By James Gilchrist to Marion Muir	0	1	6			
Item	By him to Hugh Garvan	0	9	0	0	14	6
Item	By him to Mrs. Murthland	0	4	0			
Item	By Archibald Litleton to Margaret Dunlop	0	14	0	0	14	0
Item	By John Gow to Margrat Dunlop				0	12	8
Item	By Donald Lamont to Margrat Dunlop	0	1	8	0	05	8
Item	By him to William Smaillie	0	4	0			
Item	By John Oar to Agnes Young	0	2	6	01	11	6
Item	By him to James Gloak	01	9	0			
Item	By Alexander Stewart to Jean Frances				0	8	0
					24	13	2
Item	By the said John Oar to James Smaillies wife				0	12	8

Receaved by David Tweed from Mr. Marten, Cades three dozen of Bresse buttons valued at 14s. Scotts in part of his articell of 24s. Scotts.

ACCOMPT of quhat is dew by the SHOULDIERES of Captain Patrick Ersken his Company to the persones after named INHABITANTS of IRVINE.

		Lib.	s.	d.	Lib.	s.	d.
Imprimis	By Alexander Rein to Marion Muir	0	4	0			
Item	By him to Jannet Portor	0	5	8			
Item	By him to David Tweed	0	10	0	01	10	04
Item	By him to George Watt	0	05	6			
Item	By him to Bettie Hunter	0	02	6			
Item	By him to James Nivein	0	02	8			

		£ s. d.	£ s. d.
Item	By James Montgomerie to Jannet Porter .	0 12 0	
Item	By him to Margaret Dunlop . . .	0 09 4	01 04 0
Item	By him to James Nivein . . .	0 02 8	
Item	By John Wilsone Corporall to James Steill .		0 15 0
Item	Robert Dykes to John Reoch .		01 02 0
Item	By Donald Robbisone to William Crawfourd		01 0 0
Item	By Andrew Adam to William Crawfourd .		00 16 0
Item	By John Leslie to William Craufourd	0 16 0	
Item	By him to Margrat Dunlop .	0 02 0	01 14 4
Item	By him to Agnes Young . .	0 15 0	
Item	By him to James Nivein . .	00 01 4	
Item	By Sergan Charles Hunter to Isobell Cunningham	0 18 8	
Item	By him to Samuell Hunter . .	0 08 0	01 12 0
Item	By him to Jannet Bryden . .	0 05 4	
Item	By William Stein to Isobell Cunninghame	0 4 8	00 08 8
Item	By him to Jannet Bryden .	0 4 0	
Item	By Donald M'Caskie to Agnes Young .	0 06 6	
Item	By George M'askie to Agnes Young .	0 03 0	
Item	By John Leis to William Thomsone .	01 05 6	
Item	Alexander Rein to Jannet Shaw .	00 11 0	
Item	By the said Sergant Hunter to Jannet Shaw	00 07 0	
		12 15 4	

57. *Account of Mathew Gray for repairing Newmurehouse.—September* 1702.

ACCOMPT of MATHEW GRAYIS depursments in Repairing the New mure houss (1702)

	Lib. s. d.
Imprimis Six threives straw thatched on the west syde of the barne at 12s. per threive	03 12 00
Item to expenss in casting divots to the barne and leading and one putting theirof	01 10 00
Item Eight threive of thatch sheaves at 14s. threive; and fyve threive at 12s. the threive to the houss Inde .	08 12 00
Item for ane new ash couple to the spence . . .	03 00 00
Item for two dozen and ane half of Rabeis at 20s. dozen to the spence	02 10 00
Item for ane rooff and thrie ribs at 6s. 8d. peece to the spence .	01 06 08

		Lib. s. d.
Item to ane man one day to cast divots and for leading and onputting theirof		01 10 00
Item for two load of lyme at 6s. load for casting the barne and repairing ane part of the byre, and to the man for bigging and casting both Inde . . .		01 04 00
SUMMA		23 04 08

Wee undersubscribers having by appoyntment of Magistrates and Councill perused the above accompt of Depursements extending to Twentie three pound four shilling eight pennies Scotts doe find the pryces reasonable Witnes our hands at Irving this 25th Aprile 1702 yeares
G. HAGGART.
JO. MARSHALL.

Irving 12 Decr. 1705 years :—

I the said Mathew Gray doe grant and acknowledge that the abovewrittin accompt of Tuentie three pound four shillings 8d. is allowed to me by the Magistrats and Counsell after stateing of accounts betwixt the toun and me by their act dated 10 November 1705 instant, and therefore I hereby discharge the abovewrittin soume.
MATTHEW GRAY.

58. *Order by Bailie Stevenson to William Shaw, Treasurer, to pay for 14 bolls of Lime for the New Bridge.—25th August.*

25 August Mr. William Sha thesorer pay to Robert Lokert the sum of nyn shillinges starling and fowrpence and that for six bolls leim to meilmarket and eight bools to the new Brige which maikes fortein boolls at eight pens per boll which will be alowed to you in your thesorer acounts Geiffen at Irving the twinte fift daij of Agust by   WILL: STEVENSON, baylie.

Skots acount five pund and twelve shiling Skotts mune.

59. *Account for Work by David Muir.—September 1742.*

ACCOMPT The Town of IRVINE Dr. to DAVID MUIR for Work September 1742.

Imprimis To the Loch Milne two brig stones and three pavement for the sole of the race		0 5 00
To leading them two draughts		0 1 04
To one days work of two men . .		0 2 02
To the side wall of the stable 4 bolls lymne with sand .		0 3 08

To 3 men with a server one day		0	4 00
To 2 men and a server one day		0	2 10
To leading timber from the shore for props		0	0 04
To nails		0	0 03
At the wind mill 2 bolls lymne with sand		0	2 00
To 4 draughts whinstones		0	1 02
To a man two days		0	2 02
		£1	5 11

Irvine 30th January 1745 :—

William Miller late Thesaurer of the Burgh of Irvine pay to David Muir mason in Irvine one pound five shillings and eleven pence sterling in full of the above account and the same upon his discharge shall be allowed in your Thesaurer accompts by

        John Glasgow   John Dunlop
        F. Cuninghame   John M'Cleish
        J. Boyll   John Finlay
        James Fairlie   Tho: Bigger
                John Dean

Irvine February 1st 1745 :—

Then received from William Miller Theasurer full payment of the within precept by me   DAVID MUIR.

60. *Account of Mason Work.*—1743.

Irving November 28th 1743 :—

An ACCOMPT of Masson Worke the Tune Det to JAMES GALT.

	Lib.	s.	d.
To mending a hole in the Tolbuth that the boys broke one bolle of lime and sand	0	01	00
To masson and serves work at the same	0	01	06
Mor to a Brige at the Proves Parke 11 draght of stones from the Toun at 2 pence a draght	0	01	10
To 2 Boles of lime for the same	0	01	04
To sand for the lime	0	01	00
To masson and serves worke	0	02	10
More to scull yeard dyke and olice hous casting and Kirk yeard stille bulding 6 days and one half of a masson at 14 pence a day	0	07	07
To 5 days of a serves man at 7 pence a day	0	02	11

EXCERPTS FROM BURGH ACCOUNTS.

	Lib.	s.	d.
To lime and sand 13 boles	0	13	00
To 2 draght of stones from Duntan Knoll	0	00	07
To drawing stones from the Sigetheid and the Crose to the Kirk Style	0	00	06
More to 5 foot of pathment in the Sculle at 4 pence half penie a foot	0	01	10½
	1	15	11½

June 28th 1744 :—

William Miller Thesurer of the Burgh of Irvine pay to James Galt mason junior in Irvine the above sum of one pound fifteen shillings and eleven pence halfpenny sterling and the same upon his reciept shall be allowed at clearing your Thesurer Accompts.

   John Glasgow Robert Crighton
   Thos. Bigger   James Hill
   Ja: Nisbet   James Kennedy

June 28th 1744 :—

Then received from William Miller fulle payment of the above Accompt by me
                 JAMES GALT.

61. *Various Accounts.*—1744.

12 July 1744 :—

RESAVED be me David Craige smith sevn pens for paier bans for the hall dor and deschargs the samen by me from Margrat Fergisell for hir hall dor.
                 DAVID CRAIG.

Irvine, 19 October 1744 :—

I JAMES LOCKERD shipemester in Irvene grants me to have receved from William Miller upon the acompt of Mary Dellope my sister in lawe tuo pound tuo shillings sterlen mone in pairt payment of Laim thatt sheu his furnest for the Toun of Irvene. As wittnes my hand.   JAMES LOCKHART.

Irvine 23d November 1744 :—

BAYLIE be pleased to draw a precept upon the Thesurer (payable to David Muir or John Allison in Stivenson) for five pound sterling for pen stones for the Prison and I ame yours &ca.   THO: BIGGER.

 To Baylie Fairlie.

Irvin November 23, 1744:—

Sir,—According to the above draught please pay to David Muir or John Alison five pound sterling when ye are in cash and place the same to your accompts and this shal be your warrand. JAMES FAIRLIE.

To William Miller late Treasurer.

Irvine 31st December 1744:—

Then received full payment of the above Precept by me and John Allasson is signed by DAVID MUIR.
 JOHN ALLASON.

ACCOMPT of Work done to the TOUN of IRVINE.

	Lib.	s.	d.
Ittem tuo days for puting in scleats	0	1	2
Ittem on day for tarring the prison	0	0	6
Ittem five days for clengen the market	0	2	6
	0	4	2

Irvine 13th November 1744:—

William Miller Thesarer pay George Beg four shillings and two pence sterling which with his recipt shall be allowed at stateing you accompts.
 THO: BIGGER.

Irvene 13 of November 1744:—

Receved from William Miller the contents of the within by me
 GEORGE BEGG.

62. *Account for Timber, etc.*—1744.

TOWN of IRVINE due FRANCIS CUNINGHAME Wright in Irvine.

 Sterling.
1744 September. To 63 feet firr timber at 1s. per foot for the use of the meall mercat and tolbooth . . . 3 3 0

Irvine 24th January 1745:—

William Miller.—You'll please pay Francis Cuninghame the above account of Three pound three shillings sterling which shall be allowed yow in your Thesaurer accounts by J. BOYLE.

To William Miller merchant and Thesaurer
 of the Burgh of Irvine.

Recivid from Mr. William Miller the above acomp of therie pond threi shillins sterlling this 24th of Janwary 1745 and decherges the sem by

FR. CUNINGHAME.

63. *Account for Slates and Timber.*—1744.

The TOWN of IRVINE to JOHN GLASGOW and COMPANY. Dr.

	Sterling.
1744 July. To thrie hundred and eight choice deals att six pound ten shillings per cwt.	19 18 8
To forten thousand and one hundred of slates att 15 pound Scots per thousand	17 12 6
To tuo pieces of fir timber measuring 42 foot at 12d. per foot	2 2 0
	39 13 2

Irvine 19th January 1745:—

William Miller late Thesaurer of the Burgh of Irvine pay to John Glasgow late Provost of Irvine the within sum of thirty nine pounds thirteen shillings and two pence sterling in full of the within Accompt which shall be allowed at stateing your Thesaurer Accompts by

Patt. Boyd	J. Boyll
Rob* Craig	John Dunlop
F. Cuninghame	John M'Cleish
John Dean	A. Thomson

Tho: Bigger

Irvine 29th May 1745:—

Then recieved from William Miller late Thesaurer of Irvine payment of the within Accompt which is discharged by

JOHN GLASGOW.

64. *Account for Repairs at the Meal Market.*—*February* 1745.

BURGH of IRVINE for Reparations of MEAL MERCKAT. Dr.

	£ s. d.
1745 February 9. To 63 foot of timber at 12d. per foot	3 3 0
To carriage of timber	0 1 2
To 47 dales furnishd by James Gray at 12d. per dale	2 7 0
To William Wylie and Robert Cochran for sclateing as per accompt	3 8 6
To David Craig for nails as per accompt	1 15 9
To 6 lib. of lead at 2d. per lb.	0 1 0
To 4 hundred of double plencher nails at 18d. per hundred	0 6 0

		£	s.	d.
To 11½ days work of James Gray at 14d. per day		0	13	5
To 19 days of Allexander Cuninghame at ditto .		1	2	2
To 8½ days of Thomas Boyd at do.		0	9	11
To 16½ days of Robert Kid at 12d. per day		0	16	6
To 8 days of Patrick Blair at ditto .		0	8	0
To 3 days of John Keir at ditto		0	3	0
To 3 days of David Kid at do.		0	3	0
To 7 days of David Smith at 8d. per day		0	4	8
		15	3	1
To 51 dales gott for the prison charg'd in Provost Glasgow's accompt at 13d. per dale		£2	15	3
Total of the Accompt due .	£15 3 1			
From which deduce the first article paid to Cuninghame	3 3 0			
	£12 0 1			

Irving 28th February 1745:—

William Miller Thesaurer lately of the Burgh of Irvine pay to James Gray wright in Irvine the Ballance of the within accompt extending to twelve pounds ane penny sterling which shall be allowed at stateing your Thesaurer accompts by

  J. Boyll   Tho: Bigger
  James Fairlie   Patt. Boyd
  John Dunlop   Ja: Nisbet
  John M'Cleish   John Dean
  John Glasgow   Rob' Craig

Irvene, 4 of March 1745.—I James Gray wricht in Irvene grantes me to have receved from William Miller the within Accompt and decharges the saim by me amontin to tuelve pound ane pene sterlen mone   JAMES GRAY.

65. *Accounts for Carting Materials for Building the Prison.*—1744-1745.

CARR MENS ACCOMPTS for STONES, LEADING, &c^a to the PRISON HOUSE since the first of August 1744 to the first of January 1745.

		Draughts.				
John Galt from	Stevenson	34	1	2	8	
	Seabank	22	0	18	4	
	Sclates	18	0	3	9	
	Sand	81½	0	13	6¾	
	Rubish	28	0	2	4	3 0 7¾

			Draughts.						
William Malcolm		Stiven	15	0	10	0			
		Seabank	12	0	10	0			
		Sand	39	0	6	6	1	6	6
And: M'Knight		Stiven	9	0	6	0			
		Seabank	10	0	8	4			
		Sclates	12	0	2	6			
		Sand	34	0	5	8			
	Dales and Timber		6	0	1	0	1	3	6
William Rid		Stiven	8	0	5	4			
		Seabank	16	0	13	4			
		Sclates	9	0	1	10½			
		Sand	13½	0	2	2⅔			
		Rubish	28	0	2	4	1	5	1½
Thomas Boyd		Stiven	10	0	6	8			
		Seabank	14	0	11	8			
		Sclates	10	0	2	1			
		Rubish	36	0	3	0	1	3	5
Alex^r Findlay		Stiven	28	0	18	8			
		Seabank	22	0	18	4			
		Sclates	8	0	1	8	1	18	8
Robert Muir		Stiven	16	0	10	8			
		Seabank	8	0	6	8			
		Sand	13⅓	0	2	2⅔			
		Rubbish	10	0	0	10	1	0	4⅔
Thos Kirkwood		Stiven	7	0	4	8			
		Seabank	8	0	6	8	0	11	4
Ro^{tt} Whitford		Stiven	14	0	9	4			
		Seabank	2	0	1	8			
		Timber	1	0	0	2	0	11	2
Thomas Watt		Stiven	8	0	5	4			
		Seabank	12	0	10	0	0	15	4
Hugh Miller		Stiven	9	0	6	0			
		Seabank	1	0	0	10	0	6	10
Alex^r Cuningham		Stiven	7	0	4	8			
		Seabank	5	0	4	2			
		Sand	22	0	3	8	0	12	6
William Gibson		Stiven	2	0	1	4			
		Seabank	15	0	12	6	0	13	10

		Draughts.						
Daniel Brown	Stiven	4	0	2	8			
	Seabank	8	0	6	8	0	9	4
John Muir	Stiven	12	0	8	0			
	Seabank	7	0	5	10			
	Sand	13½	0	2	2¾			
	Rubbish	4	0	0	4	0	16	4⅔
Robert Sheddcn	Stiven	8	0	5	4			
	Seabank	7	0	5	10			
	Sclats	6	0	1	3			
	Rubbish	16	0	1	4	0	13	9
Bryce Knox	Stivenson	2	0	1	4			
	Seabank	5	0	4	2	0	5	6
William Crawfurd	Stiven	9	0	6	0			
	Seabauk	10	0	8	4			
	Sclats	6	0	1	3			
	Sand	13½	0	2	2¾			
	Rubbish	4	0	0	4	0	18	1⅔
John Auld	Stiven	11	0	7	4			
	Sand	40	0	6	8	0	14	0
Edward Auld	Stivens	4	0	2	8			
	Sand	40	0	6	8	0	9	4
James Miller	Stiven	2	0	1	4			
	Seabank	5	0	4	2			
	Sclats	3	0	0	7½	0	6	1½
William Gothry	Stiven	1	0	0	8			
	Seabank	5	0	4	2	0	4	10
Mathew Brown	Stiven	5	0	3	4			
	Seabank	4	0	3	4			
	Sclats	2	0	0	5	0	7	1
William Blair	Stiven	4	0	2	8			
	Seabank	5	0	4	2	0	6	10
William Brown	Stiven	7	0	4	8			
	Seabank	1	0	0	10	0	5	6
John Thomson	Stiven	10	0	6	8			
	Seabank	8	0	6	8			
	Sand	13½	0	2	2¾			
	Rubbish	43	0	3	7	0	19	1⅔
Robert Brown	Stiven	2	0	1	4			
	Seabank	2	0	1	8	0	3	0

John Shaw		Stivens	2	0	1	4		
		Seabank	2	0	1	8	0 3 0	
Robert Tempilton		Stiven	7	0	4	8		
		Seabank	1	0	0	10		
	Dales and Timber		6	0	1	0	0 6 6	
John M'Gavan		Stiven	9	0	6	0		
		Seabank	2	0	1	8		
		Rubbish	55	0	4	7	0 12 3	
James Boyd		Stivenson	9	0	0	0	0 6 0	
David Guilkeson		Stiven	2	0	0	0	0 1 4	
Hugh Ritchie		Stiven	5	0	0	0	0 3 4	
							23 0 7	

Total of hewen stons 282 draught at 8d. per draught is	9 8 0	
Ditto of pen stons 219 draught at 10d. per draught is	9 2 6	
Sclats 74 draught at 2½d. per draught is	0 15 5	
Sand 323 draught at 2d. per draught is	2 13 10	
Rubbish 224 draught at 1d. per draught is	0 18 8	
Dales and timber 13 draught at 2d. per draught is	0 2 2	
	23 0 7	

Irvine, 31 December 1744 :—

That William Miller Thesurer of the Burgh of Irvine counted and payed the above car men of their above particular accompts is attested by me   THO: BIGGER.

66. *Account for Refreshments to the "Carriers."*—1744-1745.

ACCOMPT the Onnirbell MAGSTRETTS and TOUN COUNSILL to WILLIAM MILLER.

	Lib.	s.	d.
1744. August 1. Imprimus for 3 paints of aill by the kearrers.	00	00	6
2. Item for 3 paints of aill by the kearrers	00	00	6
6. Item for 4 paints of aill by the kearrers	00	00	8
7. Item for 4 paints of aill by the kearrers	00	00	8
23. Item for 4 paints of aill by the kearrers	00	00	8
24. Item for 3 paints of aill by the kearrers	00	00	6
September 7. Item for 7 bottells of aill by the kearrers	00	00	7
8. Item for ane paint of aill by the kearrers	00	00	2
19. Item for ane paint of aill by the kearrers	00	00	2

			Lib.	s.	d.
21.	Item for 6 paints of aill by the kearrers		00	01	0
22.	Item for ane paint of aill by the kearrers		00	00	2
26.	Item for 2 paints of aill by the kearrors		00	00	4
Octtober 4.	Item for 5 paints of aill by the kearrors		00	00	10
	Item for 3 paints of aill to the Fishiers att Norchen with the claitts		00	00	6
6.	Item for 7 bottells of aill by the kearrors		00	00	7
8.	Item for 3 bottells of aill by the kearrors		00	00	3
10.	Item for ane paint of aill by the kearrors		00	00	2
12.	Item for 3 bottells of aill by the kearrors		00	00	3
17.	Item for 3 paints of aill by the kearrors		00	00	6
22.	Item for 7 paints of aill by the kearrors		00	01	2
25.	Item for 2 paints of aill by the kearrors		00	00	4
26.	Item for ane paint of aill by the kearrors		00	00	2
29.	Item for ane paint of aill by the kearrors		00	00	2
November 3.	Item for 5 bottells of aill by the kearrors		00	00	5
5.	Item for 3 bottells of aill by the kearrors		00	00	3
10.	Item for 6 paints of aill by the kearrors		00	01	0
13.	Item for ane paint of aill by the kearrors		00	00	2
15.	Item for 3 bottells of aill by the kearrors		00	00	3
17.	Item for 3 bottells of aill by the kearrors		00	00	3
19.	Item for 3 bottells of aill by the kearrors		00	00	3
21.	Item for 3 paints of aill by the kearrors		00	00	6
26.	Item for ane paint of aill by the kearrors		00	00	2
28.	Item for 7 bottells of aill by the kearrors		00	00	7
December 1.	Item for 4 paints of aill by the kearrors		00	00	8
6.	Item for 3 bottells of aill by the kearrors		00	00	3
21.	Item for 3 bottells of aill by the kearrors		00	00	3
26.	Item for 4 paints of aill by the kearrors		00	00	8
27.	Item for 3 paints of aill by the kearrors		00	00	6
28.	Item for 5 paints of aill by the kearrors		00	00	10
29.	Item for 2 paints of aill by the kearrors		00	00	4
1745 Fibrure 8.	Item for 5 bottells of aill for the kearorrs		00	00	5
9.	Item for 4 paints of aill by the kearrors		00	00	8
11.	Item for 3 paints of aill by the kearrors		00	00	6
12.	Item for 13 bottells of aill by the karrors		00	01	1
14.	Item for 3 paints of aill by the kearrors		00	00	6
18.	Item for 4 paints of aill by the kairors		00	00	8
20.	Item for 5 bottells of aill by the kearrors		00	00	5
21.	Item for 3 paints of aill by the kearrors		00	00	6
	Kearred ofer		01	02	11

		Lib.	s.	d.
1745 Februare 22. Item for 4 paints of aill by the kearrors		00	00	8
23. Item for 3 paints of aill by the kearrors		00	00	6
25. Item for 5 paints of aill by the kearrors		00	00	10
26. Item for 4 paints of aill by the kearrors		00	00	8
27. Item for 4 paints of aill by the kairors		00	00	8
March 1. Item for 3 paints of aill by the kearors		00	00	6
2. Item for 3 paints of aill by the kearrors		00	00	6
4. Item for 3 paints of aill by the kearrors		00	00	6
6. Item for 3 bottells of aill by the kearrors		00	00	3
8. Item for 3 paints of aill by the kearrors		00	00	6
16. Item for 2 paints of aill by the kearrors		00	00	4
29. Item for 2 paints of aill by the kearrors		00	00	4
Item for 2 mor paints of aill by the kearrors		00	00	4
Aprill 25. Item for 5 bottells of aill by the kearrors		00	00	5
27. Item for 2 paints of aill by the kearrors		00	00	4
29. Item for 2 paints of aill by the kearrors		00	00	4
May 27. Item for 3 paints of aill by the kairors		00	00	6
30. Item for 7 bottells of aill by the kearrors		00	00	7
31. Item for 4 paints of aill by the kearrors		00	00	8
Juen 8. Item for 2 paints of aill by the kearrors		00	00	4
10. Item for 4 paints of aill by the kearrors		00	00	8
14. Item for 2 paints of aill by the kearrors		00	00	4
15. Item for 5 paints of aill by the kearrors		00	00	10
22. Item for 4 paints of aill by the kearrors		00	00	8
25. Item for 2 paints of aill by the kearrors		00	00	4
27. Item for 2 paints of aill by the kearrors		00	00	4
28. Item for 2 paints of aill by the kearrors		00	00	4
29. Item for 3 bottells of aill by the kearrors		00	00	3
Jully 3. Item for 3 paints of aill by the kearrors		00	00	6
4. Item for 4 paints of aill by the kearrors	.	00	00	8
5. Item for 5 paints of aill by the kearrors	.	00	00	10
6. Item for 5 paints of aill by the kairrors	.	00	00	10
8. Item for 3 paints of aill by the kearrors	.	00	00	6
10. Item for 2 paints of aill by the kearrors	.	00	00	4
12. Item for 4 paints of aill by the kearrors	.	00	00	8
13. Item for 3 paints of aill by the kearrors	.	00	00	6
15. Item for 6 bottells of aill by the keairors	.	00	01	0
16. Item for 3 paints of aill by the kearrors	.	00	00	6
19. Item for 2 paints of aill by the kearrors	.	00	00	4
29. Item for 2 paints of aill by the kearrors	.	00	00	4

		Lib.	s.	d.
31. Item spent with Baille Bigert and Robert Gillmoor ane musken spiritts in punch		00	01	2
Item for 3 bottells of aill and 4 pens for brid		00	00	7
August 12. Item for 2 paints of aill the kearrors		00	00	4
15. Item for 2 paints of aill by the kenirors		00	00	4
Item for 2 paints of aill and ane dram by Baille Bigert and Mr. Ewinge with the kearrors		00	00	6½
20. Item for 3 bottells of aill by the keairors		00	00	3
Item for 4 paints of aill by the keairors		00	00	8
26. Item for 3 paints of aill by the kearrors		00	00	6
27. Item for 3 paints by the kearrors		00	00	6
30. Item for 3 paints of aill by the kearrors		00	00	6
September 3. Item for 2 paints of aill by the kearrors		00	00	4
6. Item for 2 paints of aill by the kearrors		00	00	4
13. Item for 3 bottells of aill by the kearrors		00	00	3
14. Item for 6 bottells of aill by the kearrors		00	00	6
17. Item for 3 paints of aill by the kearrors		00	00	6
20. Item for 2 paints of aill by the kearrors		00	00	4
28. Item for 2 paints of aill by the kearrors		00	00	4
October 4. For 3 paints of aill by the kearrors		00	00	6
Item for 4 paints of aill by the kearrors		00	00	8
10. Item for 2 paints of aill by the kearrors		00	00	4
14. Item for 2 paints of aill by the kearrors		00	00	4
29. Item for ane paint of aill by the kearrors		00	00	2
		02	13	04
		00	00	2½
		2	13	6½

67. *Various Trades Accounts.*—1744-1745.

Irvine 8th September 1744 :—

WILLIAM MILLER Thesurer of the Burgh of Irvine pay to James Galt or David Muir masons five pound sterling which with either of their recipts shal be allowed at stateing your thesurer accompts   THO: BIGGER.

The above day then received from William Miller full payment of the above by me   JAMES GALT.

Irvine 27th September 1744 :—

WILLIAM MILLER Thesurer pay James Galt or David Muir ten pound sterling in part payment for building at the town-house of Irvine which with either of their recipts shall be allowed at stateing of your accompts   THO: BIGGER.

Irving October 3th 1744 :—

Then received from William Miller ten pound sterling by me
JAMES GALT.

Irvine 2d October 1744 :—

WILLIAM MILLER Thesurer pay Robert Gilmor in Saltcoats nine pound ten shillings sterling for stones furnished to the Prison House of Irvine which with his recipt shall be allowed at stateing your accompts. THO: BIGGER.

Irvine 2d October 1744 :—

Received from William Miller Thesurer payment of the above nine pound ten shillings sterling by me ROBERT GILLMOR.

Irvine 1st November 1744 :

WILLIAM MILLER Thesurer pay David Muir or James Galt masons ten pound sterling for building at Prison which with either of their recipts shall be allowed at stateing your accounts. JA: BOYLE.

November 1st 1744 :—

Then received from William Miller the above ten pounds sterling by me
JAMES GALT.

Irvine December 31st 1744 :—

SIR:—Pay Robert Gilmor three pound sterlin for stones that he is to furnishe for the Prison house of Irvine which with his receept shall be allowed in your treasurers accompts JA: BOYLE.

To William Miller late Treasurer of the Burgh of Irvine.

Irvine 31st of December 1744 :—

Receved the contents of the above from William Miller by me
ROBERT GILLMOR.

ANE Accompt of Work wrought by CHARLES SHEDDAN to the TOWN of IRVINE in the year 1744.

	£ sh. d.
Imprimis To the meal mercat of Irvine to 9 prick batts 12lib	00 03 06
Item To 27 cast 10 groat nails	00 02 03
Item To 15 lime and roof	00 01 04
Item To 3lib. 8oz. of spicks at 3½d. per lib.	00 01 00½
	00 08 01½

To Work wrought for the TOLBOOTH.

Imprimis To mending a broken crow iron		00 00 02
Item To dressing a pick and sharping 4		00 00 05
Item To 13lib. spicks att 3½ per lib.		00 03 09½
Item To 12lib. spicks att 3½ per lib.		00 03 06
Item To 9lib. 8oz. spicks att 3½ per lib.		00 02 09½
Item To 2 hundred and 27 cast 10 groat nails		00 09 02
Item To 1lib. 8oz. spicks		00 00 03
Item To a steeple		00 00 03
Item To 1 small batt		00 00 03
Item To 18 hundred mason irons sharping att 7d. per hundred		00 10 06
		01 11 03
Colum brought down		00 08 01½
		01 19 04½

Irvine January 1st 1745 :—

Sir—Pay the contents of the above account amounting to one pound nineteen shillings fourpence halfe penny sterlin salvo justo calculo and it shall be allowed to you in your treasurer account
JA: BOYLE.

To William Miller late Thesaurer of the Burgh of Irvine.

Receaved the within a count from Willim Melir and deacherges the sam bay me Jan. 1, 1745.
CHARLES SHEDDEN.

Irvine 4th June 1745 :—

WILLIAM MILLER late Thesurer of the Burgh of Irvine pay James Galt junior mason three pound sterling in part payment for building att the Prison house which with his recipt shall be allowed at stateing your accompts
THO: BIGGER.

The above day received from William Miller full payment of the above thrie pound by me
JAMES GALT.

Irvine 4th June 1745 :—

WILLIAM MILLER Thesurer of the Burgh of Irvine pay Robert Gillmor mason in Saltcoats two pound ten shillings sterling in part payment for stones furnished to the Prison house which with his recipt shall be allowed at stateing your accompts.
THO: BIGGER.

The above day received full payment of the above two pound ten shillings by me
ROBERT GILLMOR.

68. *Account of Expense of Rebuilding the Town House of Irvine.*—1745.

Coast of the Toun House of Irvine in rebuilding. Anno 1745.

To stones from Robert Gillmor according to measure by agreament	27 1 0		
To John Allison for penn stones from Seabank .	7 3 2		
To James Galt for stones from Dunton Knoll .	2 3 8	36 7 10	
To 14 thousand one hundred sclates at 25sh. per thous.		17 12 6	
To 6 hundred bolls lyme got from Mrs. Lockhart	18 9 4		
To 56 bolls lyme gott from David Muir and James Galt	1 17 4	20 6 8	
To 368 dales from Provost Glasgow at 13d. per dale out of which 51 to Meall Merckat .	17 3 5		
To 665 dales from James Gray at 1sh. per dale .	33 5 0		
To 2476 foot cuttings from ditto at 1¼ per foot .	12 17 11	63 6 4	
To 42 foot firr timber from Provost Glasgow at 1sh. per foot	2 2 0		
To 109 foot timber from Thomas Brown at 13d. per foot	5 18 1		
To 290½ foot timber from Dubline as per Thomas Robison's account . . .	16 12 7¾	24 12 8¾	
To nails, locks, bands, and snicks as per James Gray's account	9 13 4		
To iron door, batts, locks and straps as per John Robison's account . . .	14 4 7¼		
To spikes and nails, and sharping mason irons as per Charles Sheddn's account . .	1 11 3		
To nails as per Robert Armors account .	1 11 4½		
To chimnes, batts and bands spikes and prick batts, etc[a] as per David Frazer's accompt .	5 6 10		
To each bands and barrs from John Findlay .	0 16 10	33 4 2¾	
To 3st. 7lib. 12oz. sheet lead at 3sh. 4d. per stone from John Findlay for sky lights . .	0 11 6¾		
To 1st. 12lib. 12oz. sow lead for running in batts from do. at 3sh. per stone . .	0 5 4¾		
To 5st. 10lib. for sash windows from do. att 32d. per stone not made use of . .	0 15 0		

		£ s. d.	£ s. d.
To 4 hundred 12lib. weight sheat lead from Glasgow for the roof as per Mr. Craig's account		3 1 0	
To Robert Brown for carriage of do.		0 8 0	5 0 11½
To lintseed oyl from William Hunter 6 pints		0 13 0	
To a choppin from John Findlay		0 1 2	
To lintseed oyl and white lead grind from Dublin as per John Harvie's account		2 9 1	3 3 3
To sclatters and service men for stripping the old prison and sclatting the new and 8 sack full of fog as per account		6 13 2	
To glassing 10 sash windows Councill room door head and sky lights as per account		6 9 8½	13 2 10½
To masons and service men for pulling down the old and rebuilding the New Prison as per account		108 4 6½	
To account James Galt for strikeing out and putting in back windows casting out side of prison collouring hewen work of prison school bell house kirkgate mending pavement of school floor, etc.		11 9 10½	119 14 5
To service men for 29½ days' work at putting in sclates in B. Nisbet's closs cleaning the same putting out of rubbish and cleaning the street as per precepts on Thesurers		0 17 1	
To 966 draught of stones from Stivenson quary at 8d. per draught		32 4 0	
To 461 draught pen stones from Seabank at 10d. per draught		16 14 2	
To 1263 draught of sand for lyme at 2d. per draught		10 10 6	
To 262 draught of stones from Dunton Knoll at 1½ per draught		1 12 9	
To 30 draught stones from Baylie M'Leish at 1d. per draught		0 2 6	
To 74 draught of sclates from Shoar at 2¼d. per draught		0 15 5	
To 574 draught rubbish at 1d. per draught		2 7 10	
To 13 draught of dales and timber at 2d. per draught		0 2 2	64 9 4

To wrights' wages at takeing down old and putting up new work as per James Gray's account . .	42	3	10			
To 2 wheelbarrows 5 stone barrows coals for dryin wood, candle, glew, etc. furnished by James Gray as per account . . .	3	4	7	45	8	5
To incident charges laid out by overseer as per account . .				1	17	5½
TOTALL				449	4	0½

Index

ABERCROMBIE, George, 194.
Abercrombie, Walter, 193.
Aberdeen, burgh of, 21, 45, 51, 95, 96, 146, 154.
Abernethie, A., 69.
Adam, Andrew, 318.
Adam, Thomas, merchant, 42.
Adam, William, 193.
Adames, Samuel, 133.
Adamhille, laird of, 188.
Adamtoun, laird of, 236, 237, 269.
Agnew, Sir James, of Lochnaw, younger, 109.
Aird, Mr. Robert, minister at Girvan, 72.
Airds, Duncan, 41.
Airlie, Earl of, 285.
Aitken, John, 40, 242, 248.
Aitken, Patrick, 37, 41, 242, 248.
Aitkin, David, 37, 41, 248.
Aitkin, William, in Watersyde, 41.
Alexander, Robert, Stirling, 21, 22.
Alexander, Mrs., 270.
Alison, Mr. James, 144.
Alison, John, in Stevenston, 321, 322, 333.
Allan, John, 163.
Allan, Robert, councillor, 173-225.
Allasone, Mathew, 223.
Anderson, John, merchant, Glasgow, 233.
Anderson, Laurence, councillor, 79.
Anderson, Little, messenger, 249.
Anderson, Ninian, bailie, 278.
Anderson, Thomas, 140.
Anderson, William, provost of Glasgow, 233.
Andrew, ——, 41; his son, 41.
Andrew, James, 42.
Andrew, Martene, 40.
Andrew, Robert, 37, 40.
Angus, George, 14.
Annandale, earl of, 265.

Annock, water of, 54, 80.
Anstruther Easter, 46.
Arbroath, 53, 94.
Archibald, David, 39.
Ardkinglas, laird of, 73.
Ardmillan, laird of, 311.
Ardrossan, parish of, 71.
Argyle, earl of, 19, 244.
Argyll, marquis of, 74, 75.
Armer, Robert, 333.
Armour, Alexander, 226.
Armour, Edward, elder, 230.
Armour, Edward, younger, 222.
Armour, Janet, 182.
Arnot, David, 194.
Arnot (Airnet), James, 52.
Arnot, John, 24.
Arnot, William, 193, 194.
Arthurle, Mr. William, 1, 2.
Aslos, laird of, 244.
Auld, David, 229, 230, 310.
Auld, Edward, 326.
Auld, John, 3, 5, 7, 239, 242, 326.
Ayr, bailies of, 10, 28, 132, 252, 257, 261, 292.
Ayr, burgh of, 21-28, 36, 47, 52, 53, 65, 71, 73, 76, 141-145, 161, 233, 244, 245, 249, 253-256, 263, 283, 301, 306, 309, 313.

BAILLIE, Alexander, 133.
Baillie, Gawin, 20.
Baillie, John, 20.
Baillie, Margaret, 247, 249.
Baillie, Martin, 242.
Baillie, Mr., 153, 154.
Balgrey, 242.
Bangour, 217.

338　INDEX.

Bar, Archibald, in Blook, 37, 39.
Bar, Robert, 195, 207, 210.
Barclay, Alexander, 37, 133.
Barclay, David, 185, 251.
Barclay, Hugh, 314.
Barclay, Janet, 267, 269, 270.
Barclay, John, 247, 249.
Barclay, Ninian, 63, 240.
Barclay, provost, 268, 270.
Barclay, Mr. Robert, 42, 183-188, 205, 256.
Barclay, Mr. Robert, provost of Irvine, 76, 77, 79, 86, 190, 220, 228, 230, 259, 261.
Barclay, Sir Robert, 279.
Barnes, John, 241, 278.
Barnes, Robert, 181.
Barowlands, 187.
Bartancholme, 232.
Bawre, Robert, 239.
Bedland, laird of, 264.
Beg, George, 322.
Beith, 103.
Beith, barony of, 106.
Beith, brewers of, 314.
Bell, Doctor, 285.
Bell, John, in Cumroy, 41.
Bell, John, 193.
Bell, W. Dalry, 70.
Belligellie, laird of, 271.
Biggart, David, 38, 39, 195, 265.
Biggart, John, 38, 39, 243, 245, 246.
Biggart, Robert, 37.
Biggart, Thomas, 133-139, 178-187, 195, 200-232, 306, 320-327, 330-332.
Binning, Captain John, 193.
Birrell, James, 239, 240, 246, 249, 250.
Birsbane, John, of Bishoptoun, 125.
Bishopton, laird of, 284.
Black, John, 37, 242.
Black, Robert, 41, 242.
Blackburne, Alexander, 37, 41, 242.
Blackness, port of, 95.
Blair, Sir Adam, 263, 270.
Blair, Alexander, of Giffartland, 187.
Blair, Alexander, 194.
Blair, Bryce, 302, 314.
Blair, Captain, 268.
Blair, James, 11, 53, 56, 63, 74, 88, 89, 182, 186, 188, 210, 223, 230, 233, 266.

Blair, James, bailie, 87, 167, 181, 198-205, 213, 231, 254-269.
Blair, James, provost, 100, 271, 273, 275, 276, 280, 282.
Blair, John, of Burrowland, 103, 104, 185, 244, 269, 302, 312.
Blair, Jonet, 183.
Blair, laird of, 244, 251, 264, 282, 285, 286.
Blair, Lawrence, 92, 178, 179, 198, 261, 265-267.
Blair, Lawrence, bailie, 98, 205, 207, 208, 220-226, 232-236, 271, 273.
Blair, Patrick, 324.
Blair, Thomas, 295, 296.
Blair, William, 326.
Blook, 241.
Blyth, Richard, Dundee, 21, 22, 24.
Bogflatts, the, 245.
Bogis, John, 243.
Boigsyd, 187, 232.
Bolton's Acre, 231.
Bordland, Andrew, 64, 68.
Borland, Archibald, 169.
Borland, John, 136.
Boswell, Alexander, Lord Auchinleck, 141, 142, 143.
Bothwell, 254.
Bowtone, Hew, 41.
Bowtone, John, 41.
Boyd, bailie, 313.
Boyd, George, 41, 242.
Boyd, Hew, 41, 224.
Boyd, James, 42, 244, 247, 327.
Boyd, Mr. John, bailie, 103.
Boyd, John, merchant, Irvine, 119.
Boyd, John, younger of Portincroce, 37, 41.
Boyd, John, Kilmarnock, 37.
Boyd, John, Fairlie, 41.
Boyd, John, Saltcoats, 41, 241, 242, 299, 304.
Boyd, John, apprentice writer, 141.
Boyd, John, in Meinfurd, 37.
Boyd, lord, 29.
Boyd, major, 254.
Boyd, Patrick, 323, 324.
Boyd, Thomas, provost, 48, 243-250, 293.
Boyd, Thomas, 133, 242, 324, 325.
Boyd, Thomas, in Kilmarnock, 206.
Boyd, William, 41.
Boyle, Archibald, 41, 101.

Boyle, Charles, 133.
Boyle, David, 72.
Boyle, David, in Rothesay, 52.
Boyle, James, of Montgomerieston, 115.
Boyle, James, younger, of Montgomerieston, 115-121, 140.
Boyle, James, 133, 268.
Boyle, James, provost, 257, 281, 282, 293, 299, 304-332.
Boyle, John, 208.
Boyle, John, of Kelburne, 193, 194.
Boyle, Patrick, 104, 312.
Boyle, William, 41.
Boyle (Boile), ——, in Perstoune, 84.
Boys, captain, 254.
Braidmeadow, 183, 185.
Braidshaw, John, 42, 242.
Breadalbane, John, earl of, 161.
Breutene, David, 21, 26.
Brechin, bishop of, 57. See Leuchars.)
Brechin, burgh of, 96.
Bridgend, 307, 309.
Brodie, Francis, 314.
Brodie, laird of, 76.
Broomlands, laird of, Montgomerie, 302, 305, 309, 311, 313.
Broun, Alexander, 130, 131.
Broun, Charles, 168, 182, 187-189, 219, 228.
Broun, David, 39, 178, 188, 219, 220, 231, 232, 270.
Broun, George, 12.
Broun, Hew, 32, 64, 68, 84, 183, 230, 274, 276, 279.
Broun, James, 3, 5, 8-14, 37-41, 70, 166, 168, 185-191, 219, 242, 250.
Broun, John, 133, 165-173, 183, 196, 216, 220, 230, 232, 247, 304.
Broun, Margaret, 254.
Broun, Oliver, 240.
Broun, Robert, merchant, 42.
Broun, Robert, clerk of Irvine, 56, 63, 67, 68, 73-79, 86-91, 136, 177-186, 229, 247, 253, 258, 267.
Broun, Robert, of Burrowland, 246.
Broun, Robert, 326, 334.
Broun, Thomas, 12, 14, 20, 333.
Broun, Thomas, clerk of Irvine, 28, 29.
Broun, Thomas, mason, 137-139.
Broun, Mr. William, 31.

Broun, William, 116, 123, 130-133, 219, 220, 265, 275, 276, 326.
Brown, Daniel, 326.
Brown, Mathew, 326.
Bruce, William, 316
Brydeine, James, 141, 243.
Bryden, Janet, 316, 317, 318.
Bryson, George, 45.
Bryson, John, 133.
Bryson, Robert, 101, 102, 133, 219, 280-301.
Buchannan, David, 225, 292, 293, 304.
Buchannan, James, 195.
Buchannane, John, 193.
Buckill, James, 181.
Buckle, Hugh, 122, 123.
Bukillis, Janet, 241.
Buntein, major Hugh, 194.
Burns, David, 141.
Burns, John, 226.
Burnes, Peter, 226.
Burns, William, 112.
Burns, ——, 110.
Burntisland, burgh of, 46.
Busbie, laird of, 305.
Busland, 227, 230, 245, 248.
Butting, major, 274.

CADDALL, Alexander, 316.
Calander, lord, 74.
Calderwood, Andrew, councillor, 165-236.
Calderwood, David, 261, 263.
Calderwood, John, 116, 117, 123.
Caldwall, Andrew, 298.
Caldwall, David, 229, 251, 252.
Caldwall, Elizabeth, 248.
Caldwell, John, 113, 116, 123.
Caldwell, R., 53, 246, 250.
Caldwell, William, 123, 180, 251.
Caldwell, Mr. William, 53, 246, 250.
Cameron, Thomas, town clerk, 4, 5.
Campbell, Alexander, of Drumgrange, 141, 148.
Campbell, captain, 252.
Campbell, Hew, provost of Irvine, 13-15, 21, 25, 28, 29.
Campbell, James, Loudoun, 72.
Campbell, James, bailie of Irvine, 140.
Campbell, Margaret, 184, 185.
Campbell, provost, of Glasgow, 273, 282, 285.
Camphair, town of, 46, 52.

INDEX.

Caprington, laird of, 58.
Carleton, laird of, 277, 282, 285.
Carlung, laird of, 272.
Carmunnock, parish of, 112.
Carnell, laird of, 251, 266.
Carnwath, earl of, 265.
Carrick, in Galloway, 254.
Cassillis, earl of, 254, 286.
Cathcart, lord, 192, 194, 282.
Caukit acre, 230.
Cawane, Edward, 243.
Cesnock, laird of, 76, 269, 285.
Chalmer, John, 10, 12.
Chalmer, John, of Gaitgirth, 167, 193, 216.
Chalmer, Robert, 26, 193.
Chalmers, William, 202, 263, 264.
Charles II., king, 110.
Chartouris, Henry, 21, 24.
Christie, Henry, 74.
Christie, James, 74, 75.
Christmas, Thomas, 193.
Clark, John, 41, 254.
Cleland, James, 217.
Clerk's acre, 228, 232.
Clerk, John, 187.
Clerk, Mr., 160.
Clerk, William, 103.
Cloberhill, 265.
Clonbeith, 182, 188.
Clyde, water of, 45, 144.
Cochrane, Alexander, 89, 90, 178, 200-226, 234, 265, 266, 272, 281.
Cochrane, George, 21, 28, 29, 33, 36, 40.
Cochrane, Robert, 89, 90, 254, 261, 323.
Cochran, Hew, 89, 243.
Cochran, Lord, 255, 263-265.
Coilsfield, laird of, 305, 312.
Colt, Mr. Oliver, 30.
Colvill, John, 193.
Colvill, Mr. Patrick, minister at Beith, 73.
Connell, Archibald, 40.
Connell, James, 44, 202.
Connell, John, in Kilbirny, 39.
Conquerour, Dionis, 21, 22.
Cornwall, Mongow, 63.
Corsbie, laird of, 182, 188, 252.
Corsfurd, 245, 248.
Corshill, laird of, 281, 282, 295, 305.
Cotar, lieutenant-colonel, 86.

Couper, John, 37.
Cowane, John, 223.
Cowper's land, 188.
Craig, Alexander, 182.
Craig, David, 321, 323.
Craig, provost, 78, 79, 86, 263-266.
Craig, Robert, 133, 137, 138, 139, 243, 323, 324, 334.
Craig, Thomas, 42.
Craigends, laird of, 274.
Craigie, Robert, 158.
Craik, George, 296.
Craik, Peter, 9.
Craill, burgh of, 21, 22, 46.
Craufurd, Adam, 141.
Craufurd, Mr. Alexander, 102, 124, 125, 268.
Craufurd, Charles, 263.
Craufurd, David, 209.
Craufurd, Mr. Hugh, 272.
Craufurd, James, 133.
Craufurd, Thomas, 213.
Craufurde, John, in Kilmarnok, 37, 42.
Craufurde, William, 181, 182, 282, 317, 318, 326.
Craufurdston, laird of, 301.
Crawford, Alexander, of New-wark, 141.
Crawford, Archibald, of Ardmillan, 141.
Crawfurd, John, 103, 133, 216, 277, 278, 299.
Crawfurd, Moses, 122.
Crawfurd, Robert, 133, 139, 140.
Crawfurde, lady, 251.
Creag, James, 253.
Crevoch, Fairlie, 38, 39.
Crighton, Robert, 321.
Crocefurd, 187.
Cruiket acre, 228.
Cruikis, William, 42.
Cullen, harbour of, 111.
Cultoun, Andrew, 205.
Cultoun, John, 123.
Cumine, Mr. Patrick, 306.
Cuming, ———, servitor to the earl of Rothes, 193.
Cuming, John, 12, 183, 248.
Cuming, John, provost, 280, 281.
Cuming, Robert, in Balgrey, 37.
Cuming, Thomas, 241, 244, 246, 249.
Cuming, William, in Roberton, 39.

INDEX.   341

Cumming, Allan, bailie, 100, 187, 213, 262, 230, 262-273.
Cuningham, colonel, 268.
Cuningham, Isabell, 316, 317, 318.
Cuningham, Robert, 12, 98, 99.
Cuningham, Robert, councillor, 63.
Cuningham, Robert, provost, 165-267.
Cuninghame, Agnes, 257.
Cuninghame, Alexander, 133, 243, 247, 324, 325.
Cuninghame, Mr. Alexander, of Collellan, provost, 108, 111, 113-125.
Cuninghame, Allan, councillor, 86, 173, 189, 196-218, 259 ; bailie, 266.
Cuninghame, Archibald, 133.
Cuninghame, Francis, 320-323.
Cuninghame, Henry, burgess of Ayr, 133, 233.
Cuninghame, Hew, 73, 185, 186, 256, 257.
Cuninghame, Hew, bailie, 77, 79, 86, 259, 261, 266.
Cuninghame, Hew, provost, 167, 196, 268.
Cuninghame, James, in Peirston, 37.
Cuninghame, James, 133.
Cuninghame, Mr. James, sheriff-depute of Ayr, 93, 284.
Cuninghame, Joseph, 41, 72, 101.
Cuninghame, Ninian, 92, 93.
Cuninghame, Patrick, 183.
Cuninghame, Sir Alexander, of Robertland, 99.
Cuninghame, William, bailie, 21, 33, 36, 108, 116, 117.
Cuninghame, William, provost, 123, 128, 132-134.
Cuninghame, William, teacher, 154, 159.
Cuninghame, Mr. William, 185, 188.
Cuninghame, ———, provost of Ayr, 303.
Cunningham, bailiery of, 12, 16, 17, 18, 54, 60, 165, 309.
Cunningham, John, 10, 11, 258.
Cunningham, Mr. John, of Bridgehous, minister at Dalmellingtoun, 141.
Cunningham, David, 194.
Cunninghame, Jeane, 252.
Cunynghame, Adam, elder, 178, 229, 230, 257.
Cunynghame, Adam, younger, 198.
Cunynghame, Adam, 68, 182.
Cunynghame, Mr. Adam, 69, 70.
Cunynghame, major James, of Aikett, 124.
Cunynghame, Jonet, 239, 240, 249.
Cunynghame, Margaret, 247.
Cunynghame, Marion, 266, 267.
Cunynghame, Richard, 126, 127.
Cunynghamhead, laird of, 261.
Cupar in Fife, 21, 96.

Dalkeith (Decith), 255.
Dalry, 70, 71.
Dalrymple, Charles, 264.
Dalrymple's wards, 185, 188.
Dalziell, earl of, 265.
Dalziell, lieutenant, 282, 288.
Damster, Charles, 317.
Dausone, James, 193.
David, king of Scots, 50.
David II., king of Scots, 56, 57.
Davidson, Adam, 194.
Davidson, William, 123.
Davie, Cuthbert, 243.
Davie, John, 230.
Davie, William, 41.
Davison, John, 63, 69, 83, 85, 86.
Dean, John, 63, 288, 289, 323, 324.
Dean, house of, 215.
Dean of Guild, 280, 281.
Dean (Dein), John, 12, 184, 320.
Dempster, David, 241, 242.
Dick, captain Andrew, 193, 195.
Dick, Sir William, 214.
Dickie, David, 184.
Dickie, James, 316.
Dickie, John, 41, 232.
Dickie, Robert, 311.
Dickie, Thomas, 41, 216.
Dickie, Mr. William, 153, 203.
Dickson, Mr. Archibald, 269.
Dickson, John, 221.
Dieppe (Deip), 9.
Done, John, 194.
Dook, Robert, 297.
Douglas, Alexander, 193.
Douglas, William, earl of, 57.
Douglass, colonel, 291.
Dowell, William, 70.
Down county, 217.
Downie, William, 69.
Dreghorn, muir of, 60, 75, 76.
Drumlanrig, earl of, 265.
Drummond, Sir John, 48.

342   INDEX.

Drummond, Sir Patrick, 94.
Dublin, 333, 334.
Ducathoill, 229.
Duff, Mr. William, depute of Ayr, 141.
Dumfreis, 22, 27, 44, 46.
Dunbar, Mr., 269, 305.
Dunbar, 21, 24.
Dunbarton, burgh of, 21, 26, 33, 36, 43, 45, 47, 53, 243-246.
Dunbarton, castle of, 13.
Duncan, Edward, 246.
Duncan, Samuel, 113, 123, 126, 129, 130.
Duncanhill, the, 245, 248.
Dundee, burgh of, 21-24, 45, 56, 94-96.
Dundonald, 203, 290.
Dundonald, laird of, 170.
Dunlop, Alexander, 36, 43, 73.
Dunlop, Allan, bailie, 74.
Dunlop, Allan, provost, 53, 58, 190, 257, 263, 265.
Dunlop, Allan, younger of Craigie, 72, 205, 220.
Dunlop, Andrew, 244.
Dunlop, Archibald, 288.
Dunlop, Daniel, 64, 68.
Dunlop, David, councillor, 173-176, 180-233.
Dunlop, Francis, provost, 87, 262, 301.
Dunlop, John, 37, 98, 99.
Dunlop, John, Saltcoats, 42, 241.
Dunlop, John, bailie, 58, 63, 84, 137-139, 251-261, 320, 323, 324.
Dunlop, Jonet, 166.
Dunlop, laird of, 264, 269.
Dunlop, Margaret, 317, 318.
Dunlop, Martha, 317.
Dunlop (Dellope), Mary, 321.
Dunlop, Robert, treasurer, 53.
Dunlop, Robert, 109, 166, 184, 186, 229, 231.
Dunlop, Thomas, 242.
Dunlop, William, 249.
Dunscbiths, Helen, 262.
Dunton Know, the, 228-231, 298, 321, 333, 334.
Dyett, Alexander, councillor, 79, 86, 111, 116, 123, 169, 173-175, 178-180, 187, 190-298.
Dyett, Henry, 64, 68, 91, 92, 182, 186, 230, 231.
Dyett, John, 247.
Dyett, William, 173, 177-186, 197-206, 228, 231, 247.

Dykes, Robert, 318.
Dysert, Michaell, in Blair, 39.
Dysert, 27, 46.

EDGEFIELDE, lord, 148.
Elgelie, John, 212.
Edinburgh, 9, 21-32, 45-57, 68, 93-100, 115, 128, 147-157, 164, 171-173, 195-197, 209, 216, 227, 240-246, 255-276, 285, 293, 296, 298-311.
Edmonstoun, Mr. Walter, 302.
Edward, John, 175, 238.
Eglinton, Alexander, earl of, 60-69, 81, 82, 88, 101-106, 108, 141, 187, 194, 195, 250, 263-273.
Eglinton, Archibald, earl of, 161, 163.
Eglinton, Hew, earl of, 15, 18, 204.
Eglinton, Hew, master of, 15, 16, 18, 20.
Eglinton, Lady, 275.
Eglintoun, John, 194.
Eglishame, 309.
Eisat, Alexander, 86.
Eleis, Mr. John, 258.
Elgin, 27.
Elie, haven of, 27.
Elphinstone, George, 21, 24.
Elphinstone, James, 257.
England, 47, 94, 125.
English, the, 254, 257, 265.
Enterkin, laird of, 267.
Erskine, George, councillor, 103, 198, 201, 203, 217, 220-226, 233-236, 305, 309, 310.
Erskine, captain Patrick, 316, 317.
Erskine, Robert, lord, 57.
Ewing, Robert, in Southennane, 37, 41.
Ewinge, Mr., 330.

FAIR, David, Largs, 40.
Fairlie, 41, 163, 242.
Fairlie, Alexander, of Fairlie, 163.
Fairlie, bailie, 321.
Fairlie, James, 320, 322, 324.
Fairlie, Thomas, 244.
Falluslaill, John, 249.
Fergushill, George, 38.
Fergushill, Margaret, 321.
Fergushill, Robert, 38.
Fergushill, William, 38.
Fergusson, Sir Adam, of Kilkerran, 141.

INDEX.

Fergusson, bailie, 263.
Fergusson, James, 144.
Fergusson, William, 39.
Fetter, John, 136.
Findlater, earl of, 111, 140.
Findlay, John, Roberton, 37, 39.
Finlason, John, 45.
Finlay, Alexander, 42, 325.
Finlay, James, 86.
Finlay, John, 320, 333, 334.
Finlay, William, 79.
Finlaystoun, 14.
Finnie, Robert, 44.
Fischer, Andrew, 194.
Fischer, Thomas, 45.
Fleming, Captain, 278.
Fleming, Mr. Charles, 285.
Fletcher, James, provost of Dundee, 104.
Flodden, 10.
Foid, Thomas, 41.
Forbes, John, 193.
Forbes, Robert, 128.
Forbes, Thomas, 282.
Forfar, 27.
Forman, Alexander, 226.
Forres, 27.
Forrester, John, 242, 248.
Forrester, lord, 192, 195.
Forrester, Robert, 242, 248.
Foster, John, 41.
Foster, Robert, in Fairlie, 41.
Fountainhall, lord, 157.
France, 50, 52, 105.
Francis, Allan, 126-132.
Francis, David, 184.
Francis, Jean, 317.
Francis, John, 228, 229.
Francis, Robert, 92; councillor, 173-236, 273, 276, 280-282, 286.
Francis, William, 102, 184, 188, 281, 282, 296.
Frank, James, 92.
Fraser, Cuthbert, 41.
Fraser, George, 41.
Fraser, John, 317.
Frazer, David, 333.
Freir, Mr. George, 9.
Freirsmylne, 188.
Frew, John, 191.

Frew, Mathew, 310.
Fullartoun, William, of Fullartoun, 138, 183, 186, 191, 204, 229.
Fullerton, Adam, councillor, 63, 78, 79, 173-230, 267.
Fullerton, James, of that ilk, 167, 184.
Fullerton, James, 189; bailie, 190, 197, 205, 218, 229, 232, 266-280, 291-307.
Fullerton, James, of Bartanoholme, 232.
Fulton, Robert, in Kirkwode, 37, 38, 242.
Fultoun, Archibald, 39.
Fynnik, 242.

Gailis, 241.
Galbraith, James, 247.
Galloway, Mr. Patrik, 239.
Gallowhill, 184, 185.
Gallowmure, 12, 188.
Galt, Adam, 248.
Galt, Alexander, in Chap-toun, 38.
Galt, Hew, in Newmyln, 76.
Galt, James, 60-62, 75, 86, 87, 184, 186, 215, 216, 225, 236, 237, 264, 282, 296, 298, 320-334.
Galt, John, 88, 324.
Galt, Robert, 75-88.
Galt, Thomas, 198, 220, 222, 224, 225.
Galt, William, 38, 39, 63, 209.
Gardiner, Robert, 169, 183, 189.
Gardner, John, 289, 297.
Gardner, Thomas, 64, 68, 186, 229.
Gardner, William, 178-182, 198, 213, 223, 229, 230, 267.
Gargannock, lady, 286, 290.
Garrich, gudman of, 240.
Garscaddane, laird of, 183, 188.
Garvan, Thomas, 263.
Garven, George, 56, 63, 67-69, 75, 76, 86, 92, 186, 203, 234, 265-275, 287, 290.
Garven, Gilbert, 239.
Garven, Hugh, 38, 40, 108, 111, 191, 209, 212, 226, 230, 316, 317.
Garven, Janet, 287, 302, 312-315.
Gastoun, Allester, 41, 242.
Geil, Peter, 250.
Gemmell, William, 247.
Gemmill, Andrew, 108, 111, 178, 179, 198, 280, 283.

Gemmill, James, 139-141, 165, 170-175, 183, 198, 314.
Gemmill, John, 5, 7, 12, 14, 133.
Gemmill, Stevin, 31.
Gemmill, Mr. Zacharias, of Boigsyde, 123, 133.
George II., king, 144.
George, Archibald, 46, 250-252.
George, Margaret, 184.
Gib, John, 199, 264.
Gibson, ——, 8.
Gibson, Gilbert, 43.
Gibson, Henry, 36.
Gibson, John, 229.
Gibson, Thomas, 295.
Gibson, William, 325.
Giffertland, laird of, 183.
Gilbert, James, 193.
Gilchrist, James, 317.
Gilleis, James, 41.
Gillespie, Archibald, 242.
Gillespie, Robert, 42.
Gilmour, Robert, 330-333.
Girnell booth, the, 187.
Girvan, 72, 262.
Girvanmains, laird of, 69.
Girven, captain, 256, 258.
Glasgow, 20-36, 45, 47, 51, 95, 105, 149, 253-259, 272, 284, 288, 304, 305, 313, 314, 334.
Glasgow, bailie of, 273, 284.
Glasgow, official of, 1, 2.
Glasgow, provost of, 251, 324, 333.
Glasgow, John, 133, 272, 320-324.
Glasgow, Michael, 103, 113, 116, 123, 303.
Gledstons, Mr., 269, 272.
Glen, Hew, 244, 245.
Glen, Mr. Robert, 24.
Glencairn, Alexander, earl of, 13, 244, 268.
Gleneys, laird of, 305.
Glengarnock, laird of, 282.
Gloak, James, 317.
Gogeyid, Mathew, 41.
Goltray, Peter, 12.
Gooslone, the, 187.
Gordan, William, 133.
Gordon, Charles, 158.
Gordon, Hamilton, 145, 147.
Gordoun, John, 193.
Gothry, William, 326.

Gottray, John, 188, 198, 199.
Gow, John, 317.
Gowry, earl of, 29.
Granard, lord, 282, 286.
Grant, major George, 193.
Gray, Adam, 313.
Gray, Helen, 43.
Gray, James, 133, 249, 323, 324, 333, 335.
Gray, John, bailie, 106, 111, 119, 136, 176, 177, 189, 196-238, 284.
Gray, Mathew, 318, 319.
Gray, Thomas, 122.
Greg, Alexander, 254.
Greir, James, 53, 252.
Greir, Janet, 184, 262.
Guilkeson, David, 327.
Gullieland, 188.
Guschett acre, the, 228-231.
Guthrie, Mr. Alexander, 57.
Guthrie, John, bailie, 58, 84-87; provost, 179-192, 253, 258-262, 266.
Guthrie, Mr. William, 71.

HADDINGTON, burgh of, 21, 24, 25.
Haddington, provost of, 25.
Haggart, G., 319.
Hagy, Alexander, 29.
Hair Mill, the, 60.
Halkat, Mr. George, in Flanders, 27.
Hall, Adam, 21.
Hall, George, 45.
Hamilton, 254, 260.
Hamilton, Alexander, 295.
Hamilton, Arthur, town-clerk, 93, 98-101, 165, 169-175, 195, 207-209, 212, 216.
Hamilton, duke of, 78, 288, 289.
Hamilton, Edward, 298.
Hamilton, James, 271.
Hamilton, John, clerk, 103, 106-114, 126, 127, 316.
Hamilton, Robert, of Bourtriehill, 141.
Hamilton, Robert, councillor, 171, 172, 185, 188, 273.
Hamiltoun, John, of Montgomriestoun, 141.
Hamiltoun, Margaret, 250, 251.
Hamiltoun, provost, 144, 160.
Hamiltoun, Mr., 282.
Hamiltoun, captain Thomas, 193.
Hammill, Robert, 183, 217.

INDEX.

Hamuill, George, 188.
Harbert, Thomas, 41, 242, 248.
Harper, James, 68, 133.
Harper, John, 185.
Harper, Robert, 37, 42.
Hart, John, 244, 282.
Harvie, John, 246, 334.
Hastie, Robert, councillor, 113, 116, 126, 129, 134.
Hay, captain, 254.
Hay, Daniell, 29.
Hay, George, 194.
Hay, James, 104, 172, 300, 302, 312, 313.
Hay, John, drummer, 253.
Hay, John, merchant, 130, 131.
Hay, William, 298.
Hayes, Holme, 228, 231.
Hegait, W., 11, 20.
Hehous, John, 248.
Hemphill, Edward, in Fynnik, 242.
Henderson, Andrew, councillor, 79, 103, 123, 182, 200, 220, 221, 235.
Henderson, Hugh, 122, 243.
Henderson, James, 207, 233.
Henderson, John, 207.
Henderson, William, 64, 68, 145, 147, 149, 154, 155, 223.
Henry, Alexander, 172, 183, 189.
Henry, John, 169, 187, 229, 231.
Henry, Robert, 184.
Henry, William, 183, 254, 259.
"Henry," the (ship), of Londonderry, 291.
Hepburne, Janet, 188.
Heriott, Mr. David, 252, 253.
Heward, Sir Gilbert, chaplain, 1, 2.
Hiemyre, lands of, 185, 188.
Hillhouse, John, 42.
Hill, 183.
Hill, James, 140, 321.
Hingdoge, 71.
Hip acre, 230.
Hog, James, 41.
Hog, Stein, 239, 250, 252.
Hoilhouse, 188, 241.
Holland, 267.
Holme Mill, the, 81-83, 88, 108, 109, 208, 296, 301, 306, 310.
Holmes, John, 133, 134.
Holmes, Ninian, 178, 185, 188, 198, 200, 213, 220-226, 235, 236, 243.

Home, Robert, 101.
Homill, Matthew, 245.
Hopkin, Archibald, 171.
Hopkin, Robert, 169, 189.
Houlatsone, James, 193.
Houlatsone, John, 193.
Houston, Patrick, 194.
Houston, Mr. William, 21, 26, 245.
Houstoun, Hew, 183.
Houstoun, Oliver, 10, 11, 12.
Howie, Archibald, 42, 182, 241, 244.
Howie, colonel, 254.
Howie, James, 41.
Howie, William, 254.
Howy, Peter, 243.
Huchesonne, Thomas, 243.
Hude, William, 11.
Hukter, John, 253.
Humbie, lord, 70.
Hume, colonel, 70.
Hume, Robert, 42.
Hume, lord, 277.
Hunter, Andrew, of Park, 141.
Hunter, Bettie, 317.
Hunter, Charles, serjeant, 318.
Hunter, Gilbert, in Blook, 37.
Hunter, Gilbert, in Montgremane, 241.
Hunter, Hew, 273.
Hunter, James, 86, 93, 99, 225, 231, 234, 273.
Hunter, John, 37, 39, 178, 179, 209, 241.
Hunter, Patrick, of Hunterston, 101, 102.
Hunter, Robert, of Hunterston, 72, 101, 102, 273.
Hunter, Samuel, 316, 318.
Hunter, William, 40, 334.
Hunter, bailie, of Ayr, 279.
Hunterstoun, laird of, 188.
Hurrie, colonel, 271.
Hutchesone, Hugh, 305.
Hutchesone, John, 103, 289, 291.
Hutchesone, Mr., 269.

Inglis, Ninian, 241.
Inglis, captain, 285.
Innes, John, 139.
Inveraray, provost of, 272.
Inverkeithing, 46, 53.
Inverness, 27, 50.
Ireland, 88, 125, 171, 217, 241, 292.

346　　　　　　　　　　　　　INDEX.

Irnc, Moyses, 249.
Irvine, bridge of, 129, 137-139, 204, 294, 319.
Irvine, burgesses of, 2, 3, 5, 21, 31, 36, 68, etc.
Irvine, burgh of, 1, 2-15, etc.
Irvine, drum of, 295.
Irvine, green of, 233, 234.
Irvine, harbour of, 128, 129, 140, 161.
Irvine, kirk of, 146-158, 311, 321.
Irvine, kirkgate of, 262.
Irvine, magistrates of, 4, 40, 48, 78, etc.
Irvine, market cross of, 124-126, 129, 233, 321-323, 331, 333.
Irvine, mills of, 7, 8, 53, 54, 75, 79-83, 287, 288.
Irvine, prison of, 331-334.
Irvine, school of, 145-153, 311.
Irvine, town clock of, 296.
Irvine, tolbooth of, 226, 233, 251-253, 268, 271, 283, 293, 311, 320, 331.
Irvine, water of, 233.
Irving, James, 204.
Iscat, Alexander, 86.

Jack, Andrew, 110.
Jack, David, 133.
Jackson, John, 33, 36.
Jackson, Patrik, 21.
Jameson, George, 42.
Jamesone, Barbara, 250.
Jamie, John, 40.
Jamie, Robert, 41.
Jedburgh, 27.
Johnston, Fergus, 296.
Johnstoun, James, councillor, 166-200, 220, 222, 307, 309.
Jones, Hew, 241.

Kaa, Alexander, 9.
Kar, Connell, in Blook, 39.
Keir, John, 324.
Kelburne, 41, 72.
Kelburne, laird of, 281, 284, 286, 304, 309.
Kellie, William, 21.
Kello, John, 194.
Kelly bridge, 140, 162.
Kelso, Henrie, 41.
Kelso, William, 71.
Kemp, Mr. James, 145, 148, 153, 155, 158, 159.
Kennedy, George, 26.

Kennedy, James, 141, 321.
Ker, Adam, 293.
Ker, Andrew, 21, 40.
Ker, Edward, 133.
Ker, James, 194.
Kerd, Sir John, 1, 2.
Kid, David, 324.
Kid, Robert, 324.
Kid, Walter, 182.
Kidd, John, 187, 245, 248.
Kilbirnie, 71.
Kilbirnie, laird and lady of, 102, 282, 286, 290.
Kilbryde, 38, 41, 72.
Kile, Robert, 15, 247, 248.
Kilmarnock, 42, 58, 71, 72, 76, 100, 215, 222, 242, 259, 263, 300.
Kilmaurs, parish of, 72, 98, 106, 218, 223.
Kilpatrick, Hew, councillor, 173-180, 189, 209, 270.
Kilsyth, lord, 253, 290.
Kilwinning, regality of, 17, 20, 71, 100, 106, 182, 195, 204, 207, 219, 298, 313, 314.
Kilwinning, Gavin, commendator of, 9.
King, Mr. Alexander, 30.
Kingston, lord, 265.
Kirkaldy, 27, 46.
Kirkcudbryght, 27, 44, 52, 259.
Kirkwode, John, in Kilbirnie, 38, 253.
Kirkwode, William, in Southennane, 41.
Kirkwood, Thomas, 325.
Knodgerhill, lands of, 167, 187, 188, 214, 232.
Knok, Adam, 33, 36.
Knox, Bryce, 326.
Kyll, Hew, 12, 13.
Kyll, James, councillor, 171, 183, 184, 188, 200, 205-226, 232-236, 269-271.
Kyll, John, 12, 13.
Kyll, Mr. Robert, 251.
Kyll, Thomas, 12, 13.
Kyll, William, 3-7, 10, 12.

Lambert, lieut.-general, 255.
Lamont, Donald, 317.
Lamroghtoune, 273.
Lanark, burgh of, 21, 26, 44, 51, 66, 95.
Lang, Archibald, 133.
Langshaw, laird of, 286, 302.
Largs, 40, 72, 106, 254, 309.

INDEX. 347

Laurie, William, 140.
Lawder, Maurice, 21. 24.
Lawte, Adam, 29.
Lawte, David, 29.
Leis, John, 318.
Leith, 45, 47, 95.
Leslie, captain, 271.
Leslie, David, 254.
Leslie, George, 160.
Leslie, James, 194.
Leslie, John, 318.
Leslie, William, 316.
Lesly, ———, 159.
(Leuchars), Patrick, bishop of Brechin, 57.
Lillie, Adam, 253.
Lindsay, George, councillor, 165-173, 206, 221.
Linlithgow, 21, 40, 45, 48, 94-96, 105.
Linlithgow, earl of, 193, 301.
Litleton, Archibald, 317.
Livingston, lieut.-colonel, 74.
Livingston of Westquarter, 78.
Lochuylne, 208, 244, 295, 299.
Lochrig, Robert, 38, 39.
Lochwaird, 188.
Lockhart, George, 21, 24, 26.
Lockhart (Lockend), James, 321.
Lockhart, John, 10, 26.
Lockhart, Robert, 319.
Lockhart, Mrs., 333.
Logan, William, of Castlemains, 141.
Lope, Adam, 42.
Lope, Alexander, 42.
Lope, John, 239.
Lope, Michael, 42.
Lope, Peter, 42.
Lope, Thomas, 41, 245.
Lothian, earl of, 50.
Louttit, James, 133.
Love, Hugh, 108.
Lowdoun, 72.
Lowdoun, earl, 141, 194, 251, 276.
Lowrie, Alexander, 243.
Lumsdaill, James, of Buchannie, 192.
Laudie, Robert, 193.
Lunie, baillie, 281.
Luss, laird of, 285.
Lyn, Henry, bailie, 63, 98, 100, 165-236, 267, 271.
Lyn, Laurence, 247.

Lyne, Hew, 63, 195.
Lyne, William, bailie, 165-173, 187, 278, 281.
Lyntoun, Francis, 24.
Lyon herald, 266, 267.

Maggie, John, 213, 224, 225.
Mackaile, Mr. Hew, 58.
Mackie, Henrie, 193, 194.
Maghie, James, 194.
Mairtene, Stene, 21, 22.
Maitland, Mr., 317.
Makbein, William, 266.
Makkie, Mathew, 41.
Malcom, William, 136, 325.
Maldson, Robert, 194.
"Margaret" the, of Cumbrae, 125.
Marr, Archibald, 197.
Marreisland, 232.
Marschell, John, 111, 123, 125, 128, 136, 319.
Marshall, James, 132, 133, 135.
Marshall, William, 133.
Marten, Mr., 317.
Martine, Arthur, 133.
Martine, William, 123.
Massie, Mr. Andrew, 147, 157.
Mathis, Mr., 255.
Maxwell, James, burgess of Rouen, 9.
Maxwell, Robert, 312.
Maybole (Minibol), 253.
M'Alster, Duncan, 317.
M'Calzean, Thomas, 4, 5.
M'Caskie, Donald, 318.
M'Caskie, George, 318.
M'Clatchie, David, 313.
M'Cleane, John, 200.
M'Cliesh, Hugh, 133.
M'Cliesh, John, 133, 135, 136, 320, 323, 321.
M'Coage, Donald, 293.
M'Coill, Allester, 58.
Macdonald, Allaster, 259.
M'Fie, John, 141.
M'Gavan, John, 327.
M'Gibboun, Duncan, 37.
M'Gibboune, John, in Kelburn, 41, 241.
M'Gill, John, councillor, 173-199, 202-206, 220, 262.
M'Gill, Mr. James, 4, 5.
M'Gill, Thomas, 306.
M'Gleish, Robert, 309.

348   INDEX.

M'Goune, Thomas, 108, 306, 310.
M'Harg, Anthony, 161, 162.
M'Kelvie, Mary, 160.
M'Kerrell, John, 133.
M'Kerrell, Robert, 218, 220.
M'Kie, Hew, 42, 242.
M'Kinlay, Neill, 243.
M'Knight, Andrew, 325.
M'Leish, bailie, 334.
M'Lurg, William, 182, 194.
M'Murray, Hugh, 299.
M'Murray, John, 287.
M'Tagart, James, 296.
M'Taggart, William, bailie, 108-134, 209, 213, 224, 305.
M'Unsart's Hill, 188.
Meldrum, William, 293, 294, 296, 297.
Menzies, Robert, 64, 68.
Menzies, William, 21.
Millar, ——, 145-147.
Millar, Hugh, 325.
Miller, James, 326.
Miller, John, 42, 64, 68, 181.
Miller, Robert, 299.
Miller, Thomas, 148, 152.
Miller, William, treasurer, 320-332.
Millikin, James, 108, 111, 314.
Mitchell, Benjamin, 133.
Mitchell, James, 103.
Mitchell, John, 245.
Mitchell, Robert, 133.
Monckton, bailie of, 252.
Moncreiff, Agnes, 246.
Monfode, laird of, 274.
Monro, George, councillor, 113, 116, 123 - 125, 132, 303.
Monro, Hugh, 132, 133.
Montfoid, James, 37, 41.
Montgomerie, Alexander, 98, 99, 194, 244, 314.
Montgomerie, George, 262, 264, 272, 287, 303, 312.
Mongomerie, Hew, bailie, 79, 86, 87, 100-103, 132, 183, 186-188, 201, 228-231, 261, 275, 276, 280-299, 306-312.
Montgomerie, John, of Beoch, 281-287, 294, 295, 298, 300.
Montgomerie, lord, 15, 16, 60, 100, 108, 109, 123, 194, 204, 210, 254, 264, 275, 280-282, 302.

Montgomerie, Margaret, 275, 284.
Montgomerie, Matthew, 133.
Montgomerie, Patrick, 133.
Montgomeriestoun, 213.
Montgomery, Adam, 42.
Montgomery, John, 10.
Montgomery, John, bailie, 288-297, 302, 305, 312, 314.
Montgomery, Katherine, 8.
Montgomery, Robert, 41, 133, 254.
Montgomery, colonel Robert, 70, 73, 267, 278, 279.
Montgomery, major-general, 264, 282.
Montgomery, Thomas, 111.
Montgomery, William, 20, 133.
Montgomery, of Hessilhead, 194.
Montgomrie, colonel James, 263, 264, 318.
Montgrenane, 241.
Montgrenane, laird of, 251, 252.
Montrose, 27, 94, 96, 147, 151, 152, 157, 158.
Montrose, marquis of, 254.
Morris, James, in Kirkwod, 39.
Morison, William, 259.
Mortoun, George, in Barrassie, 84.
Mortoun, John, 243.
Mossman, captain, 316.
Mowat, Charles, of Busbie, 20.
Mudie, James, 264.
Muir, Bryce, 98, 99, 183, 201.
Muir, captain, 259.
Muir, James, 122, 127.
Muir (Moure), John, 255.
Muir, John, 10, 63, 182, 186, 188, 229, 231, 239, 240, 244-247, 250, 326.
Muir, Jonet, 197, 198, 246.
Muir, Marion, 316, 317.
Muir, Robert, 110, 298, 314.
Muir, Thomas, 33, 36.
Muir, William, 42, 43, 194, 247-252.
Muire, David, 133, 319, 320, 321, 322, 330, 331.
Muire, provost, 292, 309.
Mure, Archibald, 3, 7, 8, 166.
Mure, councillor, 173-181, 189, 197-209.
Mure, Hew, 42.
Mure, Quintin, 63, 249.
Mure, Robert, 111, 325.
Muling, ——, 41.
Muling, David, 242.

INDEX.

Mull, 254.
Mullivine, John, bailie, 106.
Murchie, Robert, 165.
Murchland, Robert, 277-279, 281, 282.
Murray, John, 315.
Murray, Mungo, 192, 194.
Murray, William, 194.
Murthland, Mrs., 317.

NAIRNE, James, 194.
Naper, John, 192.
Nasmyth, Gavin, 21, 25.
Nasmyth, Robert, 170, 198, 213, 219-226, 235-237, 281.
Neilson, James, 185.
Neilsoun, John, 245.
Neisbit, Mr. Alexander, 208, 210.
Neisbit, Henry, bailie, 21, 24, 334.
Neisbit, John, 246, 249.
Neisbit, Robert, provost, 21, 24, 72.
Nevein, John, 43.
Nevin, Hugh, 36, 134.
Nevin, James, 127.
Nevin, William, 187.
Newale, ——, of Polquharne, 141.
Newbottle, lord, 27.
Newmilnes, 39, 42, 75, 106, 305, 306.
Newmuir, lands of, 14, 167, 188, 214.
Newmuirehouse, 318.
Newtoun (Nitton), 256.
Nisbet, James, 106, 108-113, 122, 134, 316, 324.
Nisbet, Jonet, 323.
Nisbit, Laurence, 246.
Nithsdale, sheriff of, 263.
Nivein, James, 316, 317, 318.
Norchen, 328.
Normandie, 52.
Norris, George, 133.
Norway, 105.
Norwell, Adam, 42.

OGILVIE, Sir David, of Innerquharity, 193.
Ogilvie, James, 193.
Ogilvie, James, lord, 192.
Ogilvie, Thomas, 193.
Oliphant, James, 24.
Oliphant, John, 31.
Oliphant, Mr. William, 30.
Or, Robert, 41.

Or, William, 243.
Ormescheoch, 188.
Orr, Alexander, 178-181, 199, 219-226, 234, 235, 259.
Orr, John, Fairlie, 37, 41, 242, 248, 317.
Osburne, bailie, 305, 306, 309.

PAISLEY, 255.
Paisley, master of, 244.
Palmer, Nicoll, 22.
Park, provost, 320.
Park, John, 194.
Parker, Hew, 43, 192, 242.
Patersone, Captain Andrew, 193.
Paton, James, in Kilmernok, 39.
Paton, John, 42.
Paton, Robert, 72.
Paton, Thomas, 71.
Paton, William, 12, 242, 247.
Pearston, William, 311.
Pearstoun, laird of, 269, 276, 284, 285, 302-309.
Pearstoun, parish of, 262.
Peblis, ——, 39.
Pebles, James, of Knodgerhill, 54.
Peblis, James, in Blook, 39.
Peblis, John, 5, 7, 20, 40, 240, 247.
Peblis, Robert, 239.
Peebles, burgh of, 21, 27, 182, 183, 214.
Pells, Marion, 265.
Pennymoir, 184.
Perth, burgh of, 21-23, 28, 57, 69, 93-96.
Pervuis, William, 240.
Pettynweme, 21, 22.
Philp, David, treasurer, 21.
Picardie, 52.
Picken, James, 235.
Pinkcane, James, 170.
Pittlone, laird of, 257.
Poddock, Holme, 230.
Pond, Mr. William, 160.
Porter, Hew, in Lochlarne, 171.
Porter, James, 170, 171, 179, 189, 289, 298.
Porter (Portor), Jannet, 316, 317, 318.
Porter, John, councillor, 86, 179-183, 190, 195, 198, 200, 209-213, 218, 222, 223, 224-237, 254, 256.
Porter, Robert, 183.
Porter, William, 178, 179, 186, 219, 229, 230.

INDEX

Porterfield, Mary, 291.
Preston, Sir D., 7.
Preston, H., 7.
Preston, Mr. John, 24.
Preston, Stephen, 10.
Pringle, Robert, 148, 152.
Purves, William, 258.

Quarrell boill, 231.
Quhythorne, 27.

Rae, James, 194.
Rait (Reyte), kirk of, 23.
Ramsay, David, 21, 22.
Ramsay, James, 133.
Ramsay, William, of Montfodl, 141.
Randell, John, 247, 248.
Rankin, Mr., 279.
Rannald, John, 243.
Rannald, Thomas, 242.
Rasyde, William, 316, 317.
Reddinghill, 188.
Reid (Rid), bailie, 160, 281, 284.
Reid, Mr. George, minister at St. Evox, 141.
Reid, James, bailie, 160.
Reid, John, provost, 53, 63, 69, 70, 99, 173-237, 253, 254, 275, 276, 302, 303.
Reid, Thomas, 183.
Reidburne, 187.
Rein, Alexander, 317, 318.
Renfrew, 21, 33, 36, 45, 51.
Reoch, John, 318.
Richie, Robert, 42.
Richtpath, Thomas, 9.
Rid, William, 325.
Riddell, John, 33, 36.
Ritchard, Sara, 217.
Ritchie, Hugh, 327.
Rob, Charles, 134.
Roberts, Mathew, 160.
Robertland, laird of, 240, 269, 271.
Roberton, Sir John, 1, 2.
Robertson, James, 133.
Robertsone, Archibald, 193.
Robertsone, William, 194.
Robesone, Donald, 318.
Robesone, James, 37, 41, 212, 248.
Robesone, John, Saltcoats, 37, 41, 242, 248, 333.
Robesone, Stevin, 40, 243, 248.

Robesone, Walter, in Kilbirny, 39.
Robisone, Thomas, 333.
Roddings, lands of, 182.
Rodger, Robert, 134.
Rodger, William, 103, 299, 301.
Rodger, William, Broomlands, 314.
Rogers, Mr. Ralph, 71.
Rollok, Mr. Alexander, 69.
Roodmeidow, 188.
Roos, Master of, 271, 276.
Ros, Allan, 14, 243, 251, 252.
Ros, Andrew, in Newmuir, 14.
Ros, Finlay, 1, 2.
Ros, James, 41, 184.
Ros, John, councillor, 173, 176-180, 189, 196, 201-226, 234, 247, 249.
Ros, Ninian, 73, 180-183, 190, 196-199, 253.
Ros, William, 186, 228-235.
Ross, Hew, 77.
Ross, lord, 276, 298.
Rothes, earl of, 192-194.
Rothesay, 33, 36.
Rotten Boig, 232.
Rowallan, laird of, 261.
Russall, Mr. David, 21.
Russall, Mungo, 24.
Russallis, Johnne, 240.
Russell, John, 239-244.
Russell, William, 71.
Rutherglen, burgh of, 21, 26, 33, 36.

Saltcoats, 41, 241-245, 311, 331, 332.
Sampsone, James, in Dundonald, 203.
Scharp, Mr. William, 178.
Schort Boylets acre, 231.
Schort, Thomas, 194.
Scot, Alexander, 7, 8.
Scot, Janet, 7, 8.
Scot, John, 193.
Scot, William, 7, 8, 33, 36-43, 239, 240, 246-249.
Scotland, kingdom of, 3, 4, 5, 6, 7, 11, 12, 53, 159, 161.
Scott, Hew, 14, 15, 248, 251.
Scott, James, 4, 5, 10-12, 261.
Scott, Laurence, 30-32, 240-246.
Scott, Laurence, Sir, of Clerkington, 214.
Scott, Robert, 4, 5.
Scottswaird, 188.

INDEX.

Scrmygeour, Alexander, bailie, 21, 22.
Seabank, 333, 334.
Seagate, 188, 232, 262.
Seath, corporal, 316.
Sedserf, Archibald, 70.
Segmedow, 185.
Selkirk, 43, 47, 48, 247.
Selkrig, Mr. Robert, 285.
Semple, Margaret, 212.
Service, Robert, 91.
Session, lords of, 22, 24, 56.
Sewaltoun, laird of, 170, 282.
Sharpe, David, 69.
Shaw, Alexander, 289.
Shaw, Janet, 318.
Shaw, John, 327.
Shaw, William, 319.
Shedden, Charles, 133, 331-333.
Shedden, Martha, 316, 317.
Shedden, Robert, 326.
Shill, Mr., 59.
Shore, the, 334.
Sigetheid, 321.
Skelmorlie, laird of, 188, 236, 237.
Skeoch, Allane, 239.
Sloa, William, councillor, 42, 173-224. 234- 236.
Smaillie, John, 195, 207, 208, 216.
Smaillie, William, 317.
Small, John, 301.
Smiddie acre, 230.
Smith, David, 324.
Smith, James, 133.
Smith, Patrick, 140.
Smith, Robert, 163.
Smith, William, 282, 303, 304.
Smyth, Alexander, 182.
Smyth, Janet, 43.
Smyth, John, 98, 99, 133, 194, 218, 223.
Smyth, Thomas, 12.
Smythe, Hew, of Ridstoun, 71.
Snodgrass, John, 255, 256.
Sommer, Henry, 182.
Spark, Andrew, 108, 111, 314.
Spark, James, 133, 187, 230, 231.
Spark, John, 242.
Spark, Thomas, 183, 186, 230, 231.
Speir, Alexander, 40.
Speir, Andrew, in Colishill, 39 ; his son, 39.

Speir, David, councillor, 165-187, 228-230, 243.
Speir, John, 208.
Speir, Lawrence, 64, 68, 203, 224.
Speir, Robert, 224.
Speir, William, 45, 271.
Spens, David, bailie, 21, 26.
Spens, John, 4, 5.
Spirling, John, 183.
Spittel Meadow, 167, 185, 188, 199, 214.
Spottswood, James, 124.
Steile, John, 184.
Steill, James, 318.
Steill, John, 194.
Steill, John, councillor, 205-221.
Steill, Robert, in Balgrey, 242.
Stein, William, 318.
Steinsone, John, 224, 229, 242.
Steinsone, Robert, 187, 203.
Steinston, Allan, 241, 242.
Steinston, Bryce, 310.
Steinston, Hugh, 299.
Stene, black Joky, 42.
Stene, Thomas, 29.
Steuarde, John, 33, 36.
Stevenson, William, councillor, 108-123, 247.
Stevenson, bailie, 319.
Stevinsone, Hugh, 129.
Stevenstowne, parish of, 72, 321, 334.
Stevinston, Alexander, 37.
Stewart, Alexander, 317.
Stewart, David, 37, 38, 241.
Stewart, James, bailie of Glasgow, 33, 36.
Stewart, John, 317.
Stewart, Sir John, 70.
Stewart, major, 252.
Stewart, captain, 301.
Stewart, Robert, 86, 182, 185, 195, 210, 232, 262.
Stewart, Thomas, in Dykheid, 39.
Stewart, Walter, in Cuninghameheid, 37, 241.
Stewart, William, 38.
Stewartowne, parish of, 71, 106, 255.
Stirling, burgh of, 21-25, 29, 33, 47, 94, 95, 255.
Stirling, Mrs., 280.
St. Andrews, burgh of, 21, 27, 95.
St. Andrews, college of, 301.
St. Andrews, William, bishop of, 57.

INDEX.

St. James's land, 188.
Strachan, ——, 157.
Strachan, captain, 281, 292, 293.
Swintoun, William, councillor, 205-225, 282, 301-313.
Symontone, Allane, 243.
Symeson, John, 12, 249.
Symson, Alexander, 21, 24.
Symson, Thomas, in Haly, 41.
Symson, William, in Glenheid, 41, 133, 240.

Tailyeor, Alexander, 195.
Tailyeor, James, 206.
Tailyeor, Jeane, 206.
Tailzeour, Andrew, 42.
Tailziour, Robert, 42, 77, 184, 242.
Tait, Mr. Andrew, 112, 113.
Tannochill, Archibald, 42.
Tasker, John, of Durnest, 293, 294.
Tempill, James, 33, 36.
Tempilton, Robert, 327.
Tempiltoun, Thomas, 240.
Tempiltoun, Mrs., 253.
Templerig, 183, 184.
Templeton, James, 136.
Terbet, corporal, 268.
Thome, Patrik, 249.
Thompson, Agnes, 283.
Thompson, G., 108.
Thompsone, captaine, 197.
Thompsone, Hew, 64, 68, 168, 182-189, 198-233, 246, 249, 250, 273.
Thompsone, John, 91, 92; councillor, 108-133, 183, 186, 212, 228-231, 242-248, 313, 326.
Thomson, Mr., 258.
Thomson, Peter, 167.
Thomson, William, 37, 41; councillor, 116, 122, 123, 167-169, 189, 204-235, 248, 267, 318.
Thomsone, James, 301.
Thomsone, Robert, 249.
Thornton, Gilbert, 9.
Thorntoun, 262.
Tinehouse Burn, 233.
Tobias, surgeon, 254.
Tourlands, 305.
Towercee, laird of, 250.
Traing, Robert, 41, 89.
Tran, Mr. Alexander, 199.

Tran, Andrew, 251, 252.
Tran, Hew, 183, 241.
Tran, John, 270.
Tran, Jonet, 185.
Tran, Margaret, 242.
Tran, Patrick, 30, 241, 244.
Tran, Mr. Robert, minister, 172, 199, 246, 248, 250, 272.
Tran, Stephen, 4, 5, 10, 12.
Troon, 140, 162, 252.
Twedy, Gilbert, 21.
Twedy, John, 14.
Twedy, Robert, 14.
Tweed, David, 317.
Tweed, John, 241.
Tweydy, David, 248.

Umffald, Sir John, vicar of Kilmaurs, 1, 2.
Underwood, laird of, 266.
Urquhard, Adam, of Meldrum, 193, 194.
Urquhart, John, 194.
Urquhart, William, 293-297.

Walker, Alexander, 104.
Walker, David, 182, 194, 243.
Walker, Hugh, 230.
Walker, James, 64, 68.
Walker, James, in Crevoch, 37, 39.
Walker, John, 295.
Walkeris, ——, in Cuninghame, 39.
Wallace, Dr., 282.
Wallace, Mr., 272, 306-309.
Wallace, Anable, 262.
Wallace, Edward, 279, 283, 314.
Wallace, Hew, 181, 191, 300, 302.
Wallace, James, 216.
Wallace, John, 305, 308, 312.
Wallace, Laurence, 281, 314.
Wallace, Michael, 10.
Wallace, Robert, 187, 205, 266, 283.
Wallace, Sir Thomas, of Craigie, 216.
Wallace, William, of Failfurd, 73, 88, 180, 237, 239, 246, 249.
Wallace, William, of Symington, 251.
Walles, Edward, 26.
Watson, James, 294.
Watson, Robert, 316.
Watt, George, 316, 317.

INDEX.

Watt, Gilbert, 241, 244.
Watt, Thomas, 325.
Wauchope, John, 163.
Weir, James, 170, 171, 189, 278.
Weir, Niniane, 243.
Weir, Robert, 103, 110, 112, 281, 301-313.
Weir, Thomas, 182.
Weir, William, 292.
Weirsholme, 184.
Weymes, David, 97, 227.
Weymis, Sir John, of Bogie, 178, 202.
White, Alexander, 316.
White, Hew, 41, 88, 89, 91, 92, 244.
White, James, 133, 293, 313.
White, John, 41, 42, 194, 208, 210, 242.
White, major, 282.
White, Marioun, 53, 56.
White, William, in Newmilnes, 39.
Whitefoord, Allan, of Ballochmile, 141.
Whitefoord, James, of Dinduff, 141.
Whitefurd, John, 239.
Whitelaw, Mr. Patrik, of Newgrange, 21, 22.
Whitford, Robert, 325.
Whithorn, 27.
Whyt, Steven, 88, 182, 250.
Wick, 52.
Wigton, 22, 27, 39, 44, 45, 50, 53.
Wilkene, William, 21, 26.
Wilson, John, 3-7, 8, 12, 24, 43, 239-247, 318.
Wilson, Laurence, 228, 231.
Wilson, lieutenant, 253.

Wilson, Mathew, 41.
Wilson, Robert, 288.
Wilson, Thomas, 41, 223.
Wilson, William, 241, 244.
Wilsone, Jonet, 246.
Wilsone, Stevin, in Largs, 37, 40, 248.
Wilsone, sergeant, 260.
Wintun, Alexander, 171, 172.
Wintun, lord, 265.
Wishart, William, 63, 70-72, 79, 86, 186, 261, 266.
Wolmeidow, 185.
Wolsyid, Archibald, 41.
Wolsyd, James, 41, 89, 90; treasurer, 166, 169, 173, 174, 182, 190, 196, 199, 200-236, 281, 282.
Wood, George, 47.
Wood, Robert, 228.
Woodsyd, Robert, 173-189, 198-238.
Wricht, John, 63, 252, 253.
Wright, James, councillor, 165-175, 206, 225.
Wylie, William, 323.
Wylky, Gilbert, 86.
Wyllie, Gilbert, 79, 167, 178, 179, 195, 206, 213, 220, 221, 254, 259.
Wyllie, John, 42.
Wynrame, James, 36, 246.
Wyse, John, 21.

Young, Agnes, 317, 318.
Young, John, 182, 223, 247.
Young, Thomas, 63, 96, 97.

www.ingramcontent.com/pod-product-compliance
Lightning Source LLC
Chambersburg PA
CBHW030346230426
43664CB00007BB/547